JavaScript™

Your visual blueprint™ for building dynamic Web pages

2nd edition

by Eric Pascarello

WILEY

Wiley Publishing, Inc.

JavaScript™: Your visual blueprint™ for building dynamic Web pages, 2nd edition

Published by
Wiley Publishing, Inc.
111 River Street
Hoboken, NJ 07030-5774

Published simultaneously in Canada

Library of Congress Control Number: 2004112337

ISBN: 0-7645-7497-3

Manufactured in the United States of America

10 9 8 7 6 5 4 3 2

2V/TQ/QZ/QU/IN

Trademark Acknowledgments

Contact Us

For general information on our other products and services, please contact our Customer Care Department within the U.S. at 800-762-2974, outside the U.S. at 317-572-3993 or fax 317-572-4002. For technical support, please visit www.wiley.com/techsupport.

Torii of Itsukushima

The Torii, or gateway, of Itsukushima guards a Shinto shrine that has graced Miyajima Island since 1168. Created in 1875 by an unknown artisan, this elegant wooden gate presides over the tidal flats, where it appears to be alternately awash and adrift with the fluctuations of the tide. It is said to welcome the spirits of the departed back to the shrine. For more about Japanese landmarks and culture, explore *Frommer's Japan,* available wherever books are sold or at www.frommers.com.

U.S. Sales

Contact Wiley
at (800) 762-2974
or (317) 572-4002.

WILEY

PRAISE FOR VISUAL BOOKS...

"This is absolutely the best computer-related book I have ever bought. Thank you so much for this fantastic text. Simply the best computer book series I have ever seen. I will look for, recommend, and purchase more of the same."
—David E. Prince (NeoNome.com)

"I have several of your Visual books and they are the best I have ever used."
—Stanley Clark (Crawfordville, FL)

"I just want to let you know that I really enjoy all your books. I'm a strong visual learner. You really know how to get people addicted to learning! I'm a very satisfied Visual customer. Keep up the excellent work!"
—Helen Lee (Calgary, Alberta, Canada)

"I have several books from the Visual series and have always found them to be valuable resources."
—Stephen P. Miller (Ballston Spa, NY)

"This book is PERFECT for me - it's highly visual and gets right to the point. What I like most about it is that each page presents a new task that you can try verbatim or, alternatively, take the ideas and build your own examples. Also, this book isn't bogged down with trying to 'tell all' – it gets right to the point. This is an EXCELLENT, EXCELLENT, EXCELLENT book and I look forward purchasing other books in the series."
—Tom Dierickx (Malta, IL)

"I have quite a few of your Visual books and have been very pleased with all of them. I love the way the lessons are presented!"
—Mary Jane Newman (Yorba Linda, CA)

"I am an avid fan of your Visual books. If I need to learn anything, I just buy one of your books and learn the topic in no time. Wonders! I have even trained my friends to give me Visual books as gifts."
—Illona Bergstrom (Aventura, FL)

"I just had to let you and your company know how great I think your books are. I just purchased my third Visual book (my first two are dog-eared now!) and, once again, your product has surpassed my expectations. The expertise, thought, and effort that go into each book are obvious, and I sincerely appreciate your efforts."
—Tracey Moore (Memphis, TN)

"Compliments to the chef!! Your books are extraordinary! Or, simply put, extra-ordinary, meaning way above the rest! THANK YOU THANK YOU THANK YOU! I buy them for friends, family, and colleagues."
—Christine J. Manfrin (Castle Rock, CO)

"I write to extend my thanks and appreciation for your books. They are clear, easy to follow, and straight to the point. Keep up the good work! I bought several of your books and they are just right! No regrets! I will always buy your books because they are the best."
—Seward Kollie (Dakar, Senegal)

"I am an avid purchaser and reader of the Visual series, and they are the greatest computer books I've seen. Thank you very much for the hard work, effort, and dedication that you put into this series."
—Alex Diaz (Las Vegas, NV)

Credits

Project Editor
Jade L. Williams

Acquisitions Editor
Jody Lefevere

Product Development Manager
Lindsay Sandman

Copy Editor
Kim Heusel

Technical Editor
Namir Shammas

Editorial Manager
Robyn Siesky

Media Development Manager
Laura Carpenter VanWinkle

Permissions Editor
Laura Moss

Manufacturing
Allan Conley
Linda Cook
Paul Gilchrist
Jennifer Guynn

Production Coordinator
Maridee Ennis

Book Design
Kathie S. Rickard

Layout
Amanda Carter
Jennifer Heleine
Heather Pope

Screen Artist
Jill A. Proll

Illustrator
Rhonda David-Burroughs

Cover Illustration
David E. Gregory

Quality Control
Laura Albert
Susan Moritz

Proofreader
Vicki Broyles

Indexer
Johnna VanHoose

Special Help
Sun Microsystems, Inc.

Vice President and Executive Group Publisher
Richard Swadley

Vice President and Publisher
Barry Pruett

Composition Director
Debbie Stailey

About the Author

Eric Pascarello graduated from Penn State University in 2002 with a B.S. in Mechanical Engineering. Since then, Eric has been employed in the industry developing applications, primarily in VB.NET. The applications Eric develops focus on helpdesk support, management reporting, document management, and data recovery. In his spare time, Eric volunteers at www.JavaRanch.com, a friendly online community dedicated to helping people learn Java and Web technologies. Eric also enjoys wasting people's free time by developing JavaScript games that incorporate Artificial Intelligence.

Author's Acknowledgments

I would like to thank Tom Heine, the acquisitions editor who made this book possible. I would also like to thank Jade Williams, Jody Lefevere, Kim Heusel, and Namir Shammas, who helped me more than I could imagine through the whole writing process from start to finish. Without you, there would be no book.

The people at www.JavaRanch.com also deserve a big thank-you; especially Dr. Friedman-Hill, who helped me get noticed. Shona Feldman, hopefully my future wife, for all of your help with the last-minute, late-night edits. I know this stuff was boring to you, but you sure helped me with your input. Mark White, Praveen Prabakar, and Sriraj Rajaram deserve thanks for all of their support and interest. I need to thank my parents for allowing me to become a computer nerd. And last but not least, the aliens that abducted me and taught me how to program.

Shona, without your help, I would not have gotten this book done. Will you marry me?

TABLE OF CONTENTS

HOW TO USE THIS BOOK xii

1 INTRODUCING JAVASCRIPT .2

Introduction to JavaScript 2
Enter a JavaScript Statement into the Address Bar 4
Embed JavaScript in an HTML Document 6
Link an External JavaScript File 8
Present Content to Non-JavaScript Enabled Browsers 10
Add a Comment to JavaScript Code 12
Protect the Source Code 14

2 USING VARIABLES AND ARRAYS 16

Understand Variable Types 16
Declare Variables 18
Assign Values to Variables 19
Display Integers 20
Display Floating-Point Numbers 21
Display Booleans 22
Display Strings 23
Determine Variable Type 24
Convert Strings to Numbers 26
Convert Numbers to Strings 27
Declare an Array 28
Declare a Multidimensional Array 30
Determine the Number of Elements of an Array 32
Convert an Array into a String 34
Sort an Array 36
Remove Elements from an Array 38
Add Elements to an Array 39

3 CREATING EXPRESSIONS 40

Using the Arithmetic Operator 40
Increment and Decrement Values 42
Create Comparison Expressions 44
Create Logical Expressions 46

Identify Numbers 48

Evaluate an Expression 50

Inform the User with an Alert Dialog Box 51

Enable User Input with a Prompt Dialog Box 52

Enable User Decisions with a Confirm Dialog Box 54

4 HANDLING EVENTS 56

JavaScript Events 56

Detect a Mouse Click 58

Create Rollover Buttons 60

Detect a Key Press 62

Detect a Modifier Key Combination 64

Set and Remove Focus 66

Onchange Event 68

Handle the Page Load and Onunload Operations 70

Execute a JavaScript Statement from an HTML Link 72

Attach an Event to an Object 73

Determine the Element That Received the Event 74

Determine Which Mouse Button Was Pressed 76

Cancel Browser Events 77

5 CONTROLLING PROGRAM FLOW 78

Limit Executions with If-Else Statements 78

Using Conditional Operators 80

Optimize Performance with a Switch Statement 81

Create a For Loop 82

Continue and Break Loops 83

Handle While Loops 84

Create a Timed Interval 86

Set a Regularly Timed Interval 88

Declare and Call a Function 90

Handle Global and Local Variables 91

Pass Parameters to a Function 92

Return a Value from a Function 93

Increase Script Performance 94

TABLE OF CONTENTS

6 UTILIZING STRINGS 96

Determine the Length of a String 96
Select Portions of a String 98
Change the Case of a String 100
Extract Characters from a String 102
Escape a Text String 104
Encode a URI 105
Regular Expression 106
Match the Character in a String 108
Replace Characters in a String 110

7 WORKING WITH HTML FORMS 112

Develop HTML Forms 112
Reference Form Elements 113
Validate a Text Box Value 114
Validate a Password Field 116
Work with a Hidden Element 118
Validate Text Area Input 120
Work with a Button Element 121
Apply Reset and Submit Buttons 122
Alter Check Box Properties 124
Determine Selected Radio Button 126
Work with a Selection List 128
Basic Form Validation 130
Create a Select Element Navigation Menu 132
Block an Enter Key Invoked Form Submission 134
Advance the Text Field Focus with the Enter Key 136

8 WORKING WITH DATES AND TIMES 138

Use the Date Object to Display Dates 138
Get the Date and Time Components 140
Set the Date and Time Parts 142
Convert Dates to Strings 144
Check If a Date Is in a Range 146
Convert Between Time Zones 147
Create a Countdown Timer 148
Create a Running Clock with Images 150

9 USING THE MATH OBJECT 152

Employ Mathematical Constants 152
Apply Trigonometric Functions 154
Square Root and Power 156
Find Minimum and Maximum Values 157
Generate Random Numbers 158
Round Numbers Using Methods 160
Format Large Numbers with Commas 162

10 EXPANDING FUNCTIONALITY WITH
THE WINDOW OBJECT 164

Write Content to the Window 164
Create a Pop-Up Window 166
Detect If a Pop-Up Window Is Open 168
Reference Information from Multiple Windows 169
Close Pop-Up and Parent Windows 170
Set Window Size and Placement 172
Maximize the Browser Window 174
Center the Window on the Screen 176
Utilize an IE Modal Window 178
Create Content in a Pop-Up Window 180

11 CONTROLLING THE FRAME OBJECT 182

Create Frames 182
Reference Individual Frames 184
Determine the Frame Dimensions 186
Print Individual Frames 187
Break In and Out of Frames 188
Resize the Frames 190
Write Content to a Frame 192
Understand Frame Security 194

12 CREATING AND MANIPULATING OBJECTS 196

Reference Objects with the Document Object Model (DOM) 196
Create Custom Objects 198
Develop a Custom Object Method 200

TABLE OF CONTENTS

Create a Pseudo Hash Table 202
Manage Images with the Image Object 204
Locate All Links 206
Dissect the Location Object 207
Create a Bread Crumb Navigation Menu 208
Explore the Page History of the Browser 210
Disable the Back Button 211

13 DETERMINING ENVIRONMENT PROPERTIES 212

Detect the Browser Brand Name 212
Determine the Operating System 214
Distinguish the Default Native Browser Language 216
Identify the JavaScript Version Support 217
Verify If a Method or Object Is Supported 218
Set a Cookie Value 220
Retrieve a Cookie Value 222
Delete a Cookie Value 224
Create a Query String 226
Convert a Query String into Variables 228

14 CREATING CASCADING STYLE SHEETS 230

Link Style Sheets to a Web Page 230
Create Rules in a Style Sheet 232
Add Compliance Declaration 234
Attach Multiple CSS Rules 235
Override Rule Properties with Style Attribute 236
Modify Border Properties 237
Customize a Link Style 238
Center Content on the Web Page 240
Add a Background Image to the Document 241
Add and Alter Elements to a Web Page 242
Create a Scrollable DIV 244
Add an iFrame to the Web Page 245
Add Transparency to an Element 246
Change Style Sheet After the Page Loads 248
Turn Style Sheet Off or On 250

15 CREATING INTERACTIVE WEB PAGES WITH DHTML 252

Reference an HTML Element 252
Create New HTML Elements 254
Use innerHTML 256
Set an Element Position 257
Find Nonpositioned Element Positions 258
Show and Hide Elements 260
Find Browser Dimensions 262
Find the Mouse Position 263
Animate Elements 264
Create a Draggable Element 266
Create a Cross-Browser Layer Modal Window 270
Create a Custom Alert or Confirm Dialog Box 272

16 ADDING DYNAMIC CONTENT 276

Insert and Remove Items in a Selection List 276
Create a Double Combo Selection List 278
Add New Table Rows 280
Develop an Image Gallery 282
Produce an Autoscrolling Window 284
Construct a Navigation Tree 286
Generate a Navigation Drop-Down Menu 290
Insert Page Transition Effects 294
Incorporate Sound with a Button 296

CHAPTER 17: DEBUGGING JAVASCRIPT ERRORS 298

Detect a JavaScript Error 298
Debug through the Alert Dialog Box 300
Solve Problem with Page Onload Handlers 302
Locate Common Errors 304
Avoid Errors with Try/Catch Statements 305
Test JavaScript Code for Errors 306

APPENDIX 308

INDEX 312

How to Use This Book

JavaScript: Your visual blueprint for building dynamic Web pages, 2nd edition, uses simple, straightforward examples to teach you how to create powerful and dynamic programs.

To get the most out of this book, you should read each chapter in order, from beginning to end. Each chapter introduces new ideas and builds on the knowledge learned in previous chapters. When you become familiar with JavaScript, you can use this book as an informative desktop reference.

Who This Book Is For

If you are interested in performing death-defying feats, *JavaScript: Your visual blueprint for building dynamic Web pages,* 2nd edition, is the book for you.

What You Need to Use This Book

To program with JavaScript, you need two things: a basic text editor such as Notepad and any Web browser that supports JavaScript. There are many different browsers from which to choose, but some common browsers are Microsoft Internet Explorer, Netscape, Safari, Mozilla, and Firebird. There are many different browsers, so you should use the one you are comfortable with.

You can use a What You See Is What You Get (WYSIWYG) editor such as Front Page or Dreamweaver. You can also use text editors built for programming such as Edit Plus.

All of the examples in this book use Notepad and Microsoft Internet Explorer (version 6.0).

The Conventions in This Book

A number of typographic and layout styles have been used throughout *JavaScript: Your visual blueprint for building dynamic Web pages,* 2nd edition, to distinguish different types of information.

Courier Font

Indicates the use of HTML and JavaScript such as tags or attributes, scripting language code such as statements, operators, functions, methods, or properties.

Bold

Indicates information that you must type.

Italics

Indicates a new term.

An Apply It section usually contains a segment of code that takes the lesson you just learned one step further. Apply It sections offer inside information and pointers that you can use to enhance the functionality of your code.

Extra

An Extra section provides additional information about the task you just accomplished. Extra sections often contain interesting tips and useful tricks to make working with JavaScript easier and more efficient.

The Organization of This Book

JavaScript: Your visual blueprint for building dynamic Web pages, 2nd edition, contains 17 chapters and 1 appendix.

The first chapter, Introducing JavaScript, shows you how to add JavaScript to a Web page.

Chapter 2, Using Variables and Arrays, teaches you how to create and use different types of variables and arrays.

Chapter 3, Creating Expressions, explains how you can use arithmetic operators and create expressions so you can communicate with the user.

Chapter 4, Handling Events, enables you to add user interactivity to buttons, links, divs, text, and other HTML elements.

Chapter 5, Controlling Program Flow, teaches you how to create functions and control the flow of data and information through a program.

Chapter 6, Utilizing Strings, enables you to utilize the string object to format and manipulate strings.

Chapter 7, Working with HTML Forms, gives a detailed explanation of the form element types, explaining how you can utilize each element within a script.

Chapter 8, Working with Dates and Times, lets you handle the Date object to add validation to user input dealing with different time and date formats.

Chapter 9, Using the Math Object, explains all of the major parts of the Math object, which allows you to create random numbers, to round numbers, and to perform detailed mathematical operations.

Chapter 10, Expanding Functionality with the Window Object, gives you the power to manipulate the current window and pop-up windows so you can display information in the best possible manner.

Chapter 11, Controlling the Frame Object, provides you with a detailed explanation on how to handle and manipulate frames and their content.

Chapter 12, Creating and Manipulating Objects, teaches you how to build custom objects and methods to build dynamic Web pages that are efficient.

Chapter 13, Determining Environment Properties, permits you to determine users' properties when they visit your site, from what browser they are using to the information stored in their cookies.

Chapter 14, Creating Cascading Style Sheets (CSS), gives you the power to change the look and feel of the Web page with a minimum amount of effort.

Chapter 15, Creating Interactive Web Pages with DHTML, allows you to see all of the basic components of DHTML and how they can be used on a Web page.

Chapter 16, Adding Dynamic Content, shows you how to combine different DHTML concepts into one script, to create scripts that perform dynamic tasks that the user can interact with.

Chapter 17, Debugging JavaScript Errors, guides you through the process of finding errors in a script and how to test a script so there is a smaller chance of errors.

The final chapter, Appendix, contains useful tables of reference material.

Browser Difference

The concepts and scripts in this book are meant to be used with modern-day browsers. Modern-day browsers are Microsoft Internet Explorer 5.5+, Netscape 6+, Safari, Mozilla, Firebird, and any others that support JavaScript 1.5. Older browsers such as Netscape 4 do not support most of the concepts explained in the book.

Certain scripts in this book also inform you if certain code works with only certain browsers or operating systems. This is because there is proprietary code that is designed to only work with one browser. Microsoft Internet Explorer is the browser that normally supports proprietary code. One example in this book is transition effects which are only supported by Microsoft Internet Explorer.

Contacting the Author

To contact and ask questions directly of Eric Pascarello, visit www.JavaRanch.com and post your questions in the HTML and JavaScript forum.

Introduction to JavaScript

Web pages are written in *Hyper Text Markup Language* (HTML). HTML defines how elements on the page such as text, tables, forms, and images appear when viewed in a browser.

You can add interactivity to a Web page with JavaScript. You can use JavaScript to validate forms, display dynamic navigational menus, open pop-up windows, change elements on the page, and so on. Almost every page that you visit on the Web has some form of JavaScript embedded in the source code.

Cascading Style Sheets (CSS) allows a developer to easily modify multiple pages and to create more attractive and modern Web pages. CSS is a set of rules that affect the properties of a Web page when applied. You can use CSS to change properties of Web page elements, which can affect the colors, widths, borders, visibility, and so on. This is discussed in Chapter 14.

When JavaScript and CSS are combined to manipulate a Web page, it is called *Dynamic HTML* (DHTML). Drop-down menus, hiding layers, and changing text are a few examples of DHTML scripts that you can use on a Web page to make your user's experience pleasurable. One of the main building blocks of DHTML scripts is the *Document Object Method* (DOM). The DOM is the way to access all the elements on the page and allows you to manipulate them. For more on DHTML, see Chapter 15.

JavaScript is a client side language; therefore, it cannot interact with server elements such as databases. JavaScript was used on the server side with certain servers, but most of those servers are not in use any more. If you want to use databases, the best option is to use a server side technology like ASP, .NET, PHP, or JSP.

EXECUTE A JAVASCRIPT FUNCTION

1 Open your Web browser to view a Web page.

2 Click the right arrow link to change the month.

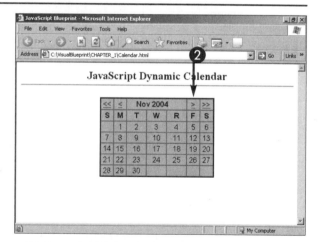

● The calendar changes the month.

VIEW THE SOURCE CODE

1 Click View➔Source.

```
View
  Toolbars                    ▶
✔ Status Bar
  Explorer Bar                ▶

  Go To                       ▶
  Stop                      Esc
  Refresh                    F5

  Text Size                   ▶
  Encoding                    ▶

  Source
  Privacy Report...
  Full Screen               F11
```
← **1**

● The Web page source code appears in the default text editor

2 Scroll down in the text editor until you see the `<script>` tag.

● The JavaScript statements placed between the `<script>` tags executes when the file is loaded or functions are called.

```
Calendar.html - Notepad                                        _ | 8 | ×
File Edit Format View Help
<script type="text/javascript">  ←  2
    var theMonths = new Array("Jan", "Feb", "Mar", "Apr", "May", "Jun", "Jul", "Aug",
        "Sep", "Oct", "Nov", "Dec")

    function GetFirstLast(xDate){
        var theDate = new Date(xDate);
        theDate.setDate(1);
        startDay = theDate.getDay();
        theDate.setMonth(theDate.getMonth() + 1);
        theDate.setDate(0);
        endDate = theDate.getDate();
        answer = new Array(startDay,endDate);
        return answer
    }

    var defDate = new Date()
    function BuildCalendar(){
        theD = GetFirstLast(defDate);
        curMonth = defDate.getMonth();
        curDate = defDate.getDate();
        curYear = defDate.getYear();
```

Extra

All modern day browsers support JavaScript, but some users may have the JavaScript option turned off for security reasons. Internet Explorer, Netscape, Mozilla, Firebird, Firefox, Safari, and Opera are the most popular browsers used to browse the Internet. Each of the browsers has multiple versions, which support different levels of JavaScript. A modern day browser supports JavaScript Version 1.5.

The downside to the wide variety of browsers is *cross browser scripting*. Cross browser scripting is trying to get the same JavaScript code to perform in the same manner across every browser. One problem that you may face is browser preparatory code. For example, Internet Explorer contains methods and events that do not follow the Web standards. Therefore, these commands do not work in other browsers since the commands do not exist in the browsers' underlying code structure. The standardization of JavaScript methods and events is making it easier to handle `cross browser scripting`.

Internet Explorer is the most popular browser for surfing the Internet, but the Mozilla based browsers — Mozilla, Firebird, and Firefox — are being used more. Dependability and security are the reasons some users have switched to Mozilla browsers. Developers tend to prefer Mozilla because it follows standards very closely.

Enter a JavaScript Statement into the Address Bar

You can work with JavaScript in three ways within the browser: hard coded into the HTML document, hard coded into a JavaScript file (.js), or entered into the address bar of the Web browser. You can run small segments of code by using the address bar to execute JavaScript commands. You can do this to test a segment of code or to manipulate a Web page.

To execute a JavaScript command in the address bar, you must first type javascript: followed by the JavaScript statement that you want to execute. You can have multiple JavaScript statements executed at the same time by placing a semicolon after each statement. The code executes in a left to right manner.

If you enter the JavaScript statement without the javascript: keyword, the browser tries to locate the keyword. For example, if you enter alert('message'); into the address bar instead of javascript:alert ('message');, the browser tries to locate alert ('message') that is most likely to cause the following message: "The Page Cannot Be Displayed".

Adding JavaScript to the address bar is used for both good and bad. JavaScript in the address bar allows you to manipulate form fields and other page properties with a single line of code. A user can easily run a statement in the browser that can alter hidden fields, make disabled fields enabled, and so on. This means that there is a lower amount of security when working with JavaScript.

If security is important, then you are going to have to develop extra checks to make sure that the user did not try to manipulate information. If you are integrating JavaScript with a server side technology, then it is important to do checks on the server side to make sure that the information is correct.

Enter a JavaScript Statement into the Address Bar

① In a Web browser, click in the address bar and delete any text that exists.

② Type **javascript:** in the address bar.

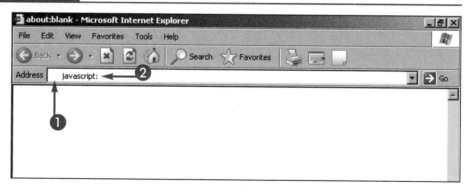

③ Enter a JavaScript statement after the javascript: keyword followed by a semicolon.

④ Enter a second JavaScript statement after the semicolon.

⑤ Press the Enter key to execute the JavaScript statements.

● The JavaScript code executes in the browser window.

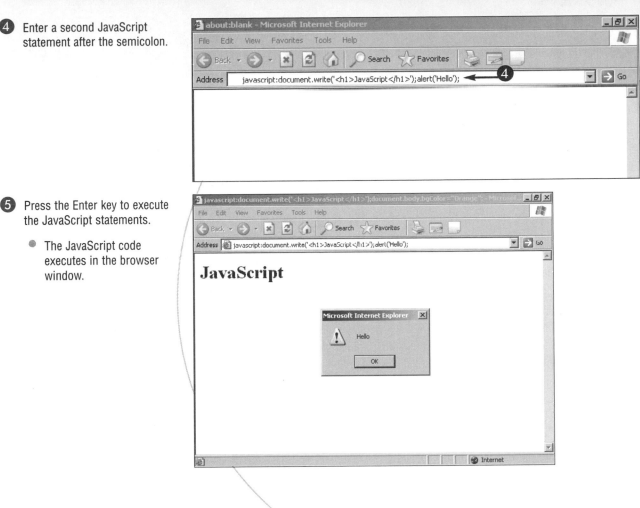

You can add JavaScript commands to the Favorites folder of your Internet browser. This is commonly referred to as bookmarklets. Almost any JavaScript command can be formed into a bookmarklet. You can create a bookmarklet by creating a blank HTML page with one link on it and then adding the JavaScript command to the href attribute. You add the JavaScript command to the href attribute the same way you add it to the address bar of the browser. It must contain javascript: followed by the statement.

Create bookmarklets

```
<a href="javascript:window.resizeTo(800,600);">Resize 800X600</a>

<a href=" javascript:void(document.
oncontextmeny=null)"> Enable Right Click</a>

<a href='javascript:alert(unescape
(unescape(document.cookie)))'>View Cookie</a>
```

Run bookmarklets

Right-click the link and select Add to Favorites. You can then run your bookmarklets by selecting them in your Favorites folder.

Embed JavaScript in an HTML Document

You can add JavaScript to a Web page's HTML source by placing the statements between `<script>` tags. This requires both opening and closing tags identical to HTML `<head>` and `<body>` tags, which both require an opening and closing tag. The `<script>` tags should not overlap any other tags on the page or the browser is going to consider it a JavaScript statement.

The `<script>` tag can have two attributes. You can set the `type` attribute to recognize the MIME type, such as `text/javascript`. The `language` attribute was the original way to specify the scripting language, but it has been phased out in the current XHTML standard. If you do not specify the script type, the browser makes a determination of what coding language is between the `<script>` tags. You should specify the script type because there are other client-side languages for which the browser

might confuse the code. For example, Microsoft Internet Explorer supports VBScript.

You can find the `<script>` tag in the `<head>` or the `<body>` tags. A Web page can contain multiple `<script>` tags, which are not required to be all in the header or all in the body. You can use multiple `<script>` tags to position JavaScript code in certain areas to write out dynamic content on a Web page. For example, you can add a JavaScript function at the bottom of the page to write out the current date in the footer. On that same page, you can have a JavaScript function between the `<head>` tags that validates a form.

JavaScript also has special event handlers that are added as attributes to HTML elements. These special JavaScript attributes do not require `<script>` tags to be placed around them. The common event handlers are `onclick`, `onmouseover`, `onmouseoff`, and `onload`.

Embed JavaScript in an HTML Document

① Click View→Source.

● The Source Code opens in the default viewer.

② Type **<script type="text/javascript">** between the `<body>` tags.

③ Press the Enter key.

④ Type the **</script>** closing tag.

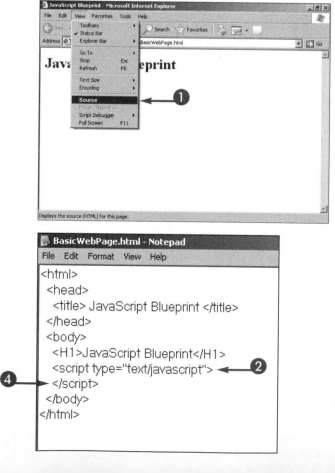

⑤ Add a JavaScript statement between the `<script>` tags.

⑥ Repeat step **5** for each JavaScript statement.

⑦ Save the document.

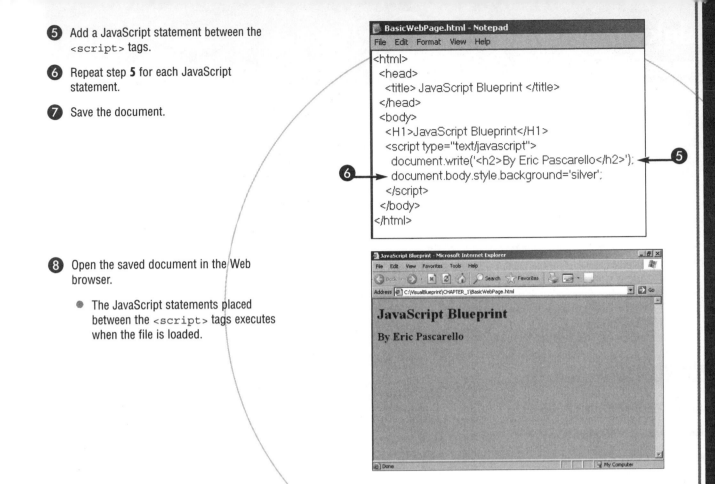

⑧ Open the saved document in the Web browser.

- The JavaScript statements placed between the `<script>` tags executes when the file is loaded.

Extra

You can use JavaScript to personalize a Web page for your visitors. To execute this example script, you will need to execute it within a set of `<script>` tags and open the saved file in a browser. The following snippet of code opens a dialog box in which the user can enter its name. The user name appears on the Web page using another JavaScript statement:

Personalize a Web Page
```
var name - window.prompt("What is
your name?");

document.write("Hello  " + name + ".
Welcome to this Web page. I hope you
find what you are looking for.");
```

You can give the user the ability to change the background color and the font color of the Web page by using a series of prompt dialog boxes. The prompt dialog box is used to gather the user's color preferences for the background and the text color. The values from the two prompt dialog boxes are then applied to the Web page.

Color Preferences
```
var theBGColor = prompt('Choose your
background color');

var theFontColor = prompt('Choose
your text color');

document.body.style.background =
theBGColor;

document.body.style.color =
theFontColor;
```

Link an External JavaScript File

You can use external JavaScript files to allow multiple pages to use the same code. This saves you time and alleviates your need to edit each individual page when you want to update your script. These files are known as external JavaScript files (`.js`). You can use multiple external JavaScript files in the Web page by linking to each one of them.

You can reference an external JavaScript file by using the source (`src`) tag. The external JavaScript file is linked to the Web pages in the same way that an HTML image is linked to the page. For example, the statement `<script src="theJavaScript.js"></script>` attaches the `theJavaScript.js` file to the Web page. You can add the `<script>` tag to the `<body>` or `<head>` tags just like a normal JavaScript code.

If you prefer to keep your JavaScript files in a separate folder, you need to add the folder name to the `src` tag. For example, the statement `src="scripts/theExample.js"` looks for the `theExample.js` in the folder called `scripts`.

You should not include any HTML or `<script>` tags in your JavaScript files. JavaScript files should only include the code that would normally go in between the `<script>` tags. This ensures that the code behaves in the same manner whether the code is in a document or in a separate JavaScript file.

When the Web page is loaded, the content in the JavaScript file acts the same as it would if it were embedded into the document. External JavaScript file code can share information with the embedded JavaScript code and vice versa. Some browsers use cached external JavaScript files when the page is loaded. Therefore, the total loading time of the Web page is quicker.

Link an External JavaScript File

RETRIEVE JAVASCRIPT CODE

1 In a text editor, cut the contents of the `<script>` tags out of a file.

2 Save the file.

BasicWebPage.html - Notepad

File   Edit   Format   View   Help

```html
<html>
 <head>
  <title> JavaScript Blueprint </title>
 </head>
 <body>
  <H1>JavaScript Blueprint</H1>
  <script type="text/javascript">
   document.write('<h2>By Eric Pascarello</h2>');
   document.body.style.background='silver';
  </script>
 </body>
</html>
```
1

CREATE A JS FILE

1 Open a new file in your text editor.

2 Paste the `<script>` tag contents into the file.

3 Save the file with the JS file extension.

theJavaScript.js - Notepad

File   Edit   Format   View   Help

```javascript
   document.write('<h2>By Eric Pascarello</h2>');
   document.body.style.background='silver';
```
2

LINK TO AN EXTERNAL FILE

① Reopen your HTML source code file.

② Add the `src` attribute to the `<script>` tag.

③ Set the `src` attribute to the external JavaScript file.

④ Save the file.

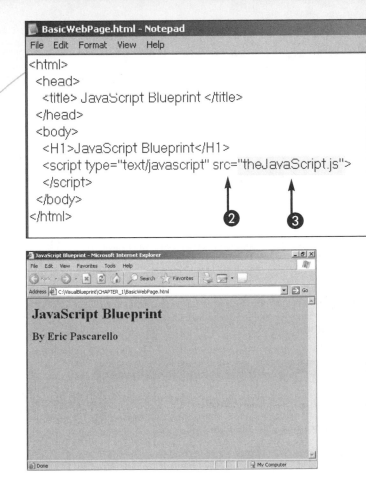

VIEW RESULTS

① Open the HTML file in a Web browser.

● The JavaScript statements still work the same as an external file.

Extra

You can have both hard-coded JavaScript code and external JavaScript code on the same page. The code can interact between the two scripts; therefore, the external JavaScript file can call the functions in the JavaScript file located in the head or the body on the HTML page. For example, you can store variables in the hard-coded JavaScript file and have the external file use them. The variables may also be stored in the external JavaScript file and used in the same manner with the JavaScript code in the HTML document.

You can run into problems when converting an error-free JavaScript code into an external file. By using the following three checks, you can normally find the cause of the error.

● Make sure that there are no `<script>` tags within the JavaScript file.

● Make sure that the source attribute is pointing to the correct directory.

● Check to see if the file has been uploaded to the correct directory.

If you are still having trouble using external JavaScript files, you can try using debugging techniques in Chapter 17 to help eliminate the problem.

Present Content to Non-JavaScript Enabled Browsers

Y ou can display text to the user, browsing your Web site that does not have JavaScript enabled on its browser, by using the `<noscript>` tags. When JavaScript is disabled by the user, your JavaScript code cannot execute. The browser ignores the code; therefore, your navigational menus, form validation, and so on cannot execute when the user is accessing your Web page.

The `<noscript>` tags are entered in between the opening and closing `<body>` tags just like normal HTML code. You can use the `<noscript>` tags to ask the user to enable JavaScript to view your Web site properly or to guide the user to a portion of your site that does not require JavaScript. For example, the statement `<noscript>This page uses JavaScript</noscript>` displays the text "This page uses JavaScript" if JavaScript is not enabled on the browser.

The common reasons why people disable JavaScript are mainly related to security issues. Pop-ups, redirection, alerts, infinite loops, and advertisements are a few reasons why people would want to disable JavaScript. The Mozilla browsers also have other options to only disable certain parts of JavaScript code that a user may find obtrusive. A few options that may be disabled are pop-up windows, resizing of the browser, animating the browser window, and many more.

You cannot force a user to use JavaScript. If JavaScript is required for the page to execute properly, then the user cannot use it. Having JavaScript disabled limits the user to what they can do while surfing the Internet. Most online forums, mail clients, shopping carts, game sites, and other general Web sites require that JavaScript be enabled.

Present Content to Non-JavaScript Enabled Browsers

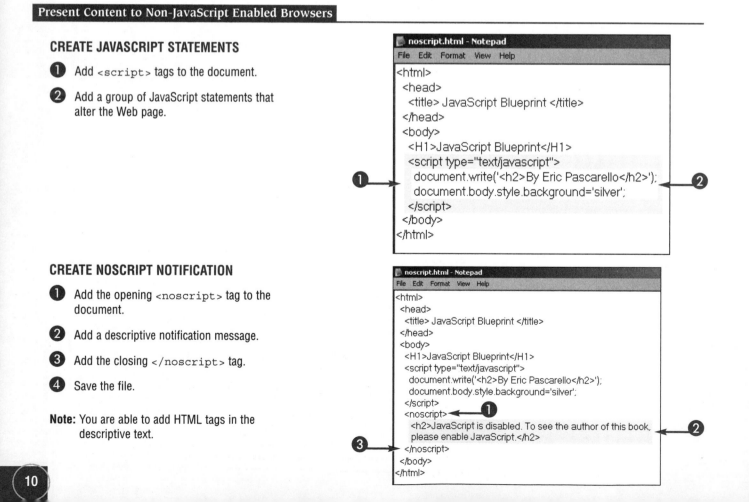

CREATE JAVASCRIPT STATEMENTS

❶ Add `<script>` tags to the document.

❷ Add a group of JavaScript statements that alter the Web page.

CREATE NOSCRIPT NOTIFICATION

❶ Add the opening `<noscript>` tag to the document.

❷ Add a descriptive notification message.

❸ Add the closing `</noscript>` tag.

❹ Save the file.

Note: You are able to add HTML tags in the descriptive text.

VIEW PAGE WITH JAVASCRIPT ENABLED

 Open the file in a Web browser with JavaScript enabled.

- The JavaScript statements executed and the content of the `<noscript>` tag is not displayed.

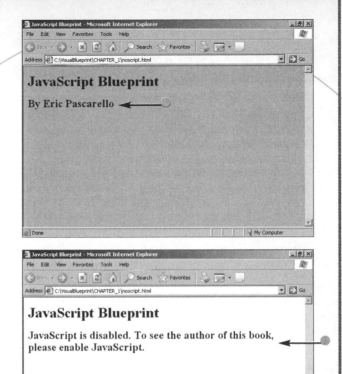

VIEW PAGE WITH JAVASCRIPT DISABLED

 Open the file in a Web browser with JavaScript disabled.

- The JavaScript statements did not execute. The content of the `<noscript>` tags is displayed.

Extra

You cannot control the browser's configuration settings; therefore, there is no way to enable JavaScript support without the user's interaction. You can only rely on the `<noscript>` tag to inform the user that JavaScript is required in order for your Web site to function properly.

Users are able to disable many other browser settings by adjusting the browser's preference settings. These settings include style sheets, Java Applets, ActiveX, scripting, cookies, certain JavaScript commands, and many more. Many Microsoft Internet Explorer users are disabling ActiveX controls since they can have major security issues including virus and spyware application downloads.

One downfall that you can find with JavaScript is you cannot adjust the user's default printer settings. Because of this restriction, you have to inform the users to change their layout to landscape if that is how your page needs to be printed. You cannot control the layout, printing background images, header or footer text, number of copies, and so on.

Security issues are the main reason for the restrictions that limit what you are able to do with the browser window. You can use ActiveX controls with Internet Explorer to get around some of these security issues, but most people disable that option. There are ActiveX controls to remove the Print dialog box, write files to your computer, and much more.

Add a Comment to JavaScript Code

You can use comments to add descriptive text to your JavaScript code, which does not execute. Comments are ignored by the parser and are only visible in the file when the user views the source code. The parser is how the browser interpolates the JavaScript and HTML code so it executes and displays the information properly on your screen.

Most developers add comments to a JavaScript file to note what a certain function's purpose is for future reference. Comments are useful to keep track of the script's version number, release date, update date, and the author of the code. Another use for comments allows developers to debug their code that contains errors. By placing comments in a particularly troublesome section, the troubleshooter can pinpoint the problem so it may be fixed. See Chapter 17 for more information.

There are two types of comments: a single line comment and a multiple line comment. A single line comment is designated with two forward slashes (//). Single line comments hide a single line of information after the two forward slashes. Multiple line comments start with a forward slash and an asterisk (/*) and end with the opposite (*/). Information that is between the comment indicators is ignored by the browser when the information is being processed.

Comments can appear anywhere within a set of <script> tags. The special markings tell the parser to ignore that portion of the code.

If you want to add comments in the HTML code instead of inside the <script> tags, you have to use a different type of syntax. HTML comments are single or multiple lines. The comment starts with (<!-) and ends with (->).

Add a Comment to JavaScript Code

ADD A SINGLE LINE COMMENT

1. Type **//** where you want a comment to appear.

2. Add text to the comment.

3. Repeat steps **1** and **2** for each line of comments.

4. Save the file.

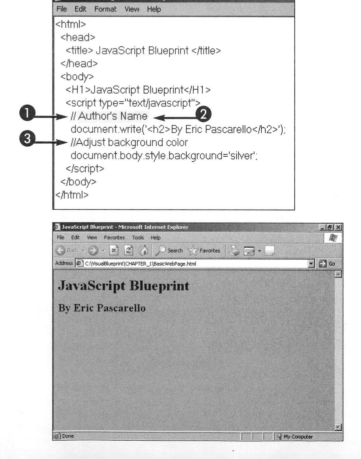

5. Open the HTML file in a browser.

● The comments do not show up in the Web page text since the Web browser ignores them when processing the page.

ADD A MULTIPLE LINE COMMENT

1️⃣ Type **/*** where you want the multiple comment to start.

2️⃣ Type ***/** where you want the multiple comment to end.

3️⃣ Repeat steps **1** and **2** for each group of comments.

4️⃣ Save the file.

5️⃣ Open the HTML file in a browser.

● The multiple line comments are not displayed on the screen because the Web browser ignores them while processing the page.

Note: The JavaScript code did not execute since the multiple line comment surrounded the code.

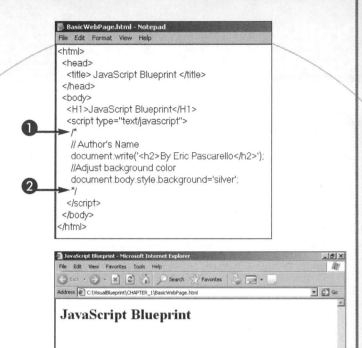

Extra

You can personalize your JavaScript code by adding a header to your JavaScript files. A header includes information about the JavaScript code. The header normally contains the script's name, the script's version, the development or update date, contact information, usage statement, and a description of what the script does. The JavaScript header information is a great way to inform users where they can check for updates to a script. They can also e-mail you if they run into problems or find an error that you may have missed during testing. People may also contact you and ask if they can host your code on their Web site.

If you use a JavaScript file that contains another developer's code, it is standard practice to leave the original header and add documentation to inform the person viewing your script that it has been changed from the original. This allows the user to find the original code if necessary and gives credit to the original author.

There are times when a particular code is copyrighted. It is always a good idea for you to check with the developer first before using the code. Often, a developer is happy that the code is being used and may even link to your Web site to show an example of how it can be used.

Protect the
Source Code

You can try to protect your JavaScript source code, but your Web page loading time may be affected. Client side coding is open source, which means you can view the underlying code. By right-clicking and selecting View Source on any Web page, you can see the source code. You can also view the source code by selecting View from the toolbar and then selecting Source. The source code opens in text editor. On a Windows machine, the text editor is normally notepad.

You can use JavaScript to disable the right-click button of the mouse. That disables the user's ability to see the source code; however, there is no way to stop a person from clicking View on the toolbar. You can also use a `bookmarklet` that disables the right-click script, attempting to block the source code useless.

A few options render the code unreadable or obfuscate. The downside to this is that it causes page-loading time to increase and obfuscation is not secure. Since obfuscating causes the code to be unreadable, the developer cannot access it later on. Therefore, before obfuscating the code, you should make sure there is a backup copy. There are many obfuscation programs on the Internet; some are free, and others you have to pay for.

Other developers try to protect images by disabling the right-click button. Images are stored in the Temporary Internet Files folder and there are programs that can retrieve all the images from a site. The best solution is to watermark the images with your name or logo or do not put them on the Web in the first place.

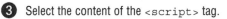

Protect the Source Code

SAFEGUARD CODE

① Click View➔Source.

   ● The source code opens in the default text editor.

② Save a backup copy of the source code.

③ Select the content of the `<script>` tag.

④ Paste the content of code in the obfuscation software of your choice.

Note: You can find free and trial versions of obfuscation software online. Since they have different processes, follow steps provided by the software developer.

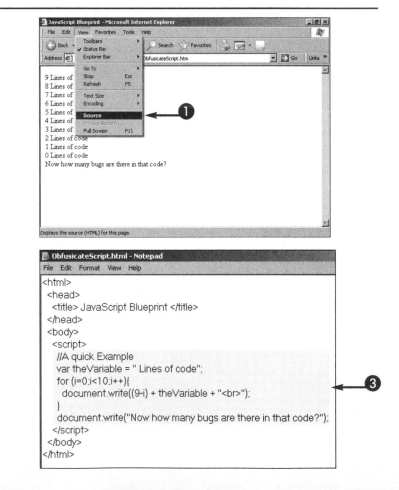

OBFUSCATED CODE

① Paste the obfuscated code from the obfuscation software output between the `<script>` tags.

② Save the file.

③ Open the HTML file.

● The output of the JavaScript code runs the same.

Note: The loading time may increase slightly for larger scripts.

```
ObfusicatedCode.html - Notepad
File  Edit  Format  View  Help

<html>
 <head>
  <title> JavaScript Blueprint </title>
 </head>
 <body>
  <script>
           S="var`1 = \" Lines of code\";for (i=0;i<10;i++){`0(9-i) +`1+ \"<br>\");} `0\"Now
how many bugs are there in that
code?\");";for(l=1;l>=0;)S=S.replace(eval('/'+l+'/g').("document.write(~ theVariable
~".split('~'))[l−]);eval(S);
  </script>
 </body>
</html>
```

①

```
JavaScript Blueprint - Microsoft Internet Explorer
File  Edit  View  Favorites  Tools  Help

Back      Search    Favorites

Address  C:\VisualBlueprint\CHAPTER_1\ObfusicatedCode.html      Go

9 Lines of code
8 Lines of code
7 Lines of code
6 Lines of code
5 Lines of code
4 Lines of code
3 Lines of code
2 Lines of code
1 Lines of code
0 Lines of code
Now how many bugs are there in that code?

Done                                    My Computer
```

Extra

You can remove toolbars from a browser window by using pop-up windows, use no right-click scripts, obfuscate the code, and many other things to protect your source code, but keep in mind you want people to come back to your site. Page loading time is a major factor if a user chooses to visit the site again. If you obfuscate a large JavaScript file, it can take the page longer to load and you may lose those impatient users on a dialup modem.

User friendliness is one of many factors that bring a user back to your Web page. If you make the experience as pleasing as possible, then the user is more likely to come back to your page instead of finding the information elsewhere.

Most successful Web sites keep user-friendly Web pages in mind. They make sure that their code is clean and bug free. They do not interfere with the user's browsing experience. They allow a user to print their page, to view the source, and to use the right-click for navigational purposes. They use JavaScript to enhance the Web page, not to make it inaccessible for the user.

Understand Variable Types

You can use variables to hold different data types when you are creating a JavaScript. Variables are like a temporary holding container for values. As values change, the variable is updated to hold the new value. Values may be changed at any point within a JavaScript document. Variables are accessed and used within functions, mathematical equations, set form field values, and so much more.

Variables can hold *constant values.* Constant values are values that do not change for the entire duration of the script. For example, you can create a variable named `hoursPerDay` and set it to `24`; within your code, you can refer to the number of hours per day using the variable `hoursPerDay`. Although, simply typing the value `24` in the code is easier, if you use a variable, the equation will have meaning when you examine it. Using variables to hold constants makes debugging and working with your code easier. However, JavaScript does not know the difference between a constant value and a normal variable. As a result, the constant variable may be overwritten if you store a value into the variable. A constant only remains constant if you do not change the value.

Variable names must meet several requirements. For example, `24` is not a good variable name because it is easily confused with a value. Variable names can include upper- and lowercase letters, numbers, and the underscore character (`_`). No other punctuation marks may be used when creating variable names. Variable names must not begin with a number and they cannot include any spaces.

Variable names in JavaScript are case-sensitive. For example, variable names such as `Hello`, `hello`, and `HeLLo` appear similar but are actually different from one another. It is best to use variable names that describe the data they hold. If you maintain consistency when naming variables, it is easier to understand your code when you look at it later.

For example, you can consistently capitalize all constant values as a way of identifying that they do not change. Several different types of variables exist, depending on the type of data that they hold. The various variable types can hold an assortment of numbers and words as values. Specifically, these types include the following:

- Integer numbers
- Floating-point numbers
- String
- Boolean

Each variable type requires a different amount of memory to store the data. A Boolean value requires the least amount of memory while a string requires the most. An integer requires less memory than a floating-point number. Therefore, if your application requires a large amount of variables, then you should use the type that helps the applications performance.

A good coding technique is to start the variable names with a letter that indicates the type of variable. This technique helps as you work with the code. For example, an integer variable is named `iVar`, a floating-point variable is `fVar`, a string variable is `sVar`, and a Boolean variable is `bVar`. This technique for naming variables is not required, only suggested. Other naming conventions include using `int` for integer, `flo` for floating-point, `str` for string, and `bool` as Boolean. You can develop your own strategy so it is easy to figure out the variable types.

Each of the variable types has its own methods and properties. These methods and properties allow you to work with the variable and extract the information that you require. Each of the properties and methods only works with its own variable type.

Integer Variables

Integer variables can hold the basic counting numbers, either positive or negative. Integer values do not have decimal places, only whole numbers. Examples of integer values include 2, 345, and -34.

These values are used with arithmetic operators such as addition, subtraction, multiplication, and division. Integer values are commonly used as counters especially in for-loops where the integer value is incremented or decremented. Integer values also make up the placement of objects and the width and height of HTML elements on the browser window.

Floating-Point Variables

Floating-point variables can hold fractional numbers that include a decimal point. You can use these variables with the standard arithmetic operators such as addition, subtraction, multiplication, and division.

Examples of floating-point values include 2.5, -34.56, and 3.121.

Floating point values are commonly used in mathematical calculations, shopping carts, form element values, and anywhere else a fractional number is required.

One thing that floating-point values do not hold in the decimal places is trailing zeros. For example, the statement `fNum = 1.23000;` is stored as a floating-point number 1.23 on the variable `fNum`.

String Variables

String variables are simply words and sentences. These variables can hold single characters or entire paragraphs. String values are usually designated with a set of quotation marks.

Examples of string values include `"hello"`, `"abcdef"`, and `'This is a test of a string'`.

The quotation marks can be single (`'`) or double (`"`), but they may not be interchanged. If the string starts with a single quote, it must end with a single quote. If the quotation marks are interchanged, then an error occurs and the script cannot be executed.

Strings can hold any type of information including alphabetical characters, numbers, and special characters. Special characters include white space, question mark, ampersand, exclamation point, dollar sign, and so on.

Boolean Variables

Boolean variables are a unique variable type that can hold only the words *true* or *false*. You can use these variables to test the condition of a statement. The number 0 is used to represent the value `false` and 1 represents the value `true`.

Booleans are normally used as flags to determine if an item is allowed to execute. Booleans are commonly used in form validation scripts to verify that the form may be submitted.

Declare Variables

JavaScript is a loosely typed language that does not require the user to declare each variable type. It enables you to combine variable types without causing an error, which other programming languages normally face. This means that you can initially use a variable as a string and later use the same variable as an integer. The freedom of this loosely typed language can lead to problems if you do not keep track of the variable types.

To declare a variable, simply type the variable name. The variable type assigned to the variable is automatically set based on what type of variable it holds. Each variable type requires a different amount of memory to hold the information. A Boolean requires the least amount of memory while a string requires a large amount of memory to hold the data.

You can specifically state variable names by using the `var` keyword in front of the variable name.

```
var int1
var int2;
```

It is a good practice for you to add a semicolon (`;`) after the variable name. The semicolon is not required for the code to function properly, but it gives a more structured format to your code. The structured format makes the code easier to debug.

You can also declare several variables at once by separating the names with a comma (`,`). For example, `var int1, int2, str1, str2;` declares four variables. Declaring the variables in one long string saves you time and space in the document and it is also a good way for you to keep track of variables' names.

When you are using variables, make sure you capitalize and spell the name correctly. A common error is misspelled variable names, which normally leads to errors in the JavaScript code.

Declare Variables

DECLARE A SINGLE VARIABLE

① Add `<script>` tags between the `<body>` tags.

② Between the `<script>` tags, add the `var` keyword, followed by a variable name, and then a semicolon (;).

③ Save the document.

DECLARE MULTIPLE VARIABLES

① Add `<script>` tags between the `<body>` tags.

② Between the `<script>` tags, add the `var` keyword, followed by a variable name, and then a comma (,).

③ To declare additional variables, add each variable name followed by a comma (,), inserting a semicolon (;) after the last variable name instead of a comma.

④ Save the document.

Note: If the semicolon is missed, the script will still execute properly.

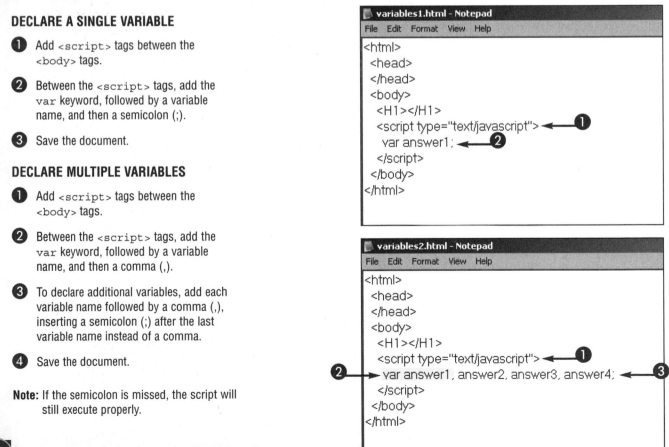

Assign Values to Variables

You can assign values to a variable by using the equal sign (=) placed to the right of the variable name. The value should always be placed on the right side of the equal sign. The value can be any of the variable types including Boolean, integer, floating-point, and string.

When storing an integer into the variable, you do not have to use quotation marks (" ") around the number. For example, the statement int1 = 24; stores the value 24 in the variable int1. If you use quotation marks, then you are creating a string.

A floating-point value is stored just like an integer without the quotation marks. Since a floating point number requires a decimal place, the statement fp1 = 12.24; stores the floating point number 12.24 into the variable fp1.

You can assign strings to a variable name if they are included in quotation marks (" "). Any string that does not have quotation marks is considered a variable name. For example, the statement str1 = "blueprint"; places the string "blueprint" in the variable str1.

You can also use single quotes to store a string. For example, the statement str1 = 'blueprint'; also stores the string 'blueprint' into the variable str1.

If the quotes are not included, the statement str1 = blueprint; searches for the variable name blueprint for the information it is to store. If blueprint is not declared, an error occurs and the script cannot execute.

When you declare a variable you can assign a value to it at that time. You just need to include the var keyword in front of the variable name. For example, the statement var int2 = 13; stores the value into the variable int2.

Assign Values to Variables

1 Add a variable declaration.

2 Add each variable name below the variable declaration and set each variable equal to a value.

3 Set each variable declaration and its equal statement in one line.

4 Add a document.write statement for each variable.

5 Save the file.

6 Open the HTML file in a Web browser.

● The values assigned to the variables appear.

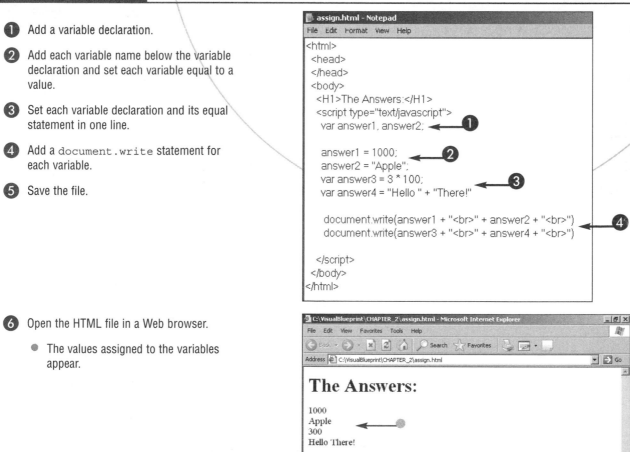

Display Integers

Integers are positive or negative values that do not have a decimal point. These values are typically referred to as whole numbers or counting numbers. Integer variables are decimal, hexadecimal, or octal. The differences between these types are the base of the number system. Decimal integers are base 10. Hexadecimal integers are base 16; the numbers above 9 are represented by the letters A to F. Hexadecimal numbers have a 0x in front of them. Octal integers are base 8 and include a leading zero. For example, 24 is a decimal number, 024 is an octal number, and 0x24 is a hexadecimal number.

Integers are commonly used in `for` loops, and hexadecimal numbers are used for Web page colors. For example, the `for-loop` statement `for(i=0;i<10;i++)` uses an integer to iterate through the loop. You also find integer values being used when accessing the width, height, and the coordinates of the elements on the browser screen. The element's coordinates, width, and height values require a whole number in order for the page to render correctly. Two problems can occur if a fractional number is used: An error can occur or the element can be misplaced on the screen.

Web page colors are made of red, green, and blue with intensity levels ranging from 0 to 256. A hexadecimal number is used to represent the intensity level of the separate colors.

When you code a Web page, you use the colors hex code to assign a color to an element. When you want an element to be white you assign it #FFFFFF.

The color white is made up of a 100 percent intensity of red, green, and blue, so the values are 256, 256, and 256. The number 256 in hexadecimal is "FF".

Display Integers

① Add a variable declaration.

② Set the value for each variable name.

③ Add the `document.write` statements to display the results.

④ Save the file.

```
numbers.html - Notepad
File  Edit  Format  View  Help
<html>
 <head>
 </head>
 <body>
  <H1>The Answers:</H1>
  <script type="text/javascript">
    var decNum, hexNum, octNum;        ——①

    decNum = 24;
    hexNum = 0x24;     ——②
    octNum = 024;

    document.write("This is a decimal number: " + decNum  + "<br>");
    document.write("This is a hexadecimal number: " + hexNum + "<br>");     ——③
    document.write("This is a octaldecimal number: " + octNum + "<br>");

  </script>
 </body>
</html>
```

⑤ Open the HTML file in a Web browser.

● The variable values appear.

Note: The values appear in the decimal equivalent.

```
C:\VisualBlueprint\CHAPTER_2\numbers.html - Microsoft Internet Explorer
File  Edit  View  Favorites  Tools  Help
Back  ·  ·  ×  ·  Search  Favorites
Address  C:\VisualBlueprint\CHAPTER_2\numbers.html
```

The Answers:

This is a decimal number: 24
This is a hexadecimal number: 36 ◄
This is a octaldecimal number: 20

Display Floating-Point Numbers

Floating-point numbers are fractional numbers that include a decimal point. These numbers are positive or negative. Floating-point numbers are used for storing or calculating numbers where the decimal point is not fixed. The decimal point moves around as needed so that the calculation takes into account significant digits. This technique enables the storage of very large and very small numbers.

Very large or very small numbers are expressed in scientific notation. Scientific notation places the letter E within the number followed by the number of places the decimal point needs to be moved. A positive value moves the decimal number to the right while a negative number moves the decimal place to the left.

For example, 7.24E6 represents the number 7,240,000 and 11.02E-4 represents the number 0.001102. Floating-point numbers that are less then 1.0E-7 or greater than 1.0E20 appear in scientific notation when they display on the screen.

JavaScript uses an IEEE double-precision 64-bit value that provides a usable number range of 2.2E-208 to 1.79E308. JavaScript treats numbers beyond these limits as *Infinity*. The IEEE method is a standard that is used to hold and calculate numeric values. The IEEE precision that JavaScript uses has a flaw that you may run into. For example, the mathematical statement of a floating-point number 99999999999.99999 X 2 should equal 1999999999999.99998, but the calculation gives a result of 1999999999999.99997. There is no way to avoid this problem.

Floating Point numbers do not hold trailing zeros, the trailing zeros are dropped when they are encountered. For example, the statement `fVal = 0.10;` stores 0.1 in the variable `fVal`.

Display Floating-Point Numbers

1 Add a variable declaration.

2 Set either a large or small floating-point value for each variable name.

3 Add a `document.write` statement to display the results.

4 Save the file.

```
float.htm - Notepad
File  Edit  Format  View  Help
<html>
 <head>
 </head>
 <body>
  <H1>The Answers:</H1>
  <script type="text/javascript">
   var largeNum, veryLargeNum, smallNum, verySmallNum;       ← 1

   largeNum = 123456789000000000000000;
   veryLargeNum = 4.321E60;                                  ← 2
   smallNum = 0.000000123;
   verySmallNum = 6.023E-23;

   document.write("Large number: " + largeNum + "<br>");
   document.write("Very large number: " + veryLargeNum + "<br>");
   document.write("Small number: " + smallNum + "<br>");    ← 3
   document.write("Very small number: " + verySmallNum + "<br>");

  </script>
 </body>
</html>
```

5 Open the HTML file in a Web browser.

● The variable values appear in a scientific format.

The Answers:

Large number: 1.23456789e+24
Very large number: 4.321e+60
Small number: 1.23e-7
Very small number: 6.023e-23

Display Booleans

Boolean values are logical values that are either true or false. In addition to the actual words, the values are set to 0 or 1, with 1 representing true and 0 representing false. The Boolean represents a logic light switch. When the light is on, the Boolean value is true. When the light is off, the Boolean value is false.

When you are storing the logic true or false into the Boolean variable, you should not include quotation marks around the keyword. For example, the statement `var bool1 = true;` stores the Boolean value `true` into the variable `bool1`. The statement `var bool2 = "true";` is not the same as the statement `var bool1 = true;`. If you were to include quotes around the `true` keyword, then the browser interprets the value as a string. As a result, the string variable cannot perform the same operations as the Boolean variable.

You can also refer to Boolean statements as flags. These flags can make great conditional statements. You can use a conditional statement to determine the flow of the program. Examples of conditional statements are `if-else` statements or `switch` statements which are explained in Chapter 5.

A Boolean value is seen visually through two types of HTML elements. The HTML check boxes and radio buttons elements have a Boolean nature. If the check box is checked or if the radio button is selected, the Boolean value is true. If the check box is unchecked or the radio button is not selected, then its Boolean value is false.

Booleans values are normally used to determine whether to execute a section of code. Booleans are commonly used in browser detection and form validations.

Display Booleans

1 Add a variable declaration.

2 Set the Boolean value for each variable name.

3 Add `document.write` statements to display the results.

4 Save the file.

```
bollean.html - Notepad
File  Edit  Format  View  Help
<html>
 <head>
 </head>
 <body>
  <H1>QUIZ</H1>
  <script type="text/javascript">
   var answer1, answer2, answer3, answer4;          ──1

   answer1 = true;
   answer2 = false;
   answer3 = 0;          ──2
   answer4 = 1;

   document.write("An adult cheatah can run 70mph? " + answer1 + "<br>")
   document.write("Monkeys will only eat bananas? " + answer2 + "<br>")
   document.write("Whales are a type of fish? " + answer3 + "<br>")          ──3
   document.write("An ostrich can run faster than a man? " + answer4 + "<br>")

  </script>
 </body>
</html>
```

5 Open the HTML file in a Web browser.

● The Boolean values appear.

```
C:\VisualBlueprint\CHAPTER_2\bollean.html - Microsoft Internet Explorer
File  Edit  View  Favorites  Tools  Help
Back ▼    ▼    Search   Favorites
Address  C:\VisualBlueprint\CHAPTER_2\bollean.html         Go
```

QUIZ

An adult cheetah can run 70mph? true
Monkeys will only eat bananas? false
Whales are a type of fish? 0
An ostrich can run faster than a man? 1

Display Strings

Y ou can use strings to hold a variety of character types. You can store a sentence in a string; you can store a single character in a string; or you can store numbers and other miscellaneous character types in a string such as underscore (_), dollar sign ($), ampersand (@), pipe (|), and so on.

String values are composed characters that are specified within a set of quotation marks. Strings are contained with double quotation marks (") or single quotation marks ('), but the beginning and ending marks must be the same. Therefore, str1="Test"; and str2='Test'; are valid and str1='Test'; and str2="Test'; are invalid. A common mistake by developers is forgetting a quotation mark when they are declaring a string, or interchanging a single quotation mark for a double quotation mark.

One problem you can face is having an extra quotation mark in the middle of the string. As a result, an error occurs causing the script on the page not to execute. For example, the statement var str3 = "Hello, I am Eric "the programmer" Pascarello"; causes an error due to the extra quotation marks inside the string.

If you want to include quotation marks within the string value, you should include a backslash (\) in front of the quotation mark that is located inside the string. For example, use the backslash in the variable's string like this: str1 = "\"Hello, my name is Eric.\""; You can avoid using the backslash by using single quotes like this: str1 = '"Hello, my name is Eric."'; The result allows the quotation mark to be displayed along with the rest of the characters in the string and the backslash symbol does not appear.

Display Strings

1 Add a variable declaration and set the variable equal to string.

2 Add a backslash (\) to escape quotes (") and apostrophes (') if necessary.

3 Repeat steps 1 and 2 as needed.

4 Add document.write statements to display variables.

5 Save the file.

```
strings.html - Notepad
File  Edit  Format  View  Help
<html>
 <head>
 </head>
 <body>
  <H1>Joke</H1>
  <script type="text/javascript">

    var str1 ='Because there weren\'t any connecting flights.'
    var str2 = "Why did the chicken cross the road?<br>";

    document.write(str2);
    document.write(str1);

  </script>
 </body>
</html>
```

6 Open the HTML file in a Web browser.

● The strings appear on the screen.

```
C:\VisualBlueprint\CHAPTER_2\strings.html - Microsoft Internet Explorer
File  Edit  View  Favorites  Tools  Help
Back          Search   Favorites
Address  C:\VisualBlueprint\CHAPTER_2\strings.html            Go
```

Joke

Why did the chicken cross the road?
Because there weren't any connecting flights.

Determine Variable Type

Y ou can determine the variable type of a variable by using the keyword `typeof`. This allows you to determine the type of character that is contained in the variable so you can perform the correct operation. Certain operations and methods require a specific variable type; if the variable type is not correct, then an error occurs.

To use the `typeof` keyword, you need to place it in front of the variable name with one space between the two words. For example, the statement `var theType = typeof theVar` returns the variable type of the variable `theVar` and stores the value into the variable `theType`.

The `typeof` keyword returns the value `number` for integers and floating-point variables, `string` for string variables, `boolean` for Boolean variables, and `undefined` if the variable type cannot be determined. For example, if the variable `int1` is assigned 6, the statement `typeof int1` returns `number`.

You can use `typeof` in a program to determine if the variable types match. This is especially useful when you combine two variables and want to make sure they are the same type. If a string and an integer are added together, you may not get the result you expected. For example, the statement `int1 = num + 13;` where `var num = "1";` stores `113` in `int1` instead of the expected answer of `14`. You can use the `parseInt()` method discussed later in this chapter to avoid this problem.

In Chapter 15, values commonly appear as strings when you want them to be integers when working with DHTML positional properties. It is useful to use `typeof` to determine what the variable holds before performing an operation. Sometimes the data received is integers and other times it is strings.

Determine Variable Type

DETERMINE VARIABLE TYPE

① Add a variable declaration.

② Set the variables equal to either a string, Boolean, or number.

③ Add `document.write` statements to display the values.

④ Add a `typeof` keyword followed by the variable name to each `document.write` statement.

⑤ Save the file.

⑥ Open the HTML file in a Web browser.

● The variable type for each variable appears.

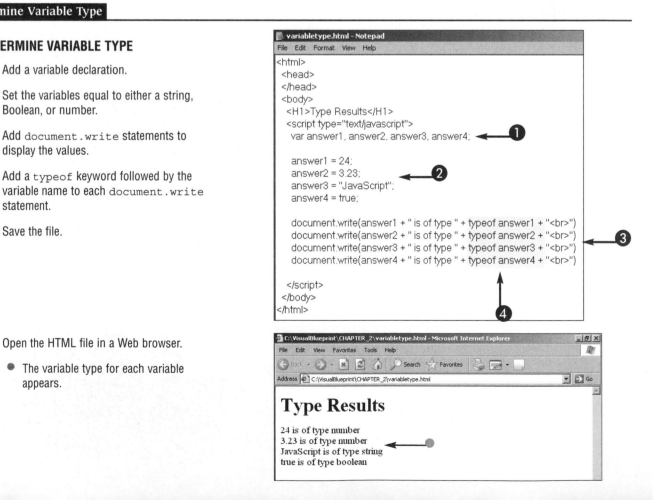

DETERMINE UNASSIGNED VARIABLES

1 Add a variable declaration and set a group of variables equal to a string, Boolean, or number.

2 Add a `document.write` statement to display the value of the `typeof` keyword statement before the variable declaration.

3 Add a `document.write` statement to display the value of the `typeof` keyword statement after the variable declaration.

4 Save the file.

5 Open the HTML file in a Web browser.

● The variable type for each variable appears.

Note: The variable type for each unassigned variable is undefined.

```
variabletype2.html - Notepad
File  Edit  Format  View  Help
<html>
 <head>
 </head>
 <body>
  <H1>Quiz Results</H1>
  <script type="text/javascript">

    document.write("Before: " + answer1 + " is of type " + typeof answer1 + "<br>")
    document.write("Before: " + answer2 + " is of type " + typeof answer2 + "<br>")

    var answer1, answer2;
    answer1 = 24;
    answer2 = true;

    document.write("After: " + answer1 + " is of type " + typeof answer1 + "<br>")
    document.write("After: " + answer2 + " is of type " + typeof answer2 + "<br>")

  </script>
 </body>
</html>
```

C:\VisualBlueprint\CHAPTER_2\variabletype2.html - Microsoft Internet Explorer

File Edit View Favorites Tools Help

Address C:\VisualBlueprint\CHAPTER_2\variabletype2.html

Quiz Results

Before: undefined is of type undefined
Before: undefined is of type undefined
After: 24 is of type number
After: true is of type boolean

Extra

If the undefined value is returned as a result of the `typeof` keyword, the variable does not exist or has not been defined yet.

If you misspell the variable name, it is not recognized and it will also return undefined.

Another case in which the undefined value is returned is if you use the `typeof` keyword before the variable value is assigned. Also, if the `typeof` keyword appears in the script before the variable or function is encountered, the `typeof` keyword returns undefined.

You can use the `typeof` keyword as a useful tool in debugging your JavaScript if you are having problems with the addition of numbers. You can place alert messages in your code to inform you of the variable types. If you find a variable type that is a string and you need it to be a number, you can use the `parseInt()` method or the `parseFloat()` method to convert the string to a number variable type. You can learn more about the `parseInt()` and `parseFloat()` methods later in this chapter.

Convert Strings to Numbers

A number in quotes when it is assigned to a variable can cause problems when you add the string to a number. For example, the statement int1 = num + 1; where var num = "1"; stores 11 in int1 instead of the expected answer of 2. To avoid this problem, JavaScript has two functions to convert a string to a number variable type. You can use parseInt() to convert the string to an integer and parseFloat() to convert the string into a floating-point number. The variable name that holds the string you want to convert should be placed between the parentheses.

For example, you can use the statement int1 = parseInt (str1); to convert the string "256" stored in the variable str1 to an integer.

The parseInt() and parseFloat() methods can extract the numbers that are from the beginning of the string. For example, if the string is str2 = "25px"; and you use the

statement int2 = parseInt(str2); the integer 25 is stored in the variable int2. If str2 contained "L25px";, then the parseInt() method returns NAN, which means Not A Number.

Another method that you can use to convert a numeric string to a number is to multiply the string by 1. For example, you can use int1 = str1 * 1; to convert the string "256" to a number. You should only use this method when you are certain that the string contains only numbers and not other characters.

When using the parseInt() method on a string or number that contains a decimal value, the parseInt() method gets rid of anything after the decimal. The parseFloat() method keeps the decimal number. For example, the statement parseFloat("1.23"); returns 1.23 while parseInt("1.23"); returns 1.

Convert Strings to Numbers

① Add a variable declaration.

② Set variables equal to a numeric string.

③ Set variables equal to parseInt() and parseFloat() adding variable names inside the parentheses.

④ Add document.write statements to display the values.

⑤ Save the file.

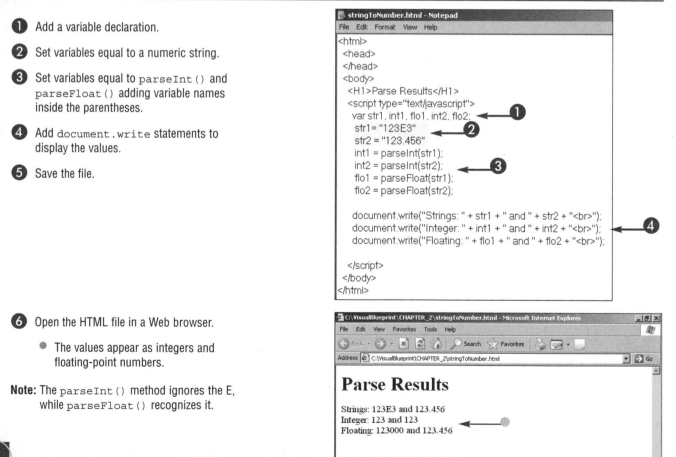

⑥ Open the HTML file in a Web browser.

● The values appear as integers and floating-point numbers.

Note: The parseInt() method ignores the E, while parseFloat() recognizes it.

Convert Numbers to Strings

You may need to convert an integer or floating-point number to a string. This allows you to perform string-based operations or append information to the front or end of the number.

JavaScript has a built-in method, toString(), to convert a number to a string. To use this method, you simply add the method to the end of the variable name with a period between them. For example, you can use the statement str1 = int1.toString(); to convert a variable int1 containing the number 36 to a string.

Another method you can use to convert a number to a string is to add a set of empty quotation marks to the variable. For example, the int2 holds the number 13. The statement str2= int2 + ""; automatically converts the number to a string.

Both methods are commonly used to convert numbers to strings. The first method is easier to recognize when viewing the source code of the script.

The second method can cause problems if the developer of the script is not careful. If the developer places a space in between the two quotation marks, then the string differs from the original number. The length is one digit longer than the string converted by the toString() method. This method is also hard for a beginner to recognize what operation is happening on the page. The toString() method clearly explains what operation is happening.

A number is also converted to a string when it is added to another string. For example, the statement str3 = int3 + "1"; adds the string str3 to the integer stored in int3. If int3 is equal to 1 then the value in str3 is 11.

Convert Numbers to Strings

① Add a variable declaration.

② Set a variable equal to a number.

③ Add the toString() method to the variable.

④ Add an empty string to the second variable.

⑤ Add document.write statements to display the values.

⑥ Save the file.

⑦ Open the HTML file in a Web browser.

● The variable type for each method appears.

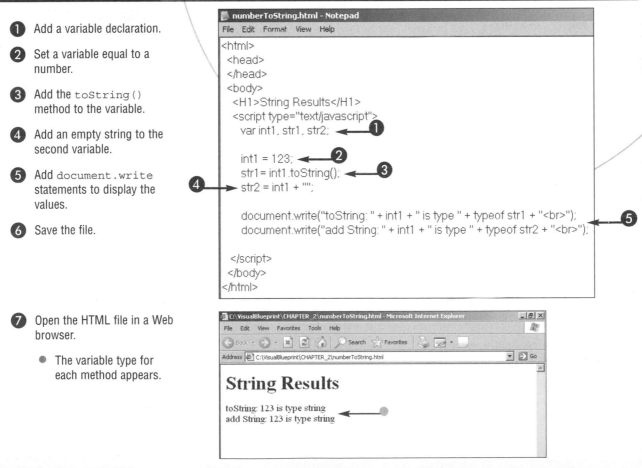

```
numberToString.html - Notepad
File  Edit  Format  View  Help
<html>
 <head>
 </head>
 <body>
  <H1>String Results</H1>
  <script type="text/javascript">
    var int1, str1, str2;              ①

    int1 = 123;                ②
    str1 = int1.toString();            ③
    str2 = int1 + "";          ④

    document.write("toString: " + int1 + " is type " + typeof str1 + "<br>");   ⑤
    document.write("add String: " + int1 + " is type " + typeof str2 + "<br>");

  </script>
 </body>
</html>
```

C:\VisualBlueprint\CHAPTER_2\numberToString.html - Microsoft Internet Explorer
File Edit View Favorites Tools Help
Back · → · ⊗ ⊠ ⌂ | Search Favorites | ⊟ ·
Address C:\VisualBlueprint\CHAPTER_2\numberToString.html   → Go

String Results

toString: 123 is type string
add String: 123 is type string

Declare an Array

You can group several variables together to form a numbered index known as an array. All variables within the array are referenced with the same name, but have a different index value. The index number is placed after the array name in square brackets ([ ]).

Arrays are created by assigning a variable name to a new Array(). You can assign the number of elements in the array by placing the number between the parentheses. For example, the statement var array0 = new Array(4); has four elements.

After an array is created, you can reference and store individual elements of the array using the array name followed by the index number. For example, array1 = new Array(10); creates an array that can hold 10 values. The first element of the array is array1[0] and the last element is array1[9]. The array starts at index zero; therefore, the last item is the length minus one.

You can store a value in each element of the array by referencing the array index. You then set the array index to the value. For example, the statement array1[0] = 123; adds the integer 123 to the first index of the array named array1.

You can use a shortcut method of storing all the array elements of the array in one line. Declare an array and instead of declaring the size, add the data separated by commas inside the parentheses. For example, the statement the items = new Array(1, "red ",true,1.23); creates a new array with four elements.

You can store multiple variable types in an array. The values are numbers, strings, or Booleans. Therefore, you can store a numeric value in the first index and strings in the other elements without any errors.

Declare an Array

CREATE AN ARRAY OF STRING VARIABLES

1. Add a new variable name and assign it to new Array(), and then assign the number of elements within the parentheses.

2. Assign each array element to a string.

3. Add a document.write statement to display the value of each array element.

4. Save the file.

5. Open the HTML file in a Web browser.

   • A string made from all the individual array elements appears.

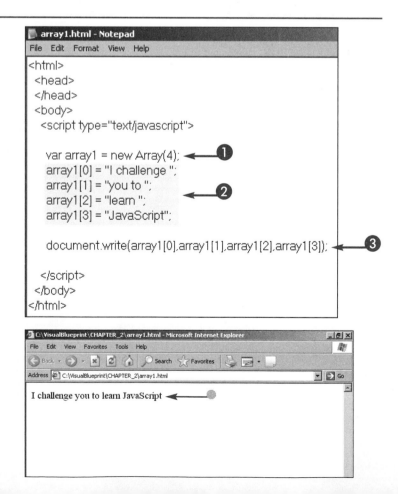

```
array1.html - Notepad
File  Edit  Format  View  Help

<html>
 <head>
 </head>
 <body>
  <script type="text/javascript">

    var array1 = new Array(4);          ①
    array1[0] = "I challenge ";
    array1[1] = "you to ";              ②
    array1[2] = "learn ";
    array1[3] = "JavaScript";

    document.write(array1[0],array1[1],array1[2],array1[3]);   ③

  </script>
 </body>
</html>
```

```
C:\VisualBlueprint\CHAPTER_2\array1.html - Microsoft Internet Explorer
File  Edit  View  Favorites  Tools  Help
Back       Search   Favorites
Address  C:\VisualBlueprint\CHAPTER_2\array1.html          Go

I challenge you to learn JavaScript
```

CREATE AN ARRAY OF NUMERIC VARIABLES

1. Add a new variable name and assign it to `new Array()`, and then assign the number of elements within the parentheses.

2. Assign a number to each array element.

3. Add a `document.write` statement to display the value of each array element.

4. Save the file.

5. Open the HTML file in a Web browser.

- A string made from all the individual array elements appears.

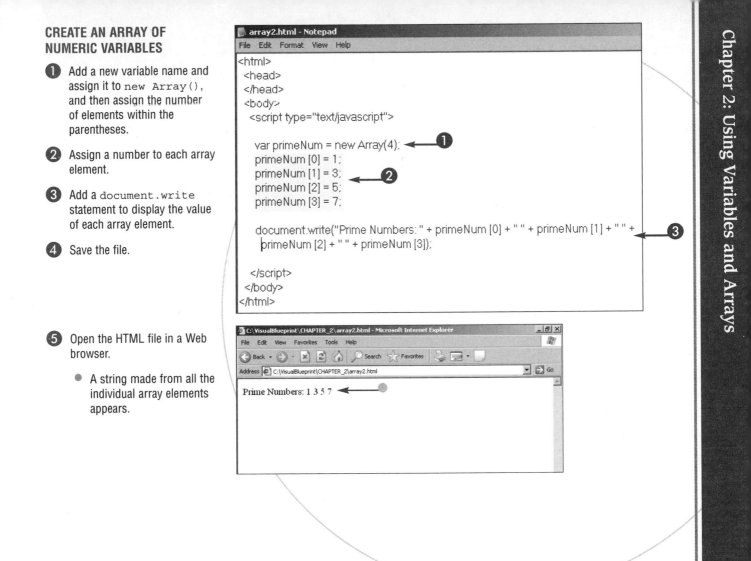

```
array2.html - Notepad
File  Edit  Format  View  Help

<html>
 <head>
 </head>
 <body>
  <script type="text/javascript">

    var primeNum = new Array(4);        1
    primeNum [0] = 1;
    primeNum [1] = 3;                   2
    primeNum [2] = 5;
    primeNum [3] = 7;

    document.write("Prime Numbers: " + primeNum [0] + " " + primeNum [1] + " " +   3
     primeNum [2] + " " + primeNum [3]);

  </script>
 </body>
</html>
```

```
C:\VisualBlueprint\CHAPTER_2\array2.html - Microsoft Internet Explorer
File  Edit  View  Favorites  Tools  Help
Back    Search  Favorites
Address  C:\VisualBlueprint\CHAPTER_2\array2.html        Go

Prime Numbers: 1 3 5 7
```

Extra

When declaring the array, you can store the actual data you want to hold instead of the number of elements. Each item is typed between the parentheses separated by commas. You can save time by typing it in this way instead of referencing every element of the array. The following example retrieves the current month name from the array and displays it on the Web page.

Store Data

```
<script type="text/javascript">
    var monthNames = new Array("January", "February", "March",
        "April", "May", "June", "July", "August", "September",
        "October", "November", "December");
    var theDate = new Date();
    var theMonth = theDate.getMonth()
    document.write(monthNames[theMonth]);
</script>
```

Declare a
Multidimensional Array

You can create a multidimensional array, which is an array that contains another array. Instead of an array being able to hold one value in each index element, you can make it hold multiple values. You can create a lookup table by holding multiple values.

The most common multidimensional array is a two-dimensional array. A two-dimensional array is represented as a table on a Web page. The array contains columns and rows. To declare a multidimensional array, you declare a one-dimensional array `var array1 = new Array(3);`. The `array1` in this example contains three elements. These three elements are the rows of the table. By declaring an array for each of the indexes of `array1`, you can make the columns of the table. Because there are three rows, you need to declare each one of them.

```
array1[0]  =  new Array(3);
array1[1]  =  new Array(3);
array1[2]  =  new Array(3);
```

The result of this is a two-dimensional array that has three rows and three columns. If you want an array that has more dimensions, you need to declare an array for each of those elements.

To access the two-dimensional array elements, you have to use two sets of square brackets (`[ ] [ ]`). The first set is the row index number; the second set is the column index number. If you want to access the third row and the first element, use the `str1 = array1[2][0];` statement.

You can use another set of brackets for each dimension that you expand the arrays. Therefore, a multidimensional array that has four dimensions would contain four brackets. The larger the array, the harder it is to keep track of the large amount of data.

Declare a Multidimensional Array

DECLARE A 2D ARRAY

① Add a new variable name and assign it to `new Array()`.

② Assign each element of the first array with a `new Array()`.

③ Assign a value to each array element.

④ Add a `document.write` statement to display the value of the array.

⑤ Save the file.

⑥ Open the HTML file in a Web browser.

● The elements in the array appear.

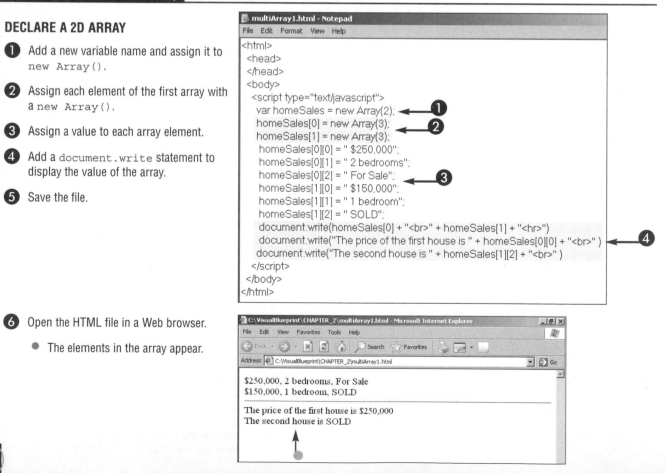

DECLARE A 3D ARRAY

① Add a new variable name and assign it to `new Array()`.

② Assign each element of the previous array to a `new Array()` statement.

③ Repeat step **2** for each new dimension added.

④ Assign a value to each array element.

⑤ Add a `document.write` statement to display the value of the array.

⑥ Save the file.

⑦ Open the HTML file in a Web browser.

● The elements in the array appear.

```
multiArray2.html - Notepad
File  Edit  Format  View  Help
<html>
 <head>
 </head>
 <body>
  <script type="text/javascript">
   var homeSales = new Array(2);        ①
   homeSales[0] = new Array(2);    ②
   homeSales[0][0] = new Array(2);      ③

   homeSales[0][0][0] = "$213,123"      ④
   homeSales[0][0][1] = "$865.95"

   document.write("Price:" + homeSales[0][0][0] + "<br>Payment:" + homeSales[0][0][1]);   ⑤

  </script>
 </body>
</html>
```

```
C:\VisualBlueprint\CHAPTER_2\multiArray2.html - Microsoft Internet Explorer
File  Edit  View  Favorites  Tools  Help
Back          Search   Favorites
Address  C:\VisualBlueprint\CHAPTER_2\multiArray2.html        Go

Price:$213,123
Payment:$865.95
```

Apply It

You may find that setting up a multidimensional array is tedious. To eliminate this problem, you can use a shortcut for setting up the array. There are two shortcuts for setting multidimensional arrays without having to declare all the new arrays. This is very helpful if you have a very large array.

The first shortcut is just like assigning values to a one-dimensional array. You can assign values to a multidimensional array when you first declare it. For each new row of data, you include it inside square brackets and separate the brackets with commas.

Set the Array
```
var array2D = new Array([1,2,3],[4,5,6],[7,8,9]);
```

The second shortcut is for when you are dynamically assigning value to the array and do not have the data available when you are first declaring it. You can use a for-loop. See Chapter 5 for more details.

Assign Values
```
var array1 = new Array(3);
var i;
for( i=0; i<array1.length; i++){
   array1[i] = new Array(3);
}
```

The code loops for the entire length of the array and assigns the array to the element creating the columns. You then have to assign the value for each of the elements in the array.

Determine the Number of Elements of an Array

I f an array is created and filled with elements as the script is executed, you may lose track of the number of elements contained within the array. Knowing the number of elements contained within the array tells you how often you need to loop through the array to process all the data.

An array is an object. Objects include properties that describe them and methods that can execute built-in functions specific to the object. Chapter 12 covers objects in more detail.

The array object includes a property named `length` that is used to return the number of elements in an array. The `length` property is a statement just like a variable. It is created by placing the length property name after the array name with a period in between them. For example, if an

array named `array1` is declared, the length of the property can be returned using the `int1 = array1.length;` statement.

The `length` property is a read-only property, so you cannot add items to the array by setting the value. If you want to add more items to the array use the `push()` method. See the Add Elements to an Array section.

The length of the array is commonly used in `for` loops to iterate through all the array's elements. By using the array length, it eliminates the need to use a hard coded value. If a hard coded value is used, the array must remain static and cannot change length. For example, the statement `for(i=0;i<array1.length;i++)` creates a `for-loop` statement that tells it to loop through all the elements contained in `array1`. The `for` loop is explained in Chapter 5.

Determine the Number of Elements of an Array

ELEMENTS IN 1D ARRAY

① Add the `length` property to the end of the array name.

② Add a `document.write` statement to view the length.

③ Open the HTML file in a Web browser.

● The number of elements appears.

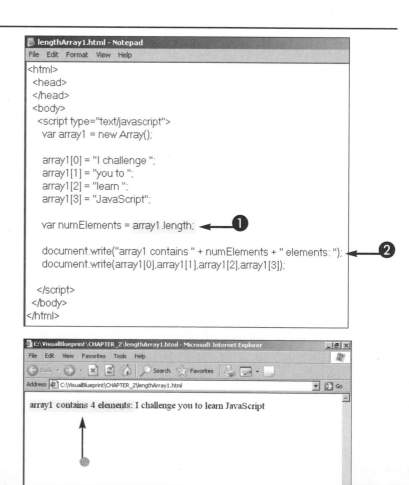

ELEMENTS IN 2D ARRAY

1. Add the `length` object to the end of the array name.

2. Repeat step 1 for each dimension.

3. Add `document.write` statements to display the array length.

4. Save the file.

5. Open the HTML file in a Web browser.

   - The length of the multidimensional array appears.

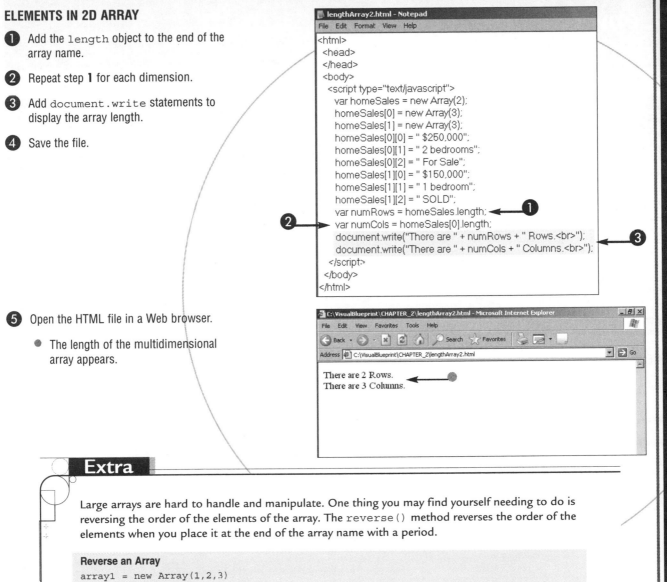

Extra

Large arrays are hard to handle and manipulate. One thing you may find yourself needing to do is reversing the order of the elements of the array. The `reverse()` method reverses the order of the elements when you place it at the end of the array name with a period.

Reverse an Array
```
array1 = new Array(1,2,3)
array2 = array1.reverse()
```

The `reverse()` method fills `array2` the opposite of `array1`. Therefore, the first position of `array2[0]` will be 3 and the last position of `array2[2]` will be 1.

If you apply the `reverse()` method to a multidimensional array, only the first dimension of the array is reversed. You can reverse additional dimensions of the array by using `for` loops. The following example reverses a two-dimensional array.

Reverse a 2D Array
```
array1 = new Array([1,2,3],[4,5,6],[7,8,9]);
array1 = array1.reverse();
for(i=0;i<array1.length;i++){
   array1[i] = array1[i].reverse();
}
```

The result of `array1` is the equivalent to `([9,8,7],[6,5,4],[3,2,1])` after it has been reversed in two dimensions.

Convert an Array into a String

Arrays are large and can contain many different elements. You may find it easy to convert the array to a string so you can display all the elements in one step without having to type each element of the entire array.

The array object includes the `join()` method, which converts the array elements to a single string. The `join()` method is compared to manually typing each element and joining them with a plus sign (+). For example, the statement `str1 = array1.join(" ");` is equivalent to the statement `str1 = array1[0] + " " + array1[1] + " " + array1[2];`. You can save time by using the `join()` method because you will not have to type every element of an array.

The `join()` method accepts a single string parameter that is inserted between each array element. You can specify the text that joins the elements together by placing the text between the parentheses. For example, if you have an array of words called `array1`, the statement `str1 = array1. join(" ");` places a space between the array elements. The result is a single string with all the words in the original array joined together with a space. If you do not include any text inside the parentheses, the default separator character used to join the array together is a comma (,).

The `join()` method is faster than adding all the individual elements together. The reason is that it does not have to locate each individual element one at a time. The `join()` method does not have to go through all the individual looks-ups, thus making the process faster.

Convert an Array into a String

DEFAULT JOIN

1 Declare a variable and set the variable equal to the array name.

2 Add the `join()` method to the end of the array name.

3 Add a `document.write` statement to display the joined array.

4 Save the file.

```
joinArray1.html - Notepad
File  Edit  Format  View  Help
<html>
 <head>
 </head>
 <body>
  <script type="text/javascript">
  var array1 = new Array();

  array1[0] = "apple";
  array1[1] = "pear";
  array1[2] = "peach";
  array1[3] = "grape";

  var str1 = array1.join();

  document.write(str1);

  </script>
 </body>
</html>
```

1 → `var str1 = array1.join();` ← 2

3 → `document.write(str1);`

5 Open the HTML file in a Web browser.

● The converted array appears separated by commas.

```
C:\VisualBlueprint\CHAPTER_2\joinArray1.html - Microsoft Internet Explorer
File  Edit  View  Favorites  Tools  Help
Back ·   ·      Search  Favorites
Address  C:\VisualBlueprint\CHAPTER_2\joinArray1.html            Go

apple,pear,peach,grape  ←
```

SPECIFY A UNIQUE SEPARATOR

① Declare a variable and set the variable equal to the array name.

② Add the `join()` method to the end of the array name

③ Add the character you want to separate the array elements between the parentheses.

④ Add a `document.write` statement to display the joined array.

⑤ Save the file.

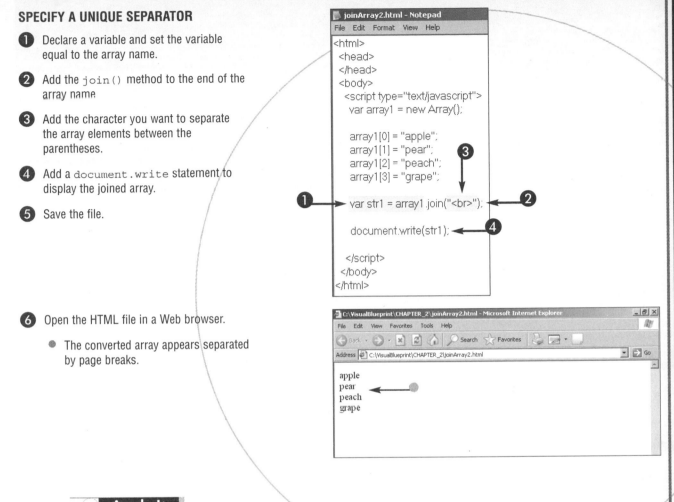

⑥ Open the HTML file in a Web browser.

● The converted array appears separated by page breaks.

Apply It

You can split a string into an array by using the `split()` method. The `split()` method works in the opposite direction of the `join()` method. The text inside the parentheses specifies where the break is made in the string to which the `split()` method is attached. The result of the `split()` method is a one-dimensional array that contains the string data. You can break a sentence into words by specifying that the breaks should be made where there is a space.

Split a String
```
str1 = "This is a sentence";
array1 = str1.split(" ");
```

The result is the first element of `array1[0]` is `This` and the last element of `array1[3]` is `sentence`.

This method is used in Chapter 13 when working with query strings. Query strings contain the separator ampersand (`&`) to separate the different variables in the query string.

The `split()` method is used to separate the values in a cookie, pull information from the browser, and alter information in form fields.

Sort an Array

T he array object includes a method to arrange the array in ascending alphabetical order. The method is called sort().

For example, if you have an array full of words named array1, you can sort the words using the array2 = array1.sort(); statement. Therefore, if the array1 contains the words orange, apple, kiwi, banana, then the order of the elements in array2 would be apple, banana, kiwi, orange.

If you want to sort in descending alphabetical order, you need to use the reverse() method that was explained earlier in the Determine the Number of Elements an Array section. You can combine the methods with the statement array3 = array1.sort().reverse();. By applying sort() and reverse() methods on array1, the result is orange, kiwi, banana, apple.

When the sort() method is used with an array of numbers, the numbers are sorted alphabetically instead of numerically. For example, an array containing 1, 2, 10, 12 will sort as 1, 10, 12, 2.

You can use the sort() method with an array that contains numeric, alphabetical, and special characters. Special characters are dollar signs, number signs, underscores, and so on. The sort() method's order of precedence is special, numeric, and alphabetical characters.

For example, an array containing the strings tree, bee, 13, $1.99, and #11 is sorted as #11, $1.99, 13, bee, tree.

If the sort() method is applied to a multidimensional array, only the first dimension of the array is sorted. The other dimensions of the array are adjusted to correspond to the first dimension. For example, the array (['base',1,2],['apple',4,2],['car',5,1]) is sorted as (['apple',4,2],['base',1,2],['car',5,1]) when the sort statement is applied to the multidimensional array.

Sort an Array

① Declare a variable and set the variable equal to the array name.

② Add the sort() method to the end of the array name.

③ Add a document.write statement to display the sorted array.

④ Save the file.

⑤ Open the HTML file in a Web browser.

● The sorted array appears separated by commas.

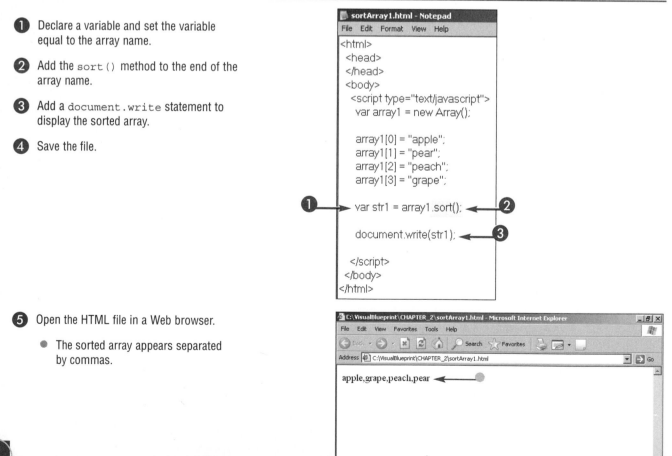

1 Declare a variable and set the variable equal to the array name.

2 Add the `sort()` method to the end of the array name.

3 Add a `document.write` statement to display the sorted array.

4 Save the file.

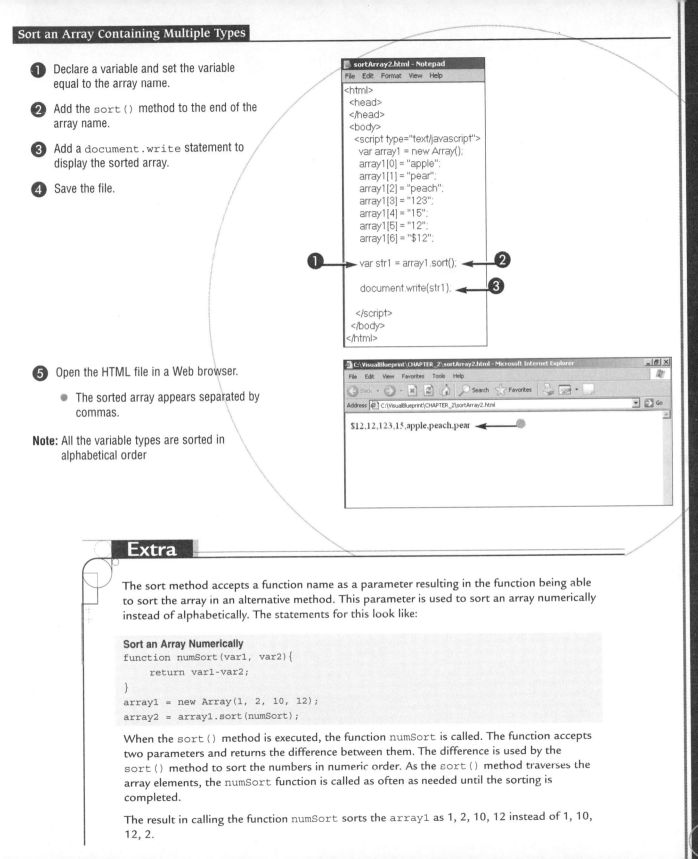

```
sortArray2.html - Notepad
File  Edit  Format  View  Help
<html>
 <head>
 </head>
 <body>
  <script type="text/javascript">
   var array1 = new Array();
   array1[0] = "apple";
   array1[1] = "pear";
   array1[2] = "peach";
   array1[3] = "123";
   array1[4] = "15";
   array1[5] = "12";
   array1[6] = "$12";

   var str1 = array1.sort();        ◄ 2

   document.write(str1);            ◄ 3

  </script>
 </body>
</html>
```

1 ►

5 Open the HTML file in a Web browser.

● The sorted array appears separated by commas.

Note: All the variable types are sorted in alphabetical order

```
C:\VisualBlueprint\CHAPTER_2\sortArray2.html - Microsoft Internet Explorer
File  Edit  View  Favorites  Tools  Help
Back ▾ ▾   Search  Favorites
Address  C:\VisualBlueprint\CHAPTER_2\sortArray2.html          ▾  Go

$12,12,123,15,apple,peach,pear   ◄
```

Extra

The sort method accepts a function name as a parameter resulting in the function being able to sort the array in an alternative method. This parameter is used to sort an array numerically instead of alphabetically. The statements for this look like:

Sort an Array Numerically
```
function numSort(var1, var2){
     return var1-var2;
}
array1 = new Array(1, 2, 10, 12);
array2 = array1.sort(numSort);
```

When the `sort()` method is executed, the function `numSort` is called. The function accepts two parameters and returns the difference between them. The difference is used by the `sort()` method to sort the numbers in numeric order. As the `sort()` method traverses the array elements, the `numSort` function is called as often as needed until the sorting is completed.

The result in calling the function `numSort` sorts the `array1` as 1, 2, 10, 12 instead of 1, 10, 12, 2.

Remove Elements from an Array

Y ou can remove individual elements of an array by using three built-in methods: `pop()`, `shift()`, and `splice()`. This allows you to edit arrays to make them hold dynamic information.

The `pop()` method returns the last element of the array and removes it. To use the method, add it to the end of the array name with a period. For example, if you have an array name `array1` and it contains five elements, the statement `int1 = array1.pop();` returns the last element of the array and removes it. Therefore, the total length of `array1` is now four elements.

The `shift()` method is just like the `pop()` method, but it returns the first element and removes it. The other elements of the array are then shifted down one spot. The statement `int2 = array1.shift();` returns the first element and removes it. Therefore, the total length of `array1` is now three elements.

The `splice()` method removes any element of the array and removes a group of elements instead of just one. The `splice()` method has two properties that need to be added between the parentheses: the index position and the number of elements to remove. For example, if you have an array named `array2` that contains ten elements and you want to remove five elements from the middle starting at the third position, the statement `int3 = array2.splice(2,5);` removes the elements. The resulting array contains only five elements.

Using `pop()`, `shift()`, and `splice()` is a great way to remove elements from an array after you have used the data. By removing the element from the array, you may not reuse the element. The three methods can assure that the data is only used one time each time the page is loaded.

Remove Elements from an Array

① Declare a variable and set the variable equal to an array.

② Add `pop()`, `shift()`, and `splice()` methods after the array names.

③ Add the index location of the deletion and the number of items to delete in the parentheses following `splice()`.

④ Add `document.write` statements to display the results.

⑤ Save the document.

⑥ Open the HTML file in a Web browser.

● The elements of the array have been removed.

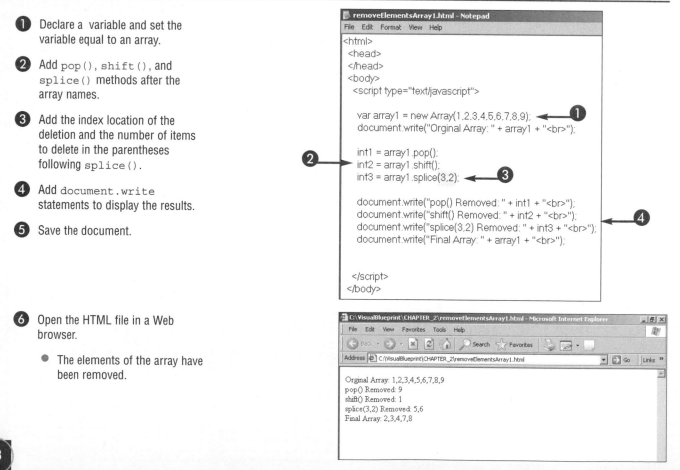

Add Elements to an Array

You can add elements to an array by using the `push()`, `unshift()`, and `splice()` methods. This allows you to create dynamic arrays by adding new information to the array.

The `push()` method adds one or more elements to the end of the array and returns its new length. The elements you want to add to the array are placed inside the parentheses separated by commas (`,`). For example, if you have an array named `array1` that contains five elements, the statement `int1 = array1.push(1,2,3);` adds three new elements to the end of `array1`. The value stored in `int1` is the new size of the array, which is 8 elements. The `unshift()` method is similar the `push()` method, but instead of adding the new elements to the end, it adds the elements to the beginning. The original elements are shifted to new indexes. For example, if you

have an array named `array2` and it contains three elements, the statement `int2 = array2.unshift ("apple", "orange");` shifts the original elements over two indexes.

The `splice()` method was introduced earlier in this chapter to remove elements, but you can also use it to add elements. The `splice()` method has three properties that need to be added between the parentheses: the index position, the number of elements to remove, and the elements that need to be added. For example, you have an array named `array3` that has four elements and you want to add two elements to the middle and not remove any elements. The statement `int3 = array3.splice(2,0,"blue","red");` adds the two new elements to the third and fourth spots and pushes the other elements two index places to the right.

Add Elements to an Array

1 Declare variables and set them equal to an array.

2 Add `push()`, `unshift()`, and `splice()` methods after the array names adding the necessary parameters.

3 Add `document.write` statements to display the results.

4 Save the document.

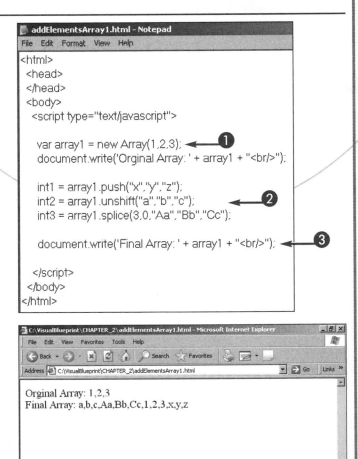

```
addElementsArray1.html - Notepad

File  Edit  Format  View  Help

<html>
 <head>
 </head>
 <body>
  <script type="text/javascript">

    var array1 = new Array(1,2,3);          ◄── 1
    document.write('Orginal Array: ' + array1 + "<br/>");

    int1 = array1.push("x","y","z");
    int2 = array1.unshift("a","b","c");     ◄── 2
    int3 = array1.splice(3,0,"Aa","Bb","Cc");

    document.write('Final Array: ' + array1 + "<br/>");   ◄── 3

  </script>
 </body>
</html>
```

5 Open the HTML file in a Web browser.

● The elements of the array are added.

```
C:\VisualBlueprint\CHAPTER_2\addElementsArray1.html - Microsoft Internet Explorer

File  Edit  View  Favorites  Tools  Help

Back ▼   ▼  ×  ⧉  ⌂   Search  ⭐ Favorites   ▼  ▼

Address  C:\VisualBlueprint\CHAPTER_2\addElementsArray1.html       ▼  → Go   Links »

Orginal Array: 1,2,3
Final Array: a,b,c,Aa,Bb,Cc,1,2,3,x,y,z
```

Using the Arithmetic Operator

You can use expressions to compose mathematical equations. These expressions compute a desired result that you can display in a Web browser. An *expression* is made of variables, numbers, and operators that compute a desired result. An operator is a built-in method in the browser that informs the browser what to do. Some example operators are addition and subtraction. When the JavaScript function uses an addition operator with two numbers, the browser recognizes that it needs to add the values.

Expressions are created with variables or literals on either side of an operator. Literals are numerical or string values. For example, the statement "qwerty" is a literal.

The expressions that are easiest to create use arithmetic operators. The four standard arithmetic operators are addition (+), subtraction (-), multiplication (*), and division (/). These operators only work if there are variables on both sides of the operator. However, the addition operator can also be used to combine strings. For example, the statement var str1 = "Java" + "Script"; stores JavaScript into the variable str1.

When a variable and a string are combined, they are joined together. For example, when an integer of 5 is added to a string with the value 5, the statement str1 = 5 + "5"; results in a string with the value of 55. You can avoid this by using parseInt() and parseFloat(), which are explained in Chapter 2.

Another less-used arithmetic operator is the modulus operator (%). This operator returns the value of the remainder after dividing two numbers. For example, 11 % 5 returns a value of 1, because 11 is divided by 5 two times with a remainder of 1.

Using the Arithmetic Operator

1 Declare variables and assign numeric values.

2 Create new variables and assign each an arithmetic operation using the variables from step **1**.

3 Add several document.write statements to display the value of the arithmetic operation.

4 Save the file.

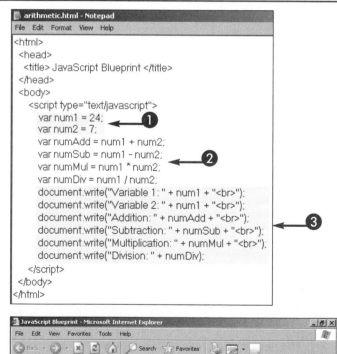

5 Open the HTML file in a Web browser.

● The value of each evaluated arithmetic expression is displayed.

Using the Modulus Operator

① Declare variables and assign numeric values.

② Create new variables and assign each the modulus operator using the variables from step **1**.

③ Add several `document.write` statements to display the value of the arithmetic operation.

④ Save the file.

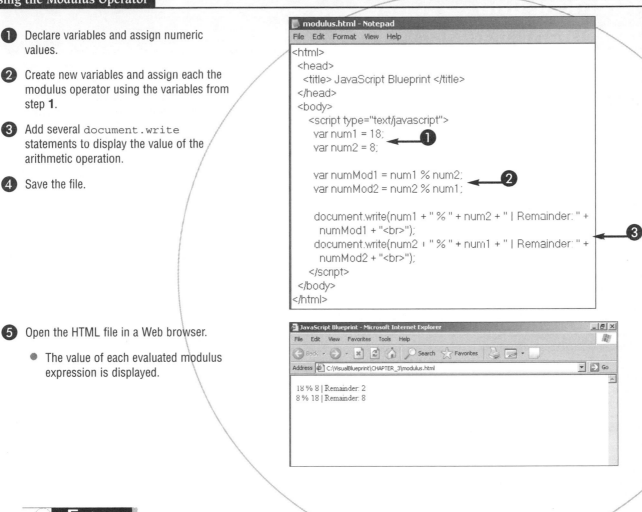

```
modulus.html - Notepad
File  Edit  Format  View  Help
<html>
 <head>
  <title> JavaScript Blueprint </title>
 </head>
 <body>
  <script type="text/javascript">
    var num1 = 18;          ①
    var num2 = 8;

    var numMod1 = num1 % num2;     ②
    var numMod2 = num2 % num1;

    document.write(num1 + " % " + num2 + " | Remainder: " +
      numMod1 + "<br>");               ③
    document.write(num2 + " % " + num1 + " | Remainder: " +
      numMod2 + "<br>");
  </script>
 </body>
</html>
```

⑤ Open the HTML file in a Web browser.

● The value of each evaluated modulus expression is displayed.

```
JavaScript Blueprint - Microsoft Internet Explorer
File  Edit  View  Favorites  Tools  Help
Back       Search   Favorites
Address  C:\VisualBlueprint\CHAPTER_3\modulus.html        Go

18 % 8 | Remainder: 2
8 % 18 | Remainder: 8
```

Extra

JavaScript evaluates operators in a specific order. This order is known as *operator precedence*. The operators with the highest precedence are evaluated first and then it moves down the line of precedence. Parentheses have the highest precedence. If you are ever in doubt of which expression to evaluate first, include the separate expressions within parentheses. If the operators have the same level of precedence, such as an expression full of addition operators, JavaScript evaluates the operators from left to right. The Arithmetic operators are broken up into two levels. That is because the precedence of multiplication (*), division (/), and modulus (%) are higher than the addition (+) and subtraction (-) operators.

PRECEDENCE	OPERATORS
1	Unary operators: ++, −, &, !
2	Arithmetic operators level 1: *, /, %
3	Arithmetic operators level 2: +, -
4	Comparison operators: >, <, >=, <=, ==
5	Logical operators: &&, ||
6	Conditional operators: ?:
7	Assignment operator: =

Increment and Decrement Values

One of the simplest expressions you can create is one that increments or decrements a variable. Incrementing expressions are useful as counters and in `for` loops. One use for incrementing and decrementing a variable is iterating through items in an array or keeping track of how many times a button is clicked.

Variables are incremented by adding 1 with the variable and assigning it to the same variable like this, `int1 = int1 + 1`. JavaScript, however, offers an easier way to increment values by attaching two plus symbols (++) to the variable.

For example, `int1++` automatically increases the value of the variable `int1` when evaluated. This is very useful to cut down on the amount of code that is needed. You can commonly find this technique used in `for` loops. For example, the statement `for(i=0;i<10;i++)` increments the variable `i` every time the loop is executed.

You can decrement the value by subtracting 1 from the variable like this, `int1 = int1 - 1` or you can use the shortcut. The variables are decremented using two minus signs (--). This character set causes the variable to be decreased by 1. For example, `int--` automatically reduces by 1 the value of `int`.

A common error occurs when only a single plus or minus sign is used instead of using double plus or minus signs. The error message normally says syntax error since it is looking for another variable after the operator.

The increment and decrement operators are *unary* operators, which means that they require a single operand instead of two like the arithmetic operators. For example, the statement `var int1 = 1 + 1;` is an expression that uses the arithmetic operator plus to add two numbers together.

Increment and Decrement Values

INCREMENT VALUES

① Assign a variable of two plus (+) signs after the variable name.

Note: The variable must be assigned a value before it can be incremented.

② Add a `document.write` statement to display the initial and incremented values.

③ Save the file.

④ Open the HTML file in a Web browser.

● The value of the variable has been incremented.

```
increment.html - Notepad
File  Edit  Format  View  Help
<html>
 <head>
  <title> JavaScript Blueprint </title>
 </head>
 <body>
   <script type="text/javascript">
     var days=1;
     document.write("Initial Value: " + days + "<br>");

     days++;          ①
     document.write("Incremented Value: " + days + "<br>");    ②
   </script>
 </body>
</html>
```

```
JavaScript Blueprint - Microsoft Internet Explorer
File  Edit  View  Favorites  Tools  Help
Back          Search   Favorites
Address  C:\VisualBlueprint\CHAPTER_3\increment.html          Go

Initial Value: 1
Incremented Value: 2

Done                              My Computer
```

DECREMENT VALUES

1. Assign a variable of two minus (-) signs after the variable name.

Note: The variable must be assigned a value before it can be decremented.

2. Add a `document.write` statement to display the initial and decremented values.

3. Save the file.

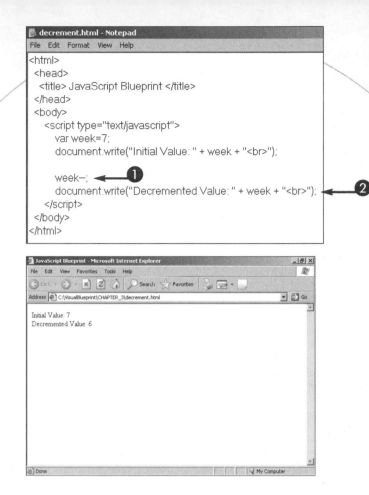

```
decrement.html - Notepad
File  Edit  Format  View  Help

<html>
 <head>
  <title> JavaScript Blueprint </title>
 </head>
 <body>
   <script type="text/javascript">
     var week=7;
     document.write("Initial Value: " + week + "<br>");

     week--;                ◄── 1
     document.write("Decremented Value: " + week + "<br>");   ◄── 2
   </script>
 </body>
</html>
```

4. Open the HTML file in a Web browser.

- The value of the variable has been decremented.

```
JavaScript Blueprint - Microsoft Internet Explorer
File  Edit  View  Favorites  Tools  Help
Back  -   -   Search   Favorites
Address  C:\VisualBlueprint\CHAPTER_3\decrement.html          Go

Initial Value: 7
Decremented Value: 6

Done                                    My Computer
```

Extra

When using the unary operators, you are not required to have the operator following the variable name. The increment or decrement operator can come before or after the variable. If the increment or decrement operator comes before the variable, like `var1 = ++var2`, `var2` gets incremented before the value is assigned to `var1`. For example, if `var2` contains the integer 5 initially, `var2` would be incremented by one to give it the value of 6. The `var1` stores `var2`'s new value of 6 as its value. If, however, the operator comes after the variable, the value of `var2` is assigned to `var1` before it is incremented or decremented. For example, the statement `var1 = var2++;` stores the `var2` value into `var1`. The `var2`'s value is then incremented. If `var2` had the value of 5 initially, `var1` contains 5 and `var2` contains 6 after the statement is executed.

You can use other shortcuts when creating expressions. The operator equals shortcuts are (+=), (-=), (*=), and (/=). For example, you can add the number 5 to a variable `var1` by simply typing the statement `var1 += 5;`.

Create Comparison Expressions

You can use comparison or relational expressions to compare the values of two variables. When evaluated, comparison expressions result in a Boolean value of either true or false.

These statements are typically used to control the program flow and are covered in more detail in Chapter 4. For example, an if statement uses comparison expressions to decide whether to execute certain statements. This allows you to validate forms to make sure a user entered in the correct data. You can also use this to make sure that a process is happening and to execute certain lines of code.

The comparison operator is designated with two equals signs (==). It is used to determine if two values are equal and is different from the assignment symbol (=). Using a single equal sign in a comparison expression is a common error in JavaScript.

Another common comparison operator compares two variables to determine if they are not equal. This operator is specified with an exclamation point in front of an equals sign (!=). The exclamation point must appear before the equal sign. If the order is switched, an error occurs causing the script to stop executing.

You can check to see if two variables are greater than (>), less than (<), greater than or equal to (>=), or less than or equal to (<=) each other. A common error that occurs is placing the equal sign in front of the less than or greater than signs. The browser requires that the less than or greater than signs appear before the equal sign.

An example of a use of this is to determine if a number is greater than another number. The statement var bool1 = 7 < 24; stores the Boolean true into the variable bool1 since 7 is less than 24.

Create Comparison Expressions

① Create comparison expressions using ==, <, <=, >, >=, and !=.

② Add a document.write statement to display the results of the comparison expressions.

③ Save the file.

Note: You can use numbers and strings with comparison expressions.

④ Open the HTML file in a Web browser.

● The expressions return the results in a form of a Boolean true or false.

● The results return three true and three false values.

Note: A result of true means the expression passed; false means the expression failed.

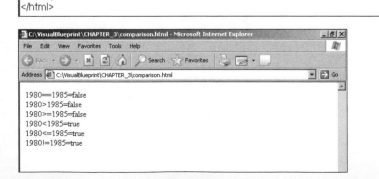

```
comparison.html - Notepad
File  Edit  Format  View  Help
<html>
 <head>
 </head>
 <body>
   <script type="text/javascript">
     var theNum1 = 1980;
     var theNum2 = 1985;
     document.write(theNum1 + "==" + theNum2 + "=" + (theNum1 == theNum2) +
     "<br>");
     document.write(theNum1 + ">" + theNum2 + "=" + (theNum1 > theNum2) +
     "<br>");
     document.write(theNum1 + ">=" + theNum2 + "=" + (theNum1 >= theNum2) +
     "<br>");
     document.write(theNum1 + "<" + theNum2 + "=" + (theNum1 < theNum2) +
     "<br>");
     document.write(theNum1 + "<=" + theNum2 + "=" + (theNum1 <= theNum2) +
     "<br>");
     document.write(theNum1 + "!=" + theNum2 + "=" + (theNum1 != theNum2) );
   </script>
 </body>
</html>
```

```
C:\VisualBlueprint\CHAPTER_3\comparison.html - Microsoft Internet Explorer
File  Edit  View  Favorites  Tools  Help
Back ·  ·   ·    Search  Favorites
Address  C:\VisualBlueprint\CHAPTER_3\comparison.html        Go

1980==1985=false
1980>1985=false
1980>=1985=false
1980<1985=true
1980<=1985=true
1980!=1985=true
```

5 Adjust the values to return different results.

6 Save the file.

```
comparison.html - Notepad
File  Edit  Format  View  Help
<html>
 <head>
 </head>
 <body>
   <script type="text/javascript">
     var theNum1 = 1980;          ← 5
     var theNum2 = 1980;
     document.write(theNum1 + "==" + theNum2 + "=" + (theNum1 == theNum2) +
     "<br>");
     document.write(theNum1 + ">" + theNum2 + "=" + (theNum1 > theNum2) +
     "<br>");
     document.write(theNum1 + ">=" + theNum2 + "=" + (theNum1 >= theNum2) +
     "<br>");
     document.write(theNum1 + "<" + theNum2 + "=" + (theNum1 < theNum2) +
     "<br>");
     document.write(theNum1 + "<=" + theNum2 + "=" + (theNum1 <= theNum2) +
     "<br>");
     document.write(theNum1 + "!=" + theNum2 + "=" + (theNum1 != theNum2) );
   </script>
 </body>
</html>
```

7 Refresh the Web page.

● The results return three `true` and three `false` values.

```
C:\VisualBlueprint\CHAPTER_3\comparison.html - Microsoft Internet Explorer
File  Edit  View  Favorites  Tools  Help
Back ·      ·     ·       Search    Favorites
Address  C:\VisualBlueprint\CHAPTER_3\comparison.html                    Go

1980==1980=true
1980>1980=false
1980>=1980=true
1980<1980=false
1980<=1980=true
1980!=1980=false
```

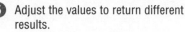
Although it is relatively easy to determine the results of a comparison expression when numbers are used, comparison operators can also use strings. When comparing strings to be equal such as `var bool1 = "happy birthday" == "Happy Birthday";`, the result is stored into the variable `bool1`. Since JavaScript is case sensitive, the result stored in `bool1` is false.

You can also use the less than and greater than operators with strings. When strings are compared, their ASCII values are compared. ASCII values assign a number to each character on the keyboard. The computer can recognize these numbers and use them to display the proper characters on the screen. The comparison results in `A` being less than `a` and `a` being less than `b`, because the ASCII value for `A` is less than the ASCII value for `a`. For example, the statement `bool2 = "apple" < "bear";` stores the Boolean `true` into the variable `bool2` since the string `apple` comes before the string `bear`. You can use this to develop your own custom sort method.

Create Logical Expressions

Y ou can use logical operators to combine several different comparison expressions together into a single complex statement. They also result in a Boolean value and are often used to control program flow. Logical operators help eliminate extra statements in a JavaScript program by allowing you to use more than one comparison statement.

The logical operators include and, which is expressed as two ampersand symbols (&&); or, which is expressed as two bar symbols (||); and not, expressed as an exclamation point (!). A common mistake is to only include one ampersand or one bar symbol. An error occurs or an invalid answer is returned.

The and operator produces a true value if both sides of the expression are true. The or operator produces a true value if either side of the expression is true. The not operator simply reverses the Boolean value.

Logical operators, when used, should appear in between statements and surrounded with parentheses. For example, the statement var theShirt = color== "red" && size=="small"; stores a true Boolean into the variable theShirt if the variable color equals red and the size equals small. If either of the two comparison expressions is not true, then the variable theShirt inherits a false Boolean value.

Logical operators follow the order of precedence. Therefore, the statement var theShirt = color== "red" && (size=="small" || brand="theFad"); first examines the two expressions in the parentheses. It then compares the result of the parentheses with the remaining statement. In order for the variable theShirt to be true, either the size has to be small or the brand has to be theFad. If either of those two statements is true, then the shirt also has to be red for the variable theShirt to be true.

Create Logical Expressions

① Add a group of if-else statements with comparison expressions.

② Add logical expressions after the comparison expressions.

③ Add a second group of comparison expressions to the right of the logical expressions.

④ Add a document.write statement to reveal the results.

⑤ Save the file.

⑥ Open the HTML file in a Web browser.

● The result appears.

Note: Because the value 85 falls between 80 and 90, the grade is a B.

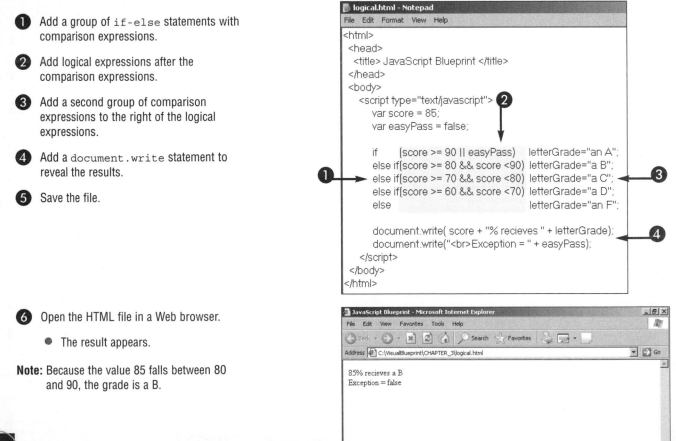

7 Change the variables to change the outcome.

8 Save the file.

```
logical.html - Notepad
File  Edit  Format  View  Help
<html>
 <head>
  <title> JavaScript Blueprint </title>
 </head>
 <body>
   <script type="text/javascript">
     var score = 85;
     var easyPass = true;                    ⟵ 7

     if      (score >= 90 || easyPass)    letterGrade="an A
     else if(score >= 80 && score <90)   letterGrade="a B"
     else if(score >= 70 && score <80)   letterGrade="a C"
     else if(score >= 60 && score <70)   letterGrade="a D"
     else                                letterGrade="an F

     document.write( score + "% recieves " + letterGrade)
     document.write("<br>Exception = " + easyPass);
   </script>
 </body>
</html>
```

9 Refresh the Web page.

● The result is changed.

```
JavaScript Blueprint - Microsoft Internet Explorer
File  Edit  View  Favorites  Tools  Help
Back       Search    Favorites
Address  C:\VisualBlueprint\CHAPTER_3\logical.html        Go

85% recieves an A
Exception = true
```

Extra

To get a better idea of the logical operators, consider the following examples.

and Operator
```
true && true = true
true && false = false
false && true = false
false && false = false
```

or Operator
```
true || true = true
true || false = true
false || true = true
false || false = false
```

not Operator
```
!true = false
!false = true
```

Logical operators evaluate the expression on each side of the logical operator first and then evaluate the logical operator. For example, the statement `(var1 > 17 && var1 < 25)` combines the two statements by comparing whether the variable is greater than 17 and less than 25. If the value of `var1` equals 18 to 24, the result of this expression is true.

Identify Numbers

JavaScript includes a unique method that is used to identify variables as numbers. This functionality is useful when you accept input from the user and want to verify that the values entered are actually numbers. Trying to evaluate a numerical expression with a string value causes an error.

The method to verify if a variable is a number actually checks to see if it is not a number. This method is `isNaN()`, which accepts a single parameter that is checked. The method `isNaN` stands for `"is not a number"`. If the variable sent to the method is a number, the method returns a false value; if the variable is not a number, a true value is returned.

For example, if a statement is defined as `var1 = 23`, the expression `isNaN(var1)` returns a false value because the value of `var1` is a number. If `var2` is equal to a string that contains the value 23, the expression `isNaN(var2)` returns false because the string only contains numbers and not other types of characters.

The `isNaN()` method is commonly used in form validation to determine if the information that the user entered into a text box or text area is a number. This check can make sure that a dollar amount entered into a price field is a number, a word field contains characters, or that the quantity field is a number.

One common thing you might see in a form field after a calculation is performed is NAN which stands for Not A Number. The NAN is a result of a variable not being a number. The variable may be a string, Boolean, or an object. The script uses NAN instead of throwing an error that stops the page from executing.

Identify Numbers

TEST TWO NUMBERS

① Create an `if-else` statement.

② Add the `isNaN()` method to the `if` statement with the variable name in the parentheses.

③ Add the conditional operator `||` to the `if` statement.

④ Add a second `isNaN()` method to the `if` statement with the variable name in the parentheses.

⑤ Save the file.

⑥ Open the HTML file in a Web browser.

● The result displays the addition of the two numbers.

Note: Even though the `isNaN()` test passed, the `parseInt` must be used on the string to convert it to a number.

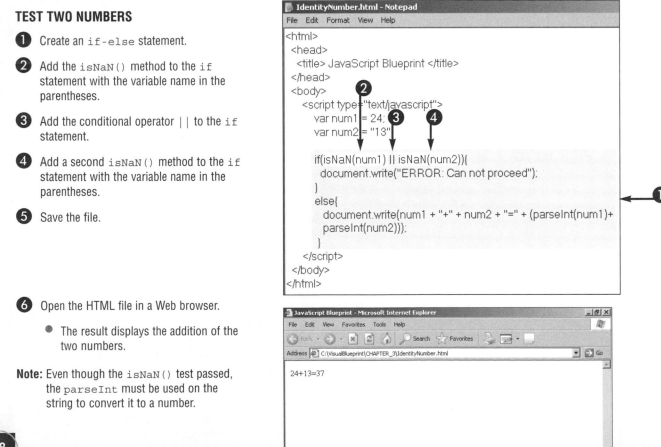

TEST A STRING AND A NUMBER

⑦ Change the values of the variables.

⑧ Save the file.

```
IdentityNumber.html - Notepad
File  Edit  Format  View  Help
<html>
 <head>
  <title> JavaScript Blueprint </title>
 </head>
 <body>
   <script type="text/javascript">
     var num1 = 24;          ←⑦
     var num2 = "Candy";

     if(isNaN(num1) || isNaN(num2)){
      document.write("ERROR: Can not proceed");
     }
     else{
      document.write(num1 + "+" + num2 + "=" + (parseInt(num1)+
      parseInt(num2)));
     }
   </script>
 </body>
</html>
```

⑨ Refresh the Web page.

● The failure message appears because a string is used.

Note: The `isNaN()` method, which returns true for a string and false for a number, is easily confused for the other way around.

```
JavaScript Blueprint - Microsoft Internet Explorer
File  Edit  View  Favorites  Tools  Help
Address C:\VisualBlueprint\CHAPTER_3\IdentityNumber.html

ERROR: Can not proceed
```

Extra

One of the best ways to use the `isNaN()` method is to validate data entered into a form. The following code computes the area of a circle, which gets the values from a form that includes two text fields. The first text field is where the user enters the radius of a circle. The `onchange` event executes the conditional statement when a number is entered and the focus of the text field is lost. The conditional statement checks the `isNaN()` method to see whether the text entered is a number. If it is, the area of the circle is computed. If not, an alert dialog box displays informing the user to input a number. If this check was not put into place, then the value displayed in the textbox would be NAN which stands for Not A Number.

Validate Data
```
<form name="form1">

   Enter the circle radius.<input type="text" name="text1"
onchange="(isNaN(this.value))?window.alert('This is not a number. Please enter a
numerical value.'):document.form1.text2.value =
(document.form1.text1.value*document.form1.text1.value*Math.PI)"/>

   Area: <input type="text" name="text2"/>

</form>
```

Sometimes expressions are contained within a string, such as when enabling the user to input an expression into a form field. You can use the `eval()` function to instruct JavaScript to evaluate the string as an expression.

For example, if a string variable name `str1` is assigned an expression such as `"128 + 62"`, displaying this variable on the screen value would be `"128 + 62"` if you would use a `document.write` statement. On the other hand, if you display `eval(str1)`, the expression is evaluated and the value of 190 appears.

The `eval()` method is commonly used in DHTML. It is normal to want to add two numbers in the middle of a large string that appears in the browser. For example, the statement `str1= "The parents bought  $" + eval(123 + 50) + " worth of candy.";` displays 173 instead of 12350.

One use for the `eval()` method is to create variables with values. For example, the statement `eval("apples=100");` creates a new variable named `apples` and stores the value as 100. This use of the `eval()` method is used with query strings, in Chapter 13, to turn the strings into a variable.

The `eval()` method is very slow compared to other JavaScript built-in methods. You can increase your script's performance by not overusing the `eval()` method. One way to not use `eval()` method is to add the variables in a separate step then combine it with the larger string, or place the variables inside the parentheses. For example, the statement `var total = "$" + (7 + 24);` stores $31 into the variable `total` and executes faster then the `eval()` method. This alternative solution to the `eval()` method only works if all the variables inside the parentheses are numbers and not strings.

Evaluate an Expression

① Assign a variable to an arithmetic operation stored as a string.

② Add the `eval()` method to the code.

③ Add the variable name inside the parentheses or the `eval()` method.

④ Save the file.

⑤ Open the HTML file in a Web browser.

● The expression in the string appears as a mathematical result.

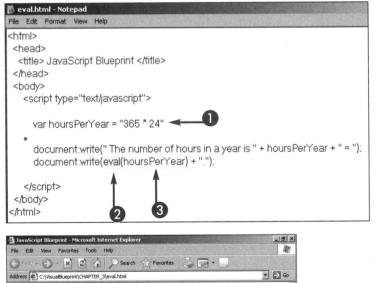

Inform the User with an Alert Dialog Box

You can use several methods that are contained in the window object to interact directly with the user. These methods make it possible to present dialog boxes to the user. The window object is the parent level of the browser that has built-in methods and properties that allow you to communicate with the user.

Many programs use dialog boxes to present information to the user. You can also use dialog boxes to collect information from the user. JavaScript includes three different types of dialog boxes: alert, prompt, and confirm. These dialog boxes are window object methods.

The simplest dialog box is an alert dialog box, which presents a text message to the user and includes a single OK button. The message is defined in quotation marks as a parameter of the `alert()` method.

For example, the statement `window.alert("Hello")` creates a dialog box with the word `Hello` in it. Clicking OK closes the dialog box.

You cannot change the `OK` text on the alert dialog box button. Furthermore, you cannot format the text in the alert dialog box's message. However, you can use `\n` to add breaks in your message so that it appears on multiple lines. The character sequence `\n` stands for a new line character. It is equivalent to using ` ` to represent a space in an HTML page. For example, the statement `window.alert ("Hello,\nWelcome to my site!")` displays an alert dialog box when the statement is executed. The string `Hello,` is displayed on the first line and the string `Welcome to my site!` is displayed on the second line.

You are not required to use the window object when referencing an alert dialog box. The statement `alert("Hello")` performs the same operation as `window.alert("Hello")`. Using the `window.alert()` method gives a more structured feel to the code.

Inform the User with an Alert Dialog Box

1 Add the `alert()` method to the file.

2 Add a message you want to display in the alert dialog box.

Note: If you are adding a string, make sure to include the message in quotes.

3 Save the file.

4 Open the HTML page in a Web browser.

● An alert dialog box appears when the page loads.

5 Click OK in the alert dialog box.

● The alert dialog box closes.

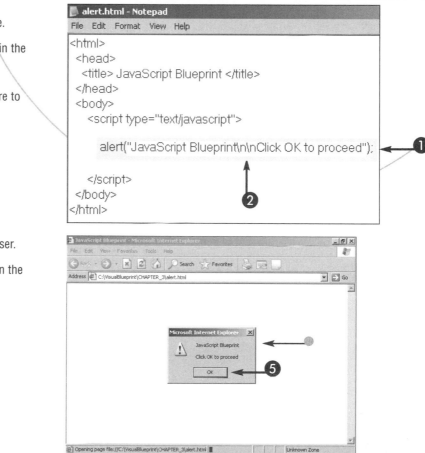

Enable User Input with a Prompt Dialog Box

You can use a prompt dialog box to enable users to type text into a text field. While an alert dialog box works well if you want to display a message to the user, it does not allow the user to input information into the script.

The window object includes a method for creating a prompt dialog box. This dialog box includes an OK button, a Cancel button, and a text field where the user can type information.

You can use the `prompt()` method to create prompt dialog boxes. This method accepts two parameters. The first parameter defines the message text that appears in the dialog box. The second is used to define the default text that appears within the text field. If OK is clicked without changing the text in the text field, then this default text is passed to the script. You can capture this text if you assign the `prompt()` method to a variable. For example,

the `statement var theItem = window.prompt("Your Name","Name");` stores the prompt value in the variable `theItem`.

If you do not want to include a default text field message that appears when the dialog box is displayed, you can simply set the second parameter of the `prompt()` method to an empty string (`""`). If you do not include the second parameter, the text `<undefined>` is displayed as the default text in the text field of the prompt dialog box.

The prompt dialog box includes an OK button and a Cancel button. If the OK button is clicked, the value within the text field of the prompt dialog box is returned to the script. However, if the Cancel button is clicked, a null value is returned to the script. You can check for a null value by using the `if (window.prompt("Input a value","10") != null)` statement.

Enable User Input with a Prompt Dialog Box

① Declare a new variable.

② Set the variable equal to the `prompt()` method.

③ Add the display message and default text by placing it between the parentheses separated by a comma.

④ Repeat steps **1** and **2** for each prompt dialog box.

⑤ Add code to handle the variables.

⑥ Save the file.

⑦ Open the HTML file in a Web browser.

● A Prompt box appears when the page loads.

⑧ Type the required information.

⑨ Click the OK button.

```
prompt.html - Notepad
File  Edit  Format  View  Help
<html>
 <head>
  <title> JavaScript Blueprint </title>
 </head>
 <body>
   <script type="text/javascript">
      var theMessage1 = "JavaScript Blueprint\nPlease Enter Your Name";
      var theTextBox1 = "Enter Your Name Here";

      var theMessage2 = "JavaScript Blueprint\nPlease Enter the name of a color";
      var theTextBox2 = "Enter a Color Name Here";

      var userName = prompt(theMessage1,theTextBox1);
      var userColor = prompt(theMessage2, theTextBox2);

      document.write("<h1>" + userName + "</h1>");
      document.body.style.background = userColor;
   </script>
 </body>
</html>
```

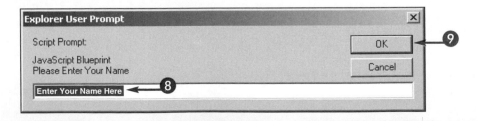

Explorer User Prompt

Script Prompt:

JavaScript Blueprint
Please Enter Your Name

Enter Your Name Here

OK

Cancel

- A second Prompt dialog box appears.

⑩ Type the required information.

⑪ Click the OK button.

- The display properties of the browser have changed.

Note: The user will have to type the information every time he or she views the Web page.

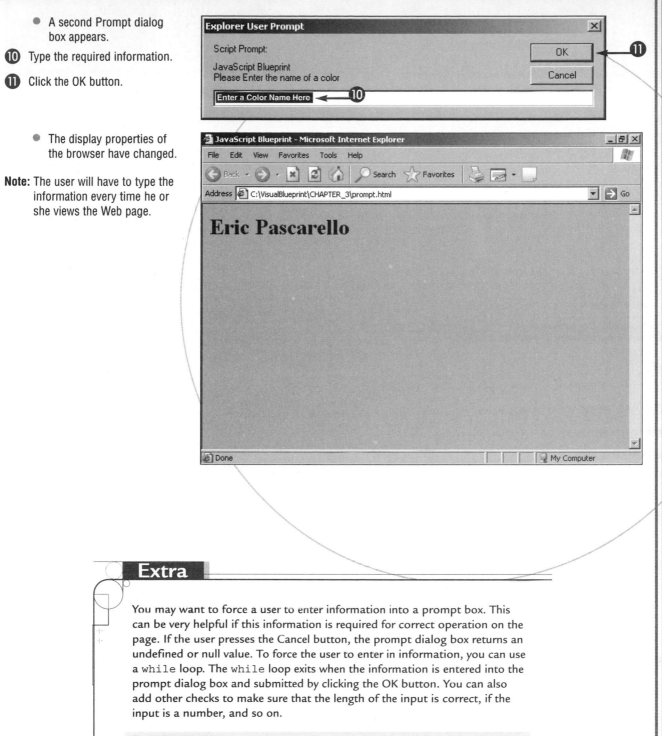

Extra

You may want to force a user to enter information into a prompt box. This can be very helpful if this information is required for correct operation on the page. If the user presses the Cancel button, the prompt dialog box returns an undefined or null value. To force the user to enter in information, you can use a `while` loop. The `while` loop exits when the information is entered into the prompt dialog box and submitted by clicking the OK button. You can also add other checks to make sure that the length of the input is correct, if the input is a number, and so on.

Force User Input
```
while(!userName){
  var userName = prompt('Enter your name');
}
document.write("Hello " + userName);
```

Enable User Decisions with a Confirm Dialog Box

You can use a confirm dialog box to ask a user questions and they can have two choices to answer it with. This dialog box includes both OK and Cancel buttons that are used to enable the user to respond to questions. One common use of the confirm dialog box is to verify a form submission; you can ask the user if one wants to submit the data.

Confirm dialog boxes are created using the confirm() method, which is part of the window object. The confirm() method can accept only a single parameter inside the parentheses that is used to display the message within the dialog box. The message in the confirm dialog box is only plain text, therefore no colors, boldness, italics, or any other HTML tag are able to be displayed.

The confirm method returns a Boolean depending on what button the user clicks. If the OK button is clicked, the confirm dialog box returns true. If the cancel button is clicked, then false is returned. You can store the result into a variable by setting the window.confirm() method equal to the variable. For example, the statement var bool1 = window.confirm("Save"); stores the result of the confirm dialog box into the variable bool1.

As with the alert and prompt dialog boxes, you cannot alter the appearance and text of the confirm dialog box. However, you can use \n to insert breaks into your message so it appears on multiple lines. For example, the string "Do you want to delete the file\nPress 'OK' to continue" is displayed on two lines.

Enable User Decisions with a Confirm Dialog Box

① Declare a variable name to store as a Boolean value.

② Add the confirm() method.

③ Add a display string between the confirm() parentheses.

④ Add if-else statements to detect which button was pressed.

⑤ Save the file.

```
confirm.htm - Notepad
File  Edit  Format  View  Help
<html>
 <head>
  <title> JavaScript Blueprint </title>
 </head>
 <body>
   <script type="text/javascript">

        var theMessage1 = "JavaScript Blueprint\nPress 'OK' if you need help.";

        var saveChanges = confirm(theMessage1);

        if(saveChanges) document.write("<h1>You need help!</h1>");
        else document.write("<h1>You do not need help!</h1>");

   </script>
 </body>
</html>
```

⑥ Open the HTML file in a Web browser.

● A confirm box appears.

⑦ Click the OK button on the confirm dialog box.

Microsoft Internet Explorer

? JavaScript Blueprint
Press 'OK' if you need help.

⑦ OK   Cancel

● The Help message appears.

8 Click the Refresh button on the Web browser to reload the Web page.

You need help! ←

9 Click the Cancel button on the confirm dialog box.

● A different message appears.

You do not need help! ←

Extra

You can apply the `confirm()` method to a form submission by using the `onsubmit()` event handler. The confirm dialog box verifies that the user wants to submit the form. If they press the OK button, the form is submitted to the next page. If they press the Cancel button, the data is not submitted and the user remains at the current page. This keeps the user from submitting wrong data. You can even display the data from the form in the confirm dialog box as the message. The user can then verify that the information is correct before submitting.

Confirm Dialog Box

```
<form name="data" onsubmit="return confirm('Submit Data')" action="SubmitTest.html">
```

JavaScript Events

When you use an operating system such as Windows or Macintosh, you are using a Graphical User Interface (GUI). This interface reacts to mouse movement, clicking on icons, clicking of buttons, and much more. You can create the same effects with JavaScript by using event handlers. JavaScript event handlers are used to create menus, rollover buttons, dynamic content, and much more.

Event handlers are built-in methods that are attached to Web page elements that react to the user's actions. For example, you can use an event handler to detect if a user clicked on a button. You can use an event handler to change an image source to display a new image. Using JavaScript event handlers can turn a static Web page into a dynamic one.

JavaScript event handlers are bits of code that link a user's actions with the JavaScript code. The user actions can execute single or multiple lines of JavaScript statements including calling functions, changing the elements' properties, and changing the page's location. The actions that can be detected are clicking the mouse, pressing a keyboard key, selecting or changing form elements, or even loading and unloading a Web page. These are just a few examples.

You can position JavaScript event handler statements within HTML tags just like the other attributes. You can set them equal to a small line of JavaScript code or to the name of a JavaScript function declared elsewhere in the Web page. When the element detects the specified event, the event handler executes the code.

For example, you can add the `onclick` event as an attribute to the `<button>` tag and set it equal to the function named `blink`, like this:

```
<button onclick="blink();">The
Button</button>
```

This tag not only displays a button on the Web page, but after you click this button, the `blink()` JavaScript function is also executed.

There are a number of different events that you can use within a Web page. However, the places where you can use them are different for each event. Some of the more common JavaScript events are covered in this chapter, including mouse events, keyboard events, and selection events. These events create dynamic forms, menus, and effects that add to the user's experience at your Web site.

Mouse Events

Mouse events fire when the user clicks or moves the mouse. If the user clicks the mouse button once, the `onclick` event fires. If the user clicks the mouse button twice, the `ondblclick` event is fired.

For more precise details, you can use the `onmousedown` event to signal when the mouse button is pressed down and the `onmouseup` event when a mouse button is released.

The `onmouseover` event detects when the mouse cursor moves over the top of an element. The `onmouseout` event detects when the mouse cursor moves off an element.

Mouse events are commonly used on images, divs, spans, and buttons to change the element's appearance and call JavaScript events. By adding an `onclick` event handler to a button, you can turn it into a link.

Keyboard Events

The onkeypress event is used to detect when a key on the keyboard is pressed. The specific key that was pressed is found in the window.event.keycode object.

Similar to the mouse button clicks, the onkeydown event detects after the key is first pressed and held down and the onkeyup event fires after the pressed key is released.

Keyboard events are commonly used in form fields to limit the keystrokes that can be entered. The keyboard events are also used to create shortcuts on navigation windows and hotkeys to perform specified JavaScript functions.

Selection Events

When an element is highlighted in the browser, it is said to have focus. The onfocus event is used to signal when an element has the focus. Pressing the Tab key or clicking on another element can change the element's focus. When an element loses the focus, the onblur event executes.

Another common event used with form elements is the onchange event. This event fires whenever the data of the form element is changed. This is commonly used on text boxes and selection lists.

Selection events are commonly used to detect changes on form elements to perform validation to verify that the information that is displayed is correct. Performing validation on the client side helps to eliminate bandwidth that a Web page can use and is another added layer in security.

Page Events

The onload event is used to detect when a Web page has completely finished loading. Similarly, the onunload event is fired when a Web page is unloaded. This happens when you leave the current page or when you click the browser's Refresh button.

When you cancel a Web page that is loading into your browser, then the onabort event is executed. When the user changes the width and height of the browser, the onchange event is fired.

Page events are used to initialize functions when something has happened to the browser whether it was opened, closed, stopped, or resized. The onload event is very common in most JavaScript applications to initialize a function when the page has been fully loaded. The onload event helps to eliminate errors by ensuring that all the necessary information is available to the JavaScript function.

Detect a Mouse Click

You can interact with the user by detecting the mouse click on Web page elements. When the user clicks elements on the Web page, he or she usually expects an operation to happen. Buttons and links are the prime target for clicking, but other Web page elements may be clicked as well. You can use the `onclick` event handler to initialize a function, open a pop-up window, validate a form, show hidden content, change the page location, and much more.

You can detect a single mouse click by using the `onclick` event. The `onclick` event then triggers a JavaScript operation.

The `onclick` event is added to Web page elements by including it as an attribute to the element. A few examples of attributes are the `src` attribute in an image and the `target` attribute of a link. For example, when the user clicks on this image `<img src="apple.jpg"`

`onclick="alert('apple')">`, an alert message appears with the word `"apple"` in it.

If you want to detect double clicks of the mouse button, you can use the `ondblclick` event. This event fires when the mouse button is clicked twice in rapid succession.

The `ondblclick` event is added to the HTML element just like the `onclick` event. For example, you can add the `ondblclick` event to a button like this `<button name="b1" value="Two" ondblclick="ClickMe()">` statement. When the button is clicked twice, the `ClickMe()` function is called.

You can add both `onclick` and `ondblclick` events in the same tag, but the `onclick` event fires every time the mouse button is clicked. Therefore, when the mouse is clicked twice, the `onclick` event fires twice, and the `ondblclick` event fires once.

Detect a Mouse Click

① Add the `onclick` handler to the `<input>` tag where you want the mouse click detected.

② Set the `onclick` event equal to a JavaScript statement that changes the button text.

③ Add the `ondblclick` handler to the `<input>` tag where you want the double click detected.

④ Set the `onclick` event equal to a JavaScript command to produce an alert message.

⑤ Save the file.

⑥ Open the HTML file in your Web browser.

⑦ Click the first button.

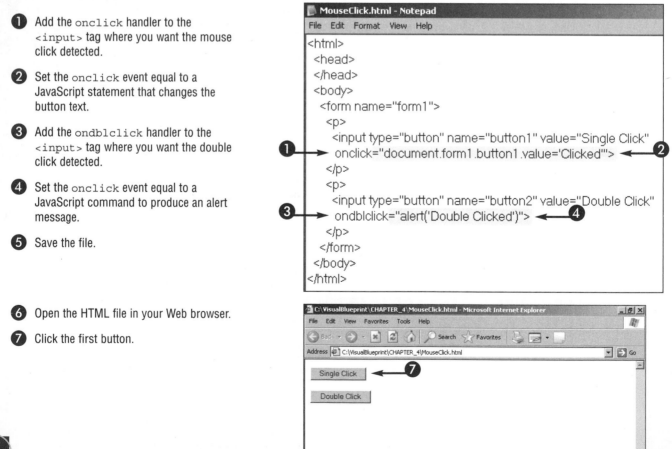

- The text displayed on the button has changed.

8 Double-click the second button.

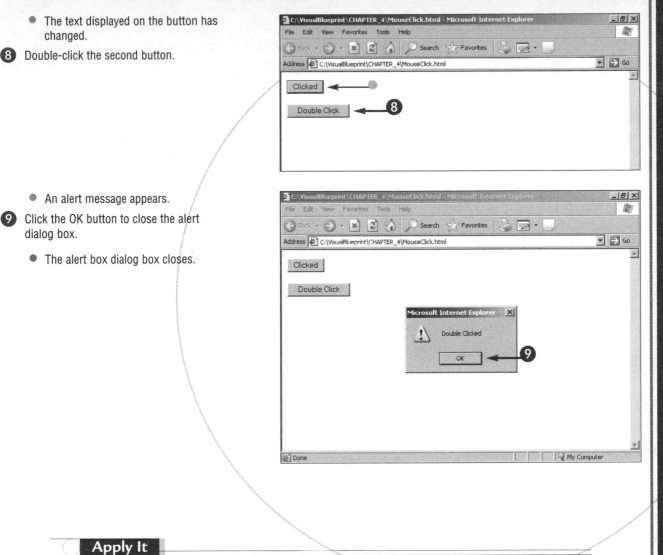

- An alert message appears.

9 Click the OK button to close the alert dialog box.

- The alert box dialog box closes.

You can use the onclick event handler to detect when the mouse button is clicked and released, but you may want to detect each operation separately to perform separate operations. You can detect the clicking and releasing actions of the mouse button by using the onmousedown and onmouseup event handlers. If a user clicks a mouse button on a page and holds it, the onclick event does not fire because it requires the mouse button to be released. The onmousedown function fires instead. You can use the following example to show the order in which the elements are fired when the HTML button is clicked.

Detect a Mouse Click

```
<form name="test">
    <button name="B1" onclick="document.test.t1.value='Fired'"
      onmousedown="document.test.t2.value='Fired'"
      onmouseup="document.test.t3.value='Fired'">TEST</button><br>
    <input type="text" name="t1">onclick<br>
    <input type="text" name="t2">onmousedown<br>
    <input type="text" name="t3">onmouseup
</form>
```

Create Rollover Buttons

To make your navigation more user friendly, you can use rollover buttons. When the mouse cursor moves over the button, the button changes its appearance. You can accomplish this by changing the source of an image or changing the Cascading Style Sheets' properties of the element. Cascading Style Sheets is referred to as CSS. You can learn more about CSS in Chapter 14.

You can create rollover buttons by using the `onmouseover` and `onmouseout` events. The events are added to the `<input>` tag of the element just like any attribute. For example, the `onmouseover` event in this statement `<img src= "Dog.jpg " onmouseover= "window.status='A dog'">` displays `A Dog` in the status bar when the cursor is placed on top of the image.

The `onmouseout` function fires when the mouse leaves the image. A common mistake for programmers is to use the term `onmouseoff` instead of `onmouseout` event. There is no event called `onmouseoff` so the code does not execute.

The `onmouseover` and `onmouseout` events are commonly used with links, buttons, text inputs, divs, and spans. The `onmouseover` and `onmouseout` events play a large role in many DHTML scripts as seen in Chapter 15.

You can change the source of an image when the mouse is placed on top of the image. To do this you need to change the image's source. For example the statement `<img src="ape.jpg" onmouseover="this.src='monkey .jpg'">` changes the image source to a new image when the cursor is over the image. If you want the image to change back to the original when the cursor leaves the image, then you need to add an `onmouseout` referencing the image's source.

A rollover button is turned into a link by using an `onclick` event handler to change the page's location.

Create Rollover Buttons

① Add the `onmouseover` event to the `<img>` tag where you want the rollover to execute.

② Set the `onmouseover` event to load another image.

③ Add the `onmouseout` event to the image tag.

④ Set the `onmouseout` event to load the original image.

⑤ Save the document.

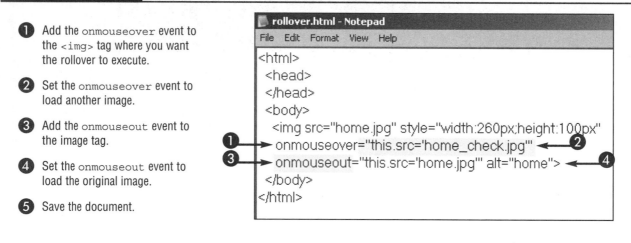

⑥ Open the HTML in your Web browser.

● The image displays the default source file set in the `src` attribute.

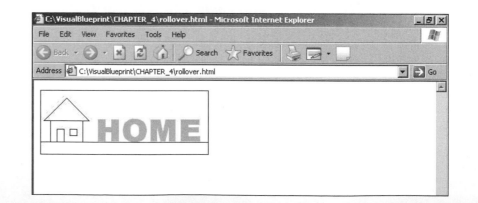

7 Position the mouse cursor over the top of the image.

- The image changes to the image specified in the `onmouseover` event.

8 Move the mouse cursor away from the image.

- The image reverts to the original look.

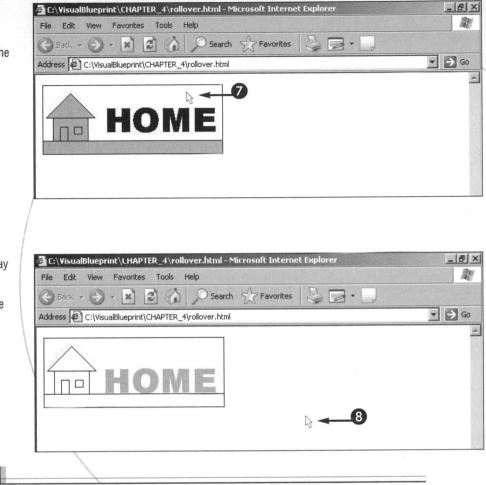

Extra

You can detect when the mouse is being moved on a Web page by using the `onmousemove` event. The event is fired whenever the mouse is moved within the Web page. If the mouse is moved outside the browser boundaries, the movement cannot be detected.

Detect Mouse Movement

```
<script>
  var IE = document.all?true:false
  if (!IE) document.captureEvents(Event.MOUSEMOVE)
  document.onmousemove = getMouseXY;
  function getMouseXY(e) {
    if (IE) {
      tempX = event.clientX + document.body.scrollLeft;
      tempY = event.clientY + document.body.scrollTop;
    } else {
      tempX = e.pageX;
      tempY = e.pageY;
    }
    document.title = "( " + tempX + "," + tempY + ")";
    return true
  }
</script>
```

Detect a Key Press

You can detect when a user pushes a key on its keyboard while your Web site is in focus. You can use the onkeypress method to determine which key was pressed. By detecting the key press, you can develop hot keys, limit text entered into a text box, block key functions, and much more.

The actual key that was pressed is identified using the window.event.keycode object. The keycode object returns a number that corresponds to that key. For example, the keycode with the number 13 corresponds to the Enter key. In Appendix A, there is a table of the keycodes mapped to the corresponding keys.

You can also use two other key press events, onkeydown and onkeyup, which detect when the user holds a key down and releases it. The onkeypress event fires only when it detects a complete stroke of a key. The onkeydown

event fires while the key is being pressed and the onkeyup event fires when the key that is being held down is released.

The key press events are added to multiple form elements on the Web page by setting the key press event as an attribute in the element's tag. The event is detected only when the element has focus. For example, the statement `<input type="text" name="T1" onkeypress="TypeFun()">` calls the function TypeFun() whenever a key is pressed while the text box T1 is in focus.

With the onkeypress event, you can assign all your interface elements a quick selection key to easily navigate through menus and forms. This enables users to navigate your interface using the keyboard instead of the mouse. It also makes your site accessible for people with disabilities.

Detect a Key Press

① Add the onkeypress event to the `<input>` tag where you want to monitor the keypress.

② Set the onkeypress event to call the function handleKeyPress().

③ Add the handleKeyPress() function between the head tags.

④ Add the cross browser code to determine how to capture the event.

⑤ Display the keyCode value and the CharacterCode value in an alert dialog box.

⑥ Set the return keyword to true to record the key press in text box.

⑦ Save the file.

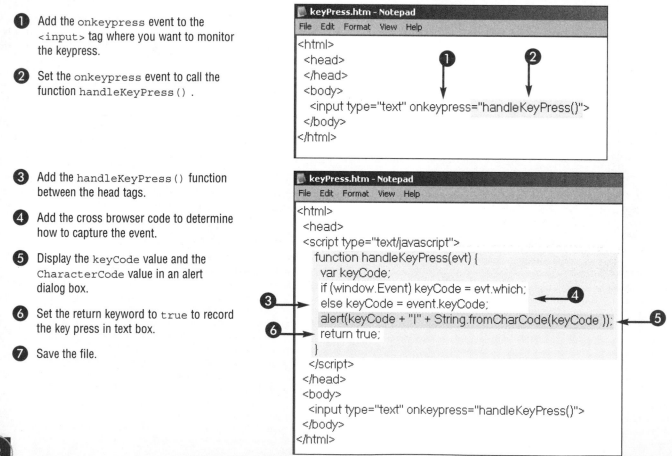

8 Open the HTML file in your Web browser.

9 Click in the text field to give it focus.

10 Enter a keyboard character.

- An alert message appears giving the key code value of the button along with what key was pressed.

11 Click the OK button to close the alert box.

- You can continue to type characters into the text box to determine the key code.

Apply It

You can limit character input in text boxes and text areas by using the onkeypress event. Not all keys on the user's keyboard can be detected or cancelled out by using JavaScript. A common key that cannot be detected is the Print Screen key. Other keys like the function keys can be detected, but you may not be able to cancel their default action. For example, the F11 key causes a Web page to become a full screen. You can detect when the key is pressed, but you cannot cancel the event.

Limit Character Input

```
<script>
 function handleKeyPress(evt) {
  var nbr, chr;
  if (window.Event) nbr = evt.which;
  else nbr = event.keyCode;
  if(nbr==13||nbr==12||nbr||11){//place key codes here
  return false;}
 }
 document.onkeydown= handleKeyPress
</script>
```

Detect a Modifier Key Combination

You can detect when a user is holding down a combination key press with a modifier key. The modifier keys are the Alt, Ctrl, and Shift keys. These keys perform special browser functions. For example, the key combination of Ctrl+N opens up a new browser instance. The property names for the keys are `altkey`, `ctrlkey`, and `shiftkey`.

You can use the modifier key combinations to perform JavaScript tasks such as opening new browser windows, opening navigation menus, filling out forms, performing special tasks, changing the page's location and so on. You have to make sure that the key combination you pick does not already have a built-in function. For example, you cannot use the Ctrl+H combination because the predefined function opens the history menu or the Ctrl+B that is used

to organize your Favorites. The default function fires when the pre-defined combination is selected. If you assigned the same combination in your code, the modifier combination may or may not be recognized depending on the browser.

Macintosh browsers have the same type of accelerator keyboard combinations as Windows. Instead of using the Ctrl key, the users use the meta key to perform their tasks. The property name of the meta key is `metakey`.

You can add a function for every key combination on the keyboard when designing your Web site; however, you should limit your choices so you do not confuse or overwhelm your users. Well-placed keyboard commands make your site's interface easier to use. You should use this as an alternative for navigating your Web site and not for the sole method of navigation.

Detect a Modifier Key Combination

① Add the `handleModifierPress` JavaScript function to the `<head>` tag.

② Add the `onkeypress` event to the entire document.

③ Set the `onkeypress` to call the `handleModifierPress` function.

④ Add the cross browser code to determine how to capture the event.

⑤ Add the statements to catch the modifier keys.

⑥ Display the key combination in a text field.

⑦ Save the file.

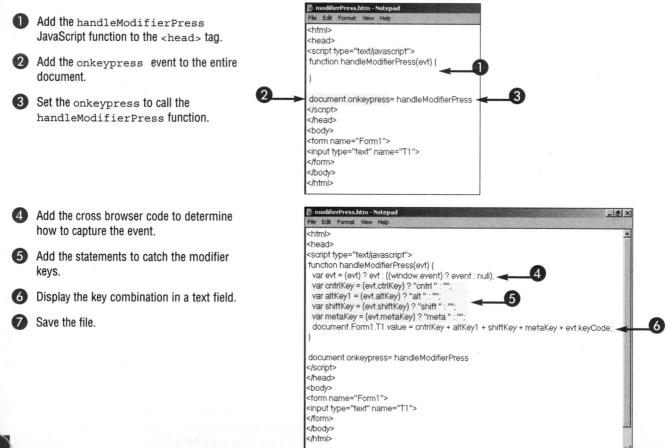

8 Open the file in a Web browser.

9 Press Shift+A.

- The text in the text box reveals what keys were pressed.

```
C:\VisualBlueprint\CHAPTER_4\modifierPress.htm - Microsoft Internet Explorer    _ 8 X
File   Edit   View   Favorites   Tools   Help
Back ▾  ➔ ▾  ✕  ⟳  ⌂   Search   Favorites   🖨  🖹 ▾  ▢
Address  C:\VisualBlueprint\CHAPTER_4\modifierPress.htm                          ➔ Go

  shift 65          ⟵──────●
```

10 Press Ctrl+Shift+V.

- The text box reveals the new key combination.

```
C:\VisualBlueprint\CHAPTER_4\modifierPress.htm - Microsoft Internet Explorer    _ 8 X
File   Edit   View   Favorites   Tools   Help
Back ▾  ➔ ▾  ✕  ⟳  ⌂   Search   Favorites   🖨  🖹 ▾  ▢
Address  C:\VisualBlueprint\CHAPTER_4\modifierPress.htm                          ➔ Go

  cntrl shift 22    ⟵──────●
```

Apply It

You can make certain keys perform special JavaScript tasks. You can change the document location, close the browser window, open a pop-up window, and more. Instead of adding the event handler to the <body> tag, you can assign the event to the entire document. For example, the following statement `document.onload = LoadValues` executes the function `LoadValues` when the document loads.

Assign an Event
```
<script>
   function handleKeyPress(evt) {
        var nbr;
        if (window.Event) nbr = evt.which;
        else nbr = event.keyCode;

        if(nbr==72){document.location.href="http://www.wiley.com";}
        else if(nbr==67){window.close();}
        else if(nbr==80){window.open("http://www.JavaRanch.com");}
        else{return true;}
    }
 document.onkeydown- handleKeyPress
</script>
```

You can alter this script to add more `else-if` statements to perform more tasks. You can also add multiple JavaScript statements in each `if` statement to perform multiple tasks per key press. By setting the JavaScript statement to `return false;`, you can keep the key press from happening.

Set and Remove Focus

You can place the cursor in any text field on the page by using the `focus()` method. For example, the statement `<body onload="document.test.text1.focus()">` places the cursor in text box named `text1` when the page loads. This method is great for pages that have a login box, because it eliminates the need for the user to click the box, thus saving the user time.

You can detect when a Web page element receives focus by using the `onfocus` event. The `onfocus` event fires when the user starts to interact with the element. By using the `onfocus()` event, you can change the background color of a form element. For example, the statement `<input type="text" name="T1" onfocus="this.style.background='yellow'">` changes the background color of the textbox `T1` when the element is focused.

If you want to remove focus from a Web page element, you can use the `blur()` method. The `blur()` method removes the focus from the element. Therefore, if the user is typing in a text box, the cursor is removed and the user can no longer type in the box. You can change the background of the element to another color after the focus has been removed from the element. For example, the statement `<input type="text" name="1" onblur="this.style.background='red'">` changes the background color of the textbox `T1` when the element's focus is removed.

When the user removes focus of an element by clicking on another part of the page or using the tab key to advance to the next element, you can detect it by using the `onblur` event. The `onblur` event is often used to validate a form element to make sure that the validation parameters are met. You can use these methods and events on frames, text boxes, text areas, pop-up windows, and the parent page.

Set and Remove Focus

① Add the `onfocus` event to the `<input>` tag.

② Set the `onfocus` event to display a new value in text box.

③ Add the `onblur` event to the `<input>` tag.

④ Set the `onblur` event to display a new value in text box.

⑤ Repeat steps **1** to **4** for each input box.

⑥ Save the file.

⑦ Open the HTML file in a Web browser.

● The text boxes have default text.

⑧ Click a text field to give it focus.

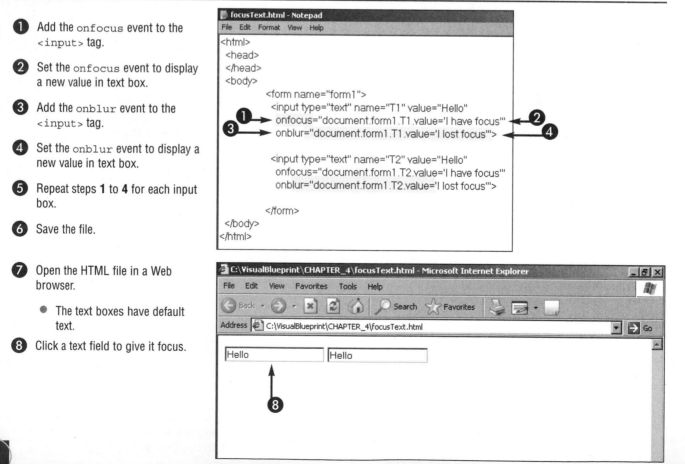

- The text updates according to the fields on focus event.

9 Click another text field.

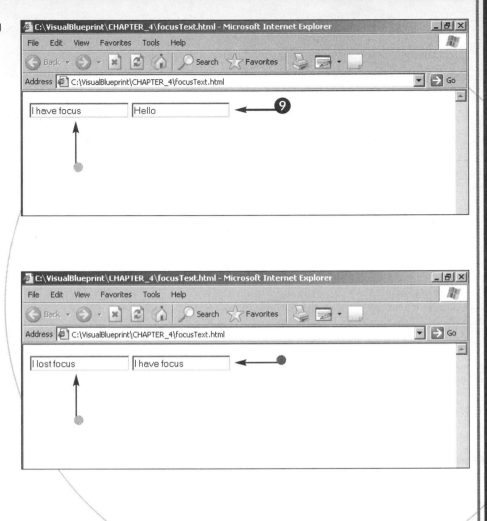

- The `onblur` event fired when the text box lost focus changing the text.

- The `onfocus` fired in the other text field after it gained focus.

Note: The `onblur` event will fire when it loses focus.

Apply It

You can move focus from element to element on a form to make it easier for a user to fill out the form. This eliminates the need for a user to have to move the mouse or use the Tab key. The following function MoveFocus() is called by the text box. You can add an onkeydown() to watch what the user types into the form fields you want. You can monitor more text boxes by adding more if statements into the function.

Move Focus
```
<script>
    function MoveFocus(name){
        if(document.form1.T1.value.length == 3 && name=='T1'){;
            document.form1.T2.focus();
        }
    }
</script>

<form name="form1">
    <input type="text" name="T1" onkeydown="MoveFocus('T1')">
    <input type="text" name="T2" >
</form>
```

Onchange Event

You can detect when the user has changed its selection in a drop-down list or even the text in a textbox with the onchange event. The onchange event is triggered when the user removes the focus from the form element. If the value of the form element is different than when the user first interacted with the element, the onchange event executes. If the value is the same as the initial value, then the onchange event handler is ignored.

The onchange event is added to the form element just like the attributes. For example, the statement `<input type="text" name="T1" onchange="Validate()">` calls the JavaScript function Validate() when the text is changed.

The onchange event handler helps to eliminate any unnecessary steps that the user would have to take when visiting your Web site. Common uses for using the

onchange event are validating forms, submitting forms, changing the page location, and calling functions without any additional user input.

A common place for the onchange event handler is with a select drop-down list. When the onchange event handler is added to the element, it is executed when a different option is selected from the list. A common script that uses the selection list with the onchange event is a navigation menu. When the option is selected in the menu, the page's location is changed. The onchange event handler eliminates the need for the user to click a button to change the page's location.

When using the onchange event with a drop-down list, it is common for the user to reselect the original value. The onchange event does not execute because the value has not changed. If you still need to detect that the user removed the focus from the element, you should use the onblur event.

Onchange Event

① Add the onchange event to the `<select>` tag.

② Set the onchange event to display price of product in text box.

③ Retrieve the value of the selected option from the drop-down menu.

④ Save the file.

⑤ Open the HTML document in a Web browser.

● The text field has the default text.

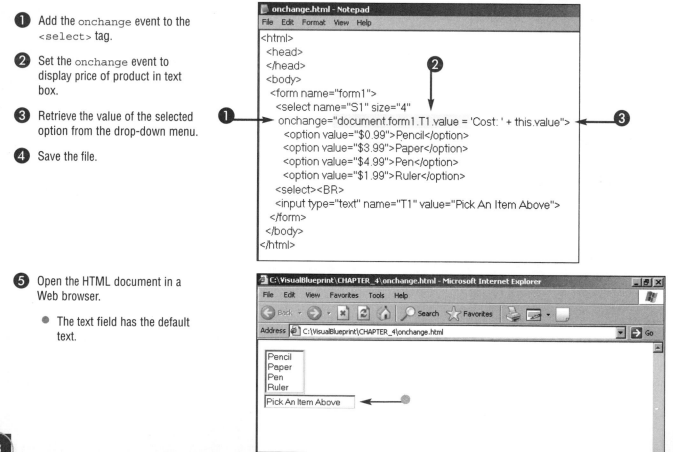

6 Click the first option in the selection list.

- The text field updates according to the onchange event.

7 Click the second option in the selection list.

- The text field updates again.

Apply It

You can use the onchange() event to validate form field elements. You can detect when the user has changed the information and call a function to verify the input. The example code checks to see if all the parameters are met. If the fields are not met, then the form value is reset and the field is refocused after an alert dialog box message is displayed. If the user does not change the value, the function does not fire again. Therefore, you may want to use the onblur() event. The onblur() event forces the user to have the correct information entered.

Validate Form Fields
```
<script>
    function Validate(){
        if(document.form1.T1.value.length < 5){
            alert('5 or more characters required');
            document.form1.T1.value = "";
            document.form1.T1.focus();
        }
    }
</script>

<form name="form1">
    <input type="text" name="T1" onchange="Validate()">
</form>
```

Handle the Page Load and Onunload Operations

Y ou can detect when a Web page has fully loaded by using the onload event handler. The onload event is normally placed as an attribute inside the <body> tag.

When the browser has loaded the last element on the Web page, the onload event is triggered. The onload event handler is typically used to initialize events after the page loads. This eliminates the chance of an error caused by the JavaScript function trying to use an object on the Web page that has not loaded. It is common to see DHTML scripts use the onload event to generate dynamic HTML elements on the page.

A similar event to the onload event is the onunload event. This event executes when the current Web page is exited. For example, the onunload event will fire for browser closings, back button, refresh button, and using links.

The onload and onunload are well known because many Web sites abuse them by opening pop-up advertisements on their Web site when you enter or leave a site.

There is no cross browser method to detect when a browser is closed. However, an Internet Explorer only event can capture the closing of the browser. The onbeforeunload event executes when exiting a page, prompting the user whether to continue ones action. There are some elaborate scripts available online that try to detect the browser's closing. Either these scripts do not work with every browser's or they increase the page loading time significantly.

You can only have one onload and onunload event handler on the page. Chapter 17 discusses ways to eliminate the problems with multiple onload and onunload event handlers.

Handle the Page Load and Onunload Operations

① Add the onload event to the <body> tag.

② Set the onload event to display welcome message.

③ Add the onunload event to the <body> tag.

④ Set the onunload event to display goodbye message.

⑤ Save the file.

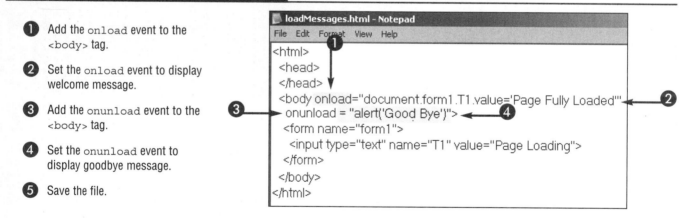

⑥ Open the file in a Web browser.

● The text box displays the loading message. Wait until Page Fully Loaded appears in the text box.

- The text box value changes.

7 Close the browser window.

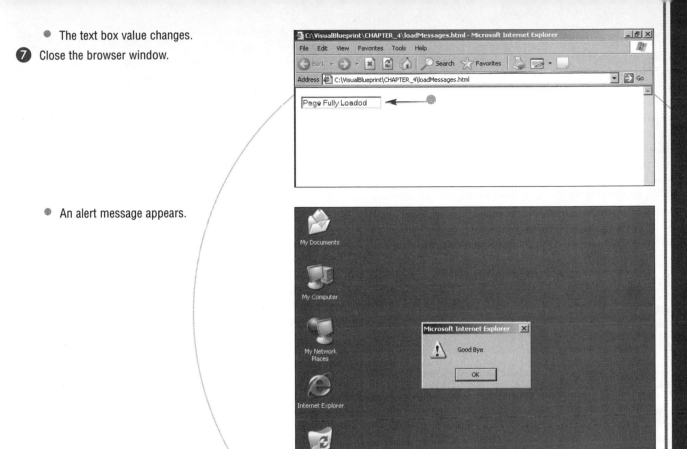

- An alert message appears.

Extra

You can detect a few more browser events including when the stop button is clicked and when the page is resized. You can use the `onabort` event to detect when the stop button is pressed on the browser. The `onabort` event is used to notify the user that the page needs to be fully loaded in order for your code to work. You add the `onabort` event handler as an attribute within the `<body>` tag. You can use the `onresize` event to detect when the user has changed the dimensions of its browser screen. Just like the `onabort` event, you add this code as an attribute in the `<body>` tag.

Detect Browser Events

```
<html>
  <head>
    <title> JavaScript  </title>
      <script>
        function ChangeSize(){
            window.resizeTo(300,300);
        }
      </script>
  </head>
  <body onResize="ChangeSize()">
    Make Page Remain 300px X 300px.
  </body>
</html>
```

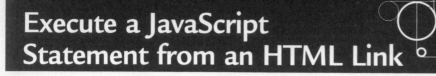

Execute a JavaScript Statement from an HTML Link

You can use an HTML link to execute a JavaScript statement or to call a function. Using links is a good way to call a JavaScript function since a user is used to clicking on them. You are also able to use CSS properties from Chapter 14 to format the links so they change properties when the mouse is over them.

There are two major ways to use a link. The first method is to add the JavaScript statement inside the href attribute of the tag. First, you need to add the javascript: keyword inside the tags, followed by colons, and then the JavaScript statement. For example, the statement `<a href="javascript:Test();">Test</a>` is a link that calls the function named Test when the link is clicked. You can add multiple JavaScript statements by placing them after the semicolon of each statement.

The second way that you can execute JavaScript statements from an HTML link is by attaching the onclick event handler to the object. You need to add a return false; statement to the end of the parameters that the onclick handler executes. This stops the link from performing its operation. You also need to include a value in the href attribute. If you do not include an href attribute, then the link does not appear as a link in the browser. For example, the statement `<a href="#" onclick="Test();return false;">Test</a>` executes the function Test when the link is clicked.

Instead of including a hash sign (#) in the href attribute of the link, you can add a page that notifies the user that the Web page requires JavaScript to be enabled. The user is redirected to that Web page since the browser ignores the onclick handler when JavaScript is disabled.

Execute a JavaScript Statement from an HTML Link

① Add the javascript: keyword to the href attribute in the link.

② Insert the JavaScript statement after the javascript: keyword.

③ Save the file.

```
link - Notepad
File  Edit  Format  View  Help
<html>
 <head>
  <title>JavaScript Blueprint</title>
 </head>
 <body>
  <a href="javascript:alert('The Link was clicked');">click this</a>
 </body>
</html>
```

④ Open the file in a Web browser.

⑤ Click the link to execute the JavaScript statement.

● The link executes the JavaScript statement displaying an alert dialog box.

```
JavaScript Blueprint - Microsoft Internet Explorer
File  Edit  View  Favorites  Tools  Help
Back    Search  Favorites
Address  C:\VisualBlueprint\CHAPTER_4\link.html        Go

click this    ⑤

   Microsoft Internet Explorer  X
      !   The Link was clicked
           OK

javascript:alert('The Link was clicked');        My Computer
```

Attach an Event to an Object

You can eliminate the need of adding the same exact event handler to every element on the page by attaching the event handler to an object. This eliminates the need to type hundreds of statements when building functions to perform validation checks or mouseover effects.

Event handlers are attached to the document, window, or any specific objects. Specific objects can include the <body> tag, text boxes, select boxes, radio buttons, and so on. A common event handler that is used with the window object is the onload event handler. The statement window.onload = Start; attaches the onload event handler to the window object and calls the Start function.

You can bind the event handler to the object by first referencing the object. Then, add the event handler after the reference and set the statement equal to the function that should be called. For example, the statement

document.form1.T1.onblur = Validate; binds the onblur event handler to the form element name T1.

By using a DOM method explained in Chapter 15, you can simplify the process by looping through all the elements and adding the event handler. Therefore, you do not have to type out hundreds of statements adding the event handler. The JavaScript function can do it for you. You can find all the elements on the page by using the getElementsByTagName() and setting the parameter inside the parentheses to the tag name. For example, the statement var theTags = document.getElementsByTagName("input"); places all the input tags into an array which you can loop through and attach the event handler. When looping through the function, you can attach the event handler with the statement theTags[i].onchange= setCount;. The event handler is added to all the tags when the array is iterated through.

Attach an Event to an Object

① Create a reference statement to the button adding the event handler to the end of the statement.

② Set the statement equal to a function name.

③ Save the file.

④ Open the file in a Web browser.

⑤ Perform the action to trigger the event handler from step **1**.

Note: This example uses the onclick handler; therefore, click the button.

● The JavaScript function was called and executed after the event handler was triggered.

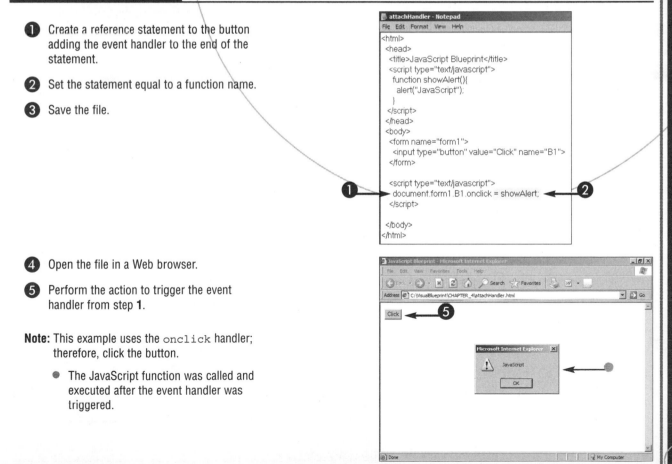

Determine the Element That Received the Event

You can detect what element received the event handler and apply this to a validation function or any other function. This method eliminates the need to have to add the element reference to each tag. Instead, you can attach the events through a JavaScript statement. This eliminates the need to type a lot of information that may be added dynamically to the page.

Microsoft Internet Explorer differs from the DOM event detection, which means you need to do some detection. Internet Explorer uses the `srcElement` event while DOM uses the target event to determine where the event came from. The statement `elem = evt.target ? evt.target : ((evt.srcElement) ? evt.srcElement : null);` determines what event the browser needs to use to detect the element.

Another problem that you face is that some other browsers such as Netscape 6 use another method to determine the element. These browsers require that you look at the parent node to find the correct element. If the statement `if(elem.nodeType == 3)` is true, then you know you have one of these special cases. You then need to use the `parentNode` property to find the element.

After you determine that the browser needs to use `srcElement` or target events, you can detect all the properties of the element. For example, the statement `var theValue = elem.value;` retrieves the value of a form element that was triggered by the event handler.

A popular reason for using this script is for form validation. You can add an `onblur` event handler to your elements and have it checked to make sure it is correct. If not, you can have the element stay focused by using the statement `elem.focus();`.

Determine the Element That Received the Event

① Add a statement that handles browser compatibility for event handling.

② Add code to determine the source element.

③ Display the element information on the page.

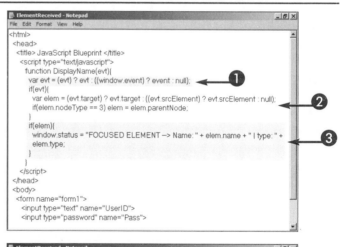

④ Add an `onfocus` event handler to a form element.

⑤ Repeat step **4** for each element of the form.

⑥ Save the file.

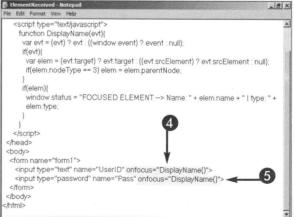

7 Open the file in a Web browser.

8 Click a form element to set the object's focus.

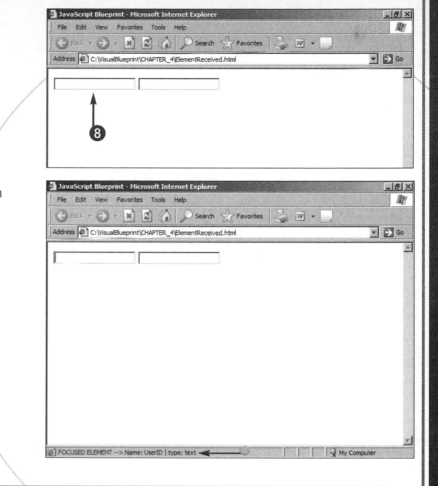

● The properties of the element that is in focus display on the screen.

Extra

You can detect where the mouse came from on a page by assigning onmouseover and onmouseout objects to the page. This allows you to determine what area of the page the mouse has come from, thereby allowing you to call functions accordingly.

Detect Mouse
```javascript
<script type="text/javascript">
  function DisplayName(evt){
    var evt = (evt) ? evt : ((window.event) ? event : null);
    if(evt){
      var oldElem = (evt.relatedTarget) ? evt.relatedTarget : ((evt.fromElement) ?
evt.fromElement : null);
      if(oldElem){
        if(oldElem.id)window.status = "Came From " + oldElem.id;
      }
    }
  }
</script>
<div id="d1" style="border:1px solid black;" onmouseout="DisplayName()">div1</div>
<div id="d2" style="border:1px solid black;" onmouseout="DisplayName()">div2</div>
```

The code shows where the cursor was moved from on the page. It uses the div ids to find the necessary information. You can use any other attribute of that form to perform any action you want.

Determine Which
Mouse Button Was Pressed

You can differentiate between what mouse button was clicked by monitoring the `onmousedown` event handler. The `onclick` and `onmouseup` event handlers do not always catch the event. Detecting the mouse button allows you to perform different actions.

The button event is an integer number that corresponds to what button was pressed on the mouse. For Internet Explorer and the DOM, the numbers of the events differ. Internet Explorer uses the number one for the left button, which is also considered the primary button. The DOM uses the number zero to correspond to the left button. The middle button on the mouse is number four for Internet Explorer and number one for DOM. The right button is number two for both Internet Explorer and DOM. When no buttons are pressed, Internet Explorer returns the number zero while DOM returns null.

Internet Explorer also detects other combination of button presses that DOM does not. A left and right button click corresponds to number three. The left and middle combination corresponds to number five, while a right and middle click correspond to number six. The last combination is a left, middle, and right button click that corresponds to the integer number seven.

When you are programming, you need to recognize that not everyone has three buttons on its mouse. Most people have two buttons. It is also common for Macs to have only one button on their mouse. Mac users have the ability to right-click objects by holding down a modifier key on the keyboard, but not everyone knows how to do this. Limiting dependability on button detection makes your script more operating system friendly.

Determine Which Mouse Button Was Pressed

① Add a statement that handles browser compatibility for event handling.

② Detect if the event is a button event.

③ Determine if the right button was pressed; if it is, `return false` to cancel it.

④ Develop `else` statement to `return true` so the function does not interfere with the other clicks.

⑤ Save the file.

⑥ Open the file in a Web browser.

⑦ Right-click the mouse anywhere on the Web page.

● An alert dialog box appears confirming that the right mouse button was clicked.

Note: The contextual menu did not appear when the button was clicked.

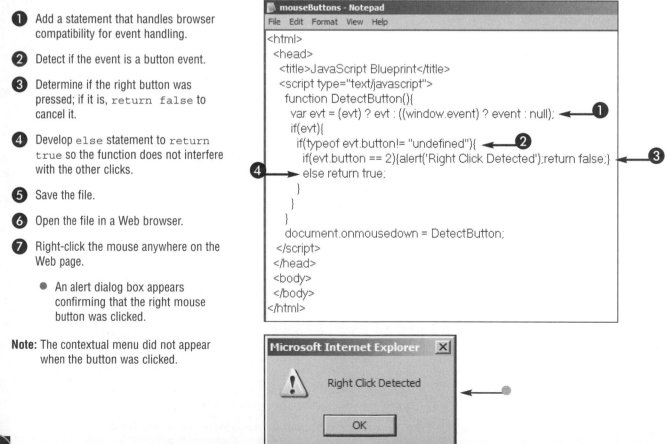

```
mouseButtons - Notepad
File  Edit  Format  View  Help
<html>
 <head>
  <title>JavaScript Blueprint</title>
  <script type="text/javascript">
   function DetectButton(){
    var evt = (evt) ? evt : ((window.event) ? event : null);   ◄── ①
    if(evt){
     if(typeof evt.button!= "undefined"){   ◄── ②
      if(evt.button == 2){alert('Right Click Detected');return false;}   ◄── ③
 ④ ─►  else return true;
      }
     }
    }
   document.onmousedown = DetectButton;
  </script>
 </head>
 <body>
 </body>
</html>
```

Microsoft Internet Explorer

⚠ Right Click Detected

OK

Cancel
Browser Events

You may want to block a user from triggering an event on the page. For example, one thing that you can block is the contextual menu, which is better known as the right-click menu. Before you block an event, you need to consider the benefit that you are giving the user by blocking the event. If you are not giving them a benefit, then you may be wasting your time and irritating the user that is visiting your site. Some people use the right mouse button as a way to navigate through a page, so by blocking this you may be alienating visitors of your site.

You can cancel an event by using the cancelBubble event. When the cancelBubble event is set to true, the event does not fire. You also need to return false at the end of the function to make sure the event is fully blocked. Not returning false allows the action to still perform.

By assigning an event at the document level, you can block most events. The event to block the right click button is to use the oncontextmenu event. By setting this to the document object and calling a function, you can disable the context menu.

If you are using this to block users from saving images, you need to remember that images are being downloaded to the user's hard drive. The images are automatically saved in the Temporary Internet Files folder. The person may be about to hot link to an image to download it. The user can disable JavaScript to download the image, use print screen, or save the document with the Save As function or a site ripper program. A determined user can steal your images or view your source code.

Cancel Browser Events

① Determine the source of the event accessing the function.

② Verify that the event was executed while accessing an image.

③ Set the cancelBubble method to true and add a return false statement to block the action fully.

④ Add a return true statement for all other events.

⑤ Attach the oncontextmenu to the document object assigning a function name.

⑥ Save the file.

⑦ Open the file in a Web browser.

⑧ Right-click the mouse on top of the image.

● The oncontextmenu browser event was blocked.

```
cancelEvent - Notepad
File  Edit  Format  View  Help
<html>
 <head>
  <title>JavaScript Blueprint</title>
  <script type="text/javascript">
   function EventBlocker(){
    var evt = (evt) ? evt : event;
    var elem = (evt.target) ? evt.target : ((evt.srcElement) ? evt.srcElement : null);
    if (elem && elem.tagName.toLowerCase() == "img"){
      if(evt.cancelBubble)evt.cancelBubble = true;
      return false;
    }
    return true;
   }
   document.oncontextmenu = EventBlocker;
  </script>
 </head>
 <body>
  <img src="image.jpg">
 </body>
</html>
```

Limit Executions with If-Else Statements

You can control the flow of the program by using `if-else` statements. The `if-else` statement limits the execution of certain steps depending on the conditions. For example, you may want a user to complete all fields in a form before submitting. If the user leaves any field blank, you can execute other statements instead of submitting the form.

The syntax of an `if` clause includes the `if` keyword followed by a conditional statement within parentheses. If only a single statement needs executed, it is positioned after the conditional statement and ended with a semicolon. If several statements need executed, you can contain them within a set of brackets.

An `else` statement is used if the `if` conditional is false and another set of statements needs executed. The `else` statement is positioned under the `if` statement and can hold a set of brackets containing several JavaScript statements. The `else` statement does not get any conditionals.

A single `if` clause is followed by several `else if` clauses, but the final `else` statement should not include the `if` keyword. If one of the `if` or `else if` conditional statements is true, then all the remaining `else if` clauses and the `else` clause in the group are ignored. Therefore, if you want every statement to be considered, you should not use the `else if` statements, instead only use `if` statements.

The conditional statement that is located in the parentheses is as simple as a Boolean or as complex as a mathematical equation. Each conditional statement is made up of multiple comparison expressions combined with conditional operators such as and `(&&)` and or `(||)`. You can find an explanation of comparison expressions and conditional operators in Chapter 3.

Limit Executions with If-Else Statements

LIMIT WITH ONE STATEMENT

1. Add an `if` statement and the statements you want to execute.

2. Place the conditional statement in the parentheses.

3. Add the `else` statement and the statements you want to execute.

4. Save the file.

```
ifelse1.html - Notepad
File  Edit  Format  View  Help
<html>
 <head>
  <title> JavaScript Blueprint </title>
 </head>
 <body>
  <h1>Games Store</h1>
  <h2>The store is
  <script type="text/javascript">
     var timeHour = 18;

     if(timeHour >= 9 && timeHour <=16){
        document.write("<span style='color:green'>OPEN</span>");
     }
     else{
        document.write("<span style='color:red'>CLOSED</span>");
     }

  </script>
  </h2>
 </body>
</html>
```

5. Open the file in a Web browser.

- The result of the `if` statement appears.

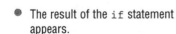

Games Store

The store is CLOSED

LIMIT WITH MULTIPLE STATEMENTS

① Add an `if` statement with the conditional parameters.

② Add an `else if` statement with the conditional parameters.

③ Repeat step **2** for each additional `else if` statement.

④ Add an `else` statement.

⑤ Save the file.

```
ifelse2.html - Notepad
File  Edit  Format  View  Help
<html>
 <head>
  <title> JavaScript Blueprint </title>
 </head>
 <body>
   <h1>Games Store</h1>
   <h2>The store is
   <script type="text/javascript">
     var timeHour = 10;

     if(timeHour >= 11 && timeHour <=12){        ◀——①
         document.write("<span style='color:red'>AT LUNCH!</span>");
     }
     else if(timeHour >= 9 && timeHour <=16){     ◀——②
         document.write("<span style='color:green'>OPEN!</span>");
     }
     else{                                        ◀——④
         document.write("<span style='color:red'>CLOSED!</span>");
     }
   </script>
   </h2>
```

⑥ Open the file in a Web browser.

- The result of the `if` statement appears showing the statement that is dependent on the variable.

```
JavaScript Blueprint - Microsoft Internet Explorer                    _ | 8 | x |
File   Edit   View   Favorites   Tools   Help
Back ▾  ▶  ▾  ✗  ↻  ⌂   Search  ⭐ Favorites   ┃  ▾  ┃
Address  C:\VisualBlueprint\CHAPTER_5\ifelse2.html              ▾  → Go
```

Games Store

The store is OPEN!

Apply It

You can nest `if` statements within one another. This enables you to drill down from general conditions to ones that are more specific. Each level of a nested `if-else` structure can contain any number of statements. By using nested `if` statements, you can pinpoint the exact criteria for which you are searching. This example drills down to specific criteria to determine the type of car the person owns. If each criterion is met, it shows the user the type of car the user wants to buy.

Nest if Statements
```
if(numberDoors == 2){
  if(numberPassengers==2){
    car="corvette";
  }
  else{
    car="mustang"
  }
}
```

When you use nested `if` statements, it is very important to keep track of the brackets. A common error arises by missing a bracket or adding it to the wrong location. It is good practice to use brackets with a single statement after the `if` statement. Using brackets with a single `if` statement creates a uniform-looking code and can help you debug your code should an error arise.

Using Conditional Operators

U sing Conditional Operators, you can use a shortcut for a single `if-else` statement to save time in development. A conditional operator is a single operator used to evaluate a conditional statement. This operator consists of a question mark (?) and a colon (:).

A conditional statement appears to the left of the question mark. If the conditional statement is true, the expression to the immediate right of the question mark is evaluated. The colon symbol is placed after the first expression and before the second expression. If the conditional statement is false, JavaScript evaluates the statement that follows the colon.

For example, the statement `(var1 == 23) ? (str2 = ' yes') : (str2 = ' no')` compares the value of var1. If this value equals 23, the variable str2 is assigned the value of yes; if the value does not equal 23, str2 is assigned no. The same statement written with an `if` statement is

`if(var1==23){str2='yes';}else{str2='no';}` which requires extra typing.

You can shorten the conditional operator statement by setting a conditional expression equal to a variable. You can change the expressions on the left and right of the colon to hold a string, Boolean, or numeric character. For example, the statement `str2 = (var1 == 23) ? 'yes' : 'no';` performs the same action as the two previous examples, which eliminates typing extra characters.

Conditional operators are commonly used in cross-browser scripting. They are typically used to determine in which browser environment the code is running. For example, the statement `evt = (evt) ? evt : ((window.event) ? event : null);` is used to determine if the object is a window event object or a W3C DOM event object.

Using Conditional Operators

1 Set a variable equal to a conditional statement.

2 Add a question mark followed by the true result.

3 Add a colon followed by the false result.

4 Save the file.

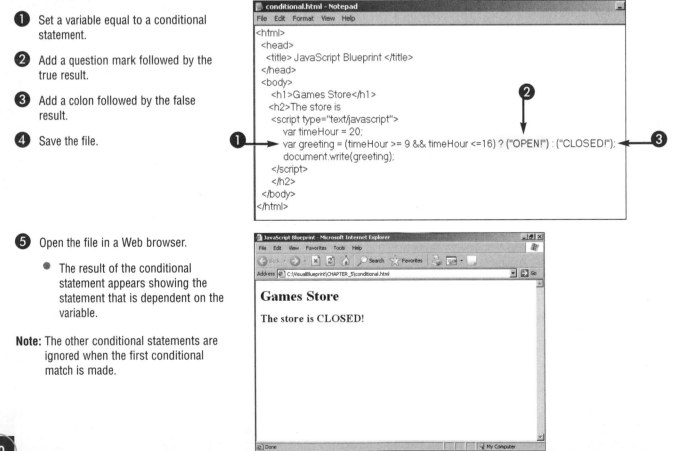

5 Open the file in a Web browser.

● The result of the conditional statement appears showing the statement that is dependent on the variable.

Note: The other conditional statements are ignored when the first conditional match is made.

Optimize Performance with a Switch Statement

You can use a `switch` statement instead of an `if` statement to compare a variable against more than three values. The `switch` statement evaluates an expression and compares the value to one or more case *clauses*. Switch statements are more efficient than `if-else` statements, and they take less time to execute.

The first line of the statement uses the `switch` keyword, followed by the expression that needs to be evaluated. The `switch` keyword is followed by parentheses. Inside the parentheses, you include a variable. The variable is used to determine which case to pick.

The case clause is similar to the `if-else` statement. The `switch` statement evaluates each case in descending order until a match is made. The case looks for a match; if there is an exact match, the statements under that case

fire until the first break is encountered. JavaScript executes all the code that follows the `switch` statement until it reaches a break point. That includes the statements that are included in other case clauses. You can use this to your benefit. You can have a case execute multiple lines of code. If you try to do the same thing with `if-else` statements, you have to repeat the code in every `if-else` statement. For example, if there are three case clauses with the third clause containing a break keyword and the first clause is a match, the statement executes the statements in all three clauses.

Just like `if-else` statements, `switch` statements have an `else` statement. If no matches are made, the `default` clause is called. When you use a `default` clause, it must be the last clause in the `switch` statement. The `default` clause does not need a break statement.

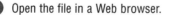

Optimize Performance with a Switch Statement

① Add the `switch` keyword with the variable you want to use as the conditional.

② Add a `case` statement along with the statements and the `break` keyword.

③ Repeat step **2** for each case.

④ Add the `default` case followed by its statements.

⑤ Save the file.

⑥ Open the file in a Web browser.

● The result of the `switch` statement selecting the correct conditional statement appears on the screen.

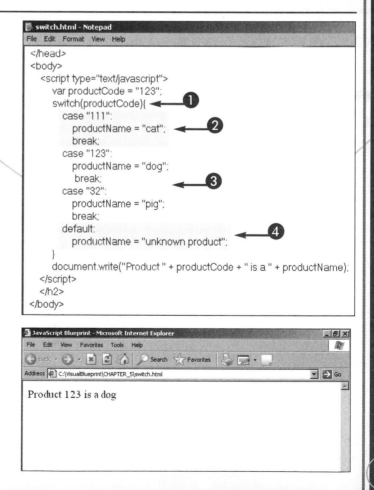

```
switch.html - Notepad
File  Edit  Format  View  Help

</head>
<body>
  <script type="text/javascript">
    var productCode = "123";
    switch(productCode){                              ①
      case "111":
        productName = "cat";                          ②
        break;
      case "123":
        productName = "dog";
        break;                                        ③
      case "32":
        productName = "pig";
        break;
      default:
        productName = "unknown product";              ④
    }
    document.write("Product " + productCode + " is a " + productName);
  </script>
  </h2>
</body>
```

```
JavaScript Blueprint - Microsoft Internet Explorer
File  Edit  View  Favorites  Tools  Help
Back        Search  Favorites
Address  C:\VisualBlueprint\CHAPTER_5\switch.html            Go

Product 123 is a dog
```

Create a For Loop

You can execute a group of statements, a given number of times, by using a for loop. A for loop typically uses a variable, called the control variable, to monitor the loop iterations. A for statement consists of three distinct parts within parentheses that are separated by semicolons. The first part defines the loop's initial condition; the second part defines the loop's terminating condition; and the final part defines how the loop is incremented.

The for loop begins at a defined initial condition and continually executes the statement or statements that follow the for statement until the termination condition is met. The for loop variable is incremented or decremented each time it iterates through the loop.

For example, the statement for(i=1;i<10;i++) begins with the loop variable i set to 1 and loops through the statements that follow, nine times before exiting the loop.

If only a single statement needs to be repeated, it is positioned after the for statement and should end with a semicolon. If several statements need executed, they are contained within a set of brackets.

The for statement loops until the end condition is met. If the end condition is never met, it is called an infinite loop. Infinite loops freeze the browser causing the user an inconvenience. You can use a counter variable with break statements to protect yourself from this problem.

You are not required to have unary operators to define how a loop is incremented such as i++ or i−. You can have an expression with arithmetic operators instead. For example, for(i=0;i<1024;i=(i+10)/(x+1)) is a valid way to increment a loop. The loop is incremented or decremented each time the loop reaches the last statement inside the loop. The incremented value is then compared to the conditional statement to continue or discontinue processing.

Create a For Loop

1 Add the for loop with the starting, ending, and increment parameter along with an opening bracket.

2 Add the statements you want to execute.

3 Close the loop with a bracket.

4 Save the file.

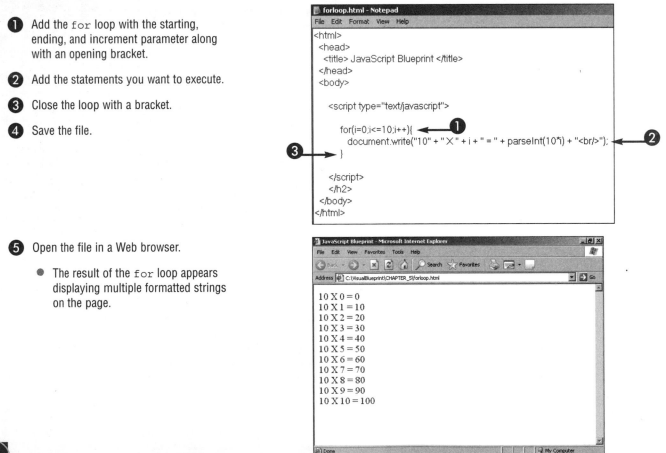

5 Open the file in a Web browser.

● The result of the for loop appears displaying multiple formatted strings on the page.

Continue and Break Loops

avaScript has built-in keywords that allow you to prematurely break a loop. This allows you to have more control over the looping process. You can use the `break` keyword to break out of an infinite loop or a loop you want to end prematurely because another parameter was met. When JavaScript encounters the `break` keyword within a loop, it automatically terminates the loop and executes the first statement that comes after the loop.

For example, if a `for` loop includes a conditional expression that is always true, such as `for(i=0; i>0;i++)`, you can break out of the loop with the `break` keyword. You just need to place the break keyword anywhere inside the loop. The loop does not process any of the remaining JavaScript statements that exist after the break statement in the loop.

You can also use another JavaScript keyword that stops the processing of a loop for one iteration, but it does not kill the looping process like the break keyword does. By using the continue keyword, you can stop the loop from processing fully and return to the top of the loop as if all the statements have been executed inside the brackets. Any statements that follow the `continue` keyword are not executed for this time through the loop.

Using the `continue` keyword enables you to check for special exceptions within the loop and skip them without interrupting the normal flow of the loop. The `continue` keyword is the equivalent of adding an `if` statement to the entire bottom contents of the loop that you do not want to execute.

For example, if the statement `for(i=0;i<=100,i++)` is executing, you can skip the execution of the step where `i` equals 50 by utilizing the statement `if(var1 == 50) continue;`.

Continue and Break Loops

① Add a `for` loop.

② Add the continue parameter where you want the loop to skip statements.

③ Add a `break` condition.

④ Save the file.

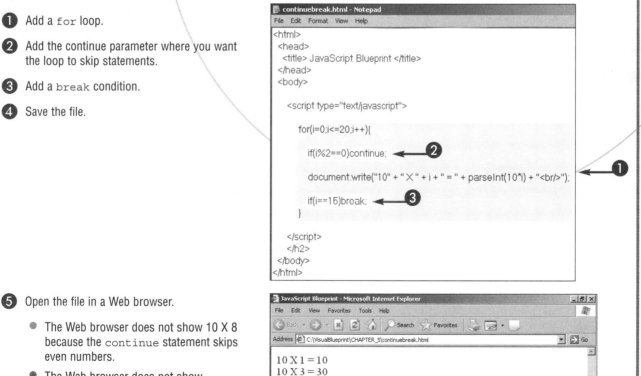

⑤ Open the file in a Web browser.

● The Web browser does not show 10 X 8 because the `continue` statement skips even numbers.

● The Web browser does not show multiplication beyond 15 because the `break` statement ends the loop.

Handle
While Loops

You can use a `while` loop to execute a statement multiple times that is not predetermined. A `while` loop is different from the `for` loop because it does not iterate to a set end condition. It simply continues to loop through the statements contained within the brackets until a conditional expression evaluates to false. The `while` loop only contains a conditional expression in parentheses that come after the `while` keyword.

When using a `while` loop, you need to make sure that the conditional statement eventually becomes false or the loop continues indefinitely. If an infinite loop occurs, the user's browser tends to freeze, causing your Web page to be inaccessible. You should also make sure that all the variables in the conditional statement are defined, so you have less of a chance of having an infinite loop.

For example, the statement `while(var1 <= 100)` executes the statements that follow until the variable, `var1`, is greater than `100`. If the statements within the loop never change the value of `var1`, then the loop continues indefinitely.

The `while` loop is a great choice if the number of iterations is not known. If the number of iterations is a set amount, the `for` loop is the preferred method to handle the situation.

Another loop is a `do-while` loop. The `do-while` loop acts exactly like the `while` loop, except that the expression is evaluated at the end of each iteration instead of at the beginning. This guarantees that at least one iteration will always happen.

You can consider the `while` loop and `do-while` loop to be slightly different versions of the same statement because everything that you can do with a `do-while` loop you can also do with a `while` loop. Because the two are so similar, a `do-while` loop is rarely seen in code.

Handle While Loops

USE A WHILE LOOP

 Add the `while` keyword along with the conditional parameter.

② Add the statements you want to execute.

③ Close the loop with a bracket.

④ Save the file.

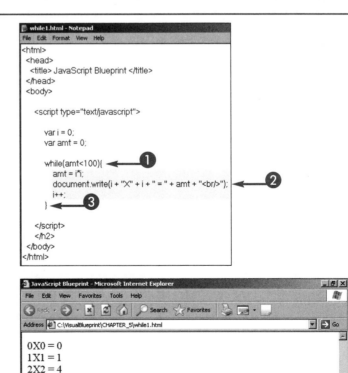

⑤ Open the file in a Web browser.

● The result of the `while` loop appears displaying a series of statements on the screen.

USE A DO-WHILE LOOP

① Add the `do` keyword.

② Add the statements you want to execute.

③ Add the `while` keyword with its parameter.

④ Save the file.

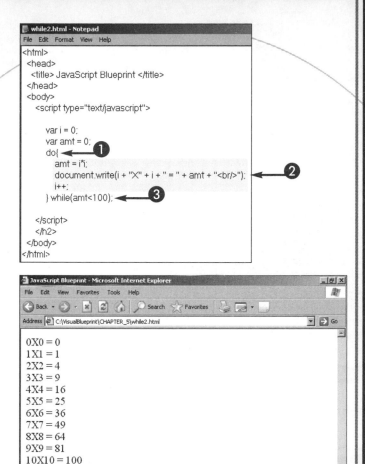

⑤ Open the file in a Web browser.

● The result of the `do-while` loop appears displaying a series of statements on the screen.

Extra

When you use `while` and `do-while` loops, you may run into the issue of having an infinite loop. An *infinite loop* is a loop that never ends. As a result, the loop can use all the memory resources allocated to the browser, which causes the browser to freeze.

You can break out of a loop two ways. You can use the `break` method or manually change the value of the variable in the comparison expression. For example, for the expression $x < 100$, you can set the variable x to equal 101 to stop the loop from performing its next iteration.

Break Out of a Loop
```
stop=0
do{
   var theError = checkError();
   stop++;
   if(stop>500)break;
}  while(!theError);
```

Create a Timed Interval

Y ou can use JavaScript to set up timers that allow certain functions to execute at different times. These are useful for timing different actions on the Web page including showing or hiding images and adding dynamic text.

The method that makes timers possible is the `window.setTimeout()` method. This method accepts two parameters. The first parameter is a JavaScript statement to execute. This may be a single statement, such as `document.body.style.background = 'blue'`, or the name of a function that is defined elsewhere in the Web page. The statement can also be several that are separated with semicolons. The statement that makes up this first parameter needs to be enclosed within quotation marks.

The second parameter accepted by the `window.setTimeout()` method is the time value to wait before the JavaScript statement is executed. This value is measured in milliseconds. For example, a value of 5000 waits 5 seconds and a value of 10000 waits 10 seconds.

You can stop a `setTimeout()` method from firing by using the `clearTimeout()` method. The `clearTimeout()` method may only be cleared internally using the `clearTimeout()` method. This method is part of the window object and is referenced in the current window as `window.clearTimeout()`. The stop button on the browser cannot stop intervals from firing; only the `clearTimeout()` method can.

To use the `clearTimeout()` method, you must name the timeout when it is set. You can name a timeout by assigning the `setTimeout()` method to a variable name. This variable name can then be used as a parameter in the `clearTimeout()` method's parentheses to terminate the timeout.

For example, if a timeout is assigned to a variable such as `timer1 = setTimeout (x++, 1000)`, the timeout is canceled at any time with the `clearTimeout (timer1)` statement.

Create a Timed Interval

① Declare a variable and set the `setTimeout()` keyword to it.

② Place the time and function call parameters in the `setTimeout()` parentheses.

③ Add an `onload` handler to call the `setTimeout()` function.

④ Save the file.

⑤ Open the file in a Web browser.

⑥ Type the answers to the questions.

⑦ Instead of clicking the Submit button, let the time run out so you can see the automatic form submission.

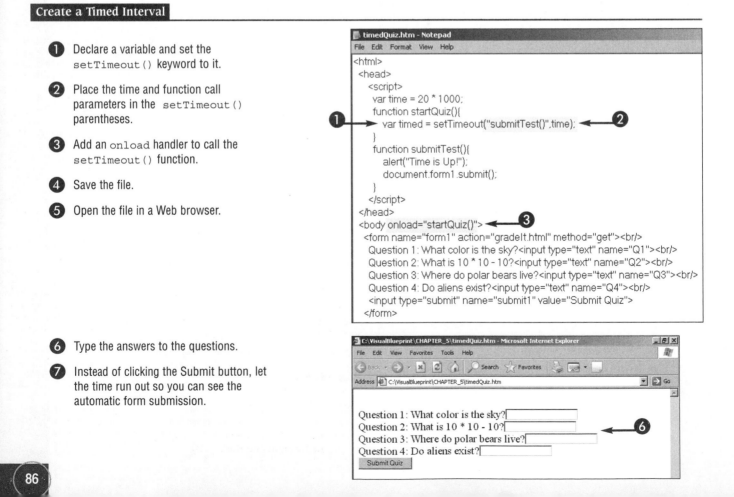

- An alert dialog box appears with a message.

⑧ Click the OK button on the alert dialog box.

Microsoft Internet Explorer

⚠ Time is Up!

OK ◄— ⑧

- The form is submitted to another Web page after the alert dialog box is closed.

C:\VisualBlueprint\CHAPTER_5\gradeIt.html - Microsoft Internet Explorer

File   Edit   View   Favorites   Tools   Help

Back ▾ ◯ ▾ ⚹ ⚹ ⚹   Search   Favorites

Address ⓔ file:///C:/VisualBlueprint/CHAPTER_5/gradeIt.html?Q1=blue&Q2=90&Q3=&Q4=   ▾ ⟶ Go

Grade Recorded

Done   💻 My Computer

Extra

You can redirect a Web page to a new location by using the JavaScript setTimeout() method. You may want to do this if you move content from your Web site to a new location. Therefore, users who have bookmarked the page that you plan to move can find the page's new location.

Redirect a Web Page
```
<body>
  <h1>The page will redirect to the new location in 5 seconds</h1>
  <script>
    var numSeconds = 5;
    var theURL = "http://www.JavaRanch.com";
    var totalTime = numSecs * 1000;
    var changeLocation = setTimeout("document.location.href=" +
theURL,totalTime);
  </script>
</body>
```

You want to give users enough time to read the page, but not too much time that they get tired of waiting. You can experiment with the amount of time by changing the variable numSeconds.

Set a Regularly Timed Interval

Y ou can have a function or statement executed in a timely matter that is equivalent to a `for` loop. Instead of having the code repeated in a rapid manner, you can use the `setTimeout()` method to specify the time it takes for each execution.

The `setInterval()` method is used to execute a function, statement, or group of statements at regular intervals repeatedly. The `setInterval()` method accepts two parameters, just like the `setTimeout()` method. The first parameter is the JavaScript statement to execute, and the second parameter is the time, in milliseconds, until the statement is executed. You must enclose the first parameter within quotation marks.

Timeouts created with the `setInterval()` method continue indefinitely unless the `clearInterval()` method is called. The `setInterval()` function has been known to behave

differently on certain computer systems with intervals ranging between 1 and 10 milliseconds.

You can end a `setinterval()` method by using the `clearInterval()` method. The `clearInterval()` method can only be cleared internally using the `clearInterval()` method. This method is part of the window object and is referenced in the current window as `window.clearInterval()`. The stop button on the browser does not stop the timed intervals from executing.

To use the `clearInterval()` method, you need to name the timeout when it is set. You can name a timeout by assigning the `setInterval()` method to a variable name. This variable name is then used as a parameter in the `clearInterval()` method's parentheses to terminate the timeout. The `setInterval()` method is used to create dynamic clocks, scrolling content, changing displays, and much more.

Set a Regularly Timed Interval

① Add the `setInterval()` method along with its parameters.

② Create the function that the `setInterval()` method calls.

③ Set parameters to display the images.

④ Add code to change the image source.

⑤ Add an event handler to the `<body>` tag to start the slide show.

⑥ Add the image to the body of the page that the JavaScript function references.

⑦ Save the file.

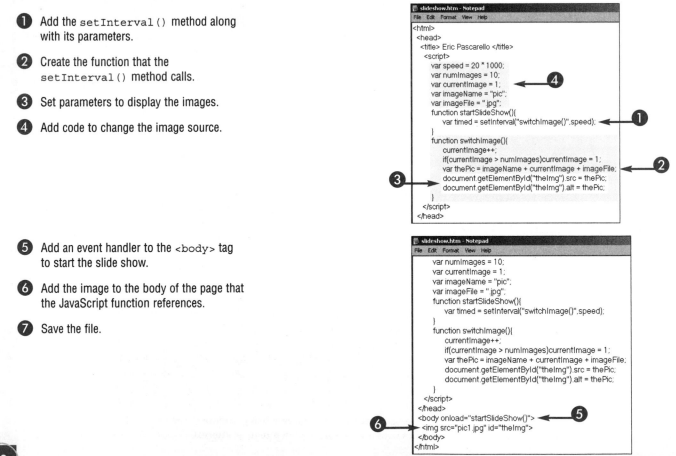

8 Open the file in a Web browser.

- The first image appears.

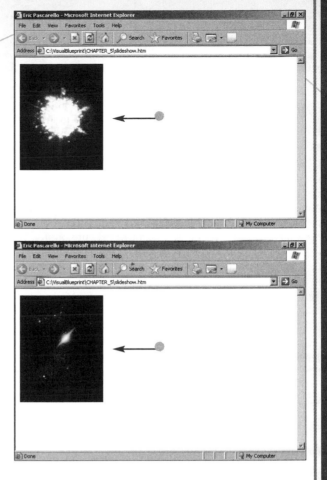

- After a set period, the image changes to next image.

Note: The images will continue to loop until the page is exited.

Apply It

You can create a clock on your Web site by using the `Date()` object. This object includes a method called `getLocaleString()` that gets the locale's current time. For more information using the `Date()` object as well as the `setInterval()` method, see Chapter 8.

Create a Clock
```
<form name="form1">
  <input type="text" name="text1" size="40">
</form>
<script>
  function setTime(){
    var time = new Date();
    document.form1.text1.value = time.toLocaleString();
  }
  var stop = setInterval("setTime()",1);
</script>
```

The code uses a form with a single text box to show the time being updated. The value of the `getLocaleString()` method is stored in the text box on a regular interval that is updated every second.

Declare and Call a Function

Y ou can group sections of code together into a structure called a function. You can call and access a function at any time. You can send parameters to functions, and the functions can return values.

You declare functions with the `function` keyword followed by the function name. Parentheses always immediately follow the function name. Parameters for the function are contained within these parentheses, but parameters are not required.

For example, the statement `function hello()` declares a function named `hello`. Function names have the same limitations and follow the same requirements as variables. They must begin with a letter; they must not contain any spaces; and they cannot use any special characters such as: +, *, /, &, %, $, #, @, or !. Also, remember that function names are case sensitive.

All JavaScript statements within the function should be contained within braces after the function declaration.

The statements that are included inside the function are not executed until the function is called. The function is called from anywhere within the document by listing the function name. You need to include parentheses when calling a function whether or not the function has parameters. For example, if a function is defined as `function hello()`, then you can execute this function with the statement `hello();`.

You can call functions by using event handlers such as `onload()`, `onclick()`, `onmouseover()`, `onmouseout()`, and so on. The event handlers are added to HTML elements to provide user functionality and dynamic content. You can learn more about event handlers in Chapter 4.

Functions are used to add structure and reusability to a Web page. You can place the JavaScript statement inside a function and call it multiple times.

Declare and Call a Function

1 Declare a function.

2 Add statements that you want to execute.

3 Add an event handler to call the function.

4 Save the file.

5 Open the file in a Web browser.

● After the function is called, the result of the `document.write` statements that are located inside the function are displayed on the screen.

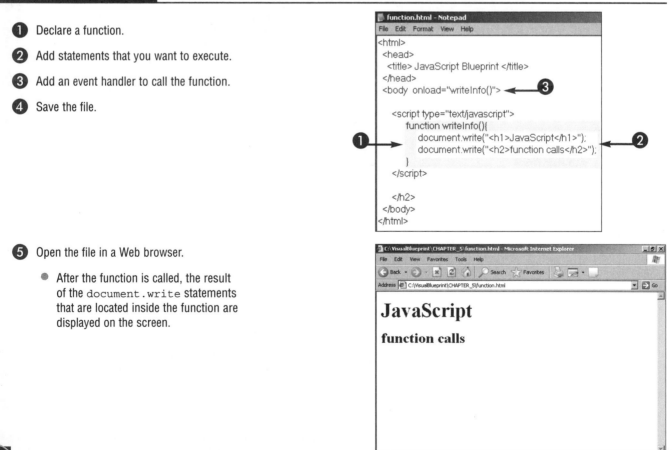

Handle Global and Local Variables

You can declare variables with the var keyword within a function. The variable is local to the function in which the variables appear. These local variables are only understood within the function and are not recognized in any JavaScript statements outside the function.

For example, if a variable named myVar1 is declared within a function using the var keyword, then that function is only able to use myVar1. If the variable is referenced outside the function it was declared in, then the value is undefined.

Variables that are implicitly declared without the var keyword in a function are global. Variables declared outside functions with or without the var keyword are also global. Global variables are used anywhere within the current document including both inside and outside functions.

You can use local variables to build functions that can easily be reused repeatedly without interfering with any global variables. For example, you can have a function that finds the location of an element. You can send multiple requests to it, and it will not interfere with any of the requests. If the variables are global, each time the script runs, it writes over the variable's value and interferes with the initial call.

By using a naming convention, you can save yourself time and trouble trying to figure out which variables are global and which are local. You can add an identifier string to the front or end of a string.

You can debug a JavaScript function that may have a global and local variable issue by using the typeof keyword. The typeof keyword allows you to differentiate between local and global variables. If the variable is local, the typeof keyword returns undefined when the variable is accessed in the global space.

Handle Global and Local Variables

① Declare a global variable outside a function.

② Declare a local variable inside a function.

③ Display the variable with the typeof keyword to avoid errors for both the local and global variables.

④ Save the file.

⑤ Open the file in a Web browser.

- The local variable is shown as undefined outside the function.

- The global variable is shown as number inside the function.

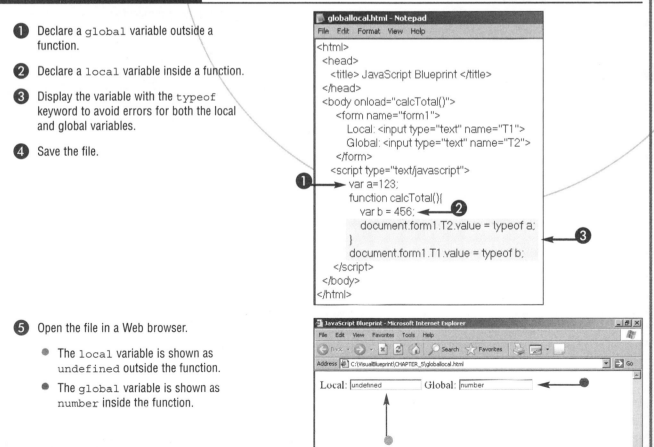

91

Pass Parameters to a Function

You can pass parameters to a function to create a more dynamic code by placing them inside the parentheses that follow the function name. Several variables may be passed to a function by separating them with commas. The parameters that may be passed are strings, numbers, Booleans, objects, and so on.

In order for your function to be able to process the parameters passed to the function name, the function definition should include the variable name for each parameter passed. You can then use these variable names within the function. The variable is local to the function and not global.

For example, if a function is defined as function sum(a, b, c), then the function called sum(16, 34, 98) places the value of 16 in the variable named a, 34 in the variable named b, and 98 in the variable named c. The values for

variables a, b, and c cannot be accessed outside the function because they are local. Therefore, the variables a, b, and c are undefined when they are accessed outside the function.

JavaScript allows you to create a function within a function. This is equivalent to local and global variables. The function that is nested inside the main function is only called within that function. A function called outside the main function results in an error. The embedded function can still use the local variables of the main function and the embedded function can overwrite the variable's values.

Nesting functions within each other is normally avoided because the other elements of the JavaScript code cannot access the nested function. Global functions are reusable and local functions are only reusable in the function in which they are nested.

Pass Parameters to a Function

① Add a function with statements that you want to execute.

② Place variables inside the function's parentheses to receive parameters.

③ Call the function with parameters in the parentheses.

④ Save the file.

⑤ Open the file in a Web browser.

● The result of the document.write() statements for each time the function is called appears.

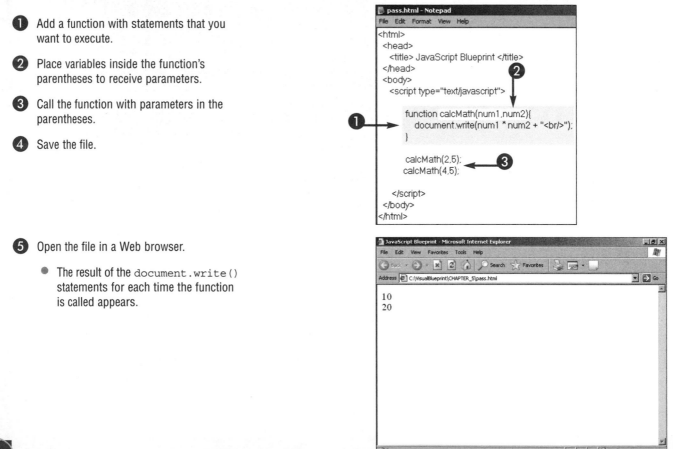

Return a Value from a Function

You can return values from a function by using the `return` keyword. The `return` keyword allows the function to determine a resulting value and send that value back to the main program without having to use global variables to get the result. This allows the function to handle multiple calls even in the same expression and pass the information to parts of the script without interfering with any of the processes. If global variables are used, the information would be constantly overwritten causing erroneous data to be transferred.

For example, if you create a function that computes a sum and the sum value is stored in a variable named `total`, then the statement `return total` sends the value of `total` back to where the function was originally called. You can call this function multiple times without any problems if all the variables contained within the

function are local. Incorporating global variables may cause problems with information being overwritten multiple times.

Because a value is being passed back to the function call, the function call must be a statement that uses the returned value. For example, `var1 = func1()` places the returned value from the `func1()` function into a variable named `var1`.

The type of data returned from a function is not restricted to numbers or strings. It can return arrays, objects, Booleans, or any other value. Common uses for returning values are used in validation scripts. For more information on returning values used in validation scripts, see Chapter 7. For more information on returning dynamic values of locations, see Chapter 15. For more information on removing extra white spaces, see Chapter 6.

Return a Value from a Function

① Add a function with the statements you want to execute.

② Add the `return` keyword with the variable to return.

③ Call the function.

④ Save the file.

⑤ Open the file in a Web browser.

● The result of the `document.write()` statement with the value returned from the function appears.

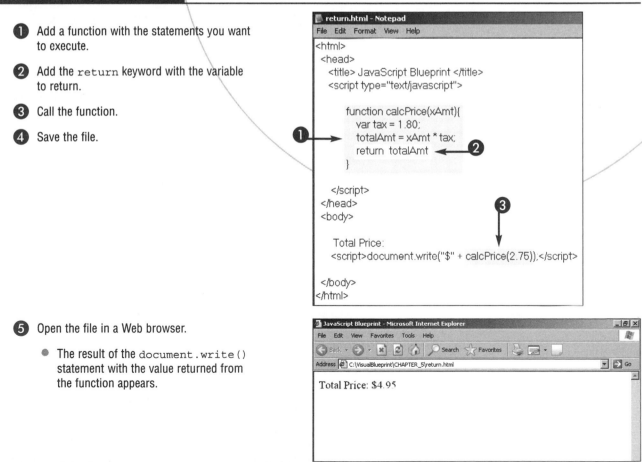

```
return.html - Notepad
File  Edit  Format  View  Help
<html>
 <head>
  <title> JavaScript Blueprint </title>
  <script type="text/javascript">

     function calcPrice(xAmt){
        var tax = 1.80;
        totalAmt = xAmt * tax;
        return  totalAmt
     }

  </script>
 </head>
 <body>

   Total Price:
   <script>document.write("$" + calcPrice(2.75));</script>

 </body>
</html>
```

```
JavaScript Blueprint - Microsoft Internet Explorer
File  Edit  View  Favorites  Tools  Help
Back  ·  ·  Search  Favorites
Address  C:\VisualBlueprint\CHAPTER_5\return.html        Go

Total Price: $4.95
```

Increase Script Performance

After developing a script, you may have slow performance. You can help speed up performance by trying to avoid a few common practices that are known to slow down performance.

The first thing that you need to look at is your `if` statements. Avoid using repetitive expression statements repeatedly when you can combine them. This eliminates unnecessary steps. Use switch statements for large `if-else` statement groupings. The look up speed of switch statements is quicker than large `if-else` statement groups.

Using many `document.write()` statements can slow down the loading of a page. By combining the `document.write()` statements into one large string, you can cut the loading time drastically. You still can have multiple statements if they are spread out across a page, but if they are in one large group, you should combine them into one statement.

If you do not have to use the `eval()` method, then do not use it. The `eval()` method takes an extended amount of time to evaluate what is inside the parentheses. Do not use the `eval()` method to join strings together; instead, you should just add them together.

Using the `with` constructor also takes a lot of the time to process information. There are places where you are forced to use it, but if you are using it to make your code look cleaner, then do not use it. The `with` constructor has to load all the information into memory before processing, which is a waste of the CPU. Instead, just try looping through the element length.

By eliminating unnecessary steps and making sure that the code is not doing any extra processes, you can eliminate the extra amount of time that a script needs to perform an action.

Increase Script Performance

① Open the source code of the file that you want to optimize.

Note: You may want to save a backup version of this file to compare to the optimized version.

② Locate the area that is slowing down the performance of the script.

③ Rewrite the code to increase the performance by eliminating bottleneck statements like `eval()`, `document.write`, and `if` statements.

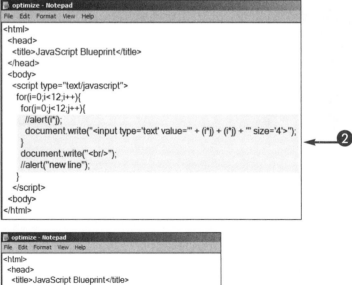

```
optimize - Notepad
File  Edit  Format  View  Help
<html>
 <head>
  <title>JavaScript Blueprint</title>
 </head>
 <body>
  <script type="text/javascript">
   for(i=0;i<12;i++){
    for(j=0;j<12;j++){
     //alert(i*j);
     document.write("<input type='text' value='" + (i*j) + (i*j) + "' size='4'>");
    }
    document.write("<br/>");
    //alert("new line");
   }
  </script>
 <body>
</html>
```
← ②

```
optimize - Notepad
File  Edit  Format  View  Help
<html>
 <head>
  <title>JavaScript Blueprint</title>
 </head>
 <body>
  <script type="text/javascript">
   var str1="";
   for(i=0;i<12;i++){
    for(j=0;j<12;j++){
     //alert(i*j);
     str1 += "<input type='text' value='" + (i*j) + "' size='4'>";
    }
    str1 += "<br/>";
    //alert("new line");
   }
   document.write(str1);
  </script>
 <body>
</html>
```
← ③

Remove any unnecessary statements that may be left over from the testing period.

Note: Unnecessary statements can increase page-loading time.

 Save the file.

```
optimize - Notepad
File  Edit  Format  View  Help
<html>
 <head>
  <title>JavaScript Blueprint</title>
 </head>
 <body>
  <script type="text/javascript">
   var str1="";
   for(i=0;i<12;i++){
    for(j=0;j<12;j++){
     //alert(i*j);              ← 4
     str1 += "<input type='text' value='" + (i*j) + "' size='4'>";
    }
    str1 += "<br/>";            ← 4
    //alert("new line");
   }
   document.write(str1);
  </script>
 <body>
</html>
```

 Open the file in a Web browser.

● The performance of the script improves slightly by avoiding common bottlenecks in the code.

```
JavaScript Blueprint - Microsoft Internet Explorer
File  Edit  View  Favorites  Tools  Help
Address  C:\VisualBlueprint\CHAPTER_5\optimize.html
```

0	0	0	0	0	0	0	0	0	0	0	0
0	1	2	3	4	5	6	7	8	9	10	11
0	2	4	6	8	10	12	14	16	18	20	22
0	3	6	9	12	15	18	21	24	27	30	33
0	4	8	12	16	20	24	28	32	36	40	44
0	5	10	15	20	25	30	35	40	45	50	55
0	6	12	18	24	30	36	42	48	54	60	66
0	7	14	21	28	35	42	49	56	63	70	77
0	8	16	24	32	40	48	56	64	72	80	88
0	9	18	27	36	45	54	63	72	81	90	99
0	10	20	30	40	50	60	70	80	90	100	110
0	11	22	33	44	55	66	77	88	99	110	121

Done   My Computer

Apply It

If you want to compare the performance of a JavaScript function, you can time how long the operation takes. The first step is to create a new Date() string on the page of the script and store the value into a variable. The second step is to create another variable and store the new Date() variable as the last line of the function. After the variable declaration, you want to subtract the first date string from the second date string. The result is the total number of milliseconds that the operation took to process. You can then use this number to find the optimized solution.

Time an Operation
```
var startTime = new Date();
var str1 = "";
for(i=0;i<26;i++){
   for(j=0;j<26;j++){
      str1 += "<input type='text' value='" + (i * j) + "' size='4'>";
   }
   str1 += "<br/>";
}
document.write(str1);
var endTime = new Date();
alert("Performance: " + (endTime-startTime) + "ms");
```

Determine the Length of a String

You can use the `length` property to return the number of characters in a string. This is used as a simple validation to verify that a form element contains a certain amount of characters. Add the length property to the end of a string of which you want to know the length. For example, `int1 = str1.length;` stores the length of `str1` in the variable `int1`.

You can also merge two strings together by using two different methods. The first is the normal addition method. For example, `var str3 = str1 + str2;` appends `str2` to the end of `str1` and stores it in the variable `str3`. The second is the `concat()` method. The `concat()` method accepts one parameter in the parentheses of the method. This parameter is added to the end of the string to which the method is attached. For example, `var str3 = str1.concat(str2);` is equivalent to the statement `var str3 = str1 + str2;`.

The string object also has numerous amounts of methods that are used to format the characters of the string. For example, you can use the `bold()` method, which returns a string of characters surrounded by an opening and closing `<b>` tag. Other string formatting methods include `big()`, `fontColor(color)`, `fontSize(size)`, `italics()`, `small()`, `strike()`, `sub()`, `sup()`, `toLowerCase()`, and `toUpperCase()`.

You can run into some issues when using some of the formatting methods. For example, the bold (`<b>`) and italics (`<i>`) tags have been depreciated in the XHTML standard. Most older browsers still support the depreciated tags. However, the browsers are not required to support the depreciated tags. Instead of using these methods to change the font color, font size, and so on, you can use CSS to format your strings. For more information on using CSS to format strings, see Chapter 14.

Determine the Length of a String

① Declare the variables and store the strings.

② Place the `length` property after the string name.

③ Add `document.write()` statements to display the results.

④ Save the file.

```
string1.html - Notepad
File  Edit  Format  View  Help

<html>
 <head>
  <title> JavaScript Blueprint </title>
 </head>
 <body>
   <script type="text/javascript">

       var str1 = "JavaScript: Your visual blueprint "      ①
       var str2 = "for building dynamic Web Pages"

       document.write("Length str1: " + str1.length + "<br/>");   ③
       document.write("Length str2: " + str2.length + "<br/>");

   </script>
 </body>
</html>
                                                            ②
```

⑤ Open the file in a Web browser.

● The length of the strings appears.

```
JavaScript Blueprint - Microsoft Internet Explorer
File  Edit  View  Favorites  Tools  Help
Back        Search    Favorites
Address  C:\VisualBlueprint\CHAPTER_6\string1.html        Go

Length str1: 34
Length str2: 30
```

① Declare the variables and store the strings.

② Combine the strings by using the addition or `concat()` methods.

③ Add `document.write()` statements to display the results.

④ Save the file.

⑤ Open the file in a Web browser.

● The combined strings segments appear.

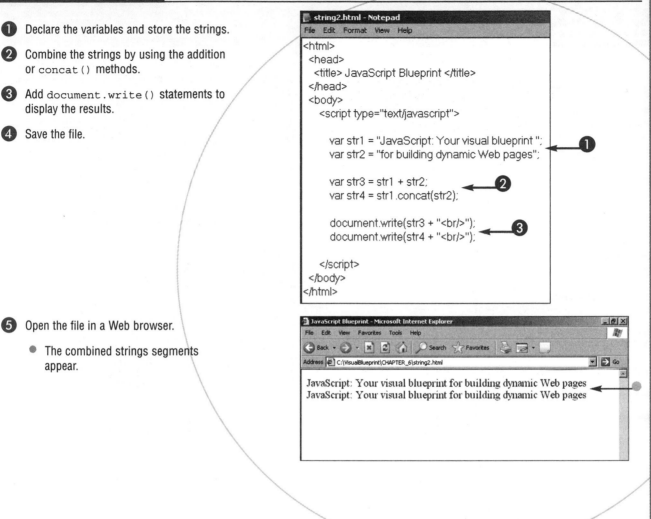

```
string2.html - Notepad
File  Edit  Format  View  Help
<html>
 <head>
  <title> JavaScript Blueprint </title>
 </head>
 <body>
   <script type="text/javascript">

       var str1 = "JavaScript: Your visual blueprint ";
       var str2 = "for building dynamic Web pages";

       var str3 = str1 + str2;
       var str4 = str1 .concat(str2);

       document.write(str3 + "<br/>");
       document.write(str4 + "<br/>");

   </script>
 </body>
</html>
```

```
JavaScript Blueprint - Microsoft Internet Explorer
File  Edit  View  Favorites  Tools  Help
Back ▾  ▾        Search  Favorites
Address  C:\VisualBlueprint\CHAPTER_6\string2.html          Go

JavaScript: Your visual blueprint for building dynamic Web pages
JavaScript: Your visual blueprint for building dynamic Web pages
```

Extra

You can format a string to produce a superscript or a subscript by using JavaScript built-in methods `sub()` and `sup()`. If an entire string is formatted using the `sub()` or `sup()` methods, it is difficult to notice how the string looks any different from a normal string unless it can be compared to another string on the page.

A more reasonable way to use the `sub()` method is to build a string: `water = "H" + "2".sub() + "O";`. This statement creates a string variable named `water` that includes an `H` and the string for `2` that is returned from the `sub()` method and an `O`. An example of the `sup()` method is `squared = "x" + int1.sup();`.

Select Portions of a String

ou can work with small portions of a large string by using two methods built into JavaScript. The methods allow you to select portions of the string by specifying certain parameters.

The first method that you can use to extract a section of string is the substring() method. The substring() method accepts two parameters to determine from where to take the partial string. The parameters are placed in parentheses separated by a comma. The first parameter is the initial point to start the cut. The second parameter decides where to end the cut. If you leave the second parameter off, the string ends the cut at the end of the main string. The method is placed behind the string variable name that you want to edit. For example, the statement var str1 = largeString.substring(13,24); cuts the 14th through the 25th letter of the variable

largeString. Just like in arrays, the starting position of a string is zero.

The second method you can use to extract part of a string is the slice() method. The slice() method accepts two parameters that are also placed in the parentheses and separated by a comma. You can use the slice() method just like the substring() method by setting the first parameter to the initial cut position and the second parameter to the position where the cut ends. A unique property of the slice method is that you can start from the end of the string instead of the beginning. You can do this by specifying both parameters as negative numbers. For example, the statement var str2 = largeString.slice(-10,-6); starts the cut at 10 characters from the end of the string and ends the cut six characters from the end of the string.

Select Portions of a String

USE THE SUBSTRING METHOD

① Declare the variables and store the strings.

② Add the substring() method to the variable name along with the selection parameters.

③ Add document.write() statements to display the results.

④ Save the file.

⑤ Open the file in a Web browser.

● The substrings appear.

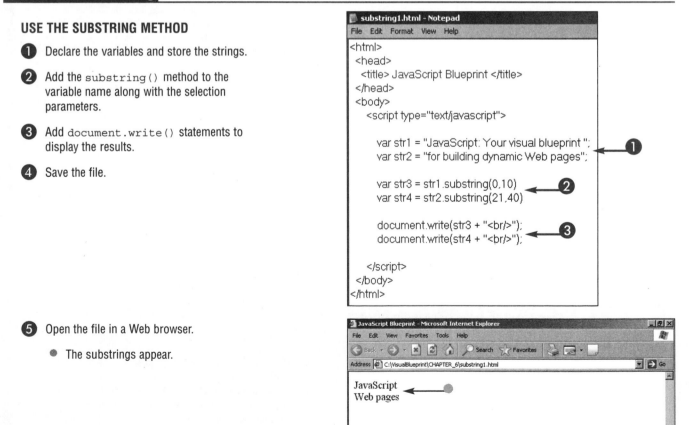

USE THE SLICE METHOD

① Declare the variables and store the strings.

② Add the `slice()` method to the variable name along with the selection parameters.

③ Add `document.write()` statements to display the results.

④ Save the file.

⑤ Open the file in a Web browser.

● The desired string portions appear.

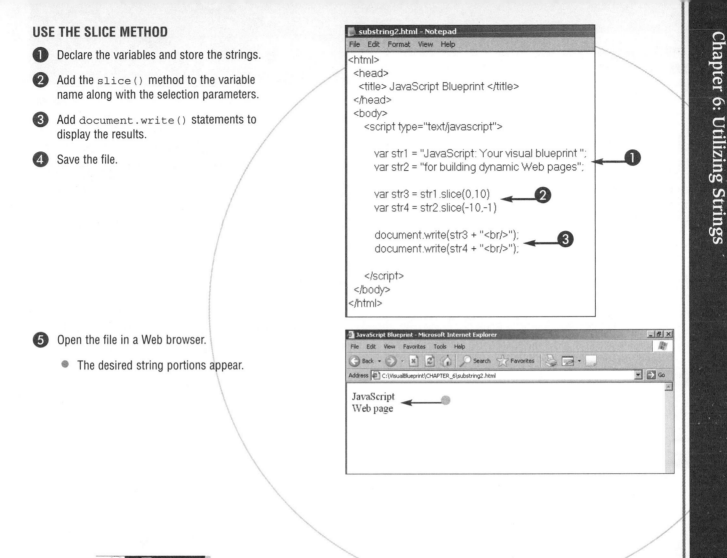

Change the Case of a String

You can change the case of a string to all uppercase or lowercase letters by using two string object methods. The methods are `toUpperCase()` and `toLowerCase()`. The methods are placed after the string name that you want to convert to the alternate case. For example the statement `var allCaps = theStr.toUpperCase();` converts the string stored in the variable `theStr` to all capital letters. The statement `var allLower = theStr.toLowerCase();` converts all of the characters in the variable `theStr` to lowercase letters and stores it in the variable `allLower`.

Both methods change the case of the letters, but they do not affect the original string to which the method is attached. If you want the original string to be overwritten by the method, you must assign the variable name equal to the method. For example, `str1 = str1.toUpperCase();`

stores a capitalized string in `str1` and permanently overwrites the variable's original value.

Common uses for the `toUpperCase()` and `toLowerCase()` methods are in form validation because JavaScript is case sensitive. Converting a string's case allows the strings `yes`, `Yes`, `yEs`, `yeS`, `Yes`, `yES`, and `YES` to equal each other in a comparison function.

The `toUpperCase()` and `toLowerCase()` methods are useful when you are using information from the browser especially when you are accessing tag names. Certain browsers tend to capitalize tags while others tend to have them in lowercase. By using either of the methods, you can verify that the string cases match in a comparison string.

You can only apply the `toUpperCase()` and `toLowerCase()` methods to strings. If the two methods are applied to any variable type other than strings, an error occurs causing the script to stop executing.

Change the Case of a String

ALL CAPS AND LOWERCASE

1 Declare the variables and store the strings.

2 Add the `toUppercase()` and `toLowerCase()` methods to the variable names.

3 Add `document.write()` statements to show the results.

4 Save the file.

5 Open the file in a Web browser.

● The strings appear in both all uppercase and lowercase.

```
changecase.html - Notepad
File  Edit  Format  View  Help
<html>
 <head>
  <title> JavaScript Blueprint </title>
 </head>
 <body>
   <script type="text/javascript">

      var str1 = "JavaScript: Your visual blueprint ";      ←— 1
      var str2 = "for building dynamic Web pages";

      var str3 = str1.toUpperCase();      ←— 2
      var str4 = str2.toLowerCase();

      document.write(str3 + "<br/>");      ←— 3
      document.write(str4 + "<br/>");

   </script>
 </body>
</html>
```

```
JavaScript Blueprint - Microsoft Internet Explorer
File  Edit  View  Favorites  Tools  Help
Back  ·        ·        Search    Favorites
Address  C:\VisualBlueprint\CHAPTER_6\changecase.html            Go

JAVASCRIPT: YOUR VISUAL BLUEPRINT
for building dynamic web pages
```

INITIAL CAPS

1 Declare the variables and store the strings.

2 Add the substring(0,1) method and the toUppercase() to the variable name and add the rest of the string with the substring(1) method.

3 Add a document.write() statement to show the result.

4 Save the file.

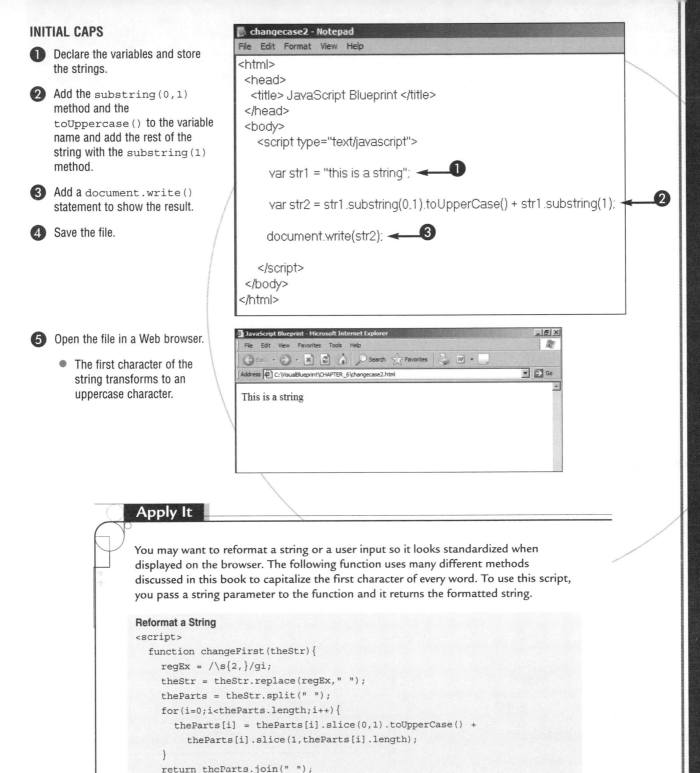

```
changecase2 - Notepad
File  Edit  Format  View  Help

<html>
 <head>
  <title> JavaScript Blueprint </title>
 </head>
 <body>
   <script type="text/javascript">

      var str1 = "this is a string";          ◄──① 

      var str2 = str1.substring(0,1).toUpperCase() + str1.substring(1);   ◄── ②

      document.write(str2);   ◄──③

   </script>
 </body>
</html>
```

5 Open the file in a Web browser.

● The first character of the string transforms to an uppercase character.

```
JavaScript Blueprint - Microsoft Internet Explorer
File  Edit  View  Favorites  Tools  Help
Back  ▼   ▼   Search   Favorites
Address  C:\VisualBlueprint\CHAPTER_6\changecase2.html     Go

This is a string
```

Apply It

You may want to reformat a string or a user input so it looks standardized when displayed on the browser. The following function uses many different methods discussed in this book to capitalize the first character of every word. To use this script, you pass a string parameter to the function and it returns the formatted string.

Reformat a String

```
<script>
  function changeFirst(theStr){
    regEx = /\s{2,}/gi;
    theStr = theStr.replace(regEx," ");
    theParts = theStr.split(" ");
    for(i=0;i<theParts.length;i++){
      theParts[i] = theParts[i].slice(0,1).toUpperCase() +
        theParts[i].slice(1,theParts[i].length);
    }
    return theParts.join(" ");
  }
  var str1 = "hello there how are you doing today?  I am doing fine!";
  document.write(changeFirst(str1));
</script>
```

Extract Characters from a String

You can extract characters out of a string by using two built-in methods. The first method returns one character from a string. You can do this by adding `charAt()` after the string name. In the parentheses, you add the index number of the character you want to extract. For example, the statement `str2 = str1.charAt(9);` extracts the 10th position of the string.

The reason why the above example is the 10th position and not the 9th is due to the numbering system of the string indexes. The first index starts at position zero and not at one. For example, the fifth character would be at the index position of four.

The second method, `charCodeAt()`, returns the *Unicode* value of one character from the string. In the parentheses, you add the index number of the character you want to find to the Unicode value. For example, the statement `var`

`theChar = str1.charCodeAt(6);` retrieves the character code of the 7th character in the string.

You can also convert a Unicode value back to a character by using the `fromCharCode()` method of the string object. The character code is placed in the parentheses of the method. The `fromCharCode()` method is called from the String object and not from a string value. For example, the statement `var str3 = String.fromCharCode(68);` returns the character.

If the `charAt()` or `charCoseAt()` methods are applied to anything but a string, an error occurs stopping the processing of the script. The descriptive error message normally reads `This object does not support this method or property`.

You can also use the `substring()`, `splice()`, and `substr()` methods to extract the value of a single character of a string by setting the range of the methods to one character.

Extract Characters from a String

EXTRACT A CHARACTER

1. Declare the variables and store the strings.

2. Add the `charCodeAt()` method to the variable name along with the position parameter.

3. Add `document.write()` statements to display the results.

```
charcode.html - Notepad
File Edit Format View Help
<html>
 <head>
  <title> JavaScript Blueprint </title>
 </head>
 <body>
  <script type="text/javascript">

    var str1 = "JavaScript: Your visual blueprint ";      ← 1
    var str2 = "for building dynamic Web pages";

    var str3 = str1.charCodeAt(12);                        ← 2
    var str4 = String.fromCharCode(str3)

    document.write("12th character from: " + str1 + "<br/>");
    document.write("charCodeAt(12): " + str3 + "<br/>");   ← 3
    document.write("fromCharCode(" + str3 + "): " + str4 + "<br/>");

  </script>
 </body>
</html>
```

4. Save the file.

5. Open the file in a Web browser.

- The specified character appears.

```
JavaScript Blueprint - Microsoft Internet Explorer
File Edit View Favorites Tools Help
Back ▼    ▼    ▼  Search  Favorites
Address  C:\VisualBlueprint\CHAPTER_6\charcode.html         Go

12th character from: JavaScript: Your visual blueprint
charCodeAt(12): 89
fromCharCode(89): Y
```

EXTRACT MULTIPLE CHARACTERS

1. Declare a variable to store a string and display the value with a `document.write()` statement.

2. Create a `for` loop to iterate through the entire string length.

3. Declare a variable and store the `charAt(i)` value along with any additional information

4. Add a `document.write()` statement to display the results.

5. Save the file.

6. Open the file in a Web browser.

   - Each character from the string extracts and appears on the screen.

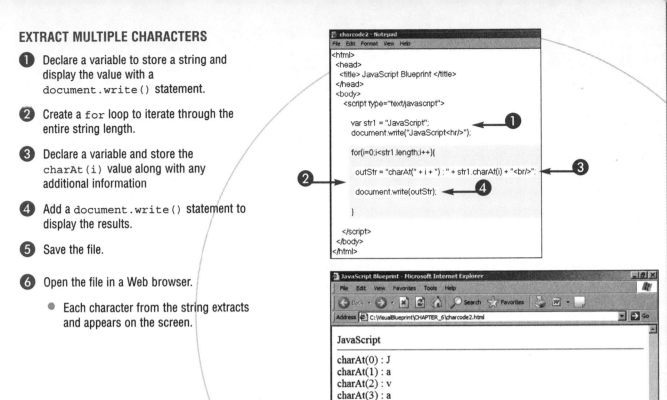

```
charcode2 - Notepad
File Edit Format View Help
<html>
 <head>
  <title> JavaScript Blueprint </title>
 </head>
 <body>
  <script type="text/javascript">

    var str1 = "JavaScript";          ①
    document.write("JavaScript<hr/>");

    for(i=0;i<str1.length;i++){

    outStr = "charAt(" + i + ") : " + str1.charAt(i) + "<br/>";    ③

    document.write(outStr);    ④

    }

  </script>
 </body>
</html>
```

```
JavaScript Blueprint - Microsoft Internet Explorer
File  Edit  View  Favorites  Tools  Help
Back ·      ·     x  2  6    Search  Favorites
Address  C:\VisualBlueprint\CHAPTER_6\charcode2.html

JavaScript
_____

charAt(0) : J
charAt(1) : a
charAt(2) : v
charAt(3) : a
charAt(4) : S
charAt(5) : c
charAt(6) : r
charAt(7) : i
charAt(8) : p
charAt(9) : t
```

Extra

You can test to see if a string exists in another string by using the `indexOf()` method. The `indexOf()` method is added to the end of the string you want to test for a match. You add the string that you want to test for inside the parentheses of the `indexOf()` method. The `indexOf()` method returns the location of the first character in the first occurrence.

You can specify where the `indexOf()` should start looking by adding a second parameter separated by a comma in the parentheses. If this parameter is not included, the search begins at the zero index of the string.

You can also search from the end of the string to the front by using the `lastIndexOf()` method. If you specify the second parameter with the `lastIndexOf()` method, it subtracts the position from the total length of the string.

Test a String
```
var str1 = "JavaScript can enhance a Web site.";
var findWord = "enhance";
var theSpot = str1.indexOf(findWord);
alert(findWord + " is located at position " + theSpot);
```

Escape a
Text String

When passing data to a server, you can escape a text string to lessen the probabilities of causing an error. Certain characters perform server-side commands such as ampersand (&) and quotation marks (" "). In order to avoid this problem, you can use the escape() method to reformat the string before passing the data.

You can use the escape() method by placing into the parentheses the string you want to convert. For example, a variable str1 containing "A 'cat' & a 'dog'"; is escaped by the statement str2 = escape(str1);. The string that is stored in str2 is A%20%27cat%27%20%26%20a%20%27dog%27.

Escaping the string converts special characters to a percentage symbol (%) followed by a two-digit Unicode value. A white space is converted to the Unicode value of 20 and the ampersand has a Unicode value of 26.

You can also convert back to the escaped character sequence by using the unescape() method. The unescape() method performs the opposite operation as the escape() method. You can place the string that you want to convert back to a readable format by placing the string between the parentheses of the unescape() method.

The unescape() method must be used if you are working with query strings. When a form is posted to a query string, the form values are automatically escaped. If you want to handle those values, you need to unescape them. query strings are discussed in Chapter 13.

The escape() method is sometimes used as a way to encode values from a user to make it harder to understand. For example, a person who does not know %27 is an apostrophe can have trouble recognizing what the string says. Every character has a Unicode value, but the escape method does not convert them all to the Unicode value. For example, %45 is the Unicode value for E and %65 is e.

Escape a Text String

1. Declare the variables and store the strings.

2. Add the escape() and unescape() methods with the string parameters that you want to encode or decode.

3. Add document.write() statements to display the results.

4. Save the file.

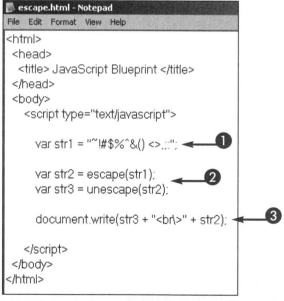

```
escape.html - Notepad
File  Edit  Format  View  Help
<html>
 <head>
  <title> JavaScript Blueprint </title>
 </head>
 <body>
   <script type="text/javascript">

     var str1 = "~!#$%^&() <>,;:";          ◄── 1

     var str2 = escape(str1);               ◄── 2
     var str3 = unescape(str2);

     document.write(str3 + "<br\>" + str2);  ◄── 3

   </script>
 </body>
</html>
```

5. Open the file in a Web browser.

• The escaped string appears on the screen with all of the special case characters converted to the new format.

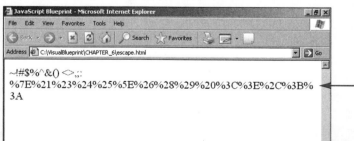

```
JavaScript Blueprint - Microsoft Internet Explorer
File  Edit  View  Favorites  Tools  Help
Back ·    ·      Search  Favorites
Address  C:\VisualBlueprint\CHAPTER_6\escape.html

~!#$%^&() <>,;:
%7E%21%23%24%25%5E%26%28%29%20%3C%3E%2C%3B%
3A
```

Encode a URI

You can use newer methods introduced in Internet Explorer 5.5 and Netscape 6, which convert a larger range of characters into Unicode format. The `encodeURI()` and `encodeURIComponent()` methods work just like the `escape()` method. To use the methods, place the string inside the parentheses of the `encodeURI()` and `encodeURIComponent()` methods. The methods return an encoded string.

The differences between the `encodeURI()` and `encodeURIComponent()` methods are based on the character sets that they convert to the URI-friendly form. The URI-friendly form is the same as the `escape()` method. It converts the character to a percentage symbol followed by the hexadecimal equivalent of the character. Normal alphabetic characters and numbers are not converted; only special characters like punctuation are converted.

The `encodeURI()` method character set that it converts is ASCII values 32 through 126, which are space " % < > [\ ] ^ ~ { | }. The `encodeURIComponent()` method character set is much larger and contains space " % < > [\ ] ^ ~ { | } : ; # $ & , / = ? @.

Each method has its own decoding method to switch back to a readable format. You can decode the `encode URI()` by using `decodeURI()` and decode `encodeURI Component()` by using `decodeURIComponent()`. To decode the string, place the string in the parentheses within two methods.

You should use the `encodeURI()` on the whole URI string and the `encodeURI()` on just the query string component of URI string.

The `encodeURI()` and `encodeURIComponent()` methods should not be used on the same string. Pick one method to perform the encoding and decoding of the URI.

Encode a URI

① Declare the variables and store the strings.

② Add the `encodeURI()` or the `encodeURIComponent()` methods depending on URI needs.

③ Add `document.write()` statements to display the results.

④ Save the file.

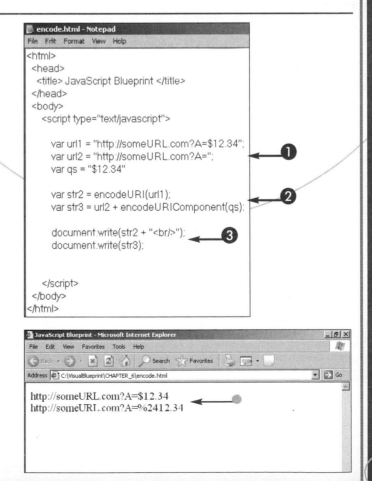

```
encode.html - Notepad
File  Edit  Format  View  Help
<html>
 <head>
  <title> JavaScript Blueprint </title>
 </head>
 <body>
   <script type="text/javascript">

      var url1 = "http://someURL.com?A=$12.34";        ①
      var url2 = "http://someURL.com?A=";
      var qs = "$12.34"

      var str2 = encodeURI(url1);                       ②
      var str3 = url2 + encodeURIComponent(qs);

      document.write(str2 + "<br/>");                   ③
      document.write(str3);


   </script>
 </body>
</html>
```

⑤ Open the file in a Web browser.

- The encoded URLs appear with the special case characters converted to the new format.

JavaScript Blueprint - Microsoft Internet Explorer

File Edit View Favorites Tools Help

Address C:\VisualBlueprint\CHAPTER_6\encode.html

http://someURL.com?A=$12.34
http://someURL.com?A=%2412.34

Regular Expression

You can use regular expressions for pattern matching and searching and replacing text. Some common uses of regular expressions are to find out if the string contains numbers, a valid date format, verifies an e-mail address format, and validates a phone number format.

A regular expression is a sequence of characters in a special format, which is used to match specific patterns in strings. You can start by defining a variable for the regular expression pattern. There are two ways to store the regular expression in this variable.

The first one is to use the regular expression class `RegExp()`. Inside the parentheses, you add the regular expression code so you can create the regular expression pattern. For example, the statement `regexZipCode = new RegExp("^\\d{5}(-\\d{4})?$");` is the regular expression pattern to test for a zip code.

The second way to store the regular expression pattern is to use a regular expression literal. You can use the forward slash (/) to signify where the regular expression pattern starts and ends. Therefore, the statement above for the zip code regular expression is defined as `regExZipCode = /^\\d{5}(-\\d{4})?$"/`; thus eliminating some of the coding involved.

In the zip code examples above, the `caret` sign (^) and the `dollar` sign ($) represent the start and end of a line. You can match the beginning of a long string by using the `caret` (^) by itself. You do not have to include the `caret` and `dollar` signs in the regular expression. You can exclude them if you want to match a string in the middle of a long text.

Use Special Tokens

You can also use special tokens to match certain character groups. A token starts out with a forward slash and is followed by a token character. A few examples of tokens are \d, which matches a number digit, \D, which matches a non-number digit, and \w, which matches a word character. You can use the table on the next page to see a list of all of the special tokens.

The forward slash is also used to indicate that a special character is being treated literally. It is the equivalent of escaping a quote in a string. For example, \$ matches a dollar sign instead of indicating the end of the line.

Match One or More Characters from a Group

You can make a group of characters by using square brackets. The characters that appear in the brackets return a positive match if found in the string being tested. For example, the statement [abcde] matches any letter in the range of a through e. The statement [a-e] also matches the range a through e. You can match any alphanumeric character by using the statement [a-zA-Z0-9] in a regular expression literal. You can also match anything except for what is in the brackets by placing a caret (^) inside the left bracket. For example, [^0-4] matches any character except for 0 to 4.

Match a Specific Group of Characters

You can match whole words or phrases by using parentheses surrounding the text. For example, if you want to match the word dog, the statement (dog) matches it. You can match different groups of words by separating them by a pipe (|). For example, the statement (dog|cat) matches either dog or cat.

Require Number of Occurrences

You can specify the number of times a token or group of tokens has to occur. You can do this by using a pair of curly brackets({ }). By including a single number parameter in the brackets, you are specifying that the token must repeat that many times. For example, the statement \d{3} specifies that a number must appear three times. By including a comma (,) after the number, you are specifying that the number has to appear that many times or more. For example, the statement \d{2,} requires that a number appear two or more times. You can specify that a token appear in a set range by including a number after the comma. The statement \d{1-5} requires between one to five occurrences of a number in order to be valid.

You can use a question mark (?) to specify that the preceding token or groups of tokens must match zero or one time only. Using the question mark is the equivalent of the statement {0,1}. Another shortcut you can use is the plus sign (+), which is another way to specify the string has to match one or more times. An asterisk (*) means that a token can match 0 or more times.

You can specify that a regular expression should be applied globally (g) and whether the pattern is case insensitive (i). They are used together if needed and are added after the last forward slash.

TOKEN	MATCHES
\b	word boundary
\B	non-word boundary
\d	numeral
\D	non-numeral
\n	new line
\r	carriage return
\s	whitespace
\S	non-whitespace
\t	tab
\w	letter, numeral, or underscore
\W	not a letter, numeral, or underscore
\0	null
.	any character except new line

Match the Character in a String

You can use regular expressions to detect if a pattern is matched within a string. This is a very valuable tool in form validation in order to make sure that an input is in correct format. For example, the statement `regEx = /^\(\d{3}\) \d{3}-\d{4}$/;` is the regular expression pattern to match a phone number `(123) 123-4567`.

To test a string you need to use either the `test()` method or the `match()` method. The `test()` method accepts the string that is tested in the parentheses. The `test()` method is attached by a period to the regular expression pattern. For example, the statement `boolean1 = regEx.test ("(123) 123-4567");` tests the string inserted in the parentheses for the `regEx` pattern. The `test()` method returns a Boolean value; true is returned if there is a match and false is returned when no match is made.

The `match()` method is different from the `test()` method. Instead of returning the Boolean, it returns an array filled with each match that the method returns. Therefore, by applying the `length` property to the variable the `match()` method is stored in, you can find the number of matches made. The parameter that goes into the parentheses is different from the `test()` method. Instead of the string, the regular expression is placed in the parentheses. The `match()` method is then attached to the string for testing by a period. For example, if the phone number is stored in a variable `phone1`, the statement `passTest = phone1. match(regEx);` tests for a match.

The `match()` method only returns the array length of 1 if the global modifier of the regular expression pattern is not set. To set the global modifier, you add it to the end of the regular expression pattern after the last forward slash (/). For example, the statement `regEx2 = /\d{2}/g;` looks for two digits that appear in a row multiple times within a string.

Match the Character in a String

① Declare a function with one parameter.

② Create a variable and add a regular expression.

③ Create a test statement using the `match()` method with the regular expression variable in the parentheses.

④ Create an `if-else` check to verify that the test passed or failed.

⑤ Add an `onchange` event handler to the form element.

⑥ Save the file.

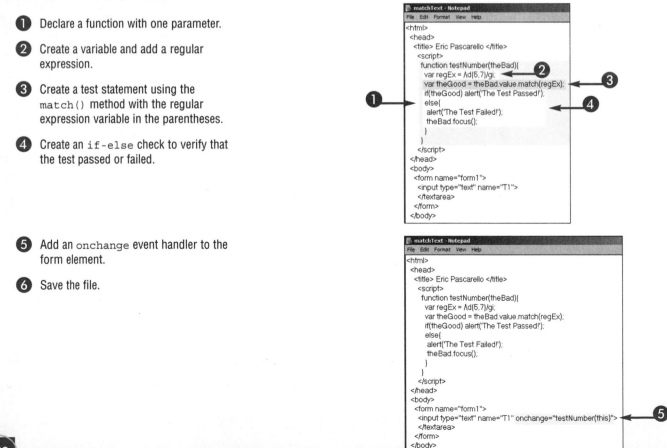

```
matchText - Notepad
File Edit Format View Help
<html>
 <head>
  <title> Eric Pascarello </title>
   <script>
    function testNumber(theBad){
     var regEx = /\d{5,7}/gi;
     var theGood = theBad.value.match(regEx);
     if(theGood) alert('The Test Passed!');
     else{
      alert('The Test Failed!');
      theBad.focus();
     }
    }
   </script>
 </head>
 <body>
  <form name="form1">
   <input type="text" name="T1">
   </textarea>
  </form>
 </body>
</html>
```

```
matchText - Notepad
File Edit Format View Help
<html>
 <head>
  <title> Eric Pascarello </title>
   <script>
    function testNumber(theBad){
     var regEx = /\d{5,7}/gi;
     var theGood = theBad.value.match(regEx);
     if(theGood) alert('The Test Passed!');
     else{
      alert('The Test Failed!');
      theBad.focus();
     }
    }
   </script>
 </head>
 <body>
  <form name="form1">
   <input type="text" name="T1" onchange="testNumber(this)">
   </textarea>
  </form>
 </body>
</html>
```

7 Open the file in a Web browser.

8 Type text in the text field.

9 Press the Tab key to remove the focus from the text box.

• The validation box appears verifying if the string was a match to the regular expression.

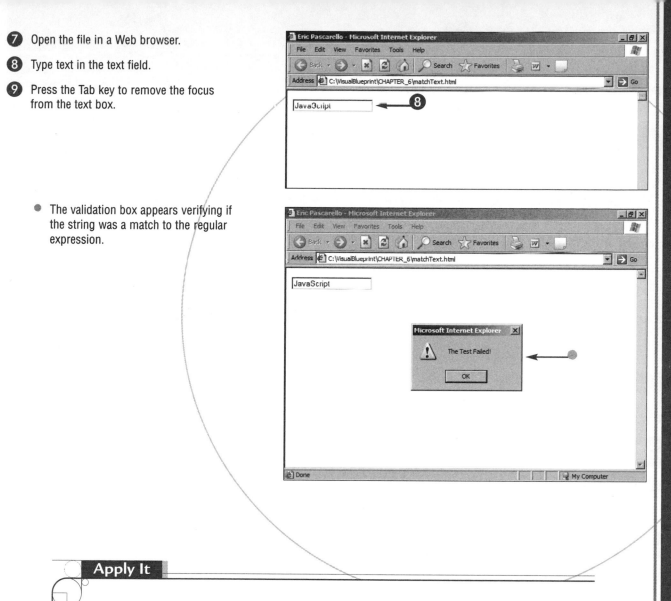

Apply It

You can verify whether the format of an e-mail address is correct by using a regular expression. Matching an e-mail address can be tricky because there are so many different formats. The main information that the e-mail address should contain is at least one character before an @ sign and one character after the @ sign. That is followed by a period and a domain address. Certain characters such as dashes and underscores should be allowed in the user name.

Verify with Regular Expression

```
function validateEmail(theEmail){
  var regEx = /^[\w\+\\'\.-]+@[\w\\'\.-]+\.[a-zA-Z]{2,}$/;
  var theFlag = regEx.test(theEmail);
  return theFlag;
}
var validEmail = validateEmail("Eric.Pascarello@hotmail.com");
alert(validEmail);
```

Replace Characters in a String

You can replace all occurrences of a character or group of characters by using the replace() method. The replace() method uses a regular expression pattern to find all of the occurrences and replaces the occurrences with the text you specify.

The replace() method is attached to the string to which you want to replace the pattern. It is added to the variable name with a period. The replace() method accepts two parameters in the parentheses separated by a comma. The first parameter is the regular expression pattern. The second parameter is the string that is to replace the pattern. For example, the statement str2 = str1.replace(regEx, "dog"); replaces the occurrence in str1 with the string dog.

In order for you to replace all of the occurrences of a pattern in the string, make sure that the regular expression modifier is set to global. You can add the global modifier

(g) to the end of the regular expression pattern after the last forward slash (/). For example, the statement regEx2 = /\s{2}/g; looks for two white spaces in a row throughout the entire string.

Another modifier that is important to the replace() method is case sensitive (i). The case-sensitive modifier is placed after the last forward slash just like the global modifier. If the case-sensitive modifier is included, the regular expression ignores the character's case when comparing strings. For example, the regular expression regExp /[a-c]/gi; matches a, b, c, A, B, or C. This is very useful when you are dealing with user inputs on forms. Instead of using toLowerCase() to change the string to a standard format, you can use the modifier to ignore the case. The original format of the initial string is not lost.

Replace Characters in a String

① Declare a function with one parameter.

② Declare a variable and add a regular expression.

③ Create a replace() method statement placing the regular expression and the replacement character in the parentheses

④ Add a return statement to return the formatted string.

⑤ Add an event handler to the textarea.

⑥ Set the textarea value equal to the replace function.

⑦ Save the file.

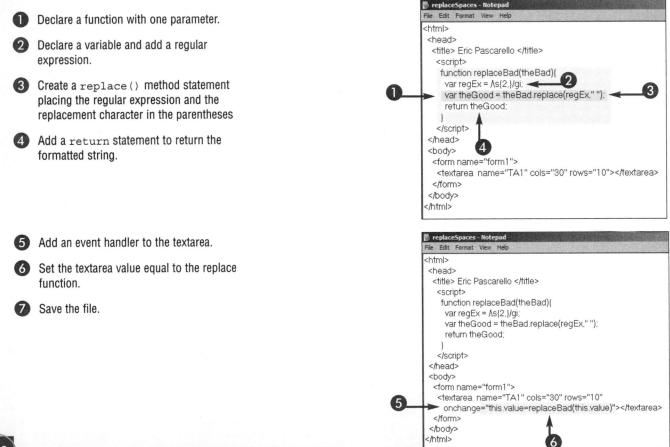

```
replaceSpaces - Notepad
File  Edit  Format  View  Help
<html>
 <head>
  <title> Eric Pascarello </title>
   <script>
    function replaceBad(theBad){
     var regEx = /\s{2,}/gi;
     var theGood = theBad.replace(regEx," ");
     return theGood;
     }
   </script>
 </head>
 <body>
  <form name="form1">
   <textarea name="TA1" cols="30" rows="10"></textarea>
  </form>
 </body>
</html>
```

```
replaceSpaces - Notepad
File  Edit  Format  View  Help
<html>
 <head>
  <title> Eric Pascarello </title>
   <script>
    function replaceBad(theBad){
     var regEx = /\s{2,}/gi;
     var theGood = theBad.replace(regEx," ");
     return theGood;
     }
   </script>
 </head>
 <body>
  <form name="form1">
   <textarea  name="TA1" cols="30" rows="10"
    onchange="this.value=replaceBad(this.value)"></textarea>
  </form>
 </body>
</html>
```

⑧ Open the file in a Web browser.

⑨ Type text in the textarea leaving extra spaces between the words.

⑩ Press the Tab key to remove the focus from the textarea.

● The textarea displays with no extra spaces because the `replace` method replaced the characters from the string.

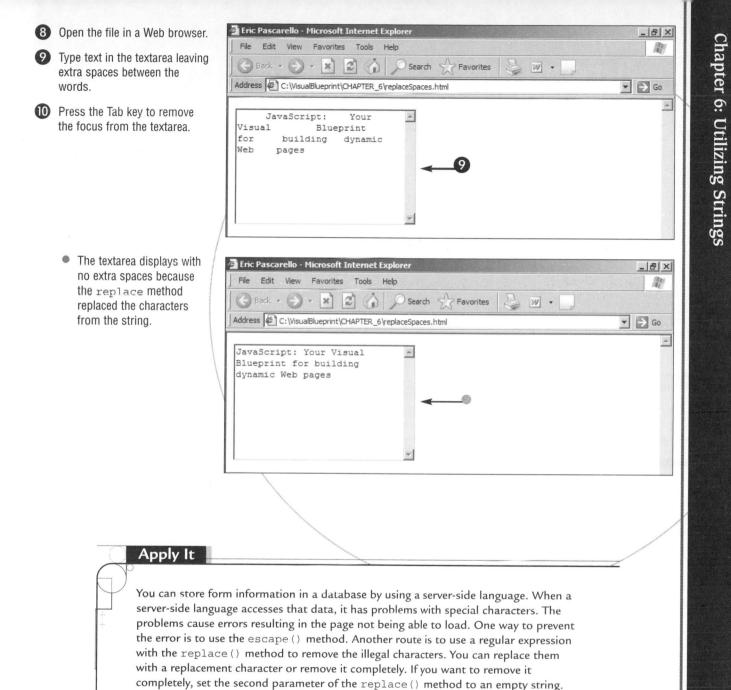

You can store form information in a database by using a server-side language. When a server-side language accesses that data, it has problems with special characters. The problems cause errors resulting in the page not being able to load. One way to prevent the error is to use the `escape()` method. Another route is to use a regular expression with the `replace()` method to remove the illegal characters. You can replace them with a replacement character or remove it completely. If you want to remove it completely, set the second parameter of the `replace()` method to an empty string.

Prevent Error
```
function replaceBad(theBad){
  var regEx = /[@#$%!^&*~]/gi;
  var replaceWith = "X"
  var theGood = theBad.replace(regEx,replaceWith);
  return theGood;
}
var newStr = replaceBad("!#@%$!&&%");
alert(newStr);
```

Develop HTML Forms

You can use HTML forms to collect information about a user or to receive content. JavaScript is used to validate form fields, limit input to form fields, disable form fields, insert dynamic data, and so on. An HTML form is defined by opening and closing `<form>` tags. The `<form>` tag can have many attributes. The `name` or `id` attribute is used to differentiate among multiple forms that are on the page. A Web page can have multiple forms, but

the forms cannot overlap each other and cannot be nested within one other. Another attribute is the `method` attribute. The `method` attribute is assigned to either `get` or `post` and determines how information is sent to the Web server. The `action` attribute determines where the Web page submits the data. The `action` attribute is normally set to another Web page where the data is processed.

User Control Groups

HTML forms can contain 13 different types of user controls. Each control has a certain function. Functions include holding characters, determining true or false statements, finding files, performing actions, and so on.

The first group of user controls holds character data. The text box collects a single line of text input. The hidden element collects a single line of text input but is hidden from a user's view. The text area allows for one or more lines of text to be entered. The last form element that collects text is the password field. The password field displays asterisks instead of the actual data to secure forms.

The second group of user controls allows users to select predefined choices. The list box, also known as a selection box or drop-down box, allows a user to select one or more items from a list of options. The radio button allows a user to select one option from a group of items. The check box allows a user to select single items.

The third group includes the buttons that perform JavaScript or predefined functions. The button is the basic element of this group. You can set the button to perform JavaScript tasks. The image button acts just like a regular button except an image replaces the actual button. The reset button resets all the form fields to the default values that are contained in the form in which the button resides. The submit button submits the form that it resides in. The file element is a mix between a button and a text field. The file button opens a system window to select a file from the computer. The file's name is placed in the text box.

The last group includes only one element. The object element creates a user-defined input control. The controls vary and may not work on every browser.

Reference
Form Elements

You can access the elements of the forms to perform validation or to collect information for a JavaScript function. You can do this by referencing the elements directly, using `document.getElementBy Id()` method, or by using the form element array.

Referencing the elements directly is the safest way of retrieving the information from a form element. Assign a name to the form, and assign individual names to each of your elements. You can use the document object to reference the element, add the form name with a period, and then the element name with a period. After the element name, you can reference the attribute of the form that you want. To retrieve the value of a text box, reference the `value` attribute. For example, the statement `str1 = document.Form1.textbox1.value` stores the `value` of the text box named `textbox1` in the form named `Form1`, which is stored in the variable `str1`.

Another way to reference the form element directly is to use `document.getElementById()`. In the parentheses, you add the element name that you want to reference. For example, the statement `document.getElement ById("textbox1").value` retrieves the value of `textbox1`. The `getElementById()` method searches the document for an `id` that contains `textbox1`. If the search for the `id` returns nothing, then the method looks for a match with the `name` attribute.

You can also use a third method to reference a form element by using the form element array. Each element in the form is in the form object array. Each form on the page is accessed by an array. For example, the statement `document.form[1].element[2].value` references the third value in the second form on the page. This method should only be used if you are looping through the form fields or the page will never be edited.

Reference Form Elements

① Declare a variable.

② Set the variables equal to the element value reference of your choice.

③ Add statements to display the textbox value.

④ Save the file.

⑤ Open the file in a Web browser.

● The value of the text box for each method appears.

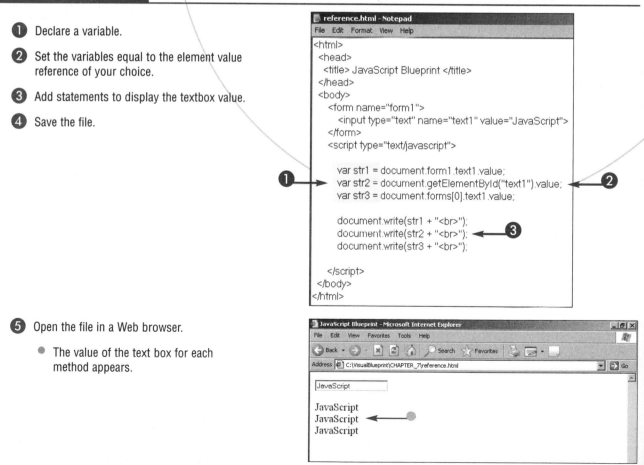

Validate a Text Box Value

You can use text boxes to allow JavaScript to interact with the user. The text box can collect a single line of text that is accessed by JavaScript. JavaScript can also set the value of the text box.

Text boxes are defined on a Web page by using the `<input>` tag. The text box is then assigned a `type` attribute set to `text`. You must give the text box a `name` attribute so you can access the element. You can also set the initial text of the text box by setting the `value` attribute of the element. You can control the number of characters that are displayed by setting the `size` attribute. The `size` attribute does not limit input character length.

To access or to set the value of a text box through JavaScript, you need to reference the element. You do this by using the syntax `document.Form1.text1.value`. The `Form1` is the name of the form in which the element is

located, and `text1` is the name of the text box. For information on other methods to reference the text box, see the section Reference Form Elements in this chapter.

You can obtain the value of a text box by storing the element's object reference in a variable. For example, the statement `var str1 = document.Form1.text1.value` stores `text1`'s value in the variable `str1`.

You can update the value of a text box by storing a number or string into the element's object reference. For example, `document.Form1.text1.value = "JavaScript"` stores JavaScript in the text box.

You can use JavaScript event handlers on the text box like `onfocus()`, `onblur()`, `onchange()`, `onkeyPress()`, and so on. You can learn more about JavaScript Event Handlers in Chapter 4.

Validate a Text Box Value

1 Declare the input field and set type to text.

2 Add an event handler to test the text box value.

3 Create a validation function.

4 Save the file.

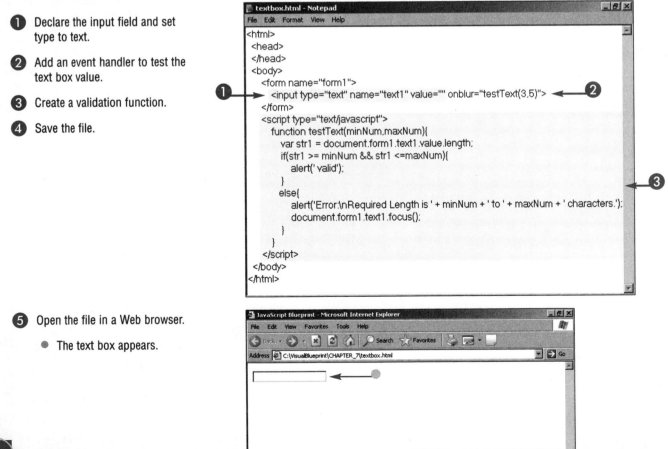

5 Open the file in a Web browser.

● The text box appears.

6 Type text into the text box.

7 Click another portion of the Web page.

● The validation message appears.

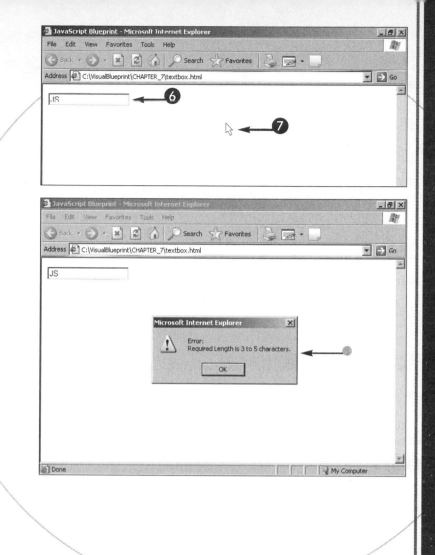

Extra

You may want to make the form more dynamic as the user fills out the form. You can change the color of the form element when the user has the text field in focus and remove the color when the user removes focus. This can add a nice effect when the user is filling out the form.

Create a Dynamic Form

```
<input type="text" name="T1"
onfocus="this.style.background=
'yellow'"
onblur="this.style.background=
'white'">
```

You may want to use a file input field in your form. The file input field contains a text field and a button. The file input field allows you to either type in the path to the file or browse to it using the button.

The text field is different from a text box since it is limited on what you are able to do with it. You are not able to set a default value by setting a value attribute or setting the value via JavaScript. This is to eliminate the developer to change the path when the form is submitted to get other information from the computer.

Validate a Password Field

Y ou can use password fields to hide sensitive data from onlookers. You may want to hide passwords, credit card numbers, and so on. The password box is similar to the text box except the characters typed are shown with an asterisk (*) instead of the actual character.

With JavaScript, you can still distinguish the text that is in the password box. You may want to use the value of the password box to validate it against another password box to make sure that the values are the same.

Password fields are defined on a Web page by using the `<input>` tag. The password field is then assigned a `type` attribute set to `password`. You must also give the password field a `name` attribute so you can access the element. You can also set the initial text of the field by setting the `value`

attribute of the element. You can control the number of characters that are displayed by setting the `size` attribute. The `size` attribute does not limit input length.

You can access the value of a password field through JavaScript by referencing the element. The syntax for accessing the value is `document.Form1.pass1.value`. The `Form1` is the name of the form the element is located in, and the `pass1` is the name of the password field. For more information on methods to reference the password field, see the section Reference Form Elements in this chapter.

The password field is not secure. If you set the `method` attribute to `get`, the password is displayed in plain text in the address bar after the form is submitted.

Validate a Password Field

① Add `<input>` tags with the type set to password.

② Add a button to the form.

③ Assign an event handler to the `<button>` tag.

④ Save the file.

⑤ Retrieve password values.

⑥ Add validation codes to verify that the passwords match.

⑦ Add methods to cause focus if the passwords do not match.

⑧ Save the file.

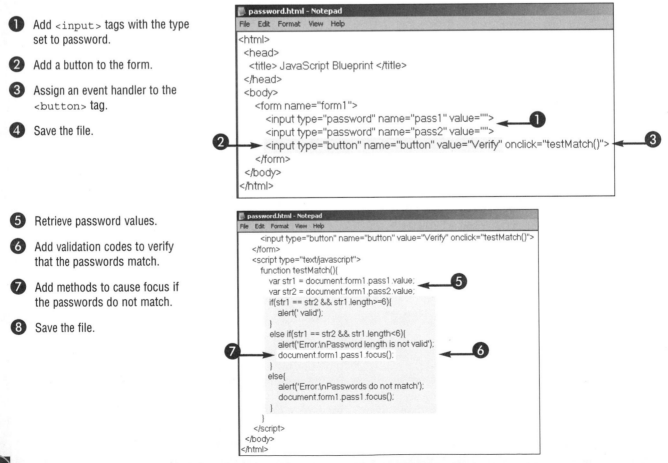

```
password.html - Notepad
File  Edit  Format  View  Help
<html>
 <head>
  <title> JavaScript Blueprint </title>
 </head>
 <body>
   <form name="form1">
     <input type="password" name="pass1" value="">          ①
     <input type="password" name="pass2" value="">
②  <input type="button" name="button" value="Verify" onclick="testMatch()">   ③
   </form>
 </body>
</html>
```

```
password.html - Notepad
File  Edit  Format  View  Help
     <input type="button" name="button" value="Verify" onclick="testMatch()">
   </form>
   <script type="text/javascript">
    function testMatch(){
      var str1 = document.form1.pass1.value;          ⑤
      var str2 = document.form1.pass2.value;
      if(str1 == str2 && str1.length>=6){
        alert(' valid');
      }
      else if(str1 == str2 && str1.length<6){
        alert('Error:\nPassword length is not valid');     ⑥
⑦      document.form1.pass1.focus();
      }
      else{
        alert('Error:\nPasswords do not match');
        document.form1.pass1.focus();
      }
    }
   </script>
 </body>
</html>
```

9 Open the file in a Web browser.

10 Type the passwords into the form password fields.

11 Click Verify.

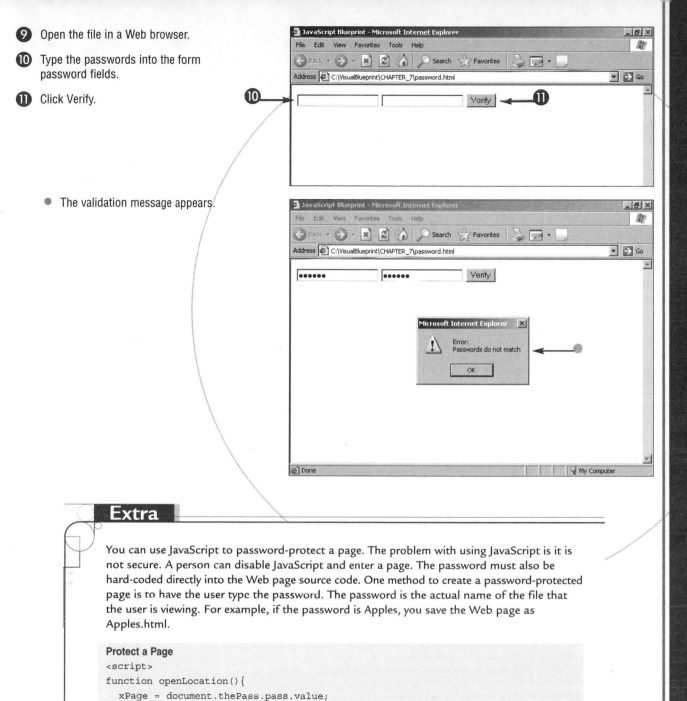

● The validation message appears.

You can use JavaScript to password-protect a page. The problem with using JavaScript is it is not secure. A person can disable JavaScript and enter a page. The password must also be hard-coded directly into the Web page source code. One method to create a password-protected page is to have the user type the password. The password is the actual name of the file that the user is viewing. For example, if the password is Apples, you save the Web page as Apples.html.

Protect a Page
```
<script>
function openLocation(){
  xPage = document.thePass.pass.value;
  document.location.href = xPage + ".html";
}
</script>
<form name="thePass">
  Members Password:
  <input type="password" name="pass">
  <input type="button" name="sub" value="submit" onclick="openLocation()">
</form>
```

Work with a Hidden Element

You can use hidden fields to hide information from the user's view and still submit the information along with the form. The information stored in the hidden field is browser settings detected by JavaScript, the time the user came to your site, the referring Web page, and so on. Users do not know what is contained in these fields unless they view the source code or use a bookmarklet.

Hidden fields are defined on a Web page by using the `<input>` tag. The hidden field is assigned a `type` attribute set to `hidden`. You must also give the hidden element field a `name` attribute so that you can access the element. You can also set the initial text of the field by setting the `value` attribute of the element. For example, the statement `<input type="hidden" name="hidden1" value=`

`"report">` creates a hidden element with the name of `hidden1` and the initial value of `report`.

The hidden element cannot be made visible, but you can read the values of the hidden element by referencing the element. The syntax for accessing the hidden element's value is `document.Form1.hidden1.value`. The `Form1` is the name of the form in which the element is located, and `hidden1` is the name of the element. For more information on methods to reference hidden field elements, see the section Reference Form Elements in this chapter.

You can use a text box if you want the hidden field to be visible. You can set the `style` attribute to `visibility:hidden` to keep the text box out of view. See Chapter 15 for more information on showing and hiding Web page elements.

Work with a Hidden Element

① Add `<input>` tags with the type set to hidden.

② Set the hidden element's value to a variable.

③ Create a function to display the hidden value when called.

④ Save the file.

⑤ Open the file in a Web browser.

● The hidden element does not appear.

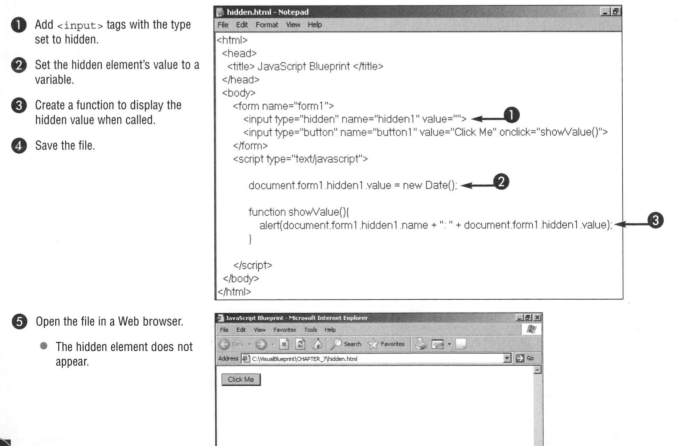

6 Click the button.

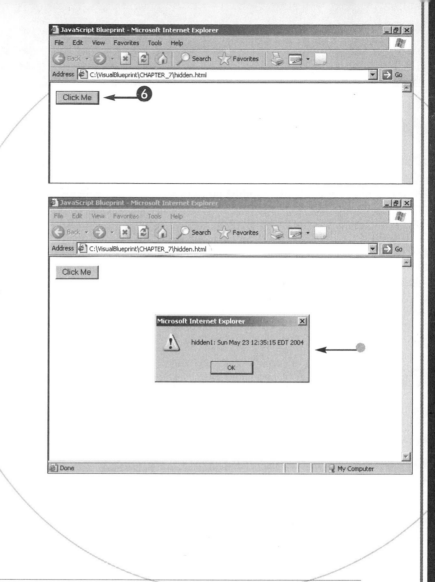

● The hidden element's value appears.

Apply It

You can view and change the values of hidden elements on any Web page by using a bookmarklet. A bookmarklet is a JavaScript statement or a group of JavaScript statements that are saved in the Favorites folder of the Web browser. The following is a bookmarklet that prompts all the hidden element values of a form and allows you to change them.

Bookmarklet:

```
<a
href="javascript:for(i=0;i<document.forms.length;i++){for(j=0;j<document.forms[i].
elements.length;j++){if(document.forms[i].elements[j].type=='hidden')document.
forms[i].elements[j].value = prompt(document.forms[i].elements[j].name,document.
forms[i].elements[j].value);}} alert('Done'); ">Change Hidden Values</a>
```

Add this link to any Web page. Open the Web page and right-click the link and add it to your favorites. You can then execute the bookmarklet by clicking on the bookmark listed in your Favorites menu. You can make any piece of JavaScript code into a bookmarklet that you find helpful.

Validate Text Area Input

You can use text areas to allow JavaScript to interact with a user. The text area can collect multiple lines of text that are accessed by a JavaScript function. JavaScript can also set the value of the text area.

Text areas are defined on a Web page by using the `<textarea>` tag. You must give the text box a `name` attribute so you can access the element. You can control the number of columns and rows that are displayed by setting the `rows` and `cols` attributes. You can also set the initial text of the text box by placing the characters between the opening and closing `<textarea>` tags.

To access or to set the value of a textarea through JavaScript, reference the element. You can do this by using the syntax `document.Form1.text1.value`. `Form1` is the name of the form in which the element is located, and

`text1` is the name of the text area. For information on other methods to reference the text area, see the section "Reference Form Elements" in this chapter.

You can obtain the value of a text area by storing the element's object reference in a variable. For example, the statement `var str1 = document.Form1.text1.value` stores `text1`'s value in the variable `str1`.

You can update the value of a text area by storing a number or string in the element's object reference. For example, `document.Form1.text1.value = "JavaScript"` stores JavaScript in the text area. If you want to break a string into multiple lines, you can type `\n` where you want the breaks to happen. For example, the statement `"JavaScript\nBlueprint"` appears as `JavaScript` on the first line and `Blueprint` on the second line.

Validate Text Area Input

① Add a `<textarea>` element to the form.

② Add an event handler to the `<textarea>` tag.

③ Create a JavaScript function to count words.

④ Save the file.

⑤ Open the file in a Web browser.

⑥ Type the text into the text area and remove focus by pressing the Tab key.

● The validation message appears after the tab key is pressed.

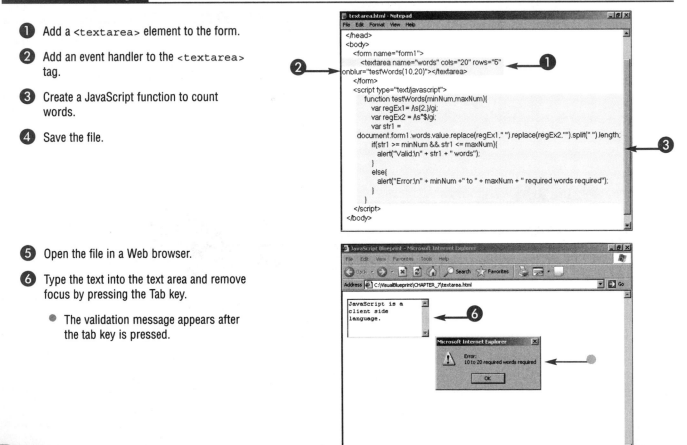

Work with a Button Element

You can create a button to initiate JavaScript functions by using event handlers like `onclick`, `onmouseover`, and so on. Buttons are defined on a Web page by using the `<input>` tag or the `<button>` tag.

If you use the `<input>` tag, the button is assigned a `type` attribute set to `button`. You also need to give the button a `name` attribute so you can access the element. You can set the text of the button by setting the `value` attribute of the element. For example, the statement `<input type="button" name="button1" value="click">` creates a button with the name of `button1` and the text click appears.

The `<button>` tag has more features then the basic `<input>` button. The `<button>` tag contains an opening and closing tag. The `<button>` tag has a `name` attribute by which to reference the button. The text that is displayed on the button is placed between the opening and closing tags. You can use HTML formatting. For example, the statement `<button name="button1">JavaScript<br><span style="color:blue">Blueprint</span></button>` appears as JavaScript on the top line and Blueprint on the bottom line. The word Blueprint appears in blue text.

You can change the text displayed on the button by changing the value. You need to reference the element to change the value. You can reference the button by using the syntax `document.Form1.button1.value = "CLICK"`. `Form1` is the name of the form, and `button1` is the name of the button. The text on the button appears as CLICK after the statement is run. For information on other methods to reference the buttons, see the section Reference Form Elements in this chapter.

Work with a Button Element

① Declare a button element.

② Reference the button.

③ Store a variable in the button reference.

④ Save the file.

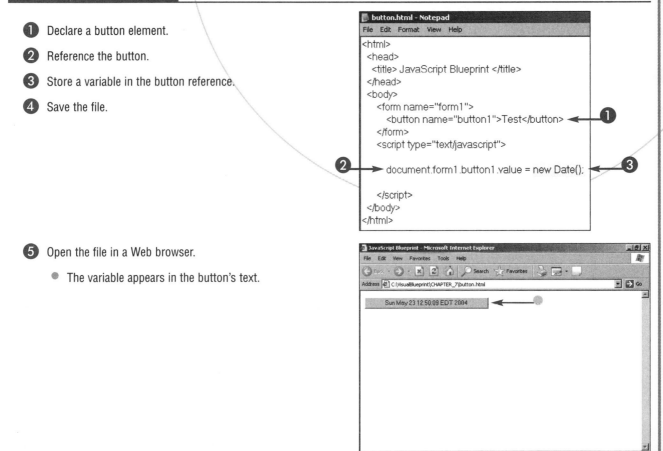

⑤ Open the file in a Web browser.

● The variable appears in the button's text.

Y ou can add a reset button to a form to reset all the element values on the page to their default values. Therefore, if users make a mistake when entering data, they can click a button to clear the whole form instead of deleting each element individually.

The reset button is added to the page by using the `<input>` tag. Set the `type` attribute to `reset`. You can give the reset button a name by using the `name` attribute. If you do not want the default text Reset on the button, you can use the reset button's `value` attribute to change it.

You can use a submit button to submit the form to the Web server. The submit button informs the browser that the information is ready to be processed. You can add the submit button to the page by using the `<input>` tag and setting the `type` attribute to `submit`. You can also set the button's name by using the `name` attribute. If you want to

change the default text that appears on the button, you can use the `value` attribute.

You do not have to use a submit button to submit a form. You can add a JavaScript built-in method to do it instead. The `submit()` method is added after the form reference. For example, `document.Form1.submit();` submits the form named `Form1` when the statement is executed. You can call the `submit()` method in any JavaScript statement. For example, you can submit a form named `Form1` by changing the value of the form element with the statement `onchange="document.Form1.submit()"`.

You can detect when the form is being selected and reset with two event handlers. The `onsubmit()` and `onreset()` event handlers fire when they detect their respective operations. The `onsubmit()` event handler is discussed later in this chapter.

Apply a Reset Button

1 Add an `input` attribute and set the type to reset.

2 Display the `button` attributes by referencing the `<input>` tag.

3 Save the file.

```
reset.html - Notepad
File  Edit  Format  View  Help
<html>
 <head>
  <title> JavaScript Blueprint </title>
 </head>
 <body>
   <form name="form1">
     <input type="reset" name="reset1" value="Reset Button">      ◀──①
   </form>
   <script type="text/javascript">

     document.write("name: " + document.form1.reset1.name + "<br\>");
     document.write("type: " + document.form1.reset1.type + "<br\>");    ◀──②
     document.write("value: " + document.form1.reset1.value + "<br\>");

   </script>
 </body>
</html>
```

4 Open the file in a Web browser.

● The Reset button's properties appear.

```
JavaScript Blueprint - Microsoft Internet Explorer
File  Edit  View  Favorites  Tools  Help
Back ·  ·  ·  Search  Favorites
Address  C:\VisualBlueprint\CHAPTER_7\reset.html                    Go

  Reset Button

name: reset1
type: reset         ◀──
value: Reset Button
```

Apply a Submit Button

① Add an `input` attribute and set the type to submit.

② Display the `button` attributes by referencing the `<input>` tag.

③ Save the file.

```
submit.html - Notepad
File  Edit  Format  View  Help

<html>
 <head>
  <title> JavaScript Blueprint </title>
 </head>
 <body>
   <form name="form1">
     <input type="submit" name="submit1" value="Submit Button">    ◀——①
   </form>
   <script type="text/javascript">

     document.write("name: " + document.form1.submit1.name + "<br\>");
     document.write("type: " + document.form1.submit1.type + "<br\>");    ◀——②
     document.write("value: " + document.form1.submit1.value + "<br\>");

   </script>
 </body>
</html>
```

④ Open the file in a Web browser.

● The Submit button's properties appear.

```
JavaScript Blueprint - Microsoft Internet Explorer
File  Edit  View  Favorites  Tools  Help
Back ▾ ⚊ ▾ ✕ ☶ ☖  Search  Favorites
Address  C:\VisualBlueprint\CHAPTER_7\submit.html                   ▾  ⟶ Go

  Submit Button

name: submit1
type: submit         ◀——
value: Submit Button
```

Apply It

You can submit a form by using the JavaScript `submit()` method. This allows you full control of how and when a form is submitted. If you combine the `submit()` method with a `setTimeout()` method, you can develop a timed quiz. The form will submit after a set period of time.

Submit a Form
```
function submitTest(){
   alert("Time is Up!");
   document.form1.submit();
}
var minute = 2;
var time = minute * 60 * 1000;
var timed = setTimeout("submitTest()",time);
```

To change the amount of minutes the user has to fill out the form, you can change the variable named minute. You can add an alert message before the submission to tell the user that time has run out as shown. If you do not use the alert message, the form submits without notifying the user.

Alter Check Box Properties

Y ou can use check boxes to allow a user to select certain items from a list. The check box is commonly used for user agreements or selecting items on a list. When using the check box for user agreements, the form cannot be submitted when the check box is not checked. Checking the check box calls a user-defined function that allows the form to be submitted.

The check box is added to the Web page by using the `<input>` tag with the `type` attribute set to `checkbox`. The check box has a `name` attribute that you can use to reference the check box. Another attribute is the `checked` attribute. When the `checked` attribute is not included, the check box is unchecked. You can also set a value to the check box by using the `value` attribute.

The check box is a Boolean. When the check box is checked, its Boolean is true; the Boolean is false when unchecked. You can detect if the text box is checked by referencing the `checked` attribute of the check box. The statement `status = document.Form1.checkbox1.checked;` stores the check box's checked Boolean from `Form1` in the variable status. To make the check box checked, the statement `document.Form1.checkbox1.checked = true;` performs that action.

When a user refreshes a page, the form values normally reset to the default values. One common problem certain browsers face is that check boxes may not reset. A common fix is to call a function on the page loading and reset the values.

Display the Check Box Properties

① Add an `input` attribute and set the type to `checkbox`.

② Display the `checkbox` attributes by referencing the `<input>` tag.

③ Save the file.

```
checkbox1.html - Notepad
File  Edit  Format  View  Help

<html>
 <head>
  <title> JavaScript Blueprint </title>
 </head>
 <body>
   <form name="form1">
     <input type="checkbox" name="cb1" value="cb1_value">   ◀──❶
   </form>
   <script type="text/javascript">

     document.write("name: " + document.form1.cb1.name + "<br\>");
     document.write("type: " + document.form1.cb1.type + "<br\>");
     document.write("value: " + document.form1.cb1.value + "<br\>");
     document.write("checked: " + document.form1.cb1.checked + "<br\>");

   </script>
 </body>
</html>
```
◀──❷

④ Open the file in a Web browser.

● The check box properties appear.

```
JavaScript Blueprint - Microsoft Internet Explorer
File  Edit  View  Favorites  Tools  Help
Back ·  ·    ·        Search    Favorites
Address  C:\VisualBlueprint\CHAPTER_7\checkbox1.html           Go

□

name: cb1
type: checkbox       ◀──
value: cb1_value
checked: false
```

Create a Check All Check Box

1️⃣ Add a group of check boxes with similar names.

2️⃣ Set the Check All check box with an event handler.

3️⃣ Create a function to check all the check boxes.

4️⃣ Save the file.

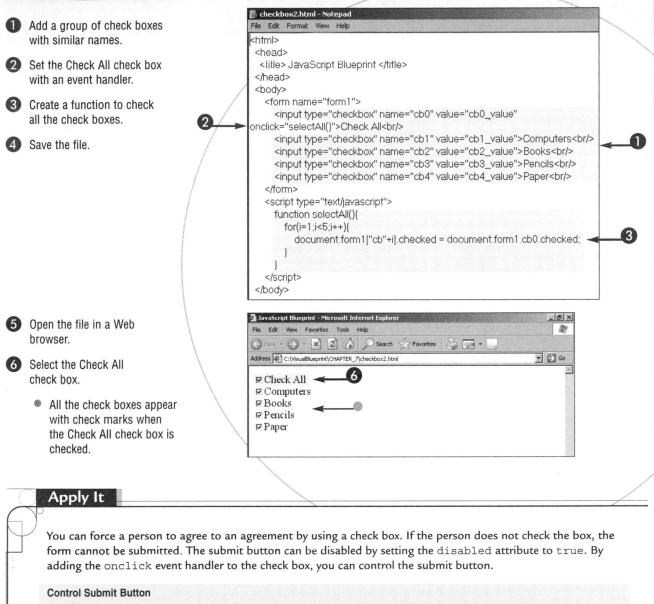

```
checkbox2.html - Notepad
File  Edit  Format  View  Help
<html>
 <head>
  <title> JavaScript Blueprint </title>
 </head>
 <body>
   <form name="form1">
     <input type="checkbox" name="cb0" value="cb0_value"
onclick="selectAll()">Check All<br/>
     <input type="checkbox" name="cb1" value="cb1_value">Computers<br/>
     <input type="checkbox" name="cb2" value="cb2_value">Books<br/>
     <input type="checkbox" name="cb3" value="cb3_value">Pencils<br/>
     <input type="checkbox" name="cb4" value="cb4_value">Paper<br/>
   </form>
   <script type="text/javascript">
     function selectAll(){
       for(i=1;i<5;i++){
         document.form1["cb"+i].checked = document.form1.cb0.checked;
       }
     }
   </script>
 </body>
```

5️⃣ Open the file in a Web browser.

6️⃣ Select the Check All check box.

● All the check boxes appear with check marks when the Check All check box is checked.

```
JavaScript Blueprint - Microsoft Internet Explorer
File  Edit  View  Favorites  Tools  Help
Back ·  ·  ·  Search  Favorites
Address  C:\VisualBluepint\CHAPTER_7\checkbox2.html   Go

☑ Check All ◄── 6
☑ Computers
☑ Books  ●
☑ Pencils ◄──
☑ Paper
```

Apply It

You can force a person to agree to an agreement by using a check box. If the person does not check the box, the form cannot be submitted. The submit button can be disabled by setting the disabled attribute to true. By adding the onclick event handler to the check box, you can control the submit button.

Control Submit Button

```
<script>
function adjustSubmit(){
  var disableIt = (document.form1.disableCB.checked) ? false : true;
  document.form1.sub1.disabled = disableIt;
}
</script>
<form name="form1">
  Accept Agreement:
  <input type="checkbox" name="disableCB" onclick="adjustSubmit()">
  <input type="submit" name="sub1" value="submit" disabled="true">
</form>
```

It is important that the check box is true when using the onclick handler. The user can click the button twice and not agree to the agreement. By not checking the checked status, you may allow a person to submit the form.

Determine Selected Radio Button

Y ou can use radio buttons to allow a user to select only one item out of a list. This enables you to limit the user's choice when filling out a form. You can initially set a radio button to be selected by adding the `checked` attribute to the radio button tag. For example, the statement `<input type="radio" name="rad1" value="r1" checked>` sets the radio button to checked as a default. If another radio button in the group also has the checked property, the last button that is loaded by the browser is selected.

A radio button is added to a Web page by using an `<input>` tag and setting the `type` attribute to `radiobutton`. The `name` attribute is used to determine what group a radio button belongs to. You can have multiple radio button groups by having different group names. Each radio button element can have different values by setting the `value` attribute in each individual `<input>` tag.

Because each radio button in a group has the same name, you must reference each one as an element in an array. The first element listed on the Web page resides at position zero. For example, the statement `bool1 = document. Form1.rad1[2].checked;` checks to see if the third radio button element in the `rad1` group in `Form1` is checked. If the radio button is selected, the Boolean `true` is stored in `rad1`. When the radio button is not selected, it returns `false`.

You can set a radio button to be checked by referencing the `checked` property and setting it to `true`. For example, the statement `document.Form1.rad1[0].checked = true;` selects the first radio button in the group `rad1`. You can unselect a radio button by setting the `checked` property to `false`.

Determine Selected Radio Button

① Declare a radio button group.

② Set the `checked` attribute to one of the group members.

③ Create a function to loop through and display the properties.

④ Save the file.

```
radiobutton.html - Notepad
File Edit Format View Help
<html>
 <head>
  <title> JavaScript Blueprint </title>
 </head>
 <body>
   <form name="form1">
     <input type="radio" name="rb1" value="rb1_value" checked>Computers<br/>
     <input type="radio" name="rb1" value="rb2_value">Books<br/>
     <input type="radio" name="rb1" value="rb3_value">Pencils<br/>
     <input type="radio" name="rb1" value="rb4_value">Paper<br/>
   </form>
   <script type="text/javascript">
     for(i=0;i<4;i++){
        document.write("Radio #" + i + "| selected: " + document.form1.rb1[i].checked +
          "<br/>");
     }
   </script>
 </body>
</html>
```

⑤ Open the file in a Web browser.

● The radio buttons appear.

● The properties of the radio buttons appear.

```
JavaScript Blueprint - Microsoft Internet Explorer
File Edit View Favorites Tools Help
Back · · ·  Search  Favorites
Address  C:\VisualBlueprint\CHAPTER_7\radiobutton.html  Go

⊙ Computers
○ Books
○ Pencils
○ Paper

Radio #0| selected: true
Radio #1| selected: false
Radio #2| selected: false
Radio #3| selected: false
```

Display Radio Button Values

1 Declare a radio button group.

2 Add an event handler to the `<radio>` button.

3 Repeat step **2** for each radio button.

4 Create a function to find each checked radio button.

5 Save the file.

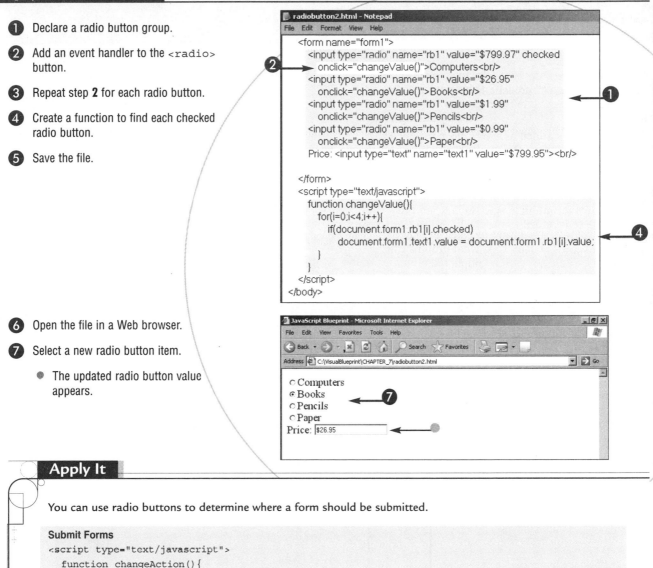

6 Open the file in a Web browser.

7 Select a new radio button item.

● The updated radio button value appears.

Apply It

You can use radio buttons to determine where a form should be submitted.

Submit Forms
```
<script type="text/javascript">
  function changeAction(){
    for(i=0;i<document.form1.R1.length;i++){
      if(document.form1.R1[i].checked){
        document.form1.action = document.form1.R1[i].value;
        document.title=document.form1.action;
      break;
      }
    }
    return true;
  }
</script>
<form name="form1" method="post" onsubmit="return changeAction()" action="Loc1.htm">
  1<input type="radio" name="R1" value="Loc1.htm"checked>
  2<input type="radio" name="R1" value="Loc2.htm">
  <input type="submit" name="submit" value="submit">
</form>
```

Work with a Selection List

You can use the drop-down list to allow users to make selections of predefined options. A selection list is set to allow one option or multiple options to be made by the user.

The drop-down list is added to a Web page by using the `<select>` tag. Each item in the drop-down list is created by using the `<option>` tag. The `<option>` tag contains a value attribute and a `selected` attribute. If the `selected` attribute is added, then the option will be highlighted in the list.

A select list allows for multiple selections when the `multiple` attribute is added to the `<select>` tag. Also, you can allow more than one option to appear by using the `size` attribute. For example, if you set the size to 4, then four items appear.

The selection list object includes a `length` property. The `length` property returns the amount of options contained in

the drop-down list. Another property is the `selectedIndex` property that returns the value of the option that is selected.

The option object is a subobject of the select object. It is an array, and each object is referred to by using its index value. For example, the first option of a selection list named `select1` in `form1` is `document.form1.select1.options[0]`.

Unlike all the other form elements, you cannot reference the selection value by adding `value` after the form name. Instead, you have to use the selected index property when only one option can be selected. First, reference the drop-down object and store it in a variable, `var sel = document.Form1.select1;`. You can then retrieve the text of the selected item with the statement `var txt = sel.options[sel.selectedIndex].text;` and the value with the statement `var opt = sel.options[sel.selected Index].value;`.

Display the Selection Box Properties

① Declare a selection element with options.

② Add code to retrieve selection box properties.

③ Add statements to display the properties.

④ Save the file.

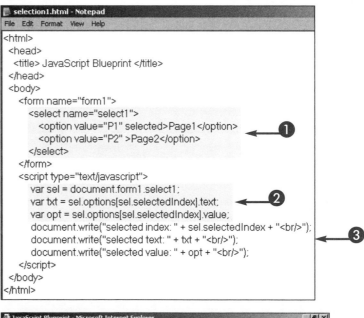

```
selection1.html - Notepad
File  Edit  Format  View  Help
<html>
 <head>
  <title> JavaScript Blueprint </title>
 </head>
 <body>
   <form name="form1">
     <select name="select1">
       <option value="P1" selected>Page1</option>          ①
       <option value="P2" >Page2</option>
     </select>
   </form>
   <script type="text/javascript">
     var sel = document.form1.select1;
     var txt = sel.options[sel.selectedIndex].text;          ②
     var opt = sel.options[sel.selectedIndex].value;
     document.write("selected index: " + sel.selectedIndex + "<br/>");
     document.write("selected text: " + txt + "<br/>");      ③
     document.write("selected value: " + opt + "<br/>");
   </script>
 </body>
</html>
```

⑤ Open the file in a Web browser.

● The selection box properties appear.

```
JavaScript Blueprint - Microsoft Internet Explorer
File  Edit  View  Favorites  Tools  Help
Back        Search   Favorites
Address  C:\VisualBlueprint\CHAPTER_7\selection1.html        Go

Page1

selected index: 0
selected text: Page1
selected value: P1
```

Detect a Value Change

① Declare a variable and set it equal to the select element object reference.

② Add statements to retrieve the text and value of the selected option.

③ Determine if the option is not the first item and display the correct message.

④ Add an onchange event handler to the select element.

⑤ Save the file.

⑥ Open the file in a Web browser.

⑦ Click here and select an item from the select element list.

● An alert dialog box appears displaying the selected item from the select element list.

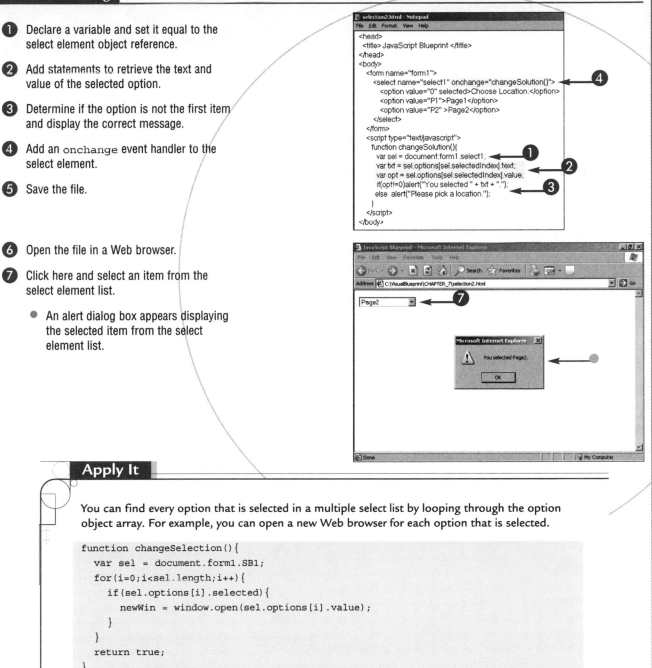

Apply It

You can find every option that is selected in a multiple select list by looping through the option object array. For example, you can open a new Web browser for each option that is selected.

```
function changeSelection(){
  var sel = document.form1.SB1;
  for(i=0;i<sel.length;i++){
    if(sel.options[i].selected){
      newWin = window.open(sel.options[i].value);
    }
  }
  return true;
}
```

You can execute the function `changeSelection()` by calling it from an event handler on the select element or from another element such as a button. The values of the options in the select element need to contain the Web page link or the page that a user will open.

```
<select name="SB1" onblur="changeSelection()" size="3" multiple>
  <option value="http://www.Wiley.com">Books</option>
  <option value="http://www.JavaRanch.com">Java</option>
  <option value="games.html">Games</option>
</select>
```

Basic Form Validation

You can validate a form so a user fills in the correct information before it reaches the server. This prevents the server from having to process any extra data, which decreases the bandwidth usage and saves a large site a lot of money. Form validation is skipped by a user if JavaScript is disabled.

The `onsubmit` event handler is added to the `<form>` tag. When the submit button is clicked, the `onsubmit` handler is called. The `onsubmit` handler determines if the form is supposed to be submitted. You can block form submissions by adding `return false` inside the value of the JavaScript event handler. However, you do not always want to not allow the form to be submitted, so instead of using false, you can have a statement or function return a Boolean value. You can add a JavaScript statement after the return

statement that returns a Boolean, but it is more common to add a function call. For example, the statement `<form name="E" onsubmit = "return jsValidate()">` will call the JavaScript function `jsValidate()` when the form is submitted.

The JavaScript function needs to return a Boolean value back to the event handler. You can return a value by using the `return` keyword. For more information, see Chapter 5.

A validation script normally checks to see if the form elements contain appropriate information. For example, a validation script can check for minimum value lengths, maximum value lengths, date ranges, and so on. Form validation usually involves regular expressions. For more information, see Chapter 6.

Basic Form Validation

1. Add an `onsubmit` handler to the `<form>` tag.

2. Create a JavaScript validation function.

3. Add statements to retrieve element properties.

4. Repeat step **3** for each element.

5. Save the file.

```
validate.html - Notepad
File  Edit  Format  View  Help
<body>
  <form name="form1" onsubmit="return validate()">         ——①
     Length 4: <input type="text" name="T1"><br/>
     Lenght 6: <input type="text" name="T2"><br/>
     <input type="submit" name="Submit" value="submit">
  </form>
  <script type="text/javascript">
     function validate(){
        submitFlag = true;
        if(document.form1.T1.value.length!=4){       ——③
           submitFlag = false;
           alert("Invalid Length  - 4 Characters Required");
        }
        if(document.form1.T2.value.length!=6){       ——②
           submitFlag = false;
           alert("Invalid Length - 6 Characters Required");
        }
        return submitFlag;
     }
  </script>
</body>
```

6. Open the file in a Web browser.

   ● The form appears.

JavaScript Blueprint - Microsoft Internet Explorer
File Edit View Favorites Tools Help
Back · · · Search Favorites
Address C:\VisualBlueprint\CHAPTER_7\validate.html

Length 4: [   ]
Lenght 6: [   ]
[submit]

7 Type text in the form.

8 Click Submit.

● The validation error message appears.

Note: The form is not submitted until all the validation parameters are met.

Extra

You can disable a form element so a user cannot edit or click it. This allows you to make sure that a form is submitted in the correct manner. To disable a form element, you add the `disabled` attribute to the tag. Adding the `disabled` attribute tag grays out the contents of the form element. To enable the form element, you must set the `disabled` attribute to `false`. For example, the statement `document.form1.text1.disabled = false;` enables a user to type text into a text box named `text1` in `form1`.

Disable a Form Element
```
<input type="text" name="text1"
value="default" disabled>
```

Another way to disable a form element is to use the `readonly` attribute. The `readonly` attribute is added to text fields that you want the user to be able to read, but do not want the user to be able to change the value of. The `readonly` attribute is set to false to disable it. For example, the statement `document.form1.text2.readOnly = false;` enables a user to type text into a text box named `text2` in `form1`.

Disable a Form Element with ReadOnly
```
<input type="text" name="text2"
value="default" readonly>
```

Create a Select Element Navigation Menu

You may see Web sites that have a select menu that allows users to move to other sections of the Web page. You can do this by implementing an event handler onclick attached to a button or with the onchange event handler on the select element. Either method creates a simple and compact menu which is easy to navigate.

The first step is to create the select menu with the values of the options being the URL. The text portion of the select menu is a descriptive value of the option. For example, the statement <option value="http://www.wiley.com">Books</option> has the URL stored in the value of the <option> tag.

The next step is to create a function that finds the value of the option selected in the drop-down list. To do this you

need to find the selected index of the option and its value. For example, the statement var num = document.form1. S1.selectedIndex; finds the option that is selected in the list. The statement theLink = document.form1. S1[num].value; finds the value of the selected option. The option is then set to change the page location or to open the link in a new window.

You then can use a button with an onclick handler to call the function, or you can use an onchange event handler on the selection list. The onchange method is the method used by most developers. It is one less step that the user has to make when using the navigation menu.

Create a Select Element Navigation Menu

① Add options to a select element setting the value equal to a Web page or a file.

② Repeat step 1 for each link you want to include in the list.

③ Create a function to handle an event handler.

④ Store the select element object reference in a variable.

⑤ Find the selected item's value from the options array.

⑥ Set the page location to the link.

⑦ Add an onchange event handler to the select element.

⑧ Save the file.

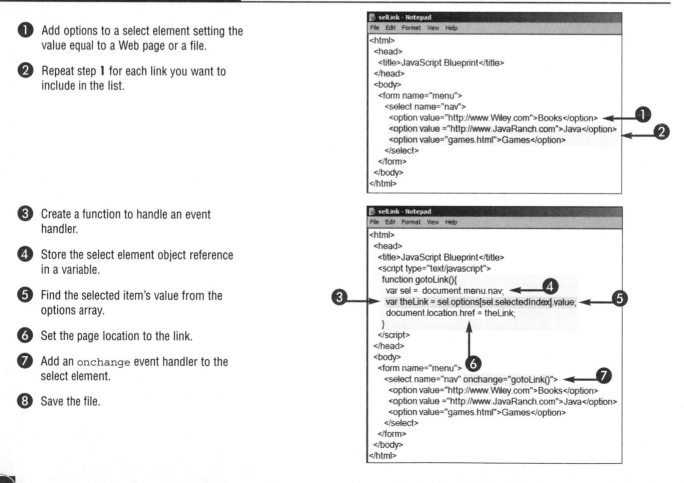

```
selLink - Notepad
File Edit Format View Help
<html>
 <head>
  <title>JavaScript Blueprint</title>
 </head>
 <body>
  <form name="menu">
   <select name="nav">
    <option value="http://www.Wiley.com">Books</option>     ①
    <option value ="http://www.JavaRanch.com">Java</option>  ②
    <option value="games.html">Games</option>
   </select>
  </form>
 </body>
</html>
```

```
selLink - Notepad
File Edit Format View Help
<html>
 <head>
  <title>JavaScript Blueprint</title>
  <script type="text/javascript">
   function gotoLink(){
    var sel = document.menu.nav;                              ④
    var theLink = sel.options[sel.selectedIndex].value;       ⑤
    document.location.href = theLink;                         ⑥
   }
  </script>
 </head>
 <body>
  <form name="menu">
   <select name="nav" onchange="gotoLink()">                  ⑦
    <option value="http://www.Wiley.com">Books</option>
    <option value="http://www.JavaRanch.com">Java</option>
    <option value="games.html">Games</option>
   </select>
  </form>
 </body>
</html>
```

9 Open the file in a Web browser.

10 Click here and select a link from the drop-down list.

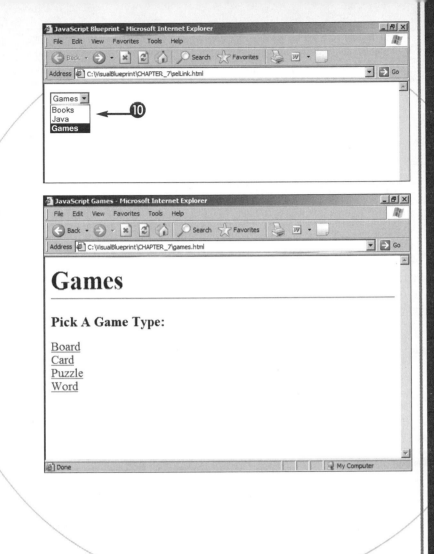

● The link opens in the browser window.

Apply It

You can give the user the option to open the window in a new window or to keep it in the same browser window. To do this you can use either a check box or a radio button. This gives the user the option on how the link opens. The JavaScript requires a check to see how the window will open by checking the checked state of a check box named CB1.

```
function gotoLink(){
  var sel =  document.menu.nav;
  var theLink = sel.options[sel.selectedIndex].value;
  if(document.menu.CB1.checked)newWin = window.open(theLink);
  else document.location.href = theLink;
}
```

Block an Enter Key Invoked Form Submission

You can block the submission of a form when the Enter key is pressed. Blocking the Enter key eliminates the chance of premature submissions of forms that can inconvenience the users on your Web site.

The default behavior of most browsers is to submit the form when the Enter key is pressed on a form that contains only one text box. This behavior is not part of the HTML standard, but most browsers adhere to it. This behavior is only convenient when there are no other fields to handle. To make sure that the form does not submit, you need to block this behavior.

To block the submission, you need to add the onkeydown event handler with the return statement. The onkeydown event calls a function that returns a true or false Boolean value. If true is returned, the key press is allowed. A false value does not allow the key press to happen.

To block the form submission, you need to block the key code of 13 or 3. The key code of 13 corresponds to the Enter key and the key code of 3 corresponds to an extra Return key on Macintosh computers. If the key code equals 13 or 3, then you need to return false. All other keys should return true.

You can also block all form submissions by setting the onsubmit handler equal to return false. The statement `<form name="form1" onsubmit="return false ">` blocks the Return key. This does not allow the form to be submitted. You can then submit the form through a JavaScript command. The statement `<input type="button" name="b1" value="submit" onclick="this.form.submit()">` submits the form when the button is clicked.

Block an Enter Key Invoked Form Submission

① Create a function that accepts one parameter.

② Store the keycode value of the key that was pressed with cross browser coding into a variable.

③ Determine if the key pressed is the Return or Enter key, returning false if it was and true if it was not.

```
blockSubmit - Notepad
File  Edit  Format  View  Help
<html>
 <head>
  <script type="text/javascript">
  function blockSubmit(evt) {
  var keyCode = (evt) ? evt.keyCode : ((window.event) ? event.which : null);   ②
  if(keyCode == 13 || keyCode == 3){
    return false;                          ③
    }
    else return true;
    }
  </script>
 </head>
 <body>
  <form name="E" onsubmit="return false">
   <input type="text" name="T1" onkeypress="return blockSubmit(event)">
   <input type="text" name="T2" onkeypress="return blockSubmit(event)">
   <input type="text" name="T3" onkeypress="return blockSubmit(event)">
   <input type="button" name="SB" value="submit" onclick="this.form.submit()">
  </form>
 </body>
</html>
```

① ③

④ Add an onsubmit handler to the form, returning false to block form submissions.

⑤ Add an onkeypress handler to the form to call function.

⑥ Repeat step **5** for each text element.

⑦ Change the submit button to a text button and add an onclick handler to submit the form.

⑧ Save the file.

```
blockSubmit - Notepad
File  Edit  Format  View  Help
<html>
 <head>
  <script type="text/javascript">
  function blockSubmit(evt) {
  var keyCode = (evt) ? evt.keyCode : ((window.event) ? event.which : null);
  if(keyCode == 13 || keyCode == 3){
    return false;
    }
    else return true;
    }
  </script>
 </head>
 <body>
  <form name="E" onsubmit="return false">                  ④
   <input type="text" name="T1" onkeypress="return blockSubmit(event)">   ⑤
   <input type="text" name="T2" onkeypress="return blockSubmit(event)">   ⑥
   <input type="text" name="T3" onkeypress="return blockSubmit(event)">
   <input type="button" name="SB" value="submit" onclick="this.form.submit()">  ⑦
  </form>
 </body>
</html>
```

9 Open the file in a Web browser.

10 Enter text into a form element and press the Enter key.

11 Fill out the rest of the form and press the Submit button.

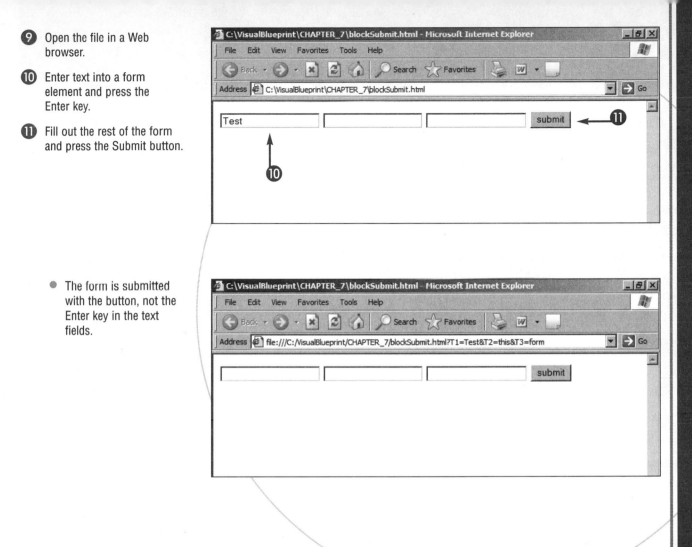

● The form is submitted with the button, not the Enter key in the text fields.

Extra

You can still validate the form even though the onsubmit handler is not returning false. Instead of using the onsubmit handler, you need to add it to the button. Inside the onclick handler you need to add an if statement that calls the form validation. If the if statement is true, then the form is submitted.

Validate the Form
```
<input type="button" name="b1"
value="submit"
onclick="if(ValidateForm())
this.form.submit()">
```

A user that has JavaScript disabled cannot submit the form. If your form depends on JavaScript validation, this is a great way to make sure that the user has JavaScript enabled and the form has been submitted correctly. If you are using a server side language, make sure that you perform validation on the server side because there are ways around JavaScript validation.

Advance the Text Field Focus with the Enter Key

You can make the Enter key in a text field give focus to the next text field. This gives the user more control when they are filling out forms. Some users may be accustomed to using the Enter key when filling out spreadsheets.

The first thing that you need to do is to set the `onsubmit` event handler to `return false`. This prevents the form from submitting when the Enter key is pressed. If you do not do this, then the form may be submitted with certain browsers.

The next step is to create a function that looks for the key press and determines if the Enter key was pressed. If the Enter key was pressed, then the next field should have the focus set. The function should accept the next form element name and also the `event` keyword. The `event` keyword is

used to detect what key was pressed. The form element name is used to set the focus of the next field.

The final step you need to do is to add an event handler to all the text elements on the page. The `onkeypress` event handler needs to catch all the key presses on the element. The event handler needs to have a `return` keyword added, which calls the function. The function call should send the form element name of the next element and the `event` keyword.

Some users are accustomed to using the Tab key to advance from text field to text field. Therefore, it is also important to add the `tabindex` attribute to all the elements. This allows the user to use the Tab key to advance form fields just like the Enter key.

Advance the Text Field Focus with the Enter Key

① Create a function that accepts three parameters.

② Store the `keycode` value of the key that was pressed with cross browser coding into a variable.

③ Determine if the `keycode` is the Enter key; if not, then return true.

④ Focus the next element by using the passed parameters and the focus method.

⑤ Add the `onkeypress` event handler passing the form object, element to be focused, and the event object as parameters.

⑥ Repeat step **5** for each element on the form.

⑦ Save the file.

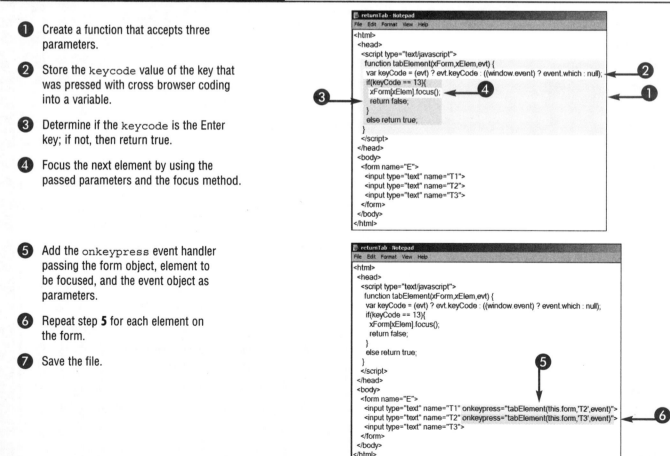

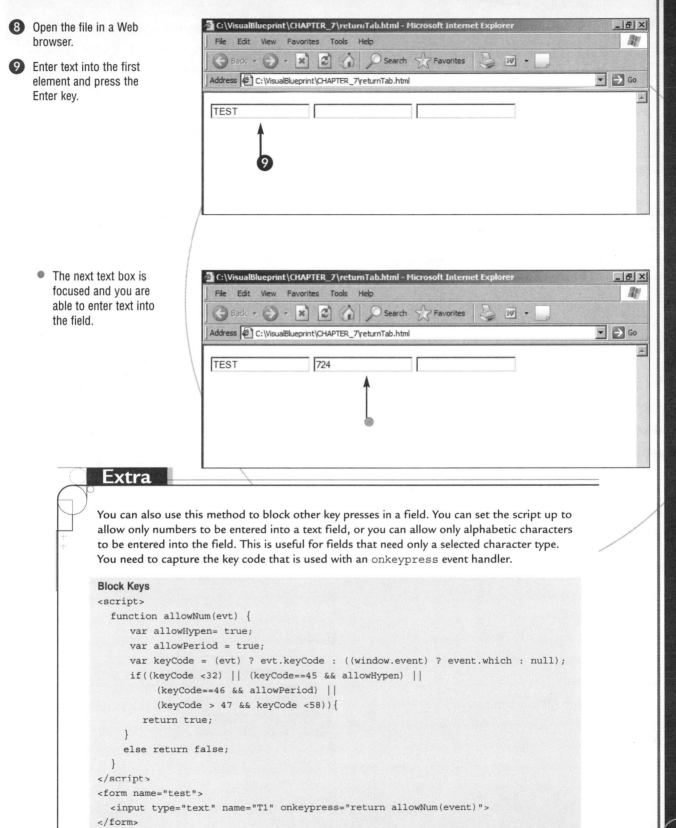

Open the file in a Web browser.

Enter text into the first element and press the Enter key.

- The next text box is focused and you are able to enter text into the field.

Chapter 7: Working with HTML Forms

Extra

You can also use this method to block other key presses in a field. You can set the script up to allow only numbers to be entered into a text field, or you can allow only alphabetic characters to be entered into the field. This is useful for fields that need only a selected character type. You need to capture the key code that is used with an `onkeypress` event handler.

```
Block Keys
<script>
  function allowNum(evt) {
    var allowHypen= true;
    var allowPeriod = true;
    var keyCode = (evt) ? evt.keyCode : ((window.event) ? event.which : null);
    if((keyCode <32) || (keyCode==45 && allowHypen) ||
        (keyCode==46 && allowPeriod) ||
        (keyCode > 47 && keyCode <58)){
      return true;
    }
    else return false;
  }
</script>
<form name="test">
  <input type="text" name="T1" onkeypress="return allowNum(event)">
</form>
```

Use the Date Object to Display Dates

Y ou can use the `Date()` object to display the current date, determine if a date is valid, determine the user's time zone, and so on. The `Date()` object relies on the time set on the user's computer. Therefore, if the wrong date or time is set on your computer, then it will also affect your script.

The `Date()` object is declared by setting the object to a variable. For example, the statement `var today = new Date();` stores the current date and time into the variable `today` in this format `Mon May 24 10:27:42 EDT 2004`.

You can specify a date by adding the date between the parentheses of the `Date()` object. You can add two main methods to the date string.

The first way is to use a date literal. A date literal is the date written in a string format either by typing the month

name and date or by using the number equivalent. For example, the statement `var date1 = new Date ("July 24, 2005 3:30PM");` and the statement `var date2 = new Date("7/24/2005 3:30PM");` can both be used to specify a date. You are not required to add the time when specifying a date. If you do not specify the time, the time will be set to midnight of that day.

The second method of specifying the date is to specify each part of the date individually. The `Date()` object can accept the year, month, day, hour, minute, second, and millisecond of the date that you want. The parameters are placed in the parentheses separated by commas: `new Date(year, month, day, hour, minute, second, millisecond);`. The hour parameter is based on the 24-hour clock. Therefore, 3 p.m. is written as 15.

Display the Current Date

① Declare a variable.

② Set the variable to a new `Date()` object.

③ Add statements to display the date.

④ Save the file.

```
date1.html - Notepad
File  Edit  Format  View  Help
<html>
 <head>
  <title> JavaScript Blueprint </title>
 </head>
 <body>
   <script type="text/javascript">

     var date1 = new Date();
     document.write(date1);

   </script>
 </body>
</html>
```

⑤ Open the file in a Web browser.

● The current date and time appear.

```
JavaScript Blueprint - Microsoft Internet Explorer
File  Edit  View  Favorites  Tools  Help
Back ·        ·       Search  Favorites
Address  C:\VisualBlueprint\CHAPTER_8\date1.html        Go

Tue May 25 17:32:12 EDT 2004
```

Display a Specific Date

① Declare the variables.

② Set the variables equal to the new `Date()` object specifying dates.

③ Add statements to display the dates.

④ Save the file.

```
date2.html - Notepad
File  Edit  Format  View  Help

<html>
 <head>
  <title> JavaScript Blueprint </title>
 </head>
 <body>
   <script type="text/javascript">

     var date1 = new Date("January 13, 2005 12:30:00PM");     ①  ②
     var date2 = new Date(2005, 0, 13, 12, 30, 00);

     document.write(date1 + "<br>");     ③
     document.write(date2 + "<br>");

   </script>
 </body>
</html>
```

⑤ Open the file in a Web browser.

● The formatted date strings appear.

Note: Both methods produce the same result.

```
JavaScript Blueprint - Microsoft Internet Explorer
File  Edit  View  Favorites  Tools  Help
Back  •          •         Search     Favorites
Address  C:\VisualBlueprint\CHAPTER_8\date2.html              Go

Thu Jan 13 12:30:00 EST 2005
Thu Jan 13 12:30:00 EST 2005
```

Apply It

You can calculate the last day of the month by using the `Date()` object. This function avoids the mess of trying to figure out if this year is a leap year. To use the function, pass the month and year to the function. The last day of the month is returned.

```
<script type="text/javascript">
  function lastDay(theMonth,theYear){
    theMonth;
    if(theMonth > 12) {theMonth = 0; theYear++;}
    var date1 = new Date(theYear,theMonth,0);
    return date1.getDate();
  }
  var theDate = lastDay(1,2004);
  alert(theDate);
</script>
```

You can change this code to return the day of the week that the last day of the month falls on by using the `getDay()` method. By replacing `getDate()` with `getDay()`, the day value is returned.

Get the Date and Time Components

You can get each of the date components by using built-in methods that are supported by the `Date()` object. You can retrieve the month, day, year, hour, minute, second, millisecond, time zone offset, and the day of the week. The `Date()` object methods return their respective values as integers.

You can retrieve the month value by using the `getMonth()` method. The method is added to the end of the `Date()` object variable. For example, the date object is stored in a variable `date1`. The statement `var theMonth = date1.getMonth();` would store the month value in `date1`. The month value ranges from 0 to 11, where 0 is January and 11 is December.

The current day of the month is found with the `getDate()` method, which returns a value between 1 and 31. You can also get the day of the week by using the `getDay()` method. The `getDay()` method returns a value between 0 and 6, where 0 is Sunday and 6 is Saturday.

To get the year of the date, you can use two methods. The first method is `getYear()`. The `getYear()` method returns different results based on the user's computer settings and the browser. Internet Explorer returns a four-digit year and Netscape returns a three-digit year. For example, the Netscape browser returns 105 for 2005. A better method to retrieve the year is `getFullYear()`, which returns a four-digit year for every browser.

The hour is retrieved by the `getHour()` method. It returns a value between 0 and 24.

You can retrieve the minute by using the `getMinute()` method, the seconds with the `getSeconds()` method, and the milliseconds with the `getMilliseconds()` method. You can also determine the number of minutes the current time zone is from Greenwich Mean Time (GMT) by using the `getTimezoneOffset()` method.

Get the Date Components

 1 Declare the date.

2 Declare variables and assign the date methods.

3 Add statements to display the date parts.

4 Save the file.

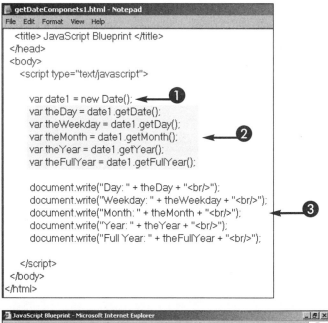

```
getDateComponets1.html - Notepad
File  Edit  Format  View  Help

  <title> JavaScript Blueprint </title>
</head>
<body>
  <script type="text/javascript">

    var date1 = new Date();            ◄── 1
    var theDay = date1.getDate();
    var theWeekday = date1.getDay();
    var theMonth = date1.getMonth();   ◄── 2
    var theYear = date1.getYear();
    var theFullYear = date1.getFullYear();

    document.write("Day: " + theDay + "<br/>");
    document.write("Weekday: " + theWeekday + "<br/>");
    document.write("Month: " + theMonth + "<br/>");   ◄── 3
    document.write("Year: " + theYear + "<br/>");
    document.write("Full Year: " + theFullYear + "<br/>");

  </script>
</body>
</html>
```

5 Open the file in a Web browser.

● Each date part appears.

① Declare the variables.

② Declare variables and assign the time methods.

③ Add statements to display the results.

④ Save the file.

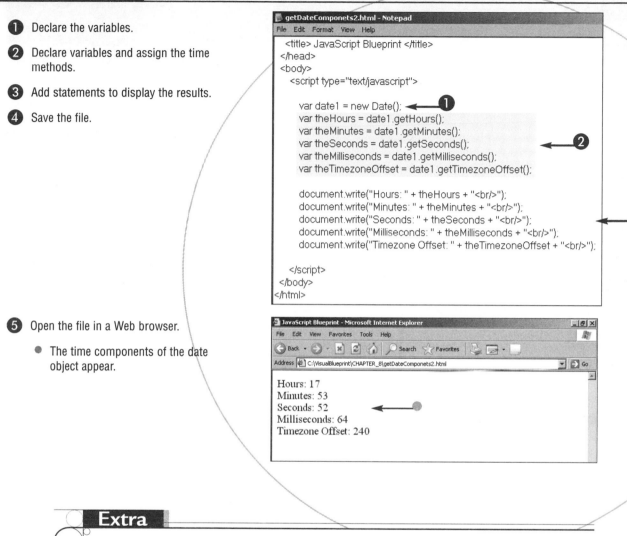

getDateComponets2.html - Notepad
File Edit Format View Help

```
   <title> JavaScript Blueprint </title>
 </head>
 <body>
   <script type="text/javascript">

     var date1 = new Date();          ①
     var theHours = date1.getHours();
     var theMinutes = date1.getMinutes();
     var theSeconds = date1.getSeconds();           ②
     var theMilliseconds = date1.getMilliseconds();
     var theTimezoneOffset = date1.getTimezoneOffset();

     document.write("Hours: " + theHours + "<br/>");
     document.write("Minutes: " + theMinutes + "<br/>");
     document.write("Seconds: " + theSeconds + "<br/>");           ③
     document.write("Milliseconds: " + theMilliseconds + "<br/>");
     document.write("Timezone Offset: " + theTimezoneOffset + "<br/>");

   </script>
 </body>
</html>
```

⑤ Open the file in a Web browser.

- The time components of the date object appear.

JavaScript Blueprint - Microsoft Internet Explorer
File Edit View Favorites Tools Help
Back ▾ ▾ ▾ Search Favorites
Address C:\VisualBlueprint\CHAPTER_8\getDateComponents2.html Go

Hours: 17
Minutes: 53
Seconds: 52
Milliseconds: 64
Timezone Offset: 240

Extra

You can use the Coordinated Universal Time (UTC) standard format, which is the time set by the World Time Standard instead of the standard time format when you retrieve the values. The UTC methods are `getUTCMonth()`, `getUTCDate()`, `getUTCDay()`, `getUTCFullYear()`, `getUTCHours()`, `getUTCMinutes()`, `getUTCSeconds()`, and `getUTCMilliseconds()`. Each of the methods acts as if the standard get methods except for the values are in the UTC format.

The correlation between the three-digit year value and the four-digit year value is based on the value 1900. By adding 1900 to the three-digit year value, you are able to get the four-digit date. For example, the statement `var newYear = 105 + 1900;` stores the value `2005` into the variable `newYear`. To avoid having to adjust the year when retrieving dates from different browsers, you can use the `getFullYear()` method.

Set the Date and Time Parts

Y**ou can set individual parts of the date to a specific month, day, year, hour, and so on without having to declare the entire date again. For example, if you develop an application and you want to add one year to the current date, you can use the setYear() method.

To use any of the set date methods, you must declare a Date() object and store it in a variable.

You can set the month by using the setMonth() method. The setMonth() method accepts a numeric parameter between 0 and 11 in the parentheses where 0 is January and 11 is December. For example, the date object is stored in a variable date1. The statement date1.setMonth(7); sets the month in date1 to August.

You can set the day of the month by using the setDate() method. The setDate() method accepts a parameter between 1 and 31. For example, if you specify June 31, the setDate() method will advance the date to July 1 because June only has 30 days.

The set date methods only have one way to set the date, which is setFullYear(). The setFullYear() method accepts a four-digit year in the parentheses.

You can set the hour by using the setHours() method. The parameter that the setHour() method accepts is based on the 24-hour clock. Therefore, you can type a value between 0 and 24.

You can also set the minutes by using the setMinutes() method, the seconds with the setSeconds() method, and the milliseconds with the setMilliseconds() method.

You can also set the date components using the Coordinated Universal Time standard. The methods are setUTCMonth(), setUTCDate(), setUTCFullYear(), setUTCHours(), setUTCMinutes(), setUTCSeconds(), and setUTCMilliseconds().

Set the Date Parts

① Declare the Date() object.

② Assign set date parameters to the date object.

③ Add statements to display the results.

④ Save the file.

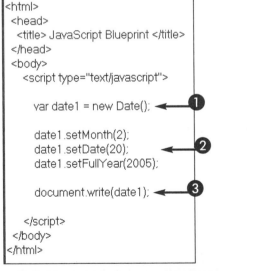

```
setDate.html - Notepad
File  Edit  Format  View  Help
<html>
 <head>
  <title> JavaScript Blueprint </title>
 </head>
 <body>
   <script type="text/javascript">

      var date1 = new Date();          ①

      date1.setMonth(2);
      date1.setDate(20);               ②
      date1.setFullYear(2005);

      document.write(date1);           ③

   </script>
 </body>
</html>
```

⑤ Open the file in a Web browser.

● The updated date appears.

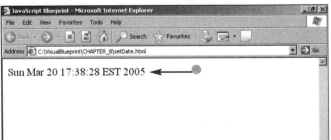

Sun Mar 20 17:38:28 EST 2005

Set the Time Parts

① Declare the `new Date()` object.

② Assign set time parameters to the date object.

③ Add statements to display the results.

④ Save the file.

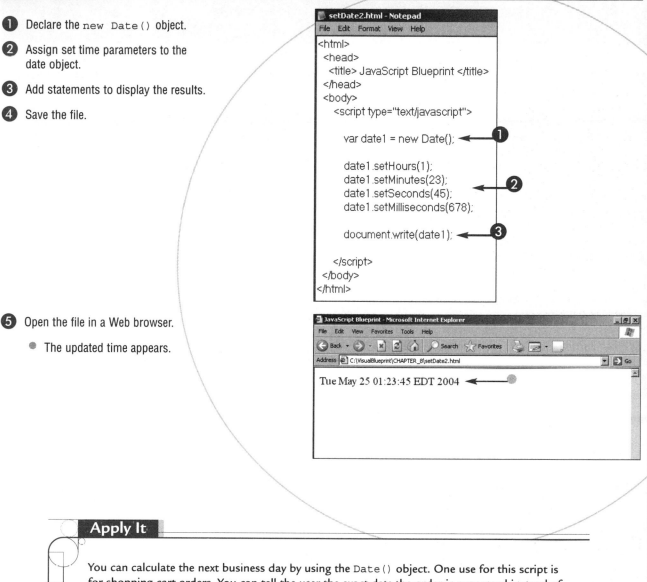

⑤ Open the file in a Web browser.

● The updated time appears.

```html
<html>
 <head>
  <title> JavaScript Blueprint </title>
 </head>
 <body>
  <script type="text/javascript">

      var date1 = new Date();           ①

      date1.setHours(1);
      date1.setMinutes(23);
      date1.setSeconds(45);             ②
      date1.setMilliseconds(678);

      document.write(date1);            ③

  </script>
 </body>
</html>
```

Tue May 25 01:23:45 EDT 2004 ◄

Apply It

You can calculate the next business day by using the `Date()` object. One use for this script is for shopping cart orders. You can tell the user the exact date the order is processed instead of simply stating the next business day. To use the function, pass the date and time to the function. The next business day is returned.

```javascript
<script type="text/javascript">
  function businessDay(busDate){
    busDate.setDate(busDate.getDate() + 1);
    var busDay = busDate.getDay();
    if(busDay==6)busDate.setDate(busDate.getDate() + 2);
    else if(busDay==0)busDate.setDate(busDate.getDate() + 1);
    return busDate;
  }
  var theDate = businessDay(new Date());
  alert(theDate);
</script>
```

Convert Dates to Strings

You can use the built-in object methods to format the string without all the hassle of separating the date object into parts. This can save you time in development and allow your application to run faster.

The `toDateString()` returns a string representing the date portion of the specified `date()` object. For example, the date object is stored in a variable `date1`. The statement `date1.toDateString()` returns the date portion of the string. If `date1` contains `Thu Jul 4 00:00:00 EDT 2004`, the returned string is `Thu Jul 4 2004`. You can just get the time portion of a date by using the `toTimeString()` method.

You can convert a date to Greenwich Mean Time (GMT) by using the `toGMTString()` method. Another method you can use is the `toUTCString()` method. The `toUTCString()` method converts the date to the Coordinated Universal Time (UTC) standard format. which is the time set by the World Time Standard.

You can display the time string in the user's local format. For example, a user in the United States may prefer to see the time expressed in a 12-hour format instead of 24-hour format. The `toLocaleString()` method will convert the date into the preferred format. The format is determined by the date and time setting on the user's computer. You can convert only the date portion by using the `toLocaleDateString()` method. You can also convert the time portion of the `Date()` object by using the `toLocaleTimeString()` method.

The `toString()` method is also used to convert the `Date()` object to a string. The `toString()` method will not change the format of the date like the `toGMTString()` or `toLocaleString()` methods do.

Convert to a Locale String

1. Declare the new `Date()` object.

2. Assign variables to the date object with the locale string methods attached.

3. Add statements to display the results.

4. Save the file.

```
datestring1.html - Notepad
File Edit Format View Help
<html>
 <head>
  <title> JavaScript Blueprint </title>
 </head>
 <body>
   <script type="text/javascript">

     var date1 = new Date();          ①

     var dateFull = date1.toLocaleString();
     var dateDate = date1.toLocaleDateString();     ②
     var dateTime = date1.toLocaleTimeString();

     document.write(dateFull + "<br/>");
     document.write(dateDate + "<br/>");          ③
     document.write(dateTime + "<br/>");

   </script>
 </body>
</html>
```

5. Open the file in a Web browser.

   ● The locale string format appears.

Note: Depending on how a computer's browser is set, the format may vary from what is shown.

```
JavaScript Blueprint - Microsoft Internet Explorer
File Edit View Favorites Tools Help
Back  Search  Favorites
Address C:\VisualBlueprint\CHAPTER_8\datestring1.html    Go

Tuesday, May 25, 2004 6:08:55 PM
Tuesday, May 25, 2004
6:08:55 PM
```

① Declare the `new Date()` object.

② Assign variables to the date object with the string methods attached.

③ Add statements to display the results.

④ Save the file.

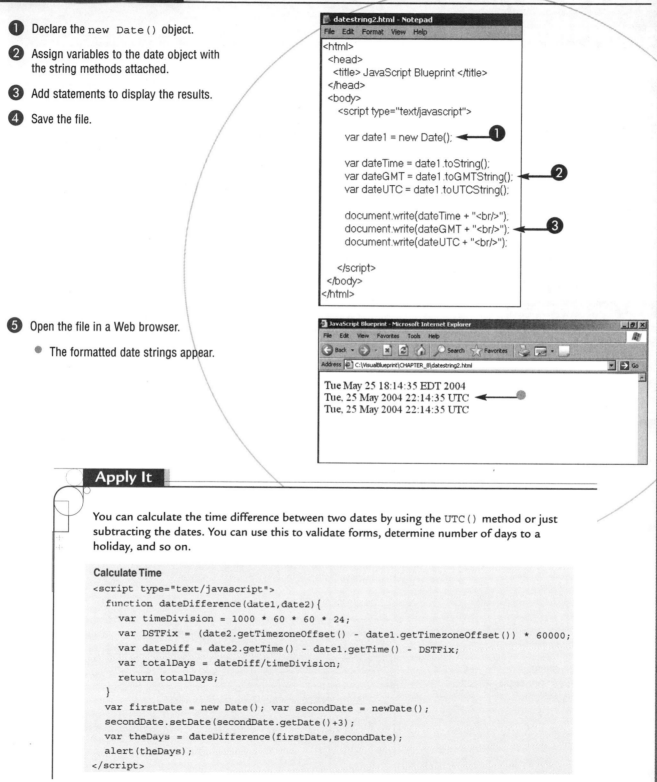

⑤ Open the file in a Web browser.

● The formatted date strings appear.

Apply It

You can calculate the time difference between two dates by using the `UTC()` method or just subtracting the dates. You can use this to validate forms, determine number of days to a holiday, and so on.

Calculate Time
```
<script type="text/javascript">
  function dateDifference(date1,date2){
    var timeDivision = 1000 * 60 * 60 * 24;
    var DSTFix = (date2.getTimezoneOffset() - date1.getTimezoneOffset()) * 60000;
    var dateDiff = date2.getTime() - date1.getTime() - DSTFix;
    var totalDays = dateDiff/timeDivision;
    return totalDays;
  }
  var firstDate = new Date(); var secondDate = newDate();
  secondDate.setDate(secondDate.getDate()+3);
  var theDays = dateDifference(firstDate,secondDate);
  alert(theDays);
</script>
```

Check If a Date Is in a Range

You can add form validation to a page to make sure that a date is within a set date range. This check makes sure that the date is valid. This check also makes sure that the date the user filled out is correct and lessens the bandwidth needed with server side validation.

The first thing that you need to do is to create three date objects. The first date object is the beginning date of the range. The second date object is the ending date of the range. The third date object is the date that the user submitted.

Then you can use a greater than or less than comparison in an if statement to find out if the date is within the set range. For example, the statement if(startDate < userDate && endDate > userDate) return true; validates the user date to make sure it falls within the set range.

You may want to limit the user to picking a date that is a certain amount of days from the present date. For this operation, you need to use the setDate() method along with the getDate() method. To calculate a date in the future you add it to the getDate() method. For example, the statement startDate.setDate(startDate.getDate() + 5); adds five days to the date stored in the startDate object.

You can also check to see if a date is a weekday or a weekend. This is important if your business is only open Monday thru Friday. You need to use the getDay() method. If the value from the getDay() method is 1 thru 5 then it is a weekday. The value 0 represents Sunday and the value 6 represents Saturday.

Check If a Date Is in a Range

① Create a function that accepts three parameters.

② Add three variables and set them equal to the new Date() object.

③ Adjust the values of the dates by adding the range values.

④ Compare the dates and return true or false.

⑤ Call the function passing the parameters.

⑥ Save the document.

⑦ Open the file in a Web browser.

- The Booleans appear verifying that the dates are in or out of the specified range of dates.

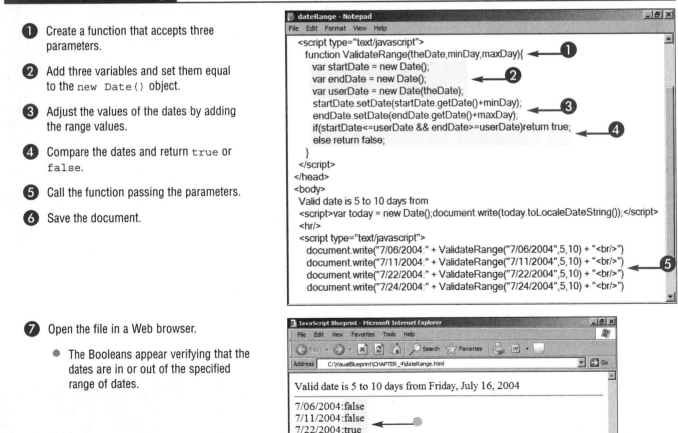

Convert Between Time Zones

You can convert between time zones to create clocks that are based in other parts of the world. This allows you to show the time in London while the user is in New York. This is great for company Web sites that have employees spread out across the globe.

The first step is to create a `new Date()` object for each time zone in which you want to have a working clock. After you create a `new Date()` object for each time zone, you need to find out what time zone the user is currently in. To do this you use the `getTimezoneOffset()` method.

The `getTimezoneOffset()` method returns the number of minutes the user's computer clock is set from the Greenwich Mean Time. You then need to know the number of hours of difference between the time zone you want to convert the user's time to and the Greenwich Mean Time. London is one hour ahead of the Greenwich Mean

Time. New York is four hours behind the Greenwich Mean Time.

To update the date object to reflect the new time zone, you need to use the `setUTCHours()` method. Inside the `setUTCHours()` parentheses, you need to assign the new hour value of the new time zone. To do this you need to get the current UTC Hour value, which you can do by using the `getUTCHours()` method. You need to add the UTC Hour to the time zone offset of the user. You also need to add the known time zone offset. For example, you would add negative four for New York.

If you want to view the whole time and date string, you can use the `toLocaleString()` method. To view the time, you can use `toLocaleTimeString()` method. The locale methods are the best to use since it puts the date into the user's everyday format.

Convert Between Time Zones

1 Create a `new Date()` object for each time zone.

2 Add the `setUTCHours()` method, the `getUTCHours()` method, the `getTimezoneOffset()` method, and the time difference.

3 Add statements to display each time zone on the screen.

4 Use a `setInterval()` method to start the clock.

5 Save the file.

6 Open the file in a Web browser.

- Two running clocks display with the adjusted time zone values.

```
tzClock - Notepad
File Edit Format View Help
<script type="text/javascript">
  function TZClock(){
    nYork = new Date();
    london = new Date();                                    ——1
    nYork.setUTCHours(nYork.getUTCHours()-4+nYork.getTimezoneOffset()/60);
    london.setUTCHours(london.getUTCHours()+1+london.getTimezoneOffset()/60);  ——2
    document.getElementById("ny").value= nYork.toLocaleTimeString();
    document.getElementById("ld").value= london.toLocaleTimeString();  ——3
  }
</script>
</head>
<body onload="setInterval('TZClock()',100)">                 ——4
<form name="TZ">
 <table border="1" cellspacing="0" cellpadding="5">
  <tr>
   <td>New York</td>
   <td>London</td>
  </tr>
  <tr>
   <td id="ny1"><input type="text" name="ny" size="10"></td>
   <td id="ld1"><input type="text" name="ld" size="10"></td>
```

```
JavaScript Blueprint - Microsoft Internet Explorer
File Edit View Favorites Tools Help
Back ·  ·  Search  Favorites  ·
Address  C:\VisualBlueprint\CHAPTER_4\tzClock.html        Go
```

New York	London
2:32:50 PM	7:32:50 PM

Create a Countdown Timer

Y ou can create a countdown timer to show how many days there are until an event. You can break the timer down to as far as you want. This is a great way to count down to a holiday.

The first step is to create a function that accepts a date parameter. The date parameter then converts to a date object. You also need to get the current date and time, so you have something to compare the event date to.

Then, you need to subtract the current date from the event date. The result of this mathematical operation is the amount of milliseconds between the two dates. If the number is negative, then the event has already happened.

Next, you need to split the number of milliseconds into time divisions. To do this, you need to know how many milliseconds there are in each time division. There are 86,400,000 milliseconds in a day, 3,600,000 milliseconds

in an hour, 60,000 milliseconds in a minute, and 1000 milliseconds in a second.

The first step is to divide by the number of milliseconds in a day to find the amount of days in that time period. You need to round the answer down by using the Math.floor() method to remove the remainder. After that step, you need to subtract that amount of time from the time difference. You then need to calculate the number of hours, minutes, and seconds remaining. The remainder after the seconds calculates is the number of milliseconds left.

You can make this countdown into a timer by using a setInterval() method. The setInterval() method needs to call the function to calculate the time difference. If you are breaking the time interval all the way down to milliseconds, then you should update the script every millisecond.

Create a Countdown Timer

① Create a group of global variables to calculate number of milliseconds in each part.

② Create a function that accepts two input parameters.

③ Create two new Date() objects with one using the current date and one using the event date.

④ Find the number of milliseconds between the two dates by subtracting the values.

⑤ Check to see if the date has already passed.

⑥ Calculate the days, minutes, seconds, and milliseconds left until the date.

⑦ Create an output string to display the result.

⑧ Display the output string on the page.

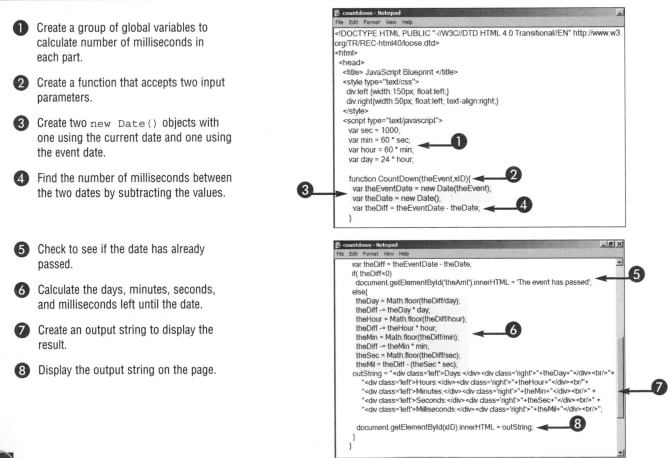

9 Use a `setInterval()` method to create a running timer placing the date parameter and output location into the function call along with the time interval.

10 Save the file.

```
        theMin = Math.floor(theDiff/min);
        theDiff -= theMin * min;
        theSec = Math.floor(theDiff/sec);
        theMil = theDiff - (theSec * sec);
      outString = "<div class='left'>Days:</div><div class='right'>"+theDay+"</div><br/>"+
        "<div class='left'>Hours:</div><div class='right'>"+theHour+"</div><br/"+
        "<div class='left'>Minutes:</div><div class='right'>"+theMin+"</div><br/>" +
        "<div class='left'>Seconds:</div><div class='right'>"+theSec+"</div><br/>" +
        "<div class='left'>Milliseconds:</div><div class='right'>"+theMil+"</div><br/>";

      document.getElementById(xID).innerHTML = outString;
    }
  }
 </script>
</head>
<body onload="setInterval('CountDown(\'12/25/2004\',\'theAmt\')',1)">    ◄── 9
 <p>Days Till Christmas<hr/>
  <div id="theAmt"></div>
 </p>
</body>
</html>
```

11 Open the file in a Web browser.

● The amount of time to the event is counting down.

Days Till Christmas

Days:	161
Hours:	10
Minutes:	25
Seconds:	0
Milliseconds:	750

Extra

You can use the count time timer to create an alarm clock type of script. You can have the window perform a specific action when the event counts down to the time. For example, you can have a new window pop up at noon to tell you that it is lunch time. The following code sample shows you how to alter the function in the example to create a daily reminder.

```
        var theEventDate = new Date();
        theEventDate.setHours(12);
        theEventDate.setMinutes(0);
        theEventDate.setSeconds(0);
        theEventDate.setMilliseconds(0);
        function CountDown(theEvent){
          var theDate = new Date();
          var theDiff = theEventDate - theDate;
          if(theDiff==0) window.open("notify.html");
          else if(theDiff<0) document.getElementById('theAmt').innerHTML = 'The
event has passed';
          else{
```

Create a Running Clock with Images

You can create a clock with images to make it appear to be a digital clock. This adds a unique feel to your site and allows you to customize the pictures to be any picture you desire.

The first step is to create an image for the numbers zero through nine, a blank holder, a dividing symbol, and AM and PM symbols. Then add an image tag for every element in the time string. This includes two image tags for the hour, one image tag to divide the hour and minute, two image tags for the minutes, one image tag to divide the minutes and seconds, two image tags for the seconds, and one image tag for the AM and PM. Each of these tags should be given a name. You can also apply CSS classes.

The next step is to create a function that puts the current time into the string format of your choosing. After the

current time is stored into a variable, you need to split the time into the hours, minutes, and seconds parts.

Then you need to apply the numbers of the time string to the images. The hour may have one or two digits for which you need to check. Checking the length of the string verifies the number of digits. If the string contains two digits, then you need to separate the two numbers from each other. You can accomplish this with the split() method. The seconds have four characters. The first two represent the numbers and the second two correspond to the AM or PM.

You need to add a setInterval() method on the page load event handler to start the clock and allow it to update on a regular interval.

Create a Running Clock with Images

① Create a function to create a running clock.

② Add a variable and set it to a new Date() object.

③ Convert the time to a string format.

④ Split the time string into the hour, minute, and second parts.

```
imageClock - Notepad
File  Edit  Format  View  Help
<!DOCTYPE HTML PUBLIC "-//W3C//DTD HTML 4.0 Transitional//EN" http://www.w3.
org/TR/REC-html40/loose.dtd>
<html>
 <head>
  <title> JavaScript Blueprint </title>
  <script type="text/javascript">
    function ImageClock(){           ①
     var thePic = "num";
     var theDate = new Date();       ②
     var theTime = theDate.toLocaleTimeString();   ③
     theTime = theTime.split(":");   ④
    }
  </script>
 </head>
 </body>
 </body>
</html>
```

⑤ Determine if you need to place a filler image in the first position and set the hour images by using the slice() method.

⑥ Determine the images to display for the minutes and seconds by using the slice() method.

⑦ Set the picture for the hour and minute division.

⑧ Determine if the time string contains AM or PM and display the correct image.

```
imageClock - Notepad
File  Edit  Format  View  Help
   theTime = theTime.split(":");
   if(theTime[0].length==1){
    document.getElementById("img0").src = thePic + "No.gif";
    document.getElementById("img1").src = thePic + theTime[0] + ".gif";
   }
   else{                            ⑤
    document.getElementById("img0").src = thePic + theTime[0].slice(0,1) + ".gif";
    document.getElementById("img1").src = thePic + theTime[0].slice(1,2) + ".gif";
   }
   document.getElementById("img2").src = thePic +  theTime[1].slice(0,1) + ".gif";
   document.getElementById("img3").src = thePic +  theTime[1].slice(1,2) + ".gif";   ⑥
   document.getElementById("img4").src = thePic +  theTime[2].slice(0,1) + ".gif";
   document.getElementById("img5").src = thePic +  theTime[2].slice(1,2) + ".gif";
   document.getElementById("dot1").src = thePic +  "dots.gif";   ⑦
   document.getElementById("dot2").src = thePic +  "dots.gif";

   if(theTime[2].length==5)                                          ⑧
    document.getElementById("img6").src = thePic + theTime[2].slice(3,5) + ".gif";
   else document.getElementById("img6").style.display = "none";
   }
  </script>
```

9 Create an `onload` handler to initialize the clock with a `setInterval()` method.

10 Create all images with the correct names to display the time.

Note: The reason for the one line of images is to avoid spaces in between the images with Internet Explorer.

11 Save the file.

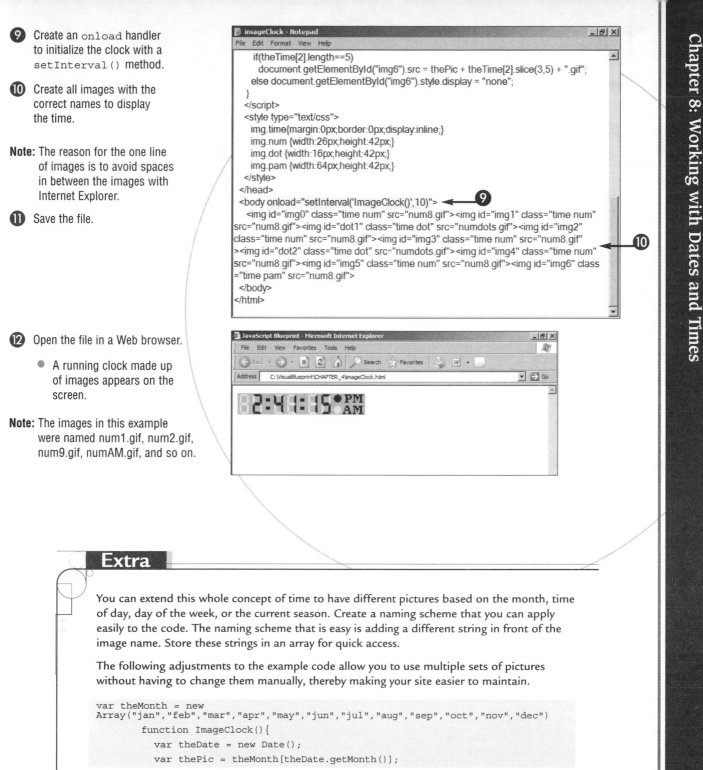

12 Open the file in a Web browser.

● A running clock made up of images appears on the screen.

Note: The images in this example were named num1.gif, num2.gif, num9.gif, numAM.gif, and so on.

Extra

You can extend this whole concept of time to have different pictures based on the month, time of day, day of the week, or the current season. Create a naming scheme that you can apply easily to the code. The naming scheme that is easy is adding a different string in front of the image name. Store these strings in an array for quick access.

The following adjustments to the example code allow you to use multiple sets of pictures without having to change them manually, thereby making your site easier to maintain.

```
var theMonth = new
Array("jan","feb","mar","apr","may","jun","jul","aug","sep","oct","nov","dec")
        function ImageClock(){
            var theDate = new Date();
            var thePic = theMonth[theDate.getMonth()];
```

Store the new leading names of the images into the array. For example, if the month was August, the image set would contain images `aug1.gif`, `aug2.gif`, `augAM.gif`, and so on.

Employ Mathematical Constants

You can use the Math object to correspond to several mathematical constants. These constants are normally used in various mathematical equations and give you uniform results when programming. For example, most people use 3.14 for the value of PI; the JavaScript constant for PI is 3.141592653589793 which returns a more accurate result in an equation. A mathematical constant allows you to get an accurate number with a minimum amount of typing. Instead of typing out a sixteen or seventeen digit number, which most of the JavaScript constants contain. You can reference the Math object with the constant keyword which is about seven to ten characters.

You can use the PI constant by using Math.PI in an equation. The JavaScript constants are inserted anywhere in an equation where a constant value would normally appear. For example, the statement cir1 = 2 * Math.PI * radius; finds the circumference of a circle.

Two other constants that JavaScript has built into the Math object are the square root of one half (Math.SQRT1_2) and the square root of two (Math.SQRT2). You can find other square root values by using the Math.SQRT() method, which is explained later in this chapter.

Other constants that the Math object contains are the Euler's constant (Math.E), the natural logarithm of 10 (Math.LN10), the natural logarithm of 2 (Math.LN2), the base-10 logarithm of Euler's constant (Math.LOG10E), and the base-2 logarithm of Euler's constant (Math.LOG2E).

You can create your own constants by creating a new object. For example, the statement var mathC = {abc:213;def:911} creates an object in which you can store the constants. To use the constant, you can reference it by using mathC.abc and mathC.def.

Employ Mathematical Constants

DISPLAY CONSTANT VALUES

① Declare the constants in document.write() statements.

② Save the file.

```
mathConstant.html - Notepad
File  Edit  Format  View  Help
<html>
 <head>
  <title> JavaScript Blueprint</title>
   </head>
 <body>
 <script type="text/javascript">
   document.write("PI = " + Math.PI + "<br/>");
   document.write("SQRT1_2 = " + Math.SQRT1_2 + "<br/>");
   document.write("SQRT2 = " + Math.SQRT2 + "<br/>");
   document.write("E = " + Math.E + "<br/>");
   document.write("LN10 = " + Math.LN10 + "<br/>");
   document.write("LN2 = " + Math.LN2 + "<br/>");
   document.write("LOG10E = " + Math.LOG10E + "<br/>");
   document.write("LOG2E = " + Math.LOG2E + "<br/>");
 </script>
 </body>
</html>
```
➊

③ Open the file in a Web browser.

● The values of the constants appear.

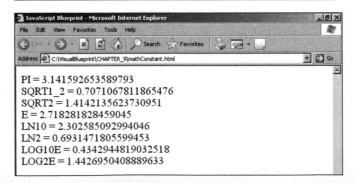

```
JavaScript Blueprint - Microsoft Internet Explorer
File  Edit  View  Favorites  Tools  Help
Back        Search    Favorites
Address  C:\VisualBlueprint\CHAPTER_9\mathConstant.html        Go

PI = 3.141592653589793
SQRT1_2 = 0.7071067811865476
SQRT2 = 1.4142135623730951
E = 2.718281828459045
LN10 = 2.302585092994046
LN2 = 0.6931471805599453
LOG10E = 0.4342944819032518
LOG2E = 1.4426950408889633
```

USE CONSTANTS IN AN EQUATION

 Add a constant declaration in the equation.

2 Repeat step **1** for each additional constant declaration.

3 Save the file.

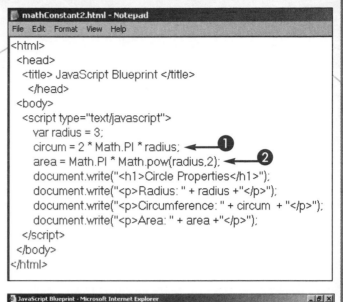

4 Open the file in a Web browser.

● The results of the equations appear.

Extra

You can use absolute values to return positive values back to the user when subtracting two numbers from the input fields. This eliminates the need to have an `if-else` check when you are doing subtraction of the numbers. The `Math.abs()` method accepts one numeric parameter in the parentheses.

```
var int1 = parseInt(document.Form1.T1.value);
var int2 = parseInt(document.Form1.T2.value);
var answer1 = Math.abs(int2 - int1)
```

The next set of statements is one way to make sure that the number in the answer is positive without using the Math object.

```
var int1 = parseInt(document.Form1.T1.value);
var int2 = parseInt(document.Form1.T2.value);
if (int1>int2){
  answer1 = int1 - int2;
}
else {
  answer1 = int2 - int1;
}
```

Apply Trigonometric Functions

You can use trigonometric functions from your trigonometry class in your JavaScript application by using the JavaScript Math object. The JavaScript Math object supports sine, cosine, and tangent functions. JavaScript also supports their opposite functions, which are arc-sine, arc-cosine, and arc-tangent.

The methods for these functions are `Math.sin()`, `Math.cos()`, `Math.tan()`, `Math.asin()`, `Math.acos()`, and `Math.atan()`. Each of these trigonometric function methods takes a single input in the parentheses. For example, the statement `ang1 = cos(Math.PI)` stores `-1` in the variable `ang1`. The numeric input should be in radians and not degrees. The result returned from the trigonometric function methods is also in radians.

You can convert degrees into radians by using the mathematical expression `radians = degrees * Math.PI / 180;`. For example, `90 degrees` is `90 * Math.PI / 180` which equals `1.5707963267948965 radians`. You can

have a more accurate result by using the Math object constant for PI, instead of the standard 3.14 that people tend to use because of the amount of significant digits.

JavaScript also has another trigonometric method that converts standard x and y coordinate values to an angular measurement. The method is `Math.atan2()`, which accepts two parameters — the x location and the y location. For example, the statement `Math.atan2(1,1)*180/Math.PI` returns `45` degrees with the `x` and `y` positions at the location `(1,1)`.

The Math object's trigonometric methods are commonly used in cursor trailing scripts and DHTML analog clocks that calculate the position of the elements from a central point. The analog clock calculates the position of the hands from the center of the dial. The mouse trailer uses the trigonometric methods to calculate the position of the element relative to the cursor's position on the screen.

Apply Trigonometric Functions

SIN COS TAN

① Add Math object declarations for sin, cos, and tan.

② Add radian values inside the parentheses.

③ Display the values using `document.write()` statements.

④ Save the file.

```html
trig1.html - Notepad
File  Edit  Format  View  Help

<html>
 <head>
  <title> JavaScript Blueprint </title>
  </head>
 <body>
  <script type="text/javascript">
    var radians = 0;
    var ansSin = Math.sin(radians);
    var ansCos = Math.cos(radians);
    var ansTan = Math.tan(radians);

    document.write("<p>sin(" + radians + ") = " + ansSin +"</p>");
    document.write("<p>cos(" + radians + ") = " + ansCos + "</p>");
    document.write("<p>tan(" + radians + ") = " + ansTan +"</p>");
  </script>
 </body>
</html>
```

⑤ Open the file in a Web browser.

● The results of the trig methods appear.

```
JavaScript Blueprint - Microsoft Internet Explorer
File  Edit  View  Favorites  Tools  Help
Back ·   ·         Search   Favorites
Address  C:\VisualBlueprint\CHAPTER_9\trig1.html          Go

sin(0) = 0

cos(0) = 1

tan(0) = 0
```

ASIN ACOS ATAN

1. Add Math object declarations for asin, acos, and atan.

2. Add radian values inside the parentheses.

3. Display the values using `document.write()` statements.

4. Save the file.

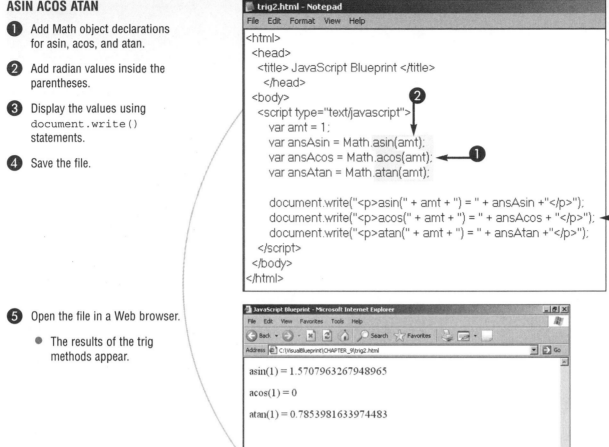

```
trig2.html - Notepad
File  Edit  Format  View  Help

<html>
 <head>
  <title> JavaScript Blueprint </title>
   </head>
 <body>
  <script type="text/javascript">
    var amt = 1;
    var ansAsin = Math.asin(amt);
    var ansAcos = Math.acos(amt);
    var ansAtan = Math.atan(amt);

    document.write("<p>asin(" + amt + ") = " + ansAsin +"</p>");
    document.write("<p>acos(" + amt + ") = " + ansAcos + "</p>");
    document.write("<p>atan(" + amt + ") = " + ansAtan +"</p>");
  </script>
 </body>
</html>
```

5. Open the file in a Web browser.

- The results of the trig methods appear.

```
JavaScript Blueprint - Microsoft Internet Explorer
File  Edit  View  Favorites  Tools  Help
Back        Search    Favorites
Address  C:\VisualBlueprint\CHAPTER_9\trig2.html        Go

asin(1) = 1.5707963267948965

acos(1) = 0

atan(1) = 0.7853981633974483
```

Apply It

You can make an image rotate around a point on a page by using trigonometric methods along with DHTML and a `setInterval()` method. By making things move on the page, you can draw the user's eye to a certain section of the page. This function animates an object around the origin located at 50 pixels from the top and bottom of the screen. You can learn more about animating objects in Chapter 16.

```
<script type="text/javascript">
  var curLocation = 0; var stepSize = 5;
  var radius = 30;
  var centerX = 50; var centerY = 50;
  function MoveImg(){
    posX = Math.cos(Math.PI/180*curLocation)*radius;
    posY = Math.sin(Math.PI/180*curLocation)*radius;
    curLocation += stepSize;
    document.getElementById("spinImg").style.left=(centerX+posX) + "px";
    document.getElementById("spinImg").style.top=(centerY+posY) + "px";
  }
  window.onload = setInterval("MoveImg()",1);
</script>
<img src="ball.gif" id="spinImg"
style="width:20px;height:20px;position:absolute;">
```

Square Root and Power

You can use methods built into JavaScript's Math object to work with square roots and powers. Square roots and powers allow you to create more powerful mathematical expressions while simplifying some of the processes.

You can compute the square root of a number by using the `Math.sqrt()` method. The square root receives a number as a parameter in the parentheses and returns its square root. The format of the number is a floating-point because it contains decimal places. For example, the statement `x = Math.sqrt(16);` takes the square root of 16, resulting in the value 4 being stored in the variable x.

An example where the square root method is used is in computing the Pythagorean theorem (the square of two sides of a triangle equals the square of the hypotenuse).

You can compute the power of a number by using the `Math.pow()` method. The power method accepts two parameters in the parentheses. The first parameter is the number, and the second parameter is the power to which the number is raised.

For example, the statement `y = Math.pow(10,3);` raises the number 10 to the power of 3, resulting in a value of 1000 being stored in the variable y.

You can also use the `Math.pow()` method to compute square roots. To do this, you have to set the power to the value of 1/2. For example, the statement `Math.pow(2,1/2)` is equivalent to `Math.sqrt(2)`.

The `Math.pow()` method is commonly used in rounding scripts to move the decimal to the right and left. For example, the statement `var bigNum = 24.5 * Math.pow(10,4)` moves the decimal point to the right 4 places. The decimal number can be moved back to the left by either dividing the result by `Math.pow(10,4)` or multiplying the result by `Math.pow(10,-4)`.

Square Root and Power

① Add the Math object for power with the parameters in the parentheses.

② Add the Math object for square root with the parameter in the parentheses.

③ Display the values using `document.write()` statements.

④ Save the file.

⑤ Open the file in a Web browser.

● The results of the power and square root methods appear.

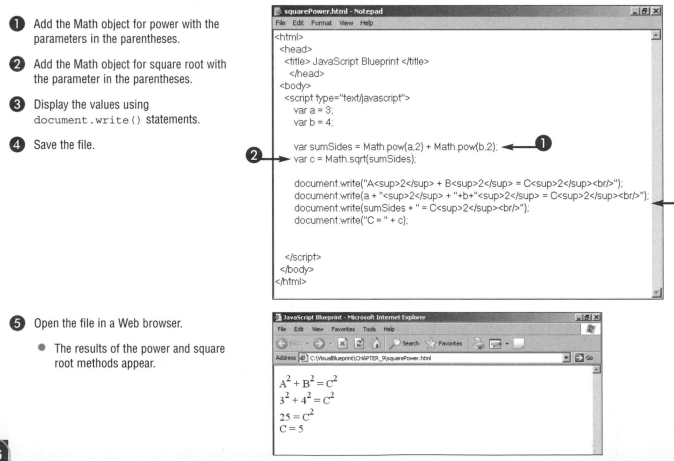

Find Minimum and Maximum Values

You can use built-in functions to find the minimum and maximum values instead of `if-else` statements. This eliminates the need for unnecessary `if` statements. These built-in methods also increase the performance of a script since it eliminates the need to use `if-else` statements, which slow down a script.

You can find the maximum value by using the `Math.max()` method. The method accepts two parameters inside the parentheses separated by a comma. The `Math.max()` method returns the value that is the greater of the two. For example, the statement `var big = Math.max(5,3);` stores the value 5 in the variable `big`.

You can find the minimum value by using the `Math.min()` method. The method also accepts two parameters separated by a comma. The `Math.min()` method returns the value that is less than the other value.

For example, the statement `var small = Math.min(5,3);` stores the value 3 in the variable `small`.

These methods are very useful with a shopping cart. You may have a special deal that has buy one item get one half off the price of equal or lesser value. Using the `Math.min()` property can help you select which item should be free. For example, the statement `var totalAmt = item1 + item2 - Math.min(item1,item2)/2;` calculates the total cost of the purchase determining which item is half price. If the sale is buy one item get one free of equal or lesser value, the statement `var total = Math.max(item1,item2);` finds the shopper's total amount due.

The `Math.min()` and `Math.max()` methods are limited to two parameters; therefore, you must either run the method multiple times or use an array with the `sort()` method. The `sort()` method is discussed in Chapter 2.

Find Minimum and Maximum Values

① Add Math object declaration for min with the two number parameters in the parentheses.

② Add Math object declaration for max with the two number parameters in the parentheses.

③ Display the values using `document.write()` statements.

④ Save the file.

⑤ Open the file in a Web browser.

● The results of the min and max methods appear.

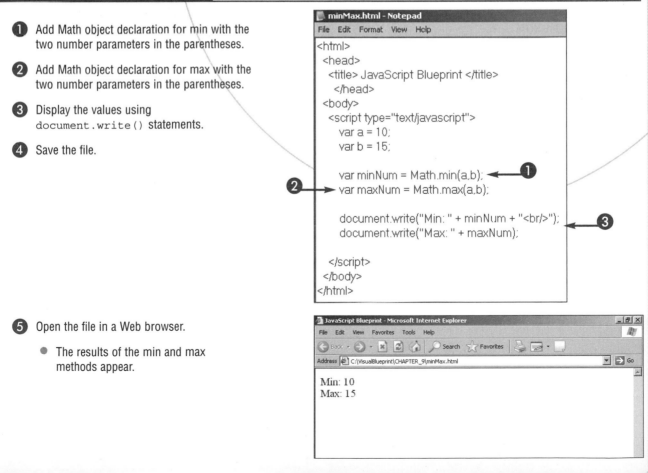

```
minMax.html - Notepad
File   Edit   Format   View   Help
<html>
 <head>
  <title> JavaScript Blueprint </title>
   </head>
 <body>
  <script type="text/javascript">
    var a = 10;
    var b = 15;

    var minNum = Math.min(a,b);        ①
    var maxNum = Math.max(a,b);    ②

    document.write("Min: " + minNum + "<br/>");   ③
    document.write("Max: " + maxNum);

  </script>
 </body>
</html>
```

```
JavaScript Blueprint - Microsoft Internet Explorer
File   Edit   View   Favorites   Tools   Help
Address  C:\VisualBlueprint\CHAPTER_9\minMax.html

Min: 10
Max: 15
```

Generate Random Numbers

Y ou can generate random numbers for a number of different purposes such as displaying different images, text, links, and so on. This can make your Web site dynamic and interesting.

The Math.round() method produces a number between 0 and 1. You can multiply this random number by another number to develop a range. The result does not produce an integer, but you can make it an integer by using the Math.floor() method. The Math.floor() method truncates the number after the decimal point. For example, the statement var x = Math.floor(Math.random() * 5); returns a random number between 0 and 4.

You are not limited to a range starting at zero. You can change the range by adding an integer to the statement. For example, the statement var x = Math.floor(Math. random() * 6 + 5); stores a random number between 5 and 10 in the variable x.

You can also make the random number negative by

multiplying by a negative number. For example, the statement var y = Math.floor(Math.random() *-20+10); produces a random number that has a range of -10 to 10.

You can use a weighted random number so there is a greater chance certain values appear more often than others. You can control how many times a number appears by using an array. Each element in the array holds a certain value. You can add more elements that contain the number, if you want the number to have better odds of appearing.

```
var theNumbers = new Array(1,2,2,3,3,3);
var x = Math.floor(Math.random() *
theNumbers.length);
var thePick = theNumbers[x];
```

The weighted random number is stored in the variable thePick. The chances of the number 1 appearing is one out of six, the number 2 is one out of four, and the number 3 is one out of two.

Generate Random Numbers

DEVELOP RANDOM NUMBERS

① Add a Math object declaration for the random method multiplying it by the number of images.

② Add a Math object declaration for the floor method to round the random number.

③ Use the random number to display an image.

④ Save the file.

DEVELOP A TIMER

① Develop the function that creates an interval to switch the random image.

② Add the onload() event handler to the <body> tag.

③ Save the file.

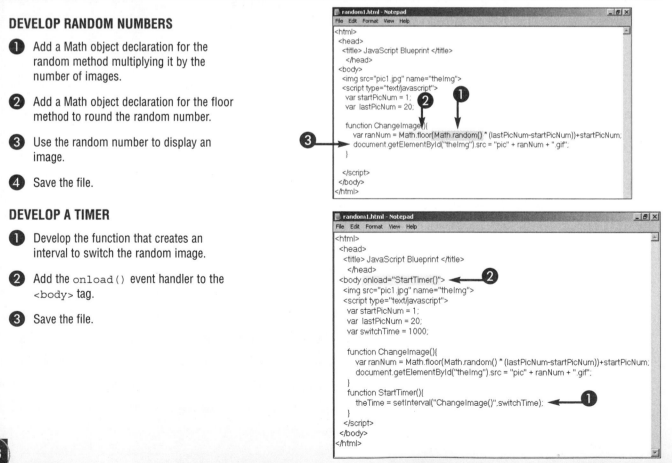

WATCH THE RANDOMNESS

 ① Open the file in a Web browser.

- An initial image appears.

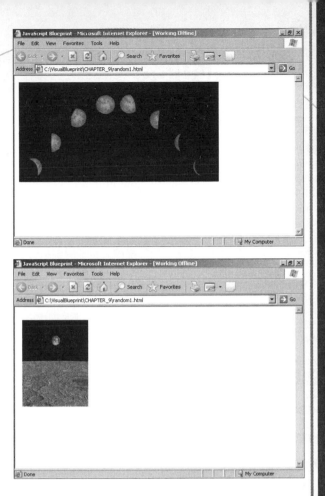

② Wait until the image changes.

- Another random image appears.

Note: The random image swap continues until the user leaves the Web page.

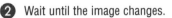
Apply It

You can display random content on the page to offer new information to the user. The random content may be quotes, links, images, banners, and so on. The basic idea behind random information is having an array filled with the different items. A random number is generated according to the length of the array. The following code uses a two-dimensional array to hold the link descriptive text and the hyperlink. The random link is written to the page wherever the script is included.

```
<script type="text/javascript">
  var linkArray = new Array();
  linkArray[0] = new Array("Programming Help","http://www.JavaRanch.com");
  linkArray[1] = new Array("Books","http://www.Wiley.com");
  linkArray[2] = new Array("Search Engine","http://www.google.com");

  var num = Math.floor(Math.random()*linkArray.length);
  document.write("<a href='" + linkArray[num][1] + "'>" +  linkArray[num][0] +
"</a>");
</script>
```

Round Numbers Using Methods

You can round a number by using a built-in method in the Math object that allows you to always have integers without decimal places. The `Math.round()` method accepts one parameter in the parentheses. The method will round to the nearest whole number. Therefore, if the first decimal place is greater than or equal to 5, the number is rounded up. If the number is less than 5, the decimal places are dropped. For example, the statement `var num = Math.round(4.5173);` stores the value of 5 in the variable `num` because the first decimal is greater than or equal to 5.

You can round a number to a specific decimal position by using the `Math.round()` method and multiplying the number by a power of 10 to move the decimal point. Then divide the result of `Math.round()` method by the same power of 10. For example, the statement `var num =`

`Math.round(theNum * 100)/100;` rounds the variable `theNum` to the second decimal place.

You can also use two other methods to round numbers up or down by using the `Math.floor()` and `Math.ceil()` methods. The `Math.floor()` rounds the number down to the nearest integer. For example, the statement `var x = Math.floor(1.56);` rounds the number `1.56` and stores the value `1` in the variable `x`. The method can also be added to negative numbers. For example, `var y = Math.floor(-2.9);` stores the value `-3` into the variable `y`.

The `Math.ceil()` method rounds the number up to the nearest integer. For example, the statement `var x = Math.ceil(1.13);` rounds the number `1.13` and stores the value `2` in the variable `x`. Another example with a negative number, `var y = Math.ceil(-2.9);`, stores `-1` into the variable `y`.

Round Numbers Using Methods

ROUND NUMBERS

① Multiply the number you want to round by the number of decimal places you want to move.

② Add the Math object declaration for rounding with the number parameter in the parentheses.

③ Divide the rounded number by the number of decimal places you want to move back.

④ Save the file.

⑤ Open the file in a Web browser.

● The results of the rounded numbers appear.

● The zero is dropped because JavaScript does not keep trailing zeros.

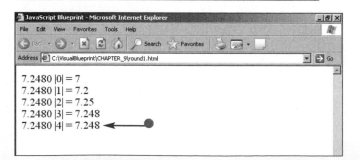

```
round1.html - Notepad
File  Edit  Format  View  Help
<html>
 <head>
  <title> JavaScript Blueprint </title>
   </head>
 <body>
  <script type="text/javascript">
   function roundNumber(theNum,places){
     var mDec = Math.pow(10,places)
     var roundNum = Math.round(theNum*mDec)/mDec;
     return roundNum
   }
   var exStr = "7.2480";
   var ex = parseFloat(exStr);
   document.write(exStr + " |0| = " + roundNumber(ex,0) + "<br/>");
   document.write(exStr + " |1| = " + roundNumber(ex,1) + "<br/>");
   document.write(exStr + " |2| = " + roundNumber(ex,2) + "<br/>");
   document.write(exStr + " |3| = " + roundNumber(ex,3) + "<br/>");
   document.write(exStr + " |4| = " + roundNumber(ex,4) + "<br/>");
  </script>
 </body>
</html>
```

```
JavaScript Blueprint - Microsoft Internet Explorer
File  Edit  View  Favorites  Tools  Help
Back         Search    Favorites
Address  C:\VisualBlueprint\CHAPTER_9\round1.html          Go

7.2480 |0| = 7
7.2480 |1| = 7.2
7.2480 |2| = 7.25
7.2480 |3| = 7.248
7.2480 |4| = 7.248
```

ROUND UP AND DOWN

① Develop a random number generator.

② Add the Math object declaration for the round, floor, and ceil methods with the number parameter in the parentheses.

③ Save the file.

④ Open the file in a Web browser.

- The results of the rounded numbers appear.

- The floor numbers are rounded down; the ceil numbers are rounded up.

```
round2.html - Notepad
File Edit Format View Help
<body>
  <table border="1" cellpadding="2" cellspacing="0">
  <tr>
   <td>Number</td>
   <td>Round</td>
   <td>Floor</td>
   <td>Ceil</td>
  </tr>
  <script type="text/javascript">
    for(i=0;i<10;i++){
      var ranNum = Math.random() * 10;        ①
      if(i==7)ranNum=7;
      document.write("<tr >");
      document.write("<td>"+ ranNum +"</td>");
      document.write("<td>"+ Math.round(ranNum) +"</td>");
      document.write("<td>"+ Math.floor(ranNum) +"</td>");
      document.write("<td>"+ Math.ceil(ranNum) +"</td>");
      document.write("</tr>");
    }
  </script>
  </table>                            ②
```

JavaScript Blueprint - Microsoft Internet Explorer
File Edit View Favorites Tools Help
Address C:\VisualBlueprint\CHAPTER_9\round2.html

Number	Round	Floor	Ceil
8.366287432694783	8	8	9
3.2050291692856354	3	3	4
2.387198247624465	2	2	3
5.940470279612028	6	5	6
2.104456305363234	2	2	3
8.832648376425067	9	8	9
7.500849226598221	8	7	8
7	7	7	7
2.22363116893331462	2	2	3
3.584483240912521	4	3	4

Apply It

You can keep the decimal places when you use the rounding method by changing the variable to a string. This keeps the trailing zeros from being dropped off. This is important to use when you are dealing with money, where you need two decimal places.

```
function holdZeros(theNumber,numPlaces){
  var num = Math.round(theNumber*numPlaces)/numPlaces;
  var strNum = num.toString();
  return strNum;
}
var amount = 13.12;
var tax = 0.055;
var theTotal = holdZeros(tax * amount,2);
alert("Your total: $" + theTotal);
```

You need to change the returned values from the function back to floating-point numbers if you want to perform any mathematical functions to them. To do this you can use the parseFloat() method. The two string values are added together instead of being joined end to end. For example, 123+123 is 246 and not 123123.

Format Large Numbers with Commas

You can display formatted numbers with commas to make it easier for the user to read. For example, it is easier for a person to read 1,000,000,000 than it is to read 1000000000. You can also use this method to add a currency sign to the beginning of the number if you desire.

The first step is to convert the number to a string using the toString() method. You need to do this to manipulate the number using string methods. If you do not convert it to a string and try using a string method, an error occurs which stops the execution of the script.

You then need to separate the string at the decimal point so you can work with the whole numbers. To do this you need to use the split() method. The statement theStr = theStr.split("."); splits the whole numbers from the fractional numbers.

The next step is to loop backwards through the whole number string and grab a sub string. You need to separate the large string into groups of three. If a group of three can be made, then you need to add a comma in front of it. If the string length that is left is less than three, then you just take that portion.

You then add the smaller portion together to build the formatted string. After the loop is finished, you can add the decimal and any currency sign that you want to the function.

Since this method converts the number to a formatted string, you cannot perform mathematical operations to this number. Either you need to keep the original version of the number in memory by using a variable or a form field, or you can remove the formatting from the string.

Format Large Numbers with Commas

1 Create a function that accepts two parameters.

2 Convert the numeric parameter to a string and store the result into a variable.

3 Split the string at the decimal point.

4 Create a variable containing a blank string.

5 Create a for loop that iterates by negative three from the end of the string to the beginning.

6 Group the characters by three if the remaining string is greater than three elements.

7 Add the remaining characters.

8 Add decimal numbers if they exist.

9 Return the formatted number.

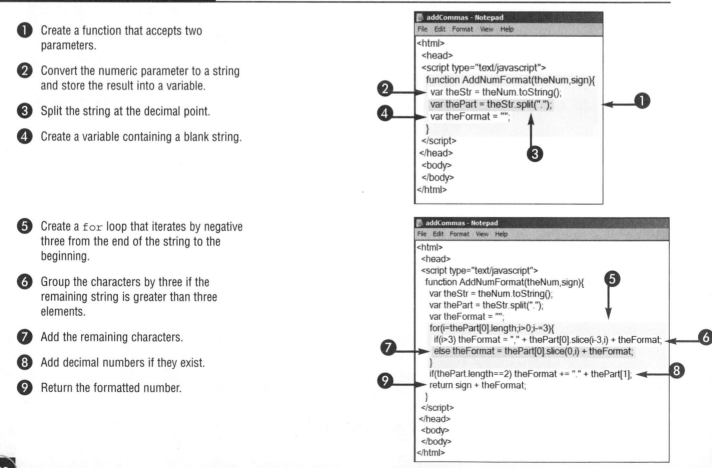

⑩ Call the function with the number and additional character parameters displaying the result with a `document.write` statement.

⑪ Save the file.

```
addCommas - Notepad
File  Edit  Format  View  Help
    var theStr = theNum.toString();
    var thePart = theStr.split(".");
    var theFormat = "";
    for(i=thePart[0].length;i>0;i-=3){
      if(i>3) theFormat = "," + thePart[0].slice(i-3,i) + theFormat;
      else theFormat = thePart[0].slice(0,i) + theFormat;
    }
    if(thePart.length==2) theFormat += "." + thePart[1];
    return sign + theFormat;
    }
  </script>
  </head>
  <body>
    <h1>Total Amount:<hr/></h1>
    <script type="text/javascript">
    var theTot = 123456789.00;
    var plusTax = theTot * 1.06;
    document.write(AddNumFormat(plusTax,"$"));   ◄── ⑩
    </script>
  </body>
</html>
```

● The formatted number appears on the screen with the dollar sign and commas.

```
C:\VisualBlueprint\CHAPTER_9\addCommas.html - Microsoft Internet Explorer
File  Edit  View  Favorites  Tools  Help
Back ▼  ▼  Search  Favorites
Address  C:\VisualBlueprint\CHAPTER_9\addCommas.html
```

Total Amount:

$130,864,196.34

Extra

You can remove the formatting from the string by using a string method. The string method `replace()` is a simple way to remove the characters that you have added to the number. The `replace()` method needs to use a regular expression to find the characters.

After the characters are stripped from the string, the string needs to be converted to a number using the `parseFloat()` method so the number can be used in mathematical calculations.

```
function RemoveFormat(theText){
  var reExp = /[,$]/gi;
  var theNum = theText.replace(reExp, "");
  return parseFloat(theNum);
}
```

To call this script, you need to set a variable equal to the function call with the formatted number inside the parentheses. The function returns a number which you are able to perform mathematical operations with.

```
var theTotal = RemoveFormat("$123,456,789.02");
var paymentDue = theTotal/2;
alert(paymentDue);
```

Write Content to the Window

You can use the window and document objects to manipulate the browser window and to determine browser properties. The window object is the top-level parent for all objects and includes the document, location, and the history objects as sub-objects.

The document object allows access to the various HTML elements that make up a Web page. In earlier chapters, the document object was used to retrieve form element values and for displaying text on the Web page by using the write() method.

The write() method outputs text and HTML code to the browser window. The write() statement is written as window.document.write() or document.write(). Both statements produce the same result. For example, the statement document.write("<h1>JavaScript<h1>"); displays the word JavaScript on the screen as a heading.

In addition to the document.write() method, JavaScript contains another method to display text on the page.

The writeln() method displays the passed parameter in the browser window along with a new line character at the end of the line. For example, the statements document. writeln("Visual"); document.writeln("Blueprint"); appear on a Web browser as JavaScript Blueprint. The Web browser interprets the new line character as a space. When you look at the source of the generated HTML code, the words JavaScript and Blueprint are displayed on separate lines.

The document.write() and document.writeln() methods are meant for using as the page is loading. You can use both the document.write() and document. writeln() methods after the page has been loaded, but the methods will overwrite all the existing HTML. You can avoid overwriting the entire HTML by using the innerHTML property in Chapter 15.

Write Content to the Window

① Add document.writeln() statements to the display strings.

② Add document.write() statements to the display strings.

③ Create a button to call the function.

④ Save the file.

```
window.html - Notepad
File  Edit  Format  View  Help
<head>
 <title> JavaScript Blueprint </title>
  </head>
<body>
  <script type="text/javascript">
    var str1 = "JavaScript:";
    var str2 = "Your visual blueprint";
    function writeContent(){
      document.writeln(str1);
      document.writeln(str2);        ①
      document.writeln("<br/>");
      document.write(str1);
      document.write(str2);          ②
      document.write("<br/>");
    }
  </script>
  <form name="F1">
    <input type="button" value="Click" onclick="writeContent()">   ③
  </form>
</body>
</html>
```

⑤ Open the file in a Web browser.

⑥ Click the button.

```
JavaScript Blueprint - Microsoft Internet Explorer
File  Edit  View  Favorites  Tools  Help
Back  ·    ·        Search    Favorites
Address  C:\VisualBlueprint\CHAPTER_10\window.html         Go

Click   ⑥
```

- Note that the `document.writeln()` string has extra spaces between the joined strings.

7 View the document source code.

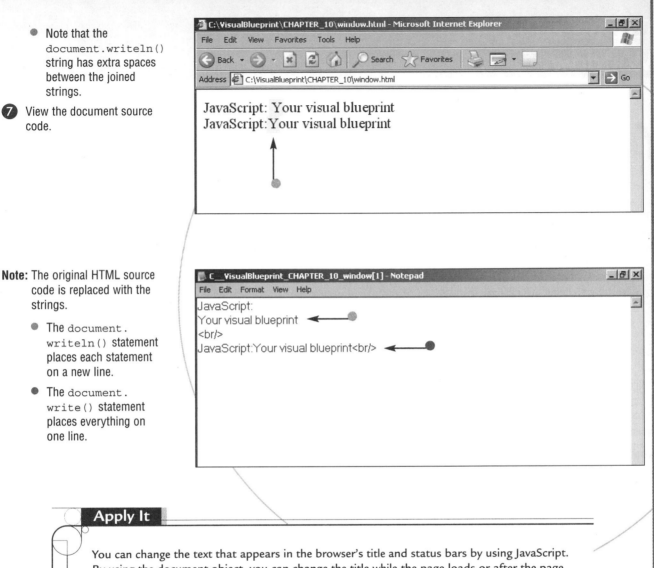

Note: The original HTML source code is replaced with the strings.

- The `document.writeln()` statement places each statement on a new line.

- The `document.write()` statement places everything on one line.

You can change the text that appears in the browser's title and status bars by using JavaScript. By using the document object, you can change the title while the page loads or after the page loads. You can reference the document object with the property `title`. By setting `document.title` to a string, the string is displayed in the browser's title bar. For example, the statement `document.title = new Date();` displays the current date in the title bar.

You can change the text in the status bar by using the window object. The `window.status` property is used to set the text in the status bar. For example, the statement `window.status = "Welcome"` displays the word `Welcome` in the status bar.

```
<body onload="setInterval('changeTime()',10)">
    <script type="text/javascript">
        document.title = "Dynamic Content";
        function changeTime(){
            var d = new Date();
            document.title = d.toLocaleString();
            window.status = d.toLocaleString();
        }
    </script>
</body>
```

Create a Pop-Up Window

You can open content in other windows so the user does not have to navigate away from the main page. Pop-up windows have a bad reputation because people often abuse the feature. Most pop-up blocker software blocks windows that are open without a click. That means most pop-up windows that open using onload(), setTimeout(), onunload(), and so on are now blocked. The window that spawned the pop-up window is considered the parent window. The pop-up window is called the child window.

You can create a pop-up window very easily. A pop-up window uses the window object. To open a window, you have to use the window.open() method. The window.open() method accepts many parameters that control the location, name, and browser properties. The parameters are added into the parentheses separated by commas.

The first parameter of the browser window is the location of the new window instance. For example, the statement window.open("http://www.javaranch. com"); opens a new browser instance to the Java Ranch's homepage when executed.

The second parameter that you can use is assigning the window a name. For example, the statement window. open("http://www.wiley.com","books"); opens the Wiley homepage in a window with the name books.

The third parameter is a group of parameters. These parameters are width, height, toolbar, location, directories, status, scrollbars, menubar, resizable, left, top, screenX, and screenY.

You can set the width and height of the new window by using the width and height parameters. The window's width and height are set in pixels (px). For most Web browsers, a pop-up window cannot be smaller then 100px x 100px.

The position of the browser window opens to any specific coordinates on the screen by using the left, top, screenX, and screenY parameters. These parameters also accept values in pixels; the top-left corner of the monitor is (0px, 0px). The location from the top of the screen is specified by top and screenY, while left and screenX set the position from the left of the screen. The reason why you need to set two parameters is for cross-browser issues. Some of the browsers use top and left, others use screenX and screenY. Just like the size restriction, some Web browsers disable the ability to make a window appear off the screen, especially in the negative x and y directions.

The rest of the parameters accept Boolean values. The value of 1 means the parameter is shown and 0 means it is not visible. You can remove or disable the toolbar, location bar, directories bar, status bar, scroll bars, menu bar, and resizable button. Other buttons and items like the close button, the minimize button, and the title bar cannot be hidden or disabled.

If any of the parameters of the group are not included, the default settings are used instead. Therefore, if the menubar parameter is not included, it is displayed. For example, the statement window.open("http:// www.wiley.com","books"," width=400px, height=350px, toolbar=0, location=0, directories=0,"); opens a browser window without the location, tool, and directory bars with a width of 400px and a height of 350px.

You can create pop-up windows to hide certain parts of the browser. The term `chromeless` means that all the available tool bars are removed from the new browser window. You can only remove toolbars from a browser window by using a pop-up window.

Some older versions of Internet explorer allow you to remove the title bar and the close and minimize

buttons due to a bug in the logic of the Web browser. Microsoft patched the Internet Explorer browsers; therefore, only non-patched users running older versions of Internet Explorer can remove these toolbars.

Web Browser Toolbars

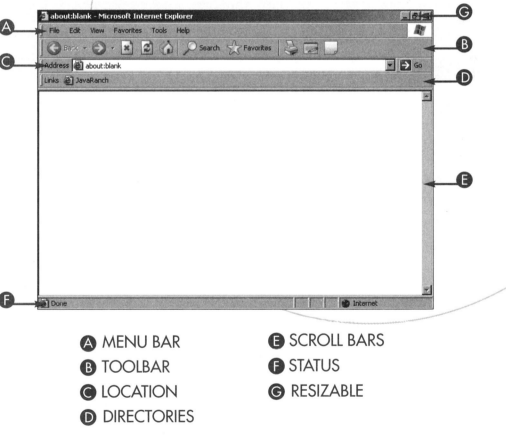

A MENU BAR
B TOOLBAR
C LOCATION
D DIRECTORIES
E SCROLL BARS
F STATUS
G RESIZABLE

Detect If a Pop-Up Window Is Open

Y ou can detect if a pop-up window is still open, from the parent window, by referencing the `window.open()` object. This allows you to replace the pop-up window with new content instead of opening a new window. You can close the window without an error, make the pop-up window the focus, and so on.

To reference the `window.open()` object, you must set the object to a variable when the window is being opened. For example, `var newWin = window.open("Wiley.com");` stores the window object in the variable `newWin`. To verify that the window has been opened, you can use an `if` statement. For example, the statement `if(newWin)` returns true when the object has been created and false when it has not been created.

The object can also determine if the window has been closed by using the `closed` property of the window

function. For example, the statement `if(!newWin.closed)` executes when the window is still open. The closed property returns true when closed and false when open. The not (`!`) operator switches the meaning of the conditional in the `if` statement.

By joining the object creation statement and the window closing statement, you can verify that a browser window is still open. For example, the statement `if(newWin && !newWin.closed)alert("Open ");` displays an alert dialog box for an open pop-up window. By adding an `else` statement, you can detect that the window is closed.

Using this logic allows you to reuse windows, refocus windows, and close child windows without any errors. For example, if you try closing a pop-up window that is already closed, the browser throws an error. The error can cause your code to stop working properly.

Detect If a Pop-Up Window Is Open

① Add statements to check to see if a window is open along with code to change the location.

② Add a statement to open up a new window if the window does not exist.

③ Create JavaScript events to open new windows by calling the function.

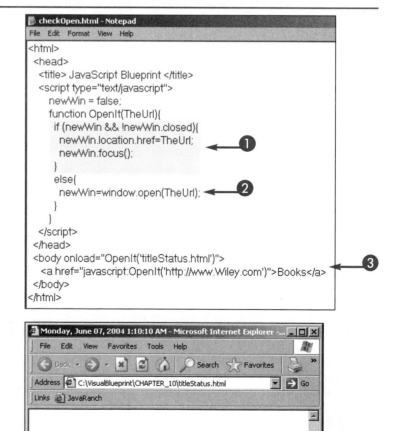

④ Open the file in a Web browser.

● The pop-up window appears.

Note: If you click the link on the parent window, the pop-up window changes to the new location.

Reference Information from Multiple Windows

You can send information to and from the child window to the parent window by referencing the window objects. This enables you to add dynamic content to your site. A common use for transferring information is with dynamic form fields. A pop-up window opens and the user can select information from the new window. That information is then sent to the parent window for processing.

You can reference the pop-up window by storing the window.open() object into a variable. You can then reference a form or the document properties by adding the variable name in front of the reference statement. For example, the statement var theWin = window.open("example.html"); opens a new browser window. You can reference a text field named T1 in a form named F1 in the child window with the statement theWin.document.F1.T1.value = "pizza";.

You can reference the parent window by using the window.opener object. You can reference a form or element the same way you would on a normal page with one exception — you must add the window.opener object in front of the form or element. For example, var theColor = window.opener.document.getElementById("Apple").style.background; stores the background information in the variable theColor.

You can reference variables in a JavaScript function from another window by using the name in which the window object is stored. For example, the statement var theNum = window.opener.guesses; stores the number of guesses into the variable theNum.

If the parent browser window is navigated away from the initial page or it is reloaded, it can keep the child window and parent window from being able to communicate with each other. There is no cross-browser method to fix the communication problem.

Reference Information from Multiple Windows

1 Store the form field value into a variable.

2 Place the form field value into the child window's text field by referencing the pop-up window.

3 Focus the child window's text field.

4 Save the file.

```
referenceWin.html - Notepad
File  Edit  Format  View  Help
<html>
 <head>
  <title> JavaScript Blueprint </title>
  <script type="text/javascript">
        var newWin=window.open("values.html");
  </script>
 </head>
 <body>
  <form name="test">
   <input type="text" name="idNum" value="112233">
  </form>
  <script type="text/javascript">
        var id = document.test.idNum.value;          ①
        newWin.document.form1.text1.value = id;       ②③
        newWin.document.form1.text1.focus();          ③
  </script>
 </body>
</html>
```

5 Open the file in a Web browser.

● The value from the parent window transfers to the child window, and the form field is in focus.

Close Pop-Up and Parent Windows

Most browsers allow you to close the pop-up and parent windows on a user's computer. This allows you to remove any unnecessary windows that the user has open.

To close a window, you can use the `close()` method of the window object. To close a pop-up window from within itself and not from the parent, you can use `window.close()`. The command is called from any event handler, JavaScript function, timer, and so on.

You can close a child window, from the parent, by setting the `window.open()` object to a variable. You can then use the variable to reference and close the window. For example, the statement `newWin.close();` closes the pop-up window whose object is stored in the variable `newWin`.

You may have a problem when trying to close the parent window. The parent window produces a warning when it is

trying to close. You can close the window from itself by using `window.close()` or from a child window by using `window.opener.close();`. Both of these methods produce a warning that allows users to select if they want to allow the operation to continue.

You can get around this security with most browsers by switching the window objects. Web browsers like Netscape 7 disable this operation. To perform this action you must set the child window to the top-level reference and switch the parent to another level. This tricks the browser into closing the parent window. For example, the statement `window.opener=window; window.close();` closes parent window.

Some users may be upset if you close their main window to remove toolbars because they will lose their history and will not be able to navigate back to the page they were viewing.

Close Pop-Up and Parent Windows

① Declare an event handler to close the pop-up window after a set period of time.

② Create a function to close the parent window.

③ Add an event handler to close the parent window.

④ Save the file.

⑤ Open the file in a Web browser.

• The pop-up window appears.

⑥ Wait for the pop-up window to close automatically.

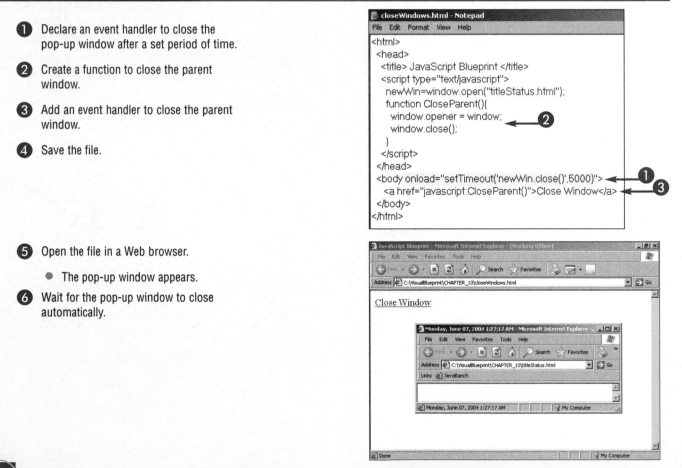

7 Click the link to close the parent window.

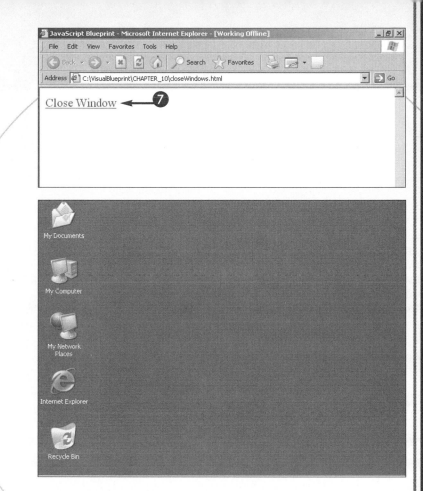

● The parent window closes without a security message.

Note: This method does not work with all browsers.

Extra

You can keep a pop-up window or a parent window on top of all the other windows by using the `onblur()` event or the `setInterval()` method. Internet Explorer has a `modal` window that always stays on top until it is closed, but it is not supported by any other browser. The `onblur()` event handler and the `setInterval()` method have to use the `focus()` method to bring the window to the top.

Add the `onblur()` event handler to the `<body>` tag. Whenever the page becomes out of focus, it brings it back into focus.

```
<body onblur= "this.focus()">
```

There is one drawback to using the `onblur()` method: It does not allow you to type data into form elements. The `setTimeout()` method is added to the `<body>` tag. You set the amount of time that it focuses the page. If the user removes focus from the page, it comes back into focus when the interval executes.

```
<body onload=
"setInterval('this.focus()',100)">
```

The problem is this method removes focus from forms when it is executed. You can come up with an elaborate method to check for focus on the page, but the best method is to use layers if the child window has forms. See Chapter 16 for more information.

Set Window Size and Placement

Y ou can place a browser window in a specific place on the monitor by using JavaScript. This allows you to control both parent and child windows. Along with being able to set the position, you can set the height and width of the window, which enables you to control the look and feel of your Web page.

The window object has two methods for you to move the window to a specific location. The first method is `moveTo()`, which accepts two positional parameters, the x and y positions. The parameters have to be integers. Certain Web browsers disable the ability for you to move the window from the viewing area of the screen. For example, the statement `window.moveTo(100,200);` moves the window 100 pixels from the left of the screen and 200 pixels from the top.

The second method is the `moveBy()` method. It also accepts two parameters, which informs the browser how many

pixels it should move in the x and y directions from its current location. For example, the statement `window.moveBy(-10,20);` moves the window 10 pixels left and 20 pixels down from its original location.

You can set the browser's width and height by using the `resizeTo()` method. The `resizeTo()` method accepts the width and height parameters, which must be integers. For example, the statement `window.resizeTo(200,150);` changes the width of the current window to 200 pixels and the height to 150 pixels. The `resizeTo()` method cannot reduce the window to a width or height smaller than 100 pixels.

The limits on the size and placement of a window are for security reasons. A malicious coder could move the window off the screen and run a harmful operation.

Set Window Size and Placement

① Add the `onload` handler and add the `resizeTo()` and `moveTo()` methods.

② Add the `onclick` event handler and add the `resizeTo()` and `moveTo()` methods.

③ Save the file.

④ Open the file in a Web browser.

● The browser window is resized and moved to new location.

⑤ Click in the text to resize and move the window.

- The browser window moves to a new location and changes size.

6 Click the maximize button.

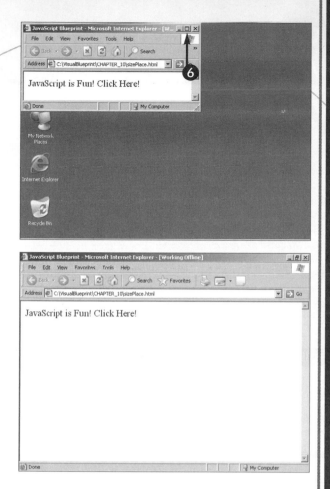

- The browser window maximizes.

Note: If clicking the maximize button returns the window to its previous position, click the maximize button a second time to maximize the browser.

Apply It

You can force a browser window to remain one standard size all the time by using the `onresize` event handler in conjunction with the `resizeTo()` method. The `onresize` handler executes when the browser size is changed. The event fires when the browser is maximized or when the user drags one of the edges of the browser window.

The `resizeTo()` method allows you to specify the exact size of the window. You do not have to go through this trouble if you are using a pop-up window. A pop-up window has the flexibility to disable the resizing feature. You do not have this convenience with the parent window.

The `onresize` event handler is added to the `<body>` tag.

```
<body onresize="window.resizeTo(300,300)">
```

The main use for the `onresize` event handler is to inform a JavaScript function that the window parameters are being adjusted. You can adjust scripts that use dynamically positioned elements accordingly to properly display the Web page. This use of the `onresize` event handler has been declining since the introduction of CSS.

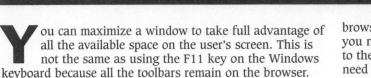

Maximize the Browser Window

You can maximize a window to take full advantage of all the available space on the user's screen. This is not the same as using the F11 key on the Windows keyboard because all the toolbars remain on the browser.

To maximize the window, you need to figure out what the available size of the screen is. The `screen.availWidth` and `screen.availHeight` properties give you the available size of the screen in pixels.

You need to use the `moveTo()` method and set the window to the top-left corner of the screen. For Microsoft Internet Explorer, you can move the window off the available viewing area of the screen. Since the border of the browser is about four pixels in size, you can move the browser off the screen to hide the border.

After the window is moved, you need to use the `resizeTo()` method to change the dimensions of the

browser window. For browsers other than Internet Explorer, you need to set the width and height of the window equal to the available width and height. For Internet Explorer, you need to add four pixels to accommodate for the pixels hanging off the left and top side of the screen and another four pixels for the top and bottom of the screen. Therefore, a total of eight pixels need to be added to the width and height of the window.

One thing that you have to remember is that certain users are running very large screen size resolutions on large monitors. These people may not want to resize their window. Therefore, do not use this script on every page just because you can. You should have a clear reason for why you want to do it. Otherwise, users may not come back to your Web site.

Maximize the Browser Window

① Create a function to maximize the window.

② Determine if the browser is Internet Explorer running on Windows and set the offset variable accordingly.

Note: You can move Microsoft Internet Explorer Browser for Windows off the screen to hide the browser border.

③ Use the `screen.availWidth` property to determine the width of the screen.

④ Use the `screen.availHeight` property to determine the height of the screen.

⑤ Use the `moveTo()` method to move the screen to the offset position.

⑥ Resize the window with the `resizeTo()` method to the screen dimensions.

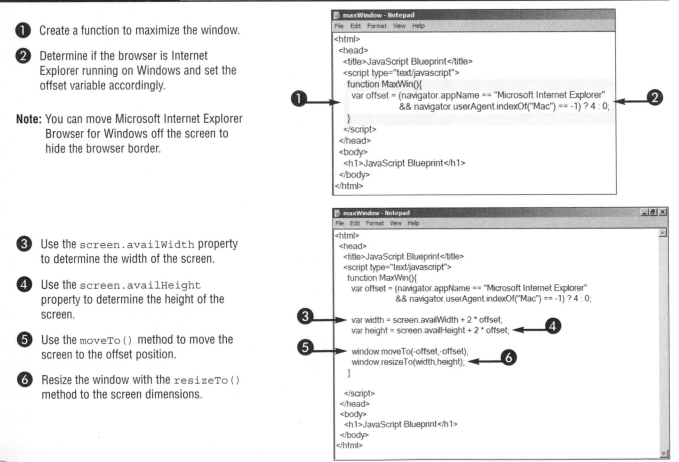

7 Attach the `onload` handler to the document object to initialize the function.

8 Save the file.

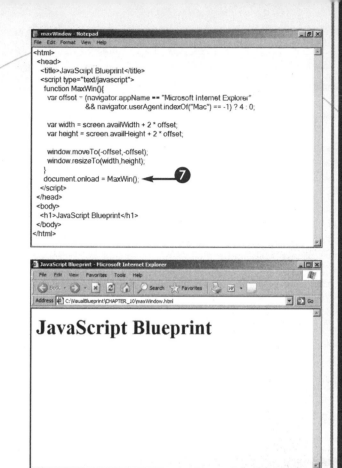

```
maxWindow - Notepad
File  Edit  Format  View  Help
<html>
 <head>
  <title>JavaScript Blueprint</title>
  <script type="text/javascript">
   function MaxWin(){
    var offset = (navigator.appName == "Microsoft Internet Explorer"
                 && navigator.userAgent.indexOf("Mac") == -1) ? 4 : 0;

    var width = screen.availWidth + 2 * offset;
    var height = screen.availHeight + 2 * offset;

    window.moveTo(-offset,-offset);
    window.resizeTo(width,height);
   }
   document.onload = MaxWin();          ◄ 7
  </script>
 </head>
 <body>
  <h1>JavaScript Blueprint</h1>
 </body>
</html>
```

9 Open the file in a Web browser.

● The browser window maximizes and fills the entire screen.

JavaScript Blueprint - Microsoft Internet Explorer
File Edit View Favorites Tools Help
Address C:\VisualBlueprint\CHAPTER_10\maxWindow.html

JavaScript Blueprint

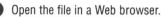

You can force the window size to remain maximized by using the `onresize` event handler. The `onresize` event handler fires whenever the browser window changes dimensions. All you need to do is add the `onresize` handler to the `<body>` tag and call the function to maximize the window.

```
<body onresize="MaxWin()">
```

You can find yourself annoyed with sites that force your window to stay maximized. You can use the address var to disable the function from happening. First, look at the source code and find the name of the function that is being called. You then need to overwrite the function name in the address bar. To block the example code, you would need to overwrite the function `MaxWin()`.

```
javascript:function MaxWin(){}
alert('Blocked');window.resizeTo
(800,600);
```

Center the Window on the Screen

Centering a window in a browser window is great when you are using pop-up windows. This assures that the content is right in the middle and the user cannot avoid seeing it. In doing this, you need to find the dimensions of the browser window along with the dimensions of window that you want to center.

First, find the available space that you have to work with on screen. To do this, you need to use the `screen.availWidth` and `screen.availHeight` properties. They return the width and height of the screen in pixels.

You then need to set the dimensions of the window in which you are working. You can use the `resizeTo()` method to set the size of the window. For example, the statement `window.resizeTo(300,400);` sets the window to a new set of dimensions.

After the window is set, you need to find the location to place this window. To do this, you need to take half of the screen width and height and subtract half of the window width and height. For example, the statement `var xLocation = (screen.availWidth - 300)/2;` finds the left position of the window.

After you find the new positional coordinates of the window, you need to move the window to that new location. You can move the window by using the `moveTo()` method. For example, the statement `window.moveTo (xLocation,yLocation);` moves the window on the screen to the new coordinates specified in the variables.

For pop-up windows, you do not have to use the `moveTo()` and `resizeTo()` methods after opening the window. You can specify the positional parameters before opening the window by setting the parameters left, top, screenX, and screenY.

Center the Window on the Screen

① Create a function to center the window on the screen.

② Use the `screen.availWidth` property to determine the width of the screen.

③ Use the `screen.availHeight` property to determine the height of the screen.

④ Create two variables and store the width and height of the browser widow.

⑤ Determine the xLocation of the browser window by subtracting the screen width from the window width and then divide by two.

⑥ Determine the yLocation of the screen.

⑦ Use the `resizeTo()` method to set the window to the default width and height values.

⑧ Use the `moveTo()` method to move the screen to the xLocation and yLocation.

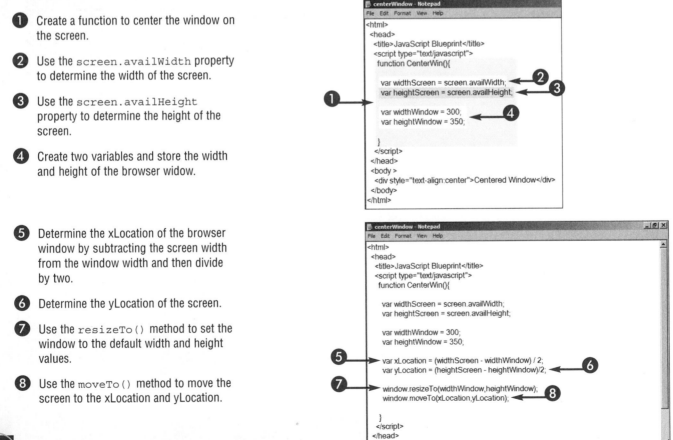

9 Attach the `onload` handler to the document object to initialize the function.

10 Save the file.

```
    var widthScreen = screen.availWidth;
    var heightScreen = screen.availHeight;

    var widthWindow = 300;
    var heightWindow = 350;

    var xLocation = (widthScreen - widthWindow) / 2;
    var yLocation = (heightScreen - heightWindow)/2;

    window.resizeTo(widthWindow,heightWindow);
    window.moveTo(xLocation,yLocation);

    }
    document.onload = CenterWin();        ◄── 9
  </script>
</head>
<body >
  <div style="text-align:center">Centered Window</div>
</body>
</html>
```

11 Open the file in a Web browser.

● The browser window repositions to the center of the screen after the page loads.

Apply It

You can animate the window to the center of the screen by using a `setInterval()` method. This can add a dynamic effect to your Web page when it first opens.

```
currentX = 0; currentY=0;
window.resizeTo(300,350);
window.moveTo(0,0);
function MoveToCenter(){ document.title = currentX
  allow=false;
  if(currentX<(screen.availWidth - 300) / 2){currentX++;allow=true;}
  if(currentY<(screen.availHeight - 350)/2){currentY++;allow=true;}
  if(!allow)clearInterval("theTime");
  window.moveTo(currentX,currentY);
}
```

You just need to initialize the function with an event handler that sets the interval.

```
<body onload='theTime = setInterval("MoveToCenter()",1);'>
```

Utilize an IE Modal Window

If your target audience is Microsoft Internet Explorer, then you can use a Modal dialog window to collect data from a user. A Modal dialog window stops the processing of the main window. Values can pass to the Modal window.

To use a Modal window you need to use the window object with the `showModalWindow()` method. The `showModal Window()` method accepts three groups of parameters. The first parameter is the link to the HTML page. The second parameter is the variable that contains objects or data references. The third parameter is the display properties of the window. A semicolon separates each of the display properties.

The display properties control the look and placement of the window. The first property is `center`, which places the Modal window in the center of the screen. It can have values of `yes`, `no`, `0`, `1`, `on`, or `off`. The `dialogLeft` and

`dialogTop` properties accept an integer value, which places the window a set number of pixels from the top corner of the screen. The `dialogLeft` and `dialogTop` properties override the `center` property.

You can specify the width and height of the Modal window by specifying the `dialogWidth` and `dialogHeight` properties. These properties accept an integer with a unit.

The `help` property is used to display the help icon in the title bar. The `status` property can be set to show or hide the status bar from the user's view. The `resizable` property allows the altering of the window size from the set dimensions. The `help`, `status`, and `resizable` properties can have the values of `yes`, `no`, `0`, `1`, `on`, or `off`.

The last property is the `edge` property. It can be set to `raised` or `sunken`. The `edge` property affects the transition style between the window border and the content.

Utilize an IE Modal Window

① Create a function with no parameters.

② Add a variable and store the form object reference into it.

③ Create a variable and store the `showModalDialog()` method with all its parameters.

④ Attach the `onload` handler to the document object to initialize the function.

⑤ Save the file.

⑥ Open the file in an Internet Explorer Web browser.

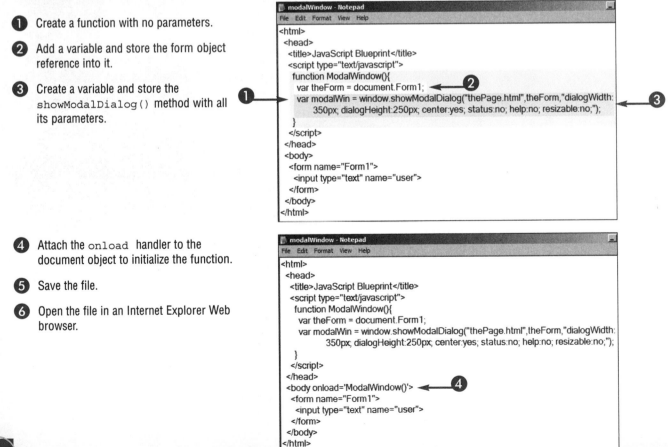

```
modalWindow - Notepad
File Edit Format View Help
<html>
 <head>
  <title>JavaScript Blueprint</title>
  <script type="text/javascript">
  function ModalWindow(){
   var theForm = document.Form1;
   var modalWin = window.showModalDialog("thePage.html",theForm,"dialogWidth:
    350px; dialogHeight:250px; center:yes; status:no; help:no; resizable:no;");
  }
 </script>
 </head>
 <body>
  <form name="Form1">
   <input type="text" name="user">
  </form>
 </body>
</html>
```

```
modalWindow - Notepad
File Edit Format View Help
<html>
 <head>
  <title>JavaScript Blueprint</title>
  <script type="text/javascript">
  function ModalWindow(){
   var theForm = document.Form1;
   var modalWin = window.showModalDialog("thePage.html",theForm,"dialogWidth:
       350px; dialogHeight:250px; center:yes; status:no; help:no; resizable:no;");
  }
 </script>
 </head>
 <body onload='ModalWindow()'>
  <form name="Form1">
   <input type="text" name="user">
  </form>
 </body>
</html>
```

- The Modal window appears on the screen.

7 Click the window to bring the main window into focus.

- The Modal window does not allow access to the main window.

8 Click the Close button to close the Modal window.

- You are now able to access the main window because the Modal window is now closed.

Extra

You can retrieve information passed to the Modal window by referencing the second parameter passed to the window. In the example code, the object passed was the form object. You are able to retrieve the values of the element of the field by referencing the element name by using the `window.dialog Arguments` property of the Modal window. The following line retrieves the value of the form element `user`.

```
document.write(window.dialogArguments.
user.value);
```

You can submit data back to the parent window by storing the value in the `window.dialogArguments` and referencing the page elements. The following example places a string into a form-field name user.

```
window.dialogArguments.user.value=
"Passed Information";
```

Create Content in a Pop-Up Window

Y ou can create dynamic content to fill a pop-up window. This allows you to develop a page that is dependent on the information provided by the parent window, without having to have it prewritten and saved on the server.

The first step that you need to do is open a new window with the `window.open()` method, with the `window.open()` object stored into a variable. For example, the statement `var winName = window.open('blank.html', 'winName');` creates a new window and stores the window object into the variable `winName`.

You have two options for the page that the `window.open()` method opens. You can use a blank HTML page that you can create, which has minimum amount of tags, or you can use `about:blank`. One problem with using `about:blank` is on pages that are on a secure site (HTTPS). If the page is opened on an HTTPS based site, a security prompt may be issued. To avoid this you should use a blank HTML page.

The second step is to create a long string that contains all the HTML tags and content of the body. To add this new HTML into the window, you need to use the `document.write()` method. Since you are writing the content to the new window, you need to reference the pop-up window object along with the `write()` method. For example, the statement `winName.document.write(htmlStr);` writes the string stored in `htmlStr` to the pop-up up window.

After the `winName.document.write()` statement, you need to include a `winName.document.close()` method. The `winName.document.close()` method does not close the window like the `window.close()` method. Instead, it closes the document to allow all the content to render correctly. If you do not close the document, then there is a chance that the images may not show up properly.

Create Content in a Pop-Up Window

① Create a function to with no parameters.

② Create a string that contains the HTML content for the new window including all the tags.

③ Add the `window.open()` method to open up `about:blank`, storing the object into a variable.

④ Reference the new window and use a `document.write()` method, adding the HTML content to the new window.

⑤ Close the document by adding a window reference with the `document.close()` method.

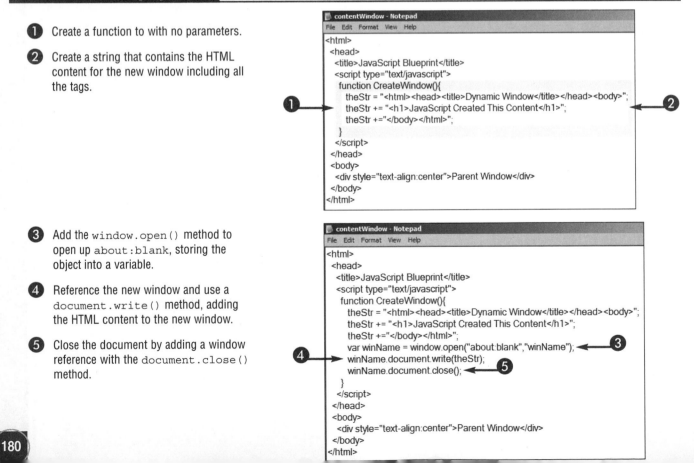

6 Attach the `onload` handler to the document object to initialize the function.

7 Save the file.

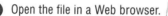

```
contentWindow - Notepad
File  Edit  Format  View  Help
<html>
 <head>
  <title>JavaScript Blueprint</title>
  <script type="text/javascript">
   function CreateWindow(){
    theStr = "<html><head><title>Dynamic Window</title></head><body>";
    theStr += "<h1>JavaScript Created This Content</h1>";
    theStr +="</body></html>";
    var winName = window.open("about:blank","winName");
    winName.document.write(theStr);
    winName.document.close();
   }
   window.onload=CreateWindow;    ◄——— 6
  </script>
 </head>
 <body>
  <div style="text-align:center">Parent Window</div>
 </body>
</html>
```

8 Open the file in a Web browser.

● The pop-up window appears with the dynamic content in the browser window.

```
JavaScript Blueprint - Microsoft Internet Explorer          _ B X
File  Edit  View  Favorites  Tools  Help
◄ Back ▾ ➔ ▾ ▾   Search   Favorites
Address  C:\VisualBlueprint\CHAPTER_10\contentWindow.html         ➔ Go

                     Parent Window
   Dynamic Window - Microsoft Internet Explorer        _ □ X
   File  Edit  View  Favorites  Tools  Help
   ◄ Back ▾ ➔ ▾ ▾   Search   Favorites
   Address  about:blank                    ➔ Go  Links »

   JavaScript Created This Content

   Done                              My Computer
Done                                My Computer
```

Extra

When you are writing content to a new window, you may notice that the operation has poor performance. Increasing the performance of the JavaScript code enables the window to load faster. To increase the performance, you can follow three main steps.

The first step is to use a single `document.write()` statement instead of a bunch of `document.write()` statements. By using one `document.write()` statement, it allows the new window to load faster. When you use multiple `document.write()` statements, the window has to do extra processing, which adds seconds to a large file loading time.

The second step is to include `<html>`, `<head>`, and `<body>` tags when creating a new window. If you do not include them in the string when you write the content to the new window, the browser assumes that you want to add the information to the body of the page. The browser automatically places the `<html>`, `<head>`, and `<body>` tags around the content, but this decreases the script's performance time.

The third step is to make sure that all the HTML tags are opened and closed properly. This ensures that the new dynamic content is displayed properly on the screen. If you miss an opening or closing tag, it may cause the page to load incorrectly.

Create Frames

Y ou can use frames to split a Web page into several different panes. Each pane is a separate HTML file that can perform separate tasks on each page. The frames are set up by using the `<frameset>` tag. The `<frameset>` tag sets up the layout for the frames. The frameset contains `name`, `cols`, and `row` attributes.

The `<frame>` tag contains the `src` and `name` attributes. The `name` attribute allows the frame to be referenced and the `src` attribute informs the browser what Web page to load into the page. You can prevent a frame from resizing by using the `noresize` attribute. For example, the statement `<frame src="page1.html" name="left" noresize="noresize">` produces a frame with the page source `page1.html` and the name `left`.

You can make your frames dynamic by using the frame object. When using the frame object, you can pass information, call functions, change locations, and so on, between the frames. If done correctly, you can make the

frame page seem like it is one HTML document instead of multiple pieces.

The frame object is referenced by the `parent` object. The `parent` object contains an array of all the frames that are located on the main frameset. For example, if a frame contains two frames, the first frame would be referenced as `parent.frame[0]` and the second one as `parent.frame[1]`.

You can also use the `name` attribute of the frame to reference the frames. Instead of using the frame index array, you use the name. For example, `parent.frames["mainBody"]` references the frame with the name `mainBody`.

Another shortcut to reference the name of the frame is to drop the frame array altogether and just use the name. For example, `parent.mainBody` also references the frame with the name `mainBody`.

Create Frames

DEVELOP FRAMESET

① Declare the frameset and add rows attribute.

② Add the frame declaration with the `src` and `name` attributes.

③ Insert a close frameset.

④ Save the file.

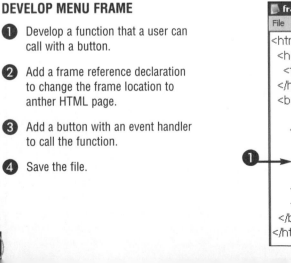

```
frameset.html - Notepad
File  Edit  Format  View  Help
<html>
 <frameset rows="50%,*">            ①
  <frame src="framePage1.html" name="frameTop">     ②
  <frame src="framePage2.html" name="frameBot">
③ </frameset>
</html>
```

DEVELOP MENU FRAME

① Develop a function that a user can call with a button.

② Add a frame reference declaration to change the frame location to anther HTML page.

③ Add a button with an event handler to call the function.

④ Save the file.

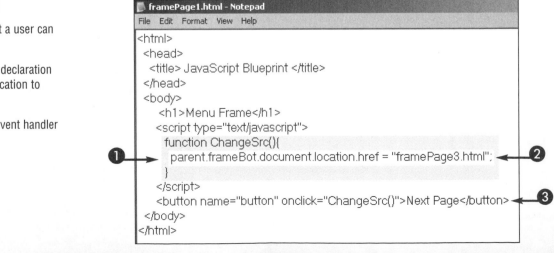

```
framePage1.html - Notepad
File  Edit  Format  View  Help
<html>
 <head>
  <title> JavaScript Blueprint </title>
 </head>
 <body>
   <h1>Menu Frame</h1>
   <script type="text/javascript">
    function ChangeSrc(){
     parent.frameBot.document.location.href = "framePage3.html";     ②
    }
   </script>
   <button name="button" onclick="ChangeSrc()">Next Page</button>     ③
 </body>
</html>
```

CHANGE THE LOCATION

 Open the frameset page.

② Click the Next Page button.

- The new Web page appears in the lower frame.

Extra

You can use the parent frame, which contains the frameset code, to control the browser properties and to find the number of frames that are present. This allows you to change the properties such as the title and status bars.

You can find the number of frames on a Web page by using the length property. You can reference the property from the parent object. For example, for a frameset with three frames, the parent.frames.length property returns a value of three.

You can find the names of the individual frames by referencing each frame. All of the frame names appear in the following code:

```
function displayNames(){
  var numFrames = parent.frames.length;
  for(i=0;i<numFrames;i++){
    document.write("frame[" + i + "] = ");
    document.write(parent.frame[i].name);
  }
}
```

Reference Individual Frames

You can reference frames to pull data from one frame to another. This allows you to pass form values, variables, and other data from frame to frame.

You can reference the frame by using the parent object either by using the frame name or the index value. By using the frame name, you are ensuring that the correct frame is being used by the browser. If you add a new frame to the page, you do not have to edit all of your functions if the frame indexes change.

Referencing form elements from one frame to another is not much different from referencing the object from its own page. You normally use the document object along with the form name and element name. The parent object and the frame name must be included. For example, the statement `parent.Frame1.document.Form1.Text1.value = "ASDF"` stores the string ASDF into the form element named Text1 in the form Form1 in the frame named Frame1.

You can reference global variables from another frame by using the same concept from above. Instead of using the document reference, you use the variable name. For example, the statement `newVar = parent.Frame1.oldVariable` stores the variable oldVariable from Frame1 into the variable newVar.

You can also call functions in other frames by using the same concept. To do this, you reference the frame using the parent object and then add the function name. For example, `parent.frame[0].OpenBrowser();` executes the function OpenBrowser() in the first frame when the statement is executed.

If the frame that is being referenced does not contain the form element, function, or variable that is being called, an error occurs. Therefore, it is important for you to make sure that the correct frame is being referenced and the correct page is located in the frame.

Reference Individual Frames

DEVELOP FUNCTION FRAME PAGE

1. Develop a function in a Web page that a user can call from another frame.

2. Add an alert dialog box that shows the information to the user.

3. Save the file.

DEVELOP CALLER FRAME PAGE

1. Add a button with an event handler.

2. Add a frame reference declaration to execute the JavaScript function in the other frame.

Note: The frame reference comes from the parent frameset the page is saved in.

3. Save the file.

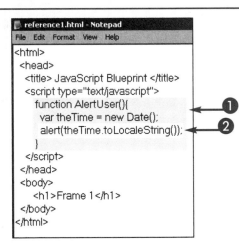

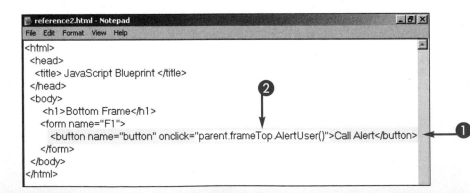

CALL JAVASCRIPT FUNCTION

 Open the frameset page.

2 Click Call Alert.

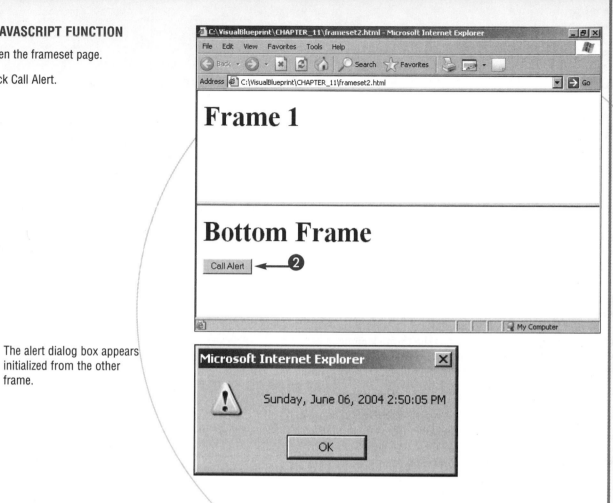

● The alert dialog box appears initialized from the other frame.

Extra

You can submit a form that is located in one frame and post the results to another frame by using the `target` attribute. This allows you to keep the form visible to the user at all times and show the results in the other frame.

The `target` attribute should be set to the frame name to which you want the form to be submitted. For example, the following form submits the results to the frame named `theResults`:

```
<form name="SearchResults"
target="theResults" method="post">

  <input type="text" name="text1">

  <input type="submit" name="submit1"
value="Get Results">

</form>
```

You can clear the form fields from another frame by using the frame reference that the form is in. For example, the following statement clears the form named `SearchResults` in the frame named `theReport`:

```
parent.theReport.SearchResults.
reset();
```

Determine the Frame Dimensions

You can determine the precise pixel dimensions of a frame after the frameset is rendered. This allows you to figure out how many pixels a percentage or wildcard actually is on the page. A wildcard is the star (*) value that is used when setting the frame dimensions. For example, the statement `<frameset name="theFrameSet" rows="100px,*">` sets the row height to one hundred pixels for the top frame and lets the bottom frame take the remaining amount of space available.

When determining the dimensions of the frames, you can use this information for JavaScript code that requires the available screen area. This is especially useful when you have dynamic content such as animations or layers.

In order to determine the frame sizes, you need to reference the frame name, which can be done using the `parent` object with the frame name, parent object with the frame array, or even by using the `getElementById()` method

with the `document` object. To get the width and height you need to use the `scrollWidth` and `scrollHeight` properties of the object. For example, the statement `var theWidth = parent.Frame2.scrollWidth;` stores the width value of the frame named `Frame2` into the variable `theWidth`.

You can also detect when a user is changing the frame dimensions by dragging the border. To detect the resizing, you can use the `onResize()` handler. The handler fires after the page has been resized and is able to execute a function that can determine the frame's new dimensions.

If you do not want a frame to be able to be resized, you can use the `noresize` attribute. The `noresize` attribute is added to the frame and not the frameset tag. For example, the statement `<frame name="example" noresize= "noresize">` creates a frame that is not able to be resized.

Determine the Frame Dimensions

① Add variables and assign them to the `scrollWidth` and `scrollHeight` properties of a frame.

② Use an alert dialog box to display the frame dimensions.

③ Add an event handler to the `<frameset>` tag to initialize the function.

④ Save the file.

⑤ Open the frameset page.

● The frame dimensions appear in the alert dialog box.

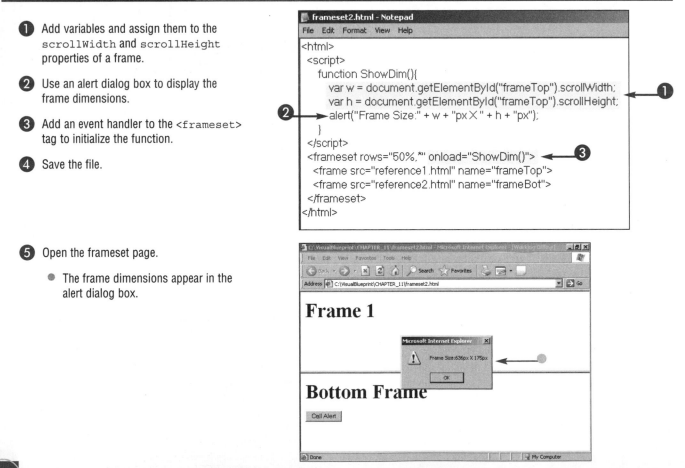

Print Individual Frames

By referencing the form object, you can change a frame's location and print a frame. This allows you to use menus to change a frame's content and allows a user to print information without printing the menus.

You can change a frame's source by using the location property and setting it to a new URL. The location property is part of the document object and needs to be assigned to the frame that you want to change. For example, the statement `parent.Frame1.document.location.href="newPage.html";` sets the frame named `Frame1` location to the HTML file `newPage`.

You can change the entire framed page to another URL by using the parent attribute without referencing a frame name. For example, the statement `parent.location.href="newPage.html"` changes the entire page to the new Web page when executed.

You can change two or more frames at once with an HTML link by using the `onclick()` event handler. For example `<a href="newPage1.html" onclick="parent.Frame2.location.href='newPage2.html'">` changes the page in the frame in which the link was clicked and also in the page of the other frame.

You can have the Web browser open the print dialog box by using the `window.print()` event. This event allows the user to print the document. You can assign the frame name to the `print()` method so only that frame is printed. For example, the statement `parent.theText.window.print()` opens the dialog box to print the frame named `theText`.

You can also print the entire frameset by using the statement `parent.window.print();`, which again opens the dialog box. You cannot avoid the dialog box with JavaScript. It is there for security reasons. If the dialog box was not there, malicious coders could print thousands of pages without the users' consent.

Print Individual Frames

① Add a frame reference with the `window.print()` method to one of the Web pages contained in the frame.

Note: You can use the name of the frames assigned in the frameset rather than using the frame array.

② Save the file.

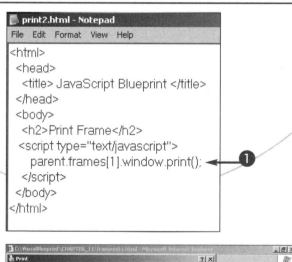

③ Open the frameset page.

● The print dialog box appears.

Note: JavaScript cannot print the page automatically since the print dialog box appears for security reasons.

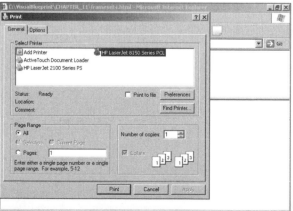

Break In and Out of Frames

You can keep your site out of another site's frames, or cause your site to break back into frames, by using JavaScript. Other sites can use frames to make it look like your content is part of theirs. You can use a frame-breaker script to avoid this.

You can break out of frames by checking to see if the top window object reference is the same as the current window reference. If it is not, then the entire frameset is replaced by your page. For example, the statement `if(top!=self) top.location.href=location.href;` changes the location of the frameset to your page when it is being framed. This JavaScript code should be added to the top of the header so it fires before the page is fully loaded.

You can include this on your own framed site, too. You must add this code to the frameset page and not on the

frame pages. If you include this on the frame pages, the frame pages end up breaking out of your own frames.

You can also break into your own frameset from a single page by using JavaScript. This forces a user to view the page in the frames and not individually. Bookmarks and search engine results are common reasons why a person may navigate to a page without using your frameset.

Putting your Web site back into frames is not as easy as breaking out of the frames. A query string has to be used to tell the browser what page it is supposed to load in the frameset. The information from the query string is then loaded into a frameset by another JavaScript function. You can also avoid the use of a query string by using session cookies.

Break In and Out of Frames

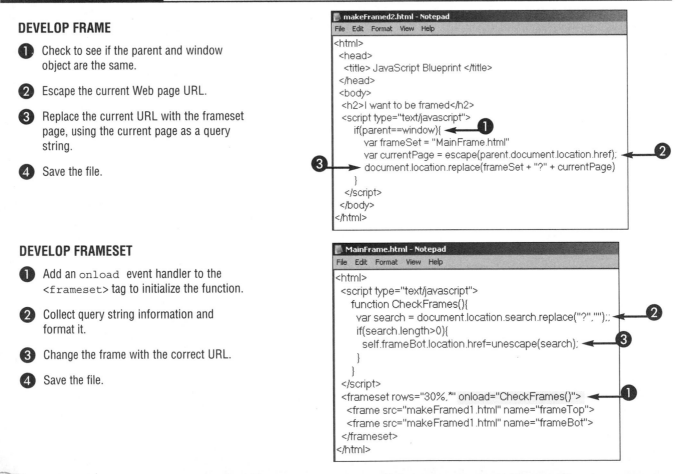

DEVELOP FRAME

1. Check to see if the parent and window object are the same.

2. Escape the current Web page URL.

3. Replace the current URL with the frameset page, using the current page as a query string.

4. Save the file.

```
makeFramed2.html - Notepad
File  Edit  Format  View  Help
<html>
 <head>
  <title> JavaScript Blueprint </title>
 </head>
 <body>
  <h2>I want to be framed</h2>
  <script type="text/javascript">
     if(parent==window){
         var frameSet = "MainFrame.html"
         var currentPage = escape(parent.document.location.href);
         document.location.replace(frameSet + "?" + currentPage)
      }
   </script>
 </body>
</html>
```

DEVELOP FRAMESET

1. Add an `onload` event handler to the `<frameset>` tag to initialize the function.

2. Collect query string information and format it.

3. Change the frame with the correct URL.

4. Save the file.

```
MainFrame.html - Notepad
File  Edit  Format  View  Help
<html>
 <script type="text/javascript">
    function CheckFrames(){
      var search = document.location.search.replace("?","");;
      if(search.length>0){
        self.frameBot.location.href=unescape(search);
      }
    }
 </script>
 <frameset rows="30%,*" onload="CheckFrames()">
  <frame src="makeFramed1.html" name="frameTop">
  <frame src="makeFramed1.html" name="frameBot">
 </frameset>
</html>
```

TEST FUNCTION

1 Open an orphaned frame Web page outside the frameset.

● The orphaned page appears in the frameset.

Resize the Frames

You can resize frames to show or hide content on the screen. This is useful for having menus that are not required to be visible all the time. Hiding the frame from view allows for more screen area to be visible when a person is reading your site content.

The first step is to create the frameset and set the cols to the default settings. If you want the menu to be hidden at the start then you should set the column width to zero pixels.

The next step is to add the `<script>` tags to the frameset HTML page. This ensures that this function is available to all the other pages all the time.

You need to create two variables; one is for the default settings of the column width and the second is for the hidden column widths. You can set the hidden width to zero pixels to hide the whole menu, or you can leave it open a few pixels to show a menu tab.

You then have to create a function that can be called from the other frames. This function needs to look at the frameset cols property and determine the state of the column widths. To reference the frameset, you must give the frameset a name.

After you detect the state of the columns, you need to apply the appropriate variable to the col property of the frameset.

You then can call the function from any of the frames. You can add the function call to a button, link, `setTimeout()` method, and so on.

You are not required to only show or hide a frame by using the columns. You can apply this same width to adjust the row height too. This can allow you to have a horizontal menu.

Resize the Frames

1. Open the source code for the frameset.

2. Declare two variables to set the default widths.

3. Create a function to change the widths.

4. Store the frame reference into a variable you want to alter.

5. Set the `cols` attribute to the column widths determining the current status.

6. Save the file.

7. Open the HTML page of the frame that is to call the function.

8. Add an event handler to a button to execute the function when clicked.

9. Save the file.

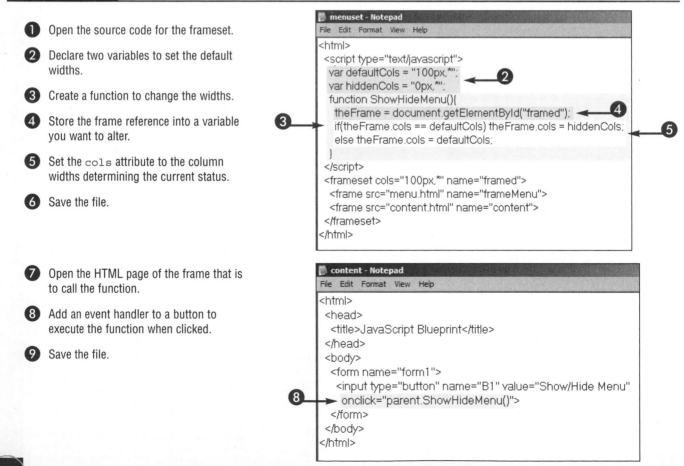

```
menuset - Notepad
File  Edit  Format  View  Help
<html>
 <script type="text/javascript">
  var defaultCols = "100px,*";            ← 2
  var hiddenCols = "0px,*";
  function ShowHideMenu(){
   theFrame = document.getElementById("framed");   ← 4
   if(theFrame.cols == defaultCols) theFrame.cols = hiddenCols;   ← 5
   else theFrame.cols = defaultCols;
  }
 </script>
 <frameset cols="100px,*" name="framed">
  <frame src="menu.html" name="frameMenu">
  <frame src="content.html" name="content">
 </frameset>
</html>
```

```
content - Notepad
File  Edit  Format  View  Help
<html>
 <head>
  <title>JavaScript Blueprint</title>
 </head>
 <body>
  <form name="form1">
   <input type="button" name="B1" value="Show/Hide Menu"
   onclick="parent.ShowHideMenu()">     ← 8
  </form>
 </body>
</html>
```

⑩ Open the frameset page.

⑪ Click the button to hide the menu frame.

● The menu frame resizes and hides from view.

Note: If you click the button again, the frame is visible.

Apply It

You can show or hide frameset rows by changing reference in the example to rows. This can allow you to have a horizontal menu on the page instead of a vertical menu that can be shown or hidden from the user's view.

```
var defaultRows = "100px,*";
var hiddenRows = "0px,*";
function ShowHideMenu(){
  theFrame = document.getElementById("framed");
  if(theFrame.rows == defaultRows) theFrame.rows = hiddenRows;
  else theFrame.rows = defaultRows;
}
</script>
```

Write Content to a Frame

You can dynamically create an HTML page and display the content in a frame. This allows you to create a dynamic Web page in which content can be built around the user's preferences or actions.

You can write the content from another frame by using the `document.write()` method. If you are writing the content from another frame, then you need to reference the frame name. For example, the statement `parent.content.document.write(htmlStr);` writes the content contained in the variable string `htmlStr` into the frame named `content`.

To speed up the process of writing the content to a new frame, it is important to use only one `document.write()` statement. Using multiple `document.write()` statements can slow down the performance of the document loading time.

After the `document.write()` method has created the document, it is important to close the document so that the information on the page can be rendered. You can do this by using the `document.close()` method. If you are adding the content from another frame, then you need to reference the frame name. The statement `parent.content.document.close();` allows the content in the frame `content` to render correctly.

If you do not close the document, then you have the chance that html elements, especially images, will not show up properly on the screen. Other ways that you can ensure that the page loads correctly and efficiently is to add the `<html>`, `<head>`, and `<body>` tags to the page. Include them into the string when writing the content to the new page. You should also make sure that all of your tags have an opening and closing tag too. This ensures that all of the information on the page is rendered correctly when the page is being loaded.

Write Content to a Frame

① Create a `<frame>` tag that contains the HTML page with the code for adding the new content to the other frame.

② Create another `<frame>` tag adding a reference name and setting the page source to `about:blank`.

③ Save the frameset page.

④ Create a new Web page and add a new function.

⑤ Create the HTML output string using the form field or any other information on the page.

⑥ Use a `document.write` statement to add content to the new frame using the frame name.

⑦ Add the `document.close()` to close the page for rendering.

⑧ Add an event handler to call the function.

⑨ Save the file.

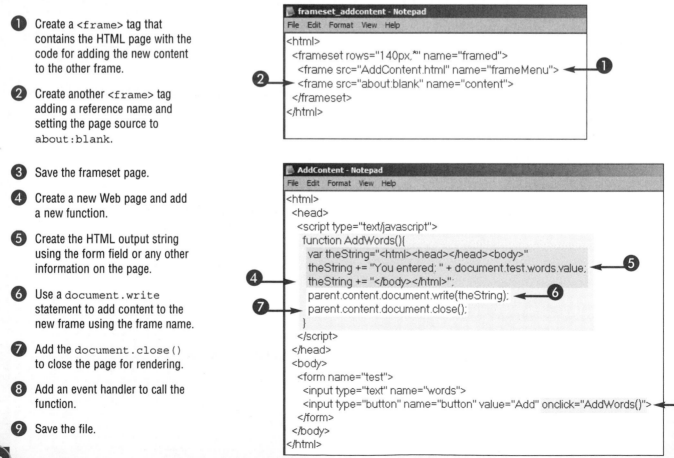

```
frameset_addcontent - Notepad
File  Edit  Format  View  Help

<html>
 <frameset rows="140px,*" name="framed">
  <frame src="AddContent.html" name="frameMenu">
  <frame src="about:blank" name="content">
 </frameset>
</html>
```

```
AddContent - Notepad
File  Edit  Format  View  Help

<html>
 <head>
  <script type="text/javascript">
   function AddWords(){
    var theString="<html><head></head><body>"
    theString += "You entered: " + document.test.words.value;
    theString += "</body></html>";
    parent.content.document.write(theString);
    parent.content.document.close();
   }
  </script>
 </head>
 <body>
  <form name="test">
   <input type="text" name="words">
   <input type="button" name="button" value="Add" onclick="AddWords()">
  </form>
 </body>
</html>
```

10 Open the frameset file in a Web browser.

11 Type text into the text box.

12 Click Add.

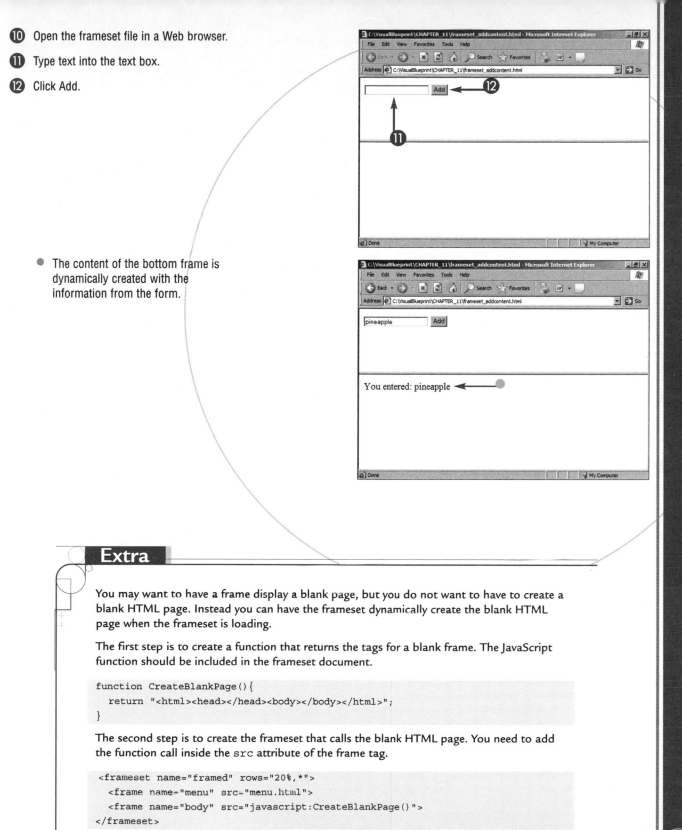

● The content of the bottom frame is dynamically created with the information from the form.

You may want to have a frame display a blank page, but you do not want to have to create a blank HTML page. Instead you can have the frameset dynamically create the blank HTML page when the frameset is loading.

The first step is to create a function that returns the tags for a blank frame. The JavaScript function should be included in the frameset document.

```
function CreateBlankPage(){
    return "<html><head></head><body></body></html>";
}
```

The second step is to create the frameset that calls the blank HTML page. You need to add the function call inside the src attribute of the frame tag.

```
<frameset name="framed" rows="20%,*">
    <frame name="menu" src="menu.html">
    <frame name="body" src="javascript:CreateBlankPage()">
</frameset>
```

Understand Frame Security

You can get security warnings such as access is denied when you try to access certain frames. There is no way to get around this warning since it is a security restriction. The reason for this warning can be that the frame is holding a page from another domain. Even sub domains from the same site have the ability to cause this error. A sub domain is a division off the main URL. For example, the URL `http://saloon.javaranch.com` targets the sub domain `saloon` from the parent domain `JavaRanch`.

The reason for the security restriction is the ability for a person to spoof another Web site. Spoofing a Web site is to make a Web site appear to be the real thing when it is actually a copy of it. If there were no security restrictions in place, then people would be able to monitor information that was being entered into fields, such as credit card numbers.

You may find that certain functions may not work properly when you have a page from another domain in the frameset. Scripts that perform actions such as Resizing, showing or hiding frames may cause security restrictions. Cookies from other sites also will not be able to work while they are in your frameset.

One way to avoid this problem is to open all links that are outside of your domain into a new window. You then do not have to worry about any errors that may occur in your frameset. You are not able to access these Web pages so it is safer to open them up in a new Window.

Hidden frames with the Microsoft Internet Explorer browser are also a security issue. Certain malicious Web sites are using frames with ActiveX controls to download information on your computer without your knowledge.

Understand Frame Security

① Create a `<frame>` tag that contains the HTML page with the code for adding the new content to the other frame.

② Create another `<frame>` tag adding a reference name and setting the page source to another domain.

③ Save the frameset page.

④ Develop a function that accesses the frame with content from the other domain.

Note: The function used here dynamically adds content to the frame.

⑤ Add an event handler to a button to call the function.

⑥ Save the file.

frameset_addcontent - Notepad
File Edit Format View Help

```html
<html>
 <frameset rows="220px,*" name="framed">
  <frame src="AddContent.html" name="frameMenu">          ①          ②
  <frame src="http://radio.javaranch.com/channel/pascarello" name="content">
 </frameset>
</html>
```

AddContent - Notepad
File Edit Format View Help

```html
<html>
 <head>
  <script type="text/javascript">
   function AddWords(){
    var theString="<html><head></head><body>"
    theString += "You entered: " + document.test.words.value;          ④
    theString += "</body></html>";
    parent.content.document.write(theString);
    parent.content.document.close();
   }
  </script>
 </head>
 <body>
  <form name="test">
   <input type="text" name="words">
   <input type="button" name="button" value="Add" onclick="AddWords()">          ⑤
  </form>
 </body>
</html>
```

7 Open the frameset file in a Web browser.

8 Type information into the text box.

9 Click the Add button.

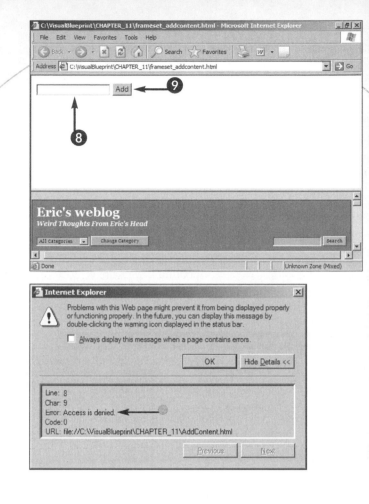

● The Error message is displayed stating the message `Access is denied.`

Note: You may have to click the icon in the status bar to view the message.

You can use frames so the Web page address in the address bar of the browser does not change. People see this as a way to add security to a page, especially when they are using query strings. The method is not secure since the user is able to right-click any one of the frames and select the property option. The property option displays the current URL of the frame, defeating the purpose of hiding the page's address.

Frames are being used less by developers since the increased use of server side languages, CSS, and JavaScript. These three technologies combined are able to create the same results that frames can implement on the page. By not using frames on your Web site, you are allowing people to bookmark Web pages easier. You also do not have to worry about the page not being loaded in the frameset. Using scrollable divs can produce the same effect as a frame if developed properly.

Reference Objects with the Document Object Model (DOM)

You need to understand the concept of objects in order to unleash the power of JavaScript. Every object is an abstract container that holds data. This data can be a single number or a complex data structure. The complete collection of JavaScript objects that refer to Web page elements is called the Document Object Model (DOM).

The DOM object can be traversed through multiple objects. Each object is considered a sub-object to its parent object. For example, the statement document.form shows that the form object is the sub-object to the document object.

In JavaScript, you can create your own objects or use predefined objects such as string, window, frame, image, and date. Objects can have properties that provide information about them. For example, the document object

has properties that can affect the title and the display properties. The property document.title="Welcome";, for example, changes the document title.

Objects can also have methods that are specific functions to the object, which performs a task. Methods are referenced like properties, such as document.write().

You can tell the difference between a property and a method by looking at the end of the statement. Any object reference that contains a set of parentheses is a method. Methods may or may not require parameters inside the parentheses. If there are no parentheses, then it is a property.

The built-in objects do not have all of the same properties and methods. The properties and methods are normally specific to the object.

Reference Objects with the Document Object Model (DOM)

REFERENCE OBJECTS WITH DOM THAT EXISTS

1. Add document.write() statements to display the objects.

2. Save the file.

document.html - Notepad

File   Edit   Format   View   Help

```html
<html>
 <head>
  <title> JavaScript Blueprint </title>
 </head>
 <body>
   <form name="form"></form>
   <script type="text\javascript">
        document.write("<br/>window: " + window);
        document.write("<br/>document: " + document);
        document.write("<br/>parent: " + parent);
        document.write("<br/>document.form: " + document.form);
        document.write("<br/>window.history: " + window.history);
   </script>
 </body>
</html>
```

3. Open the file in a Web browser.

● The objects appear in the browser window without an error.

JavaScript Blueprint - Microsoft Internet Explorer - [Working Offline]

File   Edit   View   Favorites   Tools   Help

Back ▾   ● ▾ ◙ ◙ ◚   ◯ Search ★ Favorites   ◙ ▣ ▾ ▢

Address ▣ C:\VisualBlueprint\CHAPTER_12\document.html   ▾ ▣ Go

window: [object]
document: [object]
parent: [object]
document.form: [object]
window.history: [object]

REFERENCE OBJECTS WITH DOM THAT DOES NOT EXIST

1 Add a `document.write` statement to display an object referencing a text field that does not exist.

2 Save the file.

3 Open up the file in a Web browser.

● An error message appears that explains either the element is not defined or the element is not an object.

document2.html – Notepad

File   Edit   Format   View   Help

```html
<html>
 <head>
  <title> JavaScript Blueprint </title>
 </head>
 <body>
   <form name="form"></form>
   <script type="text\javascript">
     document.write("document.form.text1.value: " + document.form.text1.value);
   </script>
 </body>
</html>
```

Internet Explorer

⚠ Problems with this Web page might prevent it from being displayed properly or functioning properly. In the future, you can display this message by double-clicking the warning icon displayed in the status bar.

☑ Always display this message when a page contains errors.

[OK]   [Hide Details <<]

```
Line: 8
Char: 2
Error: 'document.form.text1.value' is null or not an object
Code: 0
URL: file://C:\VisualBlueprint\CHAPTER_12\document2.html
```

[Previous]   [Next]

Extra

You may not remember all of the properties that an object supports, and you may not have any reference material near you. You can use a special `for` loop called the `for-in` loop. The `for-in` loop steps through the object for each property in the element.

To make the object property easier to use, you can include it as part of a function and pass the object name to it. The completed function looks like this:

```
function getProperties(obj){
  objName = prop.length;
  for (prop in obj){
    document.write(objName + prop + " = " + obj[prop] + "<br/>");
  }
}
```

You can pass the object name to the function and then all of the properties are written in the browser. Using this function helps you in the development process when you are starting out with objects. It allows you to see what parameters you have declared and what parameters may be missing.

Create Custom Objects

You can create your own custom objects that contain properties and methods. The custom object allows you to organize data with names and labels to make data easier to access. It is a good idea to use a custom object when you are frequently accessing global variables.

There are two ways to create a custom object: the long way and the short way. The long way needs a constructor function, which looks like any other function. The purpose of the constructor function is to assign the properties to their values. For example, the statement `function employee(name, department)` accepts two parameters that are converted to properties.

To convert properties to the object, you need to use the keyword `this`. The keyword `this` allows you to reference the current object. Adding the parameter name to the keyword `this` allows you to create an object property. For

example, the statement `this.name = name;` stores the variable contents of `name` into the property `this.name` when included in the constructor function.

You can create an object with its construction by invoking the function with the `new` keyword. For example, the statement `var worker = new employee("Praveen", "IT");` creates an object stored in `worker`.

You can reference the properties of the worker method with the statement `var theName = worker.name`.

The short method does not require the use of the constructor function. You can define an object inside braces. You can place the property names and values inside the braces. For example, the statement `var worker = {name: "Shona", department: "HR"};` defines an object named `worker` with the properties `name` and `department`.

Create Custom Objects

THE LONG METHOD

① Develop a custom method by declaring a function and properties.

② Declare a new custom object with values inside the parentheses.

③ Display the custom object's properties with a `document.write()` statement.

④ Save the file.

```html
<html>
 <head>
  <title> JavaScript Blueprint </title>
 </head>
 <body>
   <script type="text/javascript">
     function carSale(idNum, type, color, price){
        this.idNum = idNum;
        this.type = type;
        this.color = color;
        this.price = price;
     }

     var car1 = new carSale(123, "coupe", "red", 25450);
     document.write(car1.idNum + " | " + car1.type +
        " | " + car1.color + " | " + car1.price + "<br/>");
   </script>
 </body>
</html>
```

⑤ Open the file in a Web browser.

● The object's properties appear in the browser window.

`123 | coupe | red | 25450`

THE SHORT METHOD

1 Define the object using braces with the properties that are being defined.

2 Display the custom object's properties with a `document.write()` statement.

3 Save the file.

```
customObject2.html - Notepad
File  Edit  Format  View  Help

<html>
 <head>
  <title> JavaScript Blueprint </title>
 </head>
 <body>
   <script type="text/javascript">

     var car1 = {idNum:123, type:"coupe", color:"red", price:25450};     ◄── 1

     document.write(car1.idNum + " | " + car1.type +
        " | " + car1.color + " | " + car1.price + "<br/");              ◄── 2

   </script>
 </body>
</html>
```

4 Open the file in a Web browser.

- The object's properties appear in the browser window.

```
JavaScript Blueprint - Microsoft Internet Explorer
File  Edit  View  Favorites  Tools  Help
Back ·   ·       Search  Favorites
Address  C:\VisualBlueprint\CHAPTER_12\customObject2.html          Go

123 | coupe | red | 25450  ◄──
```

Extra

After the object is created, you can assign new property to that instance by assigning a value to the new property. For example, the statement `worker.bonus = 1000;` assigns the new property `bonus` to the `worker` object.

You can create a custom object by first assigning a blank object to a variable. You can populate the new object by assigning each parameter individually.

```
var worker = new Object();
worker.name = "Sriraj";
worker.department = "Support";
```

You can use this method to create objects, but it is normally harder to maintain than the long and short methods. Another problem with creating objects this way is the amount of space they occupy. The same object created above takes one line with the short method. A major benefit of using the constructor to define an object is that you can reference other functions when creating the object, while the short method saves on the amount of space used.

Develop a Custom Object Method

You can develop custom methods for custom objects. It is just as easy as creating the constructor function that created the object. The method has a function name followed by parentheses. For example, the statement `function getDept()` creates a method that you can use as an object.

The method can contain any type of JavaScript statement. You can reference the object by using the keyword `this` just like the constructor function. The keyword `this` references the current object that executes the method. You can retrieve any of the object parameters by attaching the keyword `this` to them. For example, the statement `this.department` pulls the data stored in the `department` property of the object.

You can also store new data in the properties by referencing the property and storing the new data. You can also create new properties in the function by assigning new property values to the object. For example, the statement `this.wage = 25.50;` creates a new property and stores the initial value.

To call a custom method, attach the method name after the object. For example, the statement `worker.getDept();` calls the method `getDept()` and uses the data from the worker object.

You should not name any of your methods after methods that already exist because it may cause errors. The same applies to the object names.

You can reference other functions within the custom method. You can call other functions to perform tasks or to return dynamic data back to the method. This allows you to make custom methods that can perform any task with one method call.

Develop a Custom Object Method

① Define the object using braces with the properties that are being defined.

② Add an additional property that calls the custom method.

③ Add a custom method calling other functions.

④ Develop another function for the custom method to call.

⑤ Declare a function that contains the custom method call.

⑥ Add a hyperlink to execute the function when clicked.

⑦ Save the file.

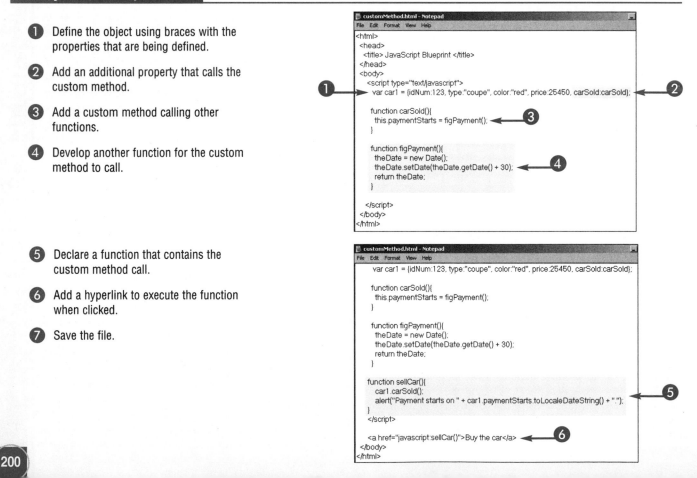

```
customMethod.html - Notepad
File  Edit  Format  View  Help
<html>
 <head>
  <title> JavaScript Blueprint </title>
 </head>
 <body>
  <script type="text/javascript">
   var car1 = {idNum:123, type:"coupe", color:"red", price:25450, carSold:carSold};

   function carSold(){
     this.paymentStarts = figPayment();
   }

   function figPayment(){
     theDate = new Date();
     theDate.setDate(theDate.getDate() + 30);
     return theDate;
   }

  </script>
 </body>
</html>
```

```
customMethod.html - Notepad
File  Edit  Format  View  Help
   var car1 = {idNum:123, type:"coupe", color:"red", price:25450, carSold:carSold};

   function carSold(){
     this.paymentStarts = figPayment();
   }

   function figPayment(){
     theDate = new Date();
     theDate.setDate(theDate.getDate() + 30);
     return theDate;
   }

   function sellCar(){
     car1.carSold();
     alert("Payment starts on " + car1.paymentStarts.toLocaleDateString() + ".");
   }
  </script>

  <a href="javascript:sellCar()">Buy the car</a>
 </body>
</html>
```

8 Open the file in a Web browser.

9 Click the link to execute the function.

● An alert dialog box appears.

Extra

You can help suppress errors when a property is null by using a shortcut operator in your constructor functions. The or (| |) operator is used when assigning values. This allows you to avoid storing nulls in the object's properties.

```
function buildObj(level, fullName){
    this.level = level || "NA";
    this.fullName = fullName || "NA";
}
```

If any of the parameters are not included when the object is being created, the property inherits the value located to the right of the or (| |) operator. If the operator is not included, you have to use if-else statements to create the same effect. The result is extra lines of code.

```
function buildObj(level, fullName){
    if(level.length > 0) this.level = level;
    else this.level = "NA";
    if(level.fullName > 0) this.fullName = fullName;
    else this.fullName = "NA";
}
```

Create a Pseudo Hash Table

Y
ou can create a pseudo hash table to produce a fast way to look up information in a two dimensional table. Instead of referencing the second dimension columns when you are looking up data, you can use a reference string.

You must first create an array that has objects. For example, the statement `cars[cars.length] = {id:'R123', style:'sport', color:'red'};` creates an array that has three objects associated with it. It is important that one object of this column is unique.

You then use this unique column to create the hash table lookup. You need to loop through the length of the array that you created. You have to store the unique column identifier as the property name of the hash table. For example, the statement `cars[cars[i].id] = cars[i];` stores the unique ID `cars[i].id` as the hash table property name.

You can then use the name of the ID to access the data in the array. For example, the statement `var theColor = cars['R123'].color;` allows you to find the color of the car with the ID `R123`. If you did not have this hash lookup on the ID, then you would have to loop through the array and find the array that matched `R123`. Then, you would have to find the value in the column for the color. The major benefit of the hash table is avoiding the `for` loop needed to match the information. Instead, you can just use the ID to pull the information without any extra steps.

It is important that the identifier column is a unique identifier. If you use an identifier that is not unique, it overwrites the data already present in the array, resulting in lost information.

Create a Pseudo Hash Table

1. Declare a `new Array`.

2. Set the new array equal to a list of object name/value pairs.

3. Repeat step **2** for each row in the array.

4. Create a `for` loop iterating through the entire length of the array.

5. Store the new value in the array using the unique identifier column.

Note: The unique column must not repeat information because the previous information is overwritten when it occurs.

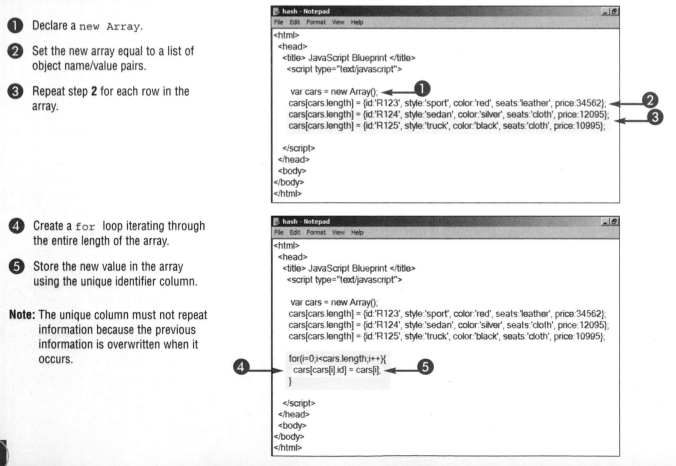

```
hash - Notepad
File  Edit  Format  View  Help
<html>
 <head>
  <title> JavaScript Blueprint </title>
   <script type="text/javascript">

    var cars = new Array();          ①
    cars[cars.length] = {id:'R123', style:'sport', color:'red', seats:'leather', price:34562};   ②
    cars[cars.length] = {id:'R124', style:'sedan', color:'silver', seats:'cloth', price:12095};
    cars[cars.length] = {id:'R125', style:'truck', color:'black', seats:'cloth', price:10995};   ③

   </script>
 </head>
 <body>
 </body>
</html>
```

```
hash - Notepad
File  Edit  Format  View  Help
<html>
 <head>
  <title> JavaScript Blueprint </title>
   <script type="text/javascript">

    var cars = new Array();
    cars[cars.length] = {id:'R123', style:'sport', color:'red', seats:'leather', price:34562};
    cars[cars.length] = {id:'R124', style:'sedan', color:'silver', seats:'cloth', price:12095};
    cars[cars.length] = {id:'R125', style:'truck', color:'black', seats:'cloth', price:10995};

    for(i=0;i<cars.length;i++){          ④  ⑤
     cars[cars[i].id] = cars[i];
    }

   </script>
 </head>
 <body>
 </body>
</html>
```

6 Add an alert dialog box statement displaying the column of the hash array using the unique identifier.

7 Save the file.

```
hash - Notepad
File Edit Format View Help

<html>
 <head>
  <title> JavaScript Blueprint </title>
   <script type="text/javascript">

   var cars = new Array();
   cars[cars.length] = {id:'R123', style:'sport', color:'red', seats:'leather', price:34562};
   cars[cars.length] = {id:'R124', style:'sedan', color:'silver', seats:'cloth', price:12095};
   cars[cars.length] = {id:'R125', style:'truck', color:'black', seats:'cloth', price:10995};

   for(i=0;i<cars.length;i++){
    cars[cars[i].id] = cars[i];
   }

   alert(cars["R123"].price);          6

  </script>
 </head>
 <body>
 </body>
</html>
```

8 Open the file in a Web browser.

● The value from the dynamically created hash table appears in an alert dialog box.

Microsoft Internet Explorer ✕

⚠ 34562

OK

Apply It

You can transform a two-dimensional array into a quick lookup hash table. The following code takes a two-dimensional array called items and turns it into a hash lookup with the name balloon.

```
var items = new Array(['red',1,1.23],['blue',2,2.25],['silver',0,3.99]);
var balloon = new Array()
for(i=0;i<items.length;i++){
  balloon[items[i][0]] = new Array();
  balloon[items[i][0]].amount = items[i][1];
  balloon[items[i][0]].cost = items[i][2];
}
alert("Cost of a Blue Balloon is $" + balloon["blue"].cost);
```

Instead of having to loop through the array to find the element that contains blue, you can reference it by the name blue. This saves time because no for loops are involved in the lookup process. If the script looks up twenty items, this function saves the script from having to process twenty loops, which is time-consuming.

Manage Images with the Image Object

You can use the image object on any page that contains at least one image. The image object is an array of all the images that are located on the page. The image object is a sub-object of the document object. You can use the image object to access all of the image properties.

The images are referred to the index, which matches the image's position on the Web page. For example, if the Web page has two images, you can refer to the first one as document.images[0] and the second one as document.images[1]. Remember that the index always begins at 0 and not at 1.

You can find the information about the image by using the image's index. Common properties that you can retrieve are the source, name, style sheet class, dimensions, and much more.

You are not restricted to using the index of the image to get its properties. You can use the name attribute to reference the image. If the image is located inside a form, you can reference it from the form object. For example, var thePic = document.Form1.theImage.src retrieves the source of the image named theImage in the form Form1.

You can also use DOM to get the image properties. You can use the getElementById() method to retrieve the values. For example, the statement document.getElementById("theImage").src references the source of the image named theImage.

The image object has no predefined methods like the form or string objects. You can change the image properties by referencing them, however. It is very common to change the source of the image or the size.

Manage Images with the Image Object

LIST ALL THE IMAGES

① Add one or more images to the document.

② Create a for loop to iterate through the image object array.

③ Retrieve the current image by referencing the object and display the result with a document.write() statement.

④ Save the file.

⑤ Open the file in a Web browser.

● The source of every image on the Web page appears.

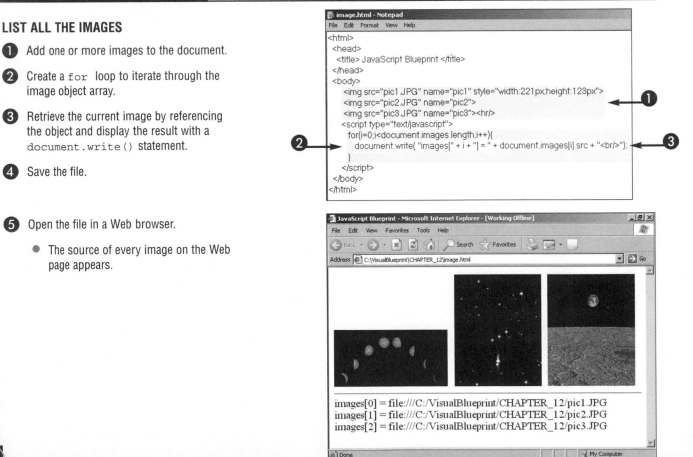

204

CHANGE ALL THE IMAGES

 ① Add one or more images that you want to change.

② Create an array to hold new image names.

③ Loop through the array and reference the image object to change the images.

④ Save the file.

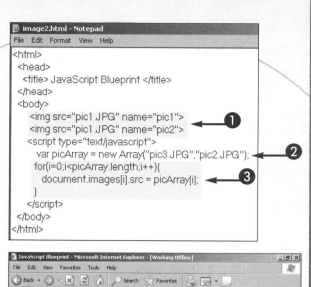

⑤ Open the file in a Web browser.

● The images from the array appear.

Apply It

You can preload images into the memory while the page is loading by using a new image object. After the image is loaded, JavaScript can reference the image object and display it immediately instead of waiting for the images to load.

A pre-loader script is great for image swaps and galleries. It increases the page loading time, but it cuts down on the amount of lag time the user may encounter.

```
var theImages = new Object();
theImages["games"] = new Image(25,40);
theImages["games"].src = "games.gif";
theImages["videos"] = new Image(25,40);
theImages["videos"].src = "videos.gif";
```

You can then access the images by using the object name.

```
document.getElementById("theImg").src = theImages["games"].src;
```

Locate All Links

You can use the link and anchor objects to reference all of the links and anchors on the Web page. Just like the image object, the links and anchors are stored in an array. The order in which the link or anchor appears on the page is the order in which they appear in the array.

For example, if the page has three links and two anchors, the first anchor would be referenced as document.anchor[0]. The last link would be referenced by document.links[2].

The anchor object includes just one property. The name property of the anchor can be changed dynamically. For example, document.anchor[1].name="end"; changes the name of the second anchor on the page to end.

The link object includes the href and target properties that are used to dynamically change a link. For example, the statement document.links[0].href = "newPage.html"; changes the location of the first link on the page to the newPage.html file.

Apply It

You can use the link array to create random links on the page. The sample code uses an array to hold the links. A random number generator picks a link and sets the href value.

```
var linkArray = new
Array("http://www.wiley.com","http://www.
JavaRanch.com","http://
www.codingforums.com");

var randomNum =
Math.floor(Math.random()*linkArray.length);
document.links[0].href = linkArray[randomNum];
```

Locate All Links

① Add one or more links to the document.

② Create a for loop to iterate through the image object array.

③ Retrieve the current link's location by referencing the object displaying its results with a document.write() statement.

④ Save the file.

link.html - Notepad
File Edit Format View Help

```
<html>
 <head>
  <title> JavaScript Blueprint </title>
 </head>
 <body>
   <a href="http://www.JavaRanch.com">JavaRanch </a><br/>
   <a href="http://www.Wiley.com">Wiley</a><br/>
   <a href="http://www.CodingForums.com">Coding Forums</a><hr/>
   <script type="text/javascript">
    for(i=0;i<document.links.length;i++){
     document.write( "links[" + i + "] = " + document.links[i].href + "<br/>");
    }
   </script>
 </body>
</html>
```

⑤ Open the file in a Web browser.

● The location of every link on the Web page appears.

JavaScript Blueprint - Microsoft Internet Explorer
File Edit View Favorites Tools Help
Back ▪ ▪ Search Favorites
Address C:\VisualBlueprint\CHAPTER_12\link.html Go

JavaRanch
Wiley
Coding Forums

links[0] = http://www.javaranch.com/
links[1] = http://www.wiley.com/
links[2] = http://www.codingforums.com/

Dissect the Location Object

You can use the location object to access the information about the link in the address bar. The location object has eight properties and three methods. The properties are used to set or get the values of the current URL.

You can set or get the URL of the current Web page by using the `href` property. For example, `var theURL = document.location.href;` stores the current Web page address into the browser.

You can determine the part of the string that is after the hash (#) sign by using the `hash` property. The hash sign is used for page anchors.

The third property is the `host` property. You can use it to set or get the host name and the port number portion of the URL. You can grab the host name part of the string by using the `hostname` property. By using the `port` property, you can determine the port portion of the URL.

The `pathname` property retrieves the filename or path to the Web page. It does not show the host name.

The `protocol` property retrieves the Web protocol name of the URL.

The last property you can use is the `search` property. The `search` property retrieves the portion of the URL after the question mark, which is known as the `query string`.

You can reload the Web page by using the `reload` method. The `reload` method reloads the existing Web page.

You can use the `replace` method to replace the existing Web page with a new page. The `replace` method does not allow the last page to be in the Web page history. The `assign` method is used to load a new Web page into the Web browser.

Dissect the Location Object

❶ Create a link that you want to evaluate.

❷ Reference the link and add the link property keywords displaying its properties with `document.write()` statements.

❸ Save the file.

Note: You can use `document.location` instead to evaluate the current Web page in the browser.

```
location.html - Notepad
File Edit Format View Help
<html>
 <head>
  <title> JavaScript Blueprint </title>
 </head>
 <body>
  <a href="http://saloon.javaranch.com/cgi-bin/ubb/ultimatebb.cgi?ubb=forum&f=20">
    JavaRanch Link</a><br>
  <script type="text/javascript">
  document.write("href: " + document.links[0].href + "<br/>")
  document.write("hash: " + document.links[0].hash + "<br/>")
  document.write("host: " + document.links[0].host + "<br/>")
  document.write("hostName: " + document.links[0].hostname + "<br/>")
  document.write("pathName: " + document.links[0].pathname + "<br/>")
  document.write("port: " + document.links[0].port + "<br/>")
  document.write("protocol: " + document.links[0].protocol + "<br/>")
  document.write("search: " + document.links[0].search + "<br/>")
  </script>
 </body>
</html>
```

❹ Open the file in a Web browser.

● The individual properties of the link appear.

```
JavaScript Blueprint - Microsoft Internet Explorer
File Edit View Favorites Tools Help
Back          Search  Favorites
Address C:\VisualBlueprint\CHAPTER_12\location.html          Go

JavaRanch Link
href: http://saloon.javaranch.com/cgi-bin/ubb/ultimatebb.cgi?
ubb=forum&f=20
hash:
host: saloon.javaranch.com:80
hostName: saloon.javaranch.com
pathName: cgi-bin/ubb/ultimatebb.cgi
port: 80
protocol: http:
search: ?ubb=forum&f=20
```

Create a Bread Crumb Navigation Menu

You can add a unique way to navigate through your Web site if each folder contains a default Web page. A bread crumb navigation menu is a link to the current page divided into each main directory leading up to it. This allows a user to backtrack to the main folder by clicking a link. For example, the following URL `http://www.somepage.com/pictures/ideas/item.html` can be broken up into the main link `www.somepage.com`, the `pictures` directory, and the `ideas` directory. Each directory can contain many HTML pages, but they should all include an index page in order for this to work correctly.

You need to store the URL in a variable, and then strip the `http:` or `https:` from the link. After that happens, you can separate the remaining portion of the link at the folder levels.

After the entire link is in pieces, you need to join them back together to build links to each folder level. To do this, you need to store the http: or https: into a variable. This variable then gets each level of the folder directory added to it by looping through the `theParts` array. Then you need to create a link to display on the page by using the folder name and adding a spacer between each of the folder levels.

The function returns the bread crumb navigation string that can be written anywhere on the page. This function accepts any URL into the field. If you want to use the current page's URL, then you should add `document.location.href` into the parentheses of the function call.

You can customize the look and feel of the links by applying Cascading Style Sheets (CSS) to the links. To learn more about CSS, see Chapter 14.

Create a Bread Crumb Navigation Menu

① Create a function that accepts one parameter.

② Use the `split()` method to split the URL at the double slash and at the single slash into two separate variables.

③ Declare two strings to hold output URL and Display Text.

④ Add the `http:` or `https:` that was sliced off to the link variable.

⑤ Declare two more variables as placeholders.

⑥ Create a `for` loop iterating through the `theParts` array.

⑦ If the loop is not run on the first time, add dividers to the string.

⑧ Add the URL part from the array to the string.

⑨ Add the next partial link to the string.

⑩ Return the string value after the loop is complete.

```
BreadCrumb - Notepad
File  Edit  Format  View  Help
<html>
 <head>
  <title> JavaScript Blueprint </title>
   <script type="text/javascript">
    function BreadCrumb(theURL){
     theURL = theURL.split("//");
     theParts = theURL[theURL.length-1].split("/");
     theStr = "| ";
     theLink = "";
     if(theURL.length>1)theLink = theURL[0] + "//";
     addDiv = "";
     addBar = "";
    }
   </script>
 </head>
 <body>
 </body>
</html>
```

```
BreadCrumb - Notepad
File  Edit  Format  View  Help
   <script type="text/javascript">
    function BreadCrumb(theURL){
     theURL = theURL.split("//");
     theParts = theURL[theURL.length-1].split("/");
     theStr = "| ";
     theLink = "";
     if(theURL.length>1)theLink = theURL[0] + "//";
     addDiv = "";
     addBar = "";
     for(i=0;i<theParts.length;i++){
      if(theStr.length != 2){
       addDiv = "/";
       addBar = " | ";
      }
      theLink += addDiv + theParts[i];
      theStr += addBar + "<a href='"+theLink+"'>"+ theParts[i] +"</a>";
     }
     return theStr;
    }
   </script>
 </head>
```

⑪ Create a `document.write()` statement that calls the function with the URL as the single parameter.

⑫ Save the file.

```
BreadCrumb - Notepad
File  Edit  Format  View  Help
        addDiv = "";
        addBar = "";
        for(i=0;i<theParts.length;i++){
          if(theStr.length != 2){
            addDiv = "/";
            addBar = " | ";
          }
          theLink += addDiv + theParts[i];
          theStr += addBar + "<a href='"+theLink+"'>"+ theParts[i] +"</a>";
        }
        return theStr;
      }
    </script>
  </head>
  <body>
   <script type="text/javascript">
     document.write("The link: http://radio.javaranch.com/channel/pascarello<br/>");
     document.write(BreadCrumb("http://radio.javaranch.com/channel/pascarello/"));      ⑪
   </script>
  </body>
</html>
```

⑬ Open the file in a Web browser.

● The bread crumb navigation menu appears on the screen separated into directory listings.

```
JavaScript Blueprint - Microsoft Internet Explorer
File  Edit  View  Favorites  Tools  Help
Back        Search  Favorites
Address  C:\VisualBlueprint\Chapter_12\BreadCrumb.html       Go

The link: http://radio.javaranch.com/channel/pascarello
| radio.javaranch.com | channel | pascarello |   ◄
```

You can display descriptive text instead of the folder names by creating an object and giving each folder a specific name. This gives the user a better feel about what the directory is, instead of a general term such as `files`. The term `files` can mean different things to different people, but the descriptive text can solve any confusion.

```
var places = new Object();
places["radio.javaranch.com"] = "Radio Home Page";
places["channel"] = "Member Blogs";
places["pascarello"] = "Eric Pascarello's Blog";
```

You need to slightly alter the bread crumb navigation script for this change to take place. You need to reference the object name with the text from the `theParts` array. Because not every folder might include this array, you need to run a check to verify that a description exists.

```
theName = (places[theParts[i]]) ? places[theParts[i]] : theParts[i];
theStr += addBar + "<a href='"+theLink+"'>"+ theName +"</a>";
```

Explore the Page History of the Browser

You can use the history object to create forward and backward buttons, just like the buttons on the browser, and make the Web page easier for the user to navigate. The history object stores all of the Web pages that the user visited in the current browser session. Once the browser window is closed, all its history information is deleted.

JavaScript has very limited access to this list of data for security reasons, but JavaScript can use the history object for navigation purposes.

You can create a Back button by using the history object's `back()` method. For example, `history.back();` moves the Web page back one page. You can also include a parameter in the parentheses to move back any number of pages. For example, `history.back(3);` sends the browser back three pages.

You can move forward in the history of the browser by using the `forward()` method, which accepts a parameter to move forward multiple pages.

Another method that is not very popular is the `go()` method. The `go()` method moves forward in history if the parameter is positive and back in history if the parameter is negative.

The history object only has one property, which is used to determine the number of elements in the history. The `length` property returns the number of items.

You cannot determine what any of the items in the history are. Therefore, you cannot determine the names or the URLs of the Web pages that the user has visited. The main reason for this high level of security is to keep prying eyes away from the surfing habits of the user. People could use the history information to determine what banks, credit card companies, and e-mail accounts a user visits.

Explore the Page History of the Browser

① Add the `history` object with the `length` property.

② Create a `document.write()` statement to display the history object.

③ Save the file.

```
history.html - Notepad
File  Edit  Format  View  Help
<html>
 <head>
  <title> JavaScript Blueprint </title>
 </head>
 <body>
   <script type="text/javascript">
   document.write("Your browser history contains " + history.length + " pages.");
   </script>
 </body>
</html>
```

④ Open the file in a Web browser.

● The number of Web pages in the history object appears.

```
JavaScript Blueprint - Microsoft Internet Explorer
File   Edit   View   Favorites   Tools   Help
Back  ·         ·         Search   Favorites
Address  C:\VisualBlueprint\CHAPTER_12\history.html        Go

Your browser history contains 3 pages.
```

Disable the
Back Button

Y ou can disable the Back button in a primitive manner by using the history object and the forward() method. By placing the history. forward() on your HTML page, the user cannot go to that Web page by pressing the Back button.

There is no way for JavaScript to disable the Back button or any other methods that a user can use to navigate through a Web page. If you use the history.forward() method and the user presses the Back button, the original page is still called.

If you can control the links in the previous pages, you can overwrite them so they never appear in the history object by using the replace() method. The replace() method is part of the location object. When you use the replace() method, it overwrites the current page in the history with the new page. Therefore, the Back button cannot go to the page because it no longer exists.

One thing you need to remember is that the user prefers the ability to move freely around a Web site. By trying to disable a user's method of navigation, he or she may get frustrated and leave. If you need to disable the Back button, it is always a good idea to look at the main reason why the Back button needs to be disabled. Redesigning part of the code may eliminate the need to remove functionality from your Web site.

There are other ways to try to disable the Back button without using JavaScript. You can use Meta tags and server-side languages like ASP, JSP, and .NET. However, not all servers will allow you to use server-side languages. The drawback with Meta tags is that they do not work 100 percent of the time.

Disable the Back Button

① Add the history object with the forward method in the header.

② Add a link to any Web page to advance the page.

③ Save the file.

disableback.html - Notepad

File Edit Format View Help

```html
<html>
 <head>
  <title> JavaScript Blueprint </title>
   <script type="text/javascript">
     history.forward();  ①
   </script>
 </head>
 <body>
  <a href="picturePage.html">Next Page</a>  ②
 </body>
</html>
```

④ Open the file in a Web browser.

⑤ Click the link.

⑥ Click the Back button.

● The Web browser returns to the last page in the history, not allowing the user to use the back button.

JavaScript Blueprint - Microsoft Internet Explorer

File Edit View Favorites Tools Help

⑥ → Back ・ ○ ・ ⊠ ② ⚛ Search Favorites

Address C:\VisualBlueprint\CHAPTER_12\disableback.html → Go

Next Page ⑤

Detect the Browser Brand Name

You may want to execute the script depending on what browser the user has available. Certain browsers handle code differently than others; therefore, you can use browser detection to determine the program flow.

The `navigator.appName` property returns a string that displays the browser. For example, the statement `var isIE = (navigator.appName == "Microsoft Internet Explorer");` stores a Boolean in the variable `isIE`. If the browser is Microsoft Internet Explorer, then the Boolean value is true. Other browsers will display false.

Not all browsers will display the true browser name. For example, you can set the Opera browser to display Netscape, Microsoft Internet Explorer, or Opera. The value that displays is based on the setting the user chooses in the options.

To verify that a browser is Opera, use the `navigator.userAgent` property. The `navigator.userAgent` property displays a more detailed view of the browser. You can test the browser to verify if it is actually Opera by utilizing the statement `var isOpera = (navigator.userAgent.indexOf("Opera") != -1);`. The statement looks for the string Opera and returns true if the browser is Opera.

The use of browser detection is no longer as important as it used to be because the browsers are now following the same standards. Cross-browser scripting has become easier, but some methods do not work between browsers. This is why browser detection is important. You can develop different versions of Web pages depending on the browser. For example, with Microsoft Internet Explorer, you can use ActiveX controls. Because other browsers do not allow you to use ActiveX controls, you must develop a Web page for IE and one for the other browsers.

Detect the Browser Brand Name

① Declare a variable and store the `navigator.appName` property.

② Create a group of expressions to check for the browser names.

③ Use a `document.write()` statement to display the browser name and expression results.

④ Save the file.

```
detectBrowser.html - Notepad
File  Edit  Format  View  Help
<html>
 <head>
  <title> JavaScript Blueprint </title>
 </head>
 <body>
   <script type="text/javascript">

     var theBrowser = navigator.appName;          ①
     var isIE = (navigator.appName == "Microsoft Internet Explorer");   ②
     var isNN = (navigator.appName == "Netscape");

     document.write("The Browser is " + theBrowser + ".<hr/>");
     document.write("MIE: " + isIE + "<br/>");     ③
     document.write("NN: " + isNN + "<br/>");

   </script>
 </body>
</html>
```

⑤ Open the file in a Web browser.

● The name of the browser appears in the browser window.

```
JavaScript Blueprint - Microsoft Internet Explorer
File  Edit  View  Favorites  Tools  Help
Back  -  x  2  Search  Favorites
Address  C:\VisualBlueprint\CHAPTER_13\detectBrowser.html    Go

The Browser is Microsoft Internet Explorer.

MIE: true
NN: false
```

1 Develop an expression to check for Microsoft Internet Explorer.

2 Add an `if` statement to redirect the user if the browser is Microsoft, and then redirect the browser to another Web page.

3 Add an `else` statement for browsers other then Microsoft, and redirect browser to another location.

4 Save the file.

5 Open the file in a Web browser.

● The page is redirected according to the browser.

```
detectBrowser2.html - Notepad
File  Edit  Format  View  Help
<html>
 <head>
  <title> JavaScript Blueprint </title>
 </head>
 <body>
   <script type="text/javascript">

     var isIE = (navigator.appName == "Microsoft Internet Explorer");    ──1

     if(isIE)document.location.href="IEVersion.html";    ──2
     else document.location.href = "OtherVersion.html";    ──3

   </script>
 </body>
</html>
```

```
JavaScript Blueprint - Microsoft Internet Explorer
File  Edit  View  Favorites  Tools  Help
Back  ▾   ▾   ✗   ⟳   ⌂   🔍 Search  ⭐ Favorites   🖨   ▾
Address  C:\VisualBlueprint\CHAPTER_13\IEVersion.html          ▾  Go
```

IE Version

Extra

Some developers tend to think that if you develop a Web page that only works with a certain browser, then you are a bad coder. These developers tend to forget that there are certain operations and objects that only certain browsers can use. For example, you can have a Web page full of ActiveX objects. Chapter 16 covers more information on ActiveX.

You can display a message to users that they need to use a specific browser in order to use a certain Web page. If you are able to offer an alternate solution, you can have the page redirected there.

```
var isIE = (navigator.appName == "Microsoft Internet Explorer");
if(isIE) document.location.replace = "theIEVersion.html";
else document.location.replace = "theOtherVersion.html";
```

You should never ban a specific browser from your site. One major reason is that you lose the traffic that comes to your Web site from other browsers. It is hard enough to get traffic to your Web site at times; by blocking browsers you can lose up to half of the traffic. By carefully coding a Web page and providing alternatives, you can support all browsers.

Determine the Operating System

You can detect the operating system of the user in order to adjust CSS properties or the JavaScript code so it performs properly for the user. One problem with Microsoft Internet Explorer is that the Windows version appears differently from the Macintosh version. You can use the navigator object to detect the operating system and adjust it accordingly.

You can use the `navigator.userAgent` property, which contains a string that allows you to determine the browser. This method has one flaw, though. The creators of the browsers never developed a standard nomenclature for the way they named the operating systems.

For example, the value for a Microsoft Windows 98 operating system may appear as `"Win98"` or `"Windows 98"`. There also can be differences in the Macintosh browser. As a result, you have to use the `indexOf()` method to determine the browser type.

All the Windows machines contain the substring `"Win"`, while the Macintosh machines contain the substring `"Mac"`. UNIX-based operating systems may be listed as `"X11"` or `"Linux"`, which adds to the problems of determining the browser.

Some browsers include more information about the operating system, such as release dates and major or minor versions of the program. Certain browsers display Windows XP as Windows NT, which can also be confusing.

Netscape 6 and later versions include the `navigator.oscpu` that returns the portion of the user agent that contains all of the possible operating systems and CPU information that it contains.

By making wise decisions, you can have a Web page that looks the same no matter what browser the user is utilizing. One application is to make the font smaller for pages viewed with Macintosh because they tend to show a larger font size.

Locate the Operating System

 Add the userAgent property in a statement to retrieve information that the browser stores inside a `document.write()` statement.

 Save the file.

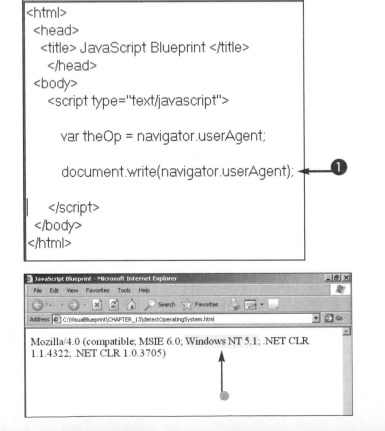

③ Open the file in a Web browser.

● The operating system appears in the middle of the string.

Determine the Operating System

1. Add a statement to compare the `userAgent` property with Windows, Macintosh, and Linux browsers.

2. Develop `document.write()` expressions to show the operating system information.

3. Save the file.

```
detectOperatingSystem2.html - Notepad
File  Edit  Format  View  Help

<html>
 <head>
  <title> JavaScript Blueprint </title>
   </head>
 <body>
  <script type="text/javascript">

    var theOp = navigator.userAgent;
    var isWin = (navigator.userAgent.indexOf("Win") != -1);
    var isMac = (navigator.userAgent.indexOf("Mac") != -1);
    var isX11 = (navigator.userAgent.indexOf("X11")  != -1 ||
                     navigator.userAgent.indexOf("Linux") != -1);    ←①

    document.write("userAgent: " + navigator.userAgent + "<hr/>");
    document.write("Win: " + isWin + "<br/>");
    document.write("Mac: " + isMac + "<br/>");    ←②
    document.write("X11: " + isX11 + "<br/>");

   </script>
 </body>
</html>
```

4. Open the file in a Web browser.

- The statements that appear show what operating system the user is using.

```
JavaScript Blueprint - Microsoft Internet Explorer
File  Edit  View  Favorites  Tools  Help

Back ▼   ▼  ×       Search    Favorites

Address  C:\VisualBlueprint\CHAPTER_13\detectOperatingSystem2.html          ▼  Go

userAgent: Mozilla/4.0 (compatible; MSIE 6.0; Windows NT 5.1; .NET
CLR 1.1.4322; .NET CLR 1.0.3705)

Win: true
Mac: false    ◄
X11: false
```

Apply It

When you develop a Web page and view it on a Macintosh computer, you may notice that the font size is larger. By detecting the operating system, you can change the size of the text on the page as it is loading. The following script will make your Web page look the same on every operating system.

```
<script type="text/javascript">
  var isMac = (navigator.userAgent.indexOf("Mac") != -1);
  var sz = (isMac) ? 12 : 10;
  document.write('<style type="text/css">');
  document.write('body {font-size: ' + sz + 'pt}');
  document.write('</style>');
</script>
```

Instead of dynamically writing the style sheet, you can add a link to an external style sheet. Depending on the operating system, this allows you to make more changes to the Web site without having to write the code dynamically on every Web page.

```
<script type="text/javascript">
  var isMac = (navigator.userAgent.indexOf("Mac") != -1);
  var sSheet = (isMac) ? "MacStyle" : "OtherStyle";
  document.write('<link rel="stylesheet" type="text/css" href="' + sSheet + '.css">');
</script>
```

Distinguish the Default Native Browser Language

Y ou can direct users to different Web page locations depending on the language that is set in the browser if you have two or more different versions of your site written in different languages. This will allow users to read your site in their native languages so your site is appealing to more users.

The `navigator.language` property allows you to determine the native language of the user. Unfortunately, each browser uses a different way to display the native language so you have to do some investigation and detection to determine the value.

To investigate the language set, you need to display the value on the page for each browser. For example, the statement `javascript:alert(navigator.language);` displays the language set for the browser when it is entered into the address bar and executed.

The code that you use to determine the language is normally a two-letter code. For example, the code `de` represents browsers that are set in `German`. You may add an optional two-letter code to the language to specify the region for which the language is tailored. For example, the code `en-us` describes `United States English`.

When trying to determine the language, it is wise to change the language code to uppercase with the `toUpperCase()` method. This helps to reduce the differences between browsers so you can make a positive match.

You can add the user language to a hidden field on a form submission. You can use this information to determine how your page responds to the user. If the form field entries seem to be from a nonnative English speaker, you can verify it with the language submission. For example, `document.formName.hiddenName.value = navigator.language;` stores the information into a form element.

Distinguish the Default Native Browser Language

① Add the statement to store the browser language.

② Develop a `document.write()` statement to show the browser language code on the screen.

③ Save the file.

```
detectLanguage.html - Notepad
File  Edit  Format  View  Help

<html>
 <head>
  <title> JavaScript Blueprint </title>
 </head>
 <body>
   <script type="text/javascript">

     var theLang = navigator.userLanguage;        ①

     document.write("The language" + theLang);     ②

   </script>
 </body>
</html>
```

④ Open the file in a Web browser.

● The native browser language code appears.

```
JavaScript Blueprint - Microsoft Internet Explorer
File  Edit  View  Favorites  Tools  Help
Back ·       ·        Search  Favorites
Address  C:\VisualBlueprint\CHAPTER_13\detectLanguage1.html        Go

The browser is set for en-us  ←
```

Identify the JavaScript Version Support

You may want to detect the JavaScript version in order to verify that a browser is able to support the necessary code. When the JavaScript version changes, older browsers do not support the newest objects, methods, properties, and syntax that are available in the new version. As a result, you may want to develop a way to detect the browser version in use.

There is no built-in method to determine the JavaScript version like there is for detecting the version of the browser. You have to create your own method to test for the JavaScript version. To do this you need to understand how a browser knows to read the code.

When you define a JavaScript `<script>` tag, you can specify the version of code that it contains. For example, the statement `<script language="JavaScript1.4" type="text/javascript">` allows older browsers to determine what the language is. A browser that does not support `version 1.4` ignores the code.

By using this behavior of ignoring the JavaScript code, you can determine what version of JavaScript the browser can run. The first thing you need to do is define a `<script>` tag without a version. For example, the statement `<script language="JavaScript" type="text/javascript">` defines a segment of code without specifying the version. Inside the `<script>` tags you want to define a function that you can call.

Next, you need to add a second function under the first function. This time you need to specify a version. You also need to add the same function name as you listed above. This is important because calling that function's name determines the browser version.

If the browser supports the version, it overwrites the function that is stored in the browser's memory from the first `<script>` tag.

Identify the JavaScript Version Support

① Create a function that does not have a specific JavaScript version set by not including the version.

② Create another function that has the same name as in step **1** and set a specific JavaScript version in the `<script>` tags.

③ Add a JavaScript statement to call the function name that exists in both scripts from steps **1** and **2.**

④ Save the file.

⑤ Open the file in a Web browser.

● A dialog box appears showing the version that is supported.

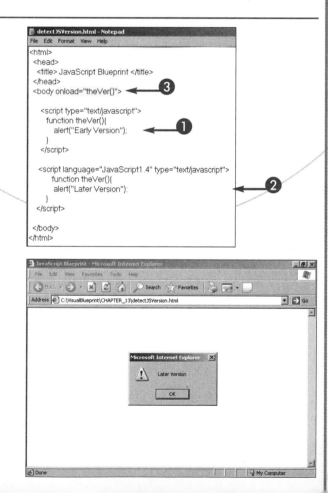

Verify If a Method or Object Is Supported

You can detect a browser's method and object support to allow a JavaScript function to degrade well depending on the browser brand and version. If an object or method does not exist, it causes an error that stops the execution of any other JavaScript statement. You can use method and object detection to protect yourself from this problem.

You can use an `if` statement to test for an object to see if the browser recognizes the object. For example, the statement `if(document.getElementById)` executes the `if` statement if the browser returns `true` for the conditional `document.getElementById`.

Determining properties are a little different from an object because an error occurs in a browser that does not have the specific object. Therefore, you need to include the object along with the property in the `if` statement's conditional.

For example, `if(objectName && objectName.property);` verifies that the object and property both exist.

Checking to see if a method is valid is just like testing for a property. Remember that the method does not get the parentheses when you test it for existence. For example, the statement `if(objectName && objectMethod)` verifies that it can use the method specified in the conditional.

When you look at DHTML scripts, you commonly see a conditional statement such as `var isW3C = (document.getElelementById) ? true:false;`. This conditional statement allows the programmer to use `isW3C` instead of `document.getElementById` in the `if` statement. It saves time and space while coding the application and makes more sense as you read the `if` statements. For example, the statement `if(isW3C)` executes the `if` statement if the Boolean value is `true`.

Verify If a Method or Object Is Supported

① Add an `if` statement to check whether the object is loaded before declaring the object by placing the object reference in the `if` statement.

② Add an `if` statement after the object to verify whether the object has been loaded by placing the object name in the `if` statement.

③ Save the file.

```
detectMethod.html - Notepad
File  Edit  Format  View  Help
<html>
 <head>
  <title> JavaScript Blueprint </title>
   </head>
 <body>
   <form name="form1">
   <script type="text/javascript">
    elemLoad=false;
    if(document.form1.T1)elemLoad = true;      ①
    alert("Element Loaded: " + elemLoad);
  </script>
   <input type="text" name="T1">
   <script type="text/javascript">
    elemLoad=false;
    if(document.form1.T1)elemLoad = true;      ②
    alert("Element Loaded: " + elemLoad);
  </script>
  </form>
 </body>
</html>
```

④ Open the file in a Web browser.

● The alert dialog box appears saying that the object has not been loaded when it encounters the first `if` statement.

⑤ Click OK in the alert dialog box.

```
Microsoft Internet Explorer            [X]

  ⚠     Element Loaded: false

             [   OK   ]   ⑤
```

- The alert dialog box appears again saying that the object has been loaded when it encounters the second `if` statement.

6 Click OK in the alert dialog box.

Microsoft Internet Explorer
⚠ Element Loaded: true
OK ← **6**

- The Done message appears in the status bar showing no errors because the object detection avoided the error.

Note: If you reference the element before it is loaded without the if-statement check, an error appears.

Extra

When you look at older DHTML scripts, there are three lines that tend to appear often: `document.getElementById`, `document.all`, and `document.layers`. These three lines are ways that certain browsers handle the objects in the browser. The `document.getElementById` object is the standard way to access Web page elements that are supported by every modern-day browser. Browsers like Mozilla only use `document.getElementById`; other statements result in errors.

The object `document.layers` is supported by Netscape's major browser version 4 and older. The earlier versions of the browser require more work to perform simple tasks. Netscape browsers 4 and older are considered outdated by a majority of programmers and are not being placed as a specification. Netscape 4 and older do not support CSS and JavaScript fully, which limits the ability to code.

The `document.all` object is the way earlier versions of Microsoft Internet Explorer can handle browser elements. The current version of Internet Explorer still supports the `document.all` object along with the `document.getElementById` object. Browsers that only support `document.all` are also considered outdated by the standards of the programming community.

Set a Cookie Value

A cookie is a variable that you can store on a computer. You can access it as long as the cookie does not expire and the cookie is not deleted from the cache. You can use cookies to keep track of user information to avoid reentering information each time a user visits your site.

The user has the ability to disable cookies so they are not fully reliable. Some users see cookies as a way you can spy on them, so they disable cookies. You cannot enable the user's cookies with JavaScript; the user must do this manually.

The cookie is stored in the `document.cookie` object. A cookie consists of a reference name, a value, and an expiration date. The `setCookie()` function that you create stores the name, value, and expiration date in the cookie

object with this statement: `document.cookie = nameOfCookie + "=" + escape(value) + "; expires=" + expireDate;`.

The name is the reference value that JavaScript uses to grab the cookie information. The value is the data you want to store. The value must escape to eliminate the possibility of errors. The expiration date is the end of the date range from the current date when the cookie is no longer useful. If you want the cookie to last for a long time, make the cookie good for years.

The value that the cookie can store is 4000 characters, but you have to remember that you have to escape the value of the cookie so that 4000 characters is more likely 2000 to 2500 characters. You are also limited to about 20 different name/value pairs of cookies per domain name.

Set a Cookie Value

① Create a function that can accept three parameters.

② Add a cookie declaration to store the name, value, and expiration date.

```
setCookie.html - Notepad
File  Edit  Format  View  Help
<html>
 <head>
  <title> JavaScript Blueprint </title>
   </head>
 <body>
  <script type="text/javascript">

    function setCookie(nameOfCookie, theValue, expireDate){          ①
      document.cookie = nameOfCookie + "=" + escape(theValue) +      ②
                ";expires=" + expireDate;
    }

  </script>
 </body>
</html>
```

③ Add a declaration to call the function to store the cookie.

④ Add an alert statement to see if the stored information is in the cookie.

⑤ Repeat steps **3** and **4** for each cookie you want to store.

⑥ Save the file.

```
setCookie.html - Notepad
File  Edit  Format  View  Help
<html>
 <head>
  <title> JavaScript Blueprint </title>
   </head>
 <body>
  <script type="text/javascript">

    function setCookie(nameOfCookie, theValue, expireDate){
      document.cookie = nameOfCookie + "=" + escape(theValue) +
                ";expires=" + expireDate;
    }

    setCookie("JavaScript_BP","read",new Date("1/1/2008"));          ③
    alert(document.cookie);                                          ④
    setCookie("Second_Name","data",new Date("1/13/2006"));
    alert(document.cookie);                                          ⑤

  </script>
 </body>
</html>
```

7 Open the file in a Web browser.

- An alert dialog box appears showing the stored value in the cookie.

8 Click OK.

- Another alert dialog box appears.

- The first name/value pair is stored in the cookie that you created.

- The second name/value pair is stored in the cookie that you created.

Extra

You can check to see if a user has cookies enabled on their browser by using the `navigator` object. The `navigator` object uses the `cookieEnabled` property that works for Internet Explorer 4 or newer and Netscape 6 or newer. The `navigator.cookieEnabled` returns `true` if cookies are enabled and `false` if they are disabled.

```
if(navigator.cookieEnabled){
  //cookie code
}
else {
  alert("Please enable cookie to use this functionality ");
}
```

You can still test for cookies with earlier versions of a browser by checking for a value stored in a cookie. If the value does not hold in the cookie, then you know that the cookies are disabled.

```
var isCookieEnabled = false;
if(typeof document.cookie == "string"){
  if(document.cookie.length == 0){
    document.cookie = "test enabled";
    isCookieEnabled = (document.cookie == "test enabled");
    document.cookie = "";
  }
  else{
    isCookieEnabled = true;
  }
}
```

Retrieve a Cookie Value

You can retrieve the values of a cookie to display text on the page so the user does not have to continuously fill out forms or log on to pages. You can retrieve information from a cookie by referencing the `document.cookie` object along with the cookie name. The first thing that is important is to do a basic check to see if cookies exist for the domain. You can do this by checking the length of the cookie object. For example, the conditional statement `document.cookie.length > 0` returns `true` if the Web page has any cookies stored.

The cookie is made of the name, the value, and the expiration date that are stored in one long string. The expiration date is not required for all cookies. Because the cookie is stored in one string, you need to break it up into parts in order to get the value that you want.

The first thing you need to do is find the position of the name in the cookie by using the `indexOf` method. For example, the statement `document.cookie.indexOf (nameOfCookie+"=")` returns the position of the name in the cookie. You then add the length of the cookie name along with the equals sign (=) to get the starting position of the value. The statement `startC += nameOfCookie. length+1;` finds the starting point.

You can find the end position of the value by using the `indexOf()` method. The statement `endC = document. cookie.indexOf(";", startC);` finds the ending position of the value. If the value returns `-1`, then make the ending position the last position in the cookie by using the cookie's length.

Because you have the starting and ending points of the value that you want to retrieve, you can use the `substring()` method to extract the value. You also can use the `unescape()` value.

Retrieve a Cookie Value

① Add a statement to make sure that a cookie exists for the page.

② Create a statement to find the position of the variable name for which you want the value.

③ Insert statements to find the value `substring`.

④ Add a `return null` statement if the cookie does not exist.

⑤ Add a JavaScript statement to initialize the function to retrieve the value from the cookie.

⑥ Repeat step **5** for each name/value pair in the cookie.

⑦ Save the file.

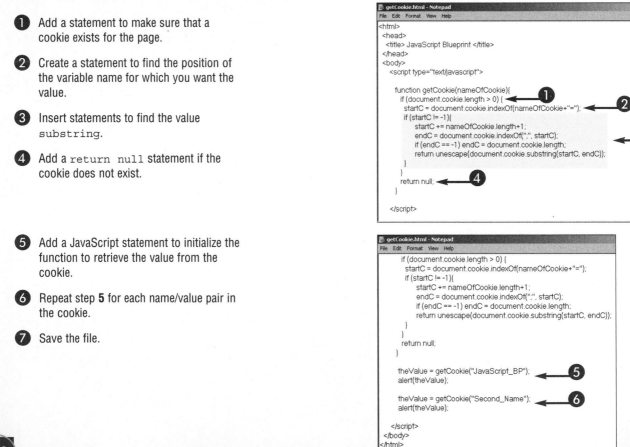

8 Open the file in a Web browser.

● The first cookie value appears in an alert dialog box.

9 Click OK.

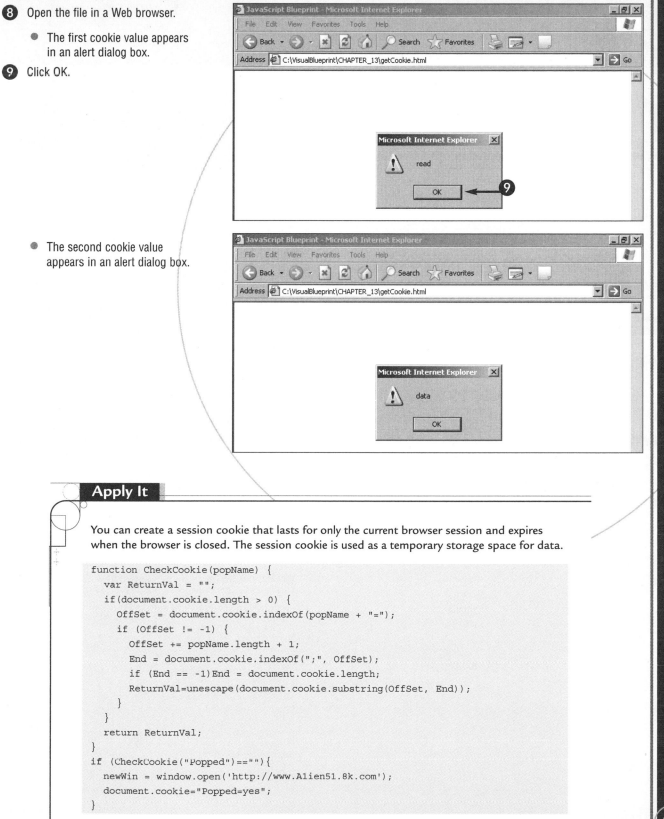

● The second cookie value appears in an alert dialog box.

Apply It

You can create a session cookie that lasts for only the current browser session and expires when the browser is closed. The session cookie is used as a temporary storage space for data.

```
function CheckCookie(popName) {
  var ReturnVal = "";
  if(document.cookie.length > 0) {
    OffSet = document.cookie.indexOf(popName + "=");
    if (OffSet != -1) {
      OffSet += popName.length + 1;
      End = document.cookie.indexOf(";", OffSet);
      if (End == -1)End = document.cookie.length;
      ReturnVal=unescape(document.cookie.substring(OffSet, End));
    }
  }
  return ReturnVal;
}
if (CheckCookie("Popped")==""){
  newWin = window.open('http://www.Alien51.8k.com');
  document.cookie="Popped=yes";
}
```

Delete a Cookie Value

You can delete the cookies that your Web page has created to log a user out of your site, or to provide added security. One big drawback to cookies is that the information is stored on the computer. If the computer is public, anyone can see that information. You can add a button on your page that removes the cookie information and helps protect the user's privacy.

When you want to delete a cookie, first make sure that the cookie exists. You can easily find out if the cookie exists by using the getCookie() function created earlier in this chapter.

Store the cookie again with the name and the expiration date stored somewhere in the past. A common date that many developers use is Thu, 01-Jan-70 00:00:01 GMT.

Because the current date is greater than the expiration date, the cookie is removed. You can use any date that is less than the current date to expire the cookie.

The time that a cookie is removed from the history depends on the user's browser. A cookie is removed from the history of some browsers when the browser is closed; in others, the cookie can be deleted when the browser is still running. Most browsers will not let you access the cookie if it has expired.

If you find yourself deleting cookies during the closing of the page, you may want to consider using session cookies. A browser session starts when the browser opens and ends when the browser closes. The browser session is not dependent on Web sites the user visits.

Delete a Cookie Value

① Add the getCookie() function to your script.

Note: To add a getCookie() function, repeat steps **1** to **4** in the previous task, Retrieve a Cookie Value.

② Create a check using the getCookie() function to see if a cookie exists.

③ Change the expiration date of the cookie to a date in the past to expire the cookie.

④ Call the delCookie() function with the name of a cookie value you want to delete.

⑤ Save the file.

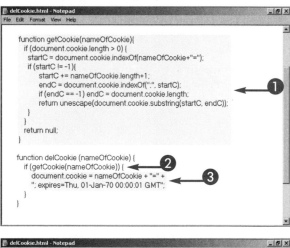

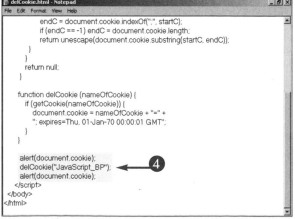

- Open the file in a Web browser.
- The alert dialog box appears showing the values stored in the cookie.

6 Click OK.

- Another alert dialog box appears and shows the cookie with the value removed.

Note: The cookie name is removed from the browser's cache after the browser window is closed.

JavaScript Blueprint - Microsoft Internet Explorer

File Edit View Favorites Tools Help

Back · · · Search Favorites

Address C:\VisualBlueprint\CHAPTER_13\delCookie.html Go

Microsoft Internet Explorer

JavaScript_BP=read; Second_Name=data

OK ← **6**

JavaScript Blueprint - Microsoft Internet Explorer

File Edit View Favorites Tools Help

Back · · · Search Favorites

Address C:\VisualBlueprint\CHAPTER_13\delCookie.html Go

Microsoft Internet Explorer

JavaScript_BP; Second_Name=data

OK

Apply It

You can create, read, and delete cookies from your own domain, but you cannot touch the cookies from other domains. This is done for security reasons. In this sense, cookies are safe because no other domain can read other cookies from another domain, but the user has a little bit more control over the cookie situation.

A user can look at the cookies stored on the computer either by using a text editor or a program that is made to handle cookies. The user can edit and change the cookie at this level without any major problems. Therefore, the user can see what information you are storing and can edit the values.

The user can open a Web site and view the cookie on any page by using a bookmarklet. The bookmarklet formats the cookie into readable text so the user can see what is stored in it without having to file the actual cookie file.

```
javascript:alert(unescape(unescape(document.cookie)).replace(/;/gi,"\n\n"));
```

The bookmarklet code above shows that cookies are not secure since you are able to access the data. If you need to keep track of a user and keep it secure, then you must use a server-side language.

Create a Query String

You can use query strings to pass information from page to page by using forms or by appending the information to the end of the URL. This allows you to keep track of information.

The first way to create a query string is by posting a form. Set the `method` attribute equal to `post`. When you submit the form, a query string is added to the end of the URL.

The query string begins with a question mark to denote the query string. The query string is followed by the first element name in the form object array with its corresponding value. An equals sign (=) separates the name from the value. Each of the form elements is separated by an ampersand symbol (&). For example, the statement `C:\VisualBlueprint\CHAPTER_13\popup.html? T1= fun&T2=games&submit=submit` contains a query string that has three form fields. The fields are `T1`, `T2`, and `submit`.

A form field element appears in the query string when it has a value. If a field is left null, then it will not appear in the query string. A multiple select box shows the name and value for each option that is selected. For example, the query string `?S1=1&S1=1&S1=2&S1=3` shows that three options were selected from the multiple list box.

If a checkbox does not contain a value to place in the query string, the query string keeps the value `on` when it is checked.

You can add the values to the URL by appending them to the end of the URL. For example, the statement `document.location.href = "thePage.html?thePage=" + thePage;` adds a variable to the end of the URL.

Create a Query String

① Create an HTML form that contains different elements.

② Set the `action` attribute to the page where you want to submit the information.

③ Set the `method` attribute to `post`.

④ Save the file.

setQS.html - Notepad

File Edit Format View Help

```html
<html>
 <head>
  <title> Eric Pascarello </title>
 </head>
 <body>
  <form name="test" action="getQS.html" method="post">
    <input type="text" name="ABC"><br/>
    <input type="checkbox" name="CB1"><br/>
    <input type="radio" name="R1" value="1" checked><br/>
    <input type="radio" name="R1" value="2"><br/>
    <input type="submit" name="submit" value="Submit Form">
  </form>
 </body>
</html>
```

⑤ Open the file in a Web browser.

⑥ Complete the form by filling in the appropriate information.

⑦ Click Submit.

Eric Pascarello - Microsoft Internet Explorer

File Edit View Favorites Tools Help

Address C:\VisualBlueprint\CHAPTER_13\setQS.html

123

Submit Form

- The browser window is set to the location in the action attribute.
- The text box name and value appear.
- The checkbox name shows that the checkbox is checked.
- The radio button name and value appear.

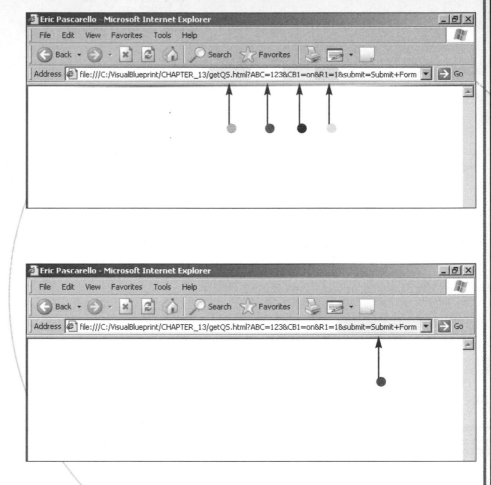

- The submit button name and value appear.
- Because the value has a space between the words, they are joined by a plus sign (+).

Note: The query string begins with a question mark, and the name/value pairs are separated by ampersand symbols.

Apply It

You cannot rely on the information of query strings to be the same as it was intended to be. Because you can manipulate query strings in the address bar of the browser, users can change the values or even remove them. If a person removes the values from the query string, it can cause your application to stop working or produce the wrong results.

One way to protect yourself from this is to add protection in your code that checks to see if all of the parameters exist. If any of the parameters are missing, then the script does not execute.

```
<script>
   numElements = 3;
   theQS = document.location.search;
   theParts = theQS.split("&");
   if(numElements != theParts.length){
       alert('Invalid information provided');
   }
   else{
       //perform action
   }
</script>
```

Convert a Query String into Variables

You can pull information from a query string in order to use the values in a JavaScript program. The values are strings or integers that are submitted from a form or added by the user.

The location object contains the `search` property, which separates the query string from the BASE URL. For example, the statement `var qStr = document.location.search;` stores the query string into a variable `qStr`.

The first character of the query string is a question mark (?) that must be removed. You can remove it by using the `substring()` method. For example, the statement `qStr = qStr.substring(1,qStr.length);` removes the question mark from the string.

You can split the string into variable/value pairs by using the `split()` method. For example, the statement `theVar = QS.split("&");` divides the query string into an array of variable/value pairs.

You can split each pair of values into a new array that results in a two-dimensional array. You need to create a `for` loop that loops through the length of the array splitting the elements apart using this statement: `theVar[i] = theVar[i].split("=");` where `i` is the looping increment variable. You can get the length of the array by using the `length` property.

If you know the order in which the values are submitted to the page, you can access the values of the array by using the index. For example, the statement `var thePic = theVar[2][1];` extracts the third value from the query string.

If you do not know the order of the values being returned, then you must use the names of the variables stored in the first index of the array. You can develop a `for` loop that compares the name and stores the value.

Convert a Query String into Variables

① Use the `location.search` property to retrieve the search parameters.

② Use the `substring()` method to remove the leading question mark.

③ Use the `split()` method to separate the formatted query string at the ampersand symbols.

Note: If you send special characters in the query string, you need to `unescape()` the query string.

④ Create a `for` loop to access the elements of the new array you created.

⑤ Add quotation marks around the value portion of the variable to format the string.

⑥ Add the `eval()` method to evaluate the new string part.

⑦ Access the variable values by using the element names from the form stored in the query string.

⑧ Save the file.

```
getQS.html - Notepad
File  Edit  Format  View  Help

<html>
 <head>
  <title> Eric Pascarello </title>
  <script type="text/javascript">

   qStr = document.location.search;          ①
   qStr = qStr.substring(1,qStr.length)      ②

   theParts = qStr.split("&");               ③

  </script>
 </head>
 <body>
 </body>
</html>
```

```
getQS.html - Notepad
File  Edit  Format  View  Help

<html>
 <head>
  <title> Eric Pascarello </title>
  <script type="text/javascript">

   qStr = document.location.search;
   qStr = qStr.substring(1,qStr.length)

   theParts = qStr.split("&");

   for(i=0;i<theParts.length;i++){           ④
    theParts[i] = theParts[i].replace("=","=") + "";   ⑤
    eval(theParts[i]);                       ⑥
   }

   alert("Number of Elements: " + theParts.length);    ⑦
   alert(ABC);

  </script>
 </head>
 <body>
```

9 Develop a form and submit the form to this page to create a query string.

Note: To develop the form, repeat steps **1** to **4** in the previous task, Create a Query String.

● A text box appears showing the number of query string elements.

10 Click OK.

● An alert dialog box appears showing the value of the variable ABC.

● You can verify that the value in the alert dialog box is the same as the value in the query string.

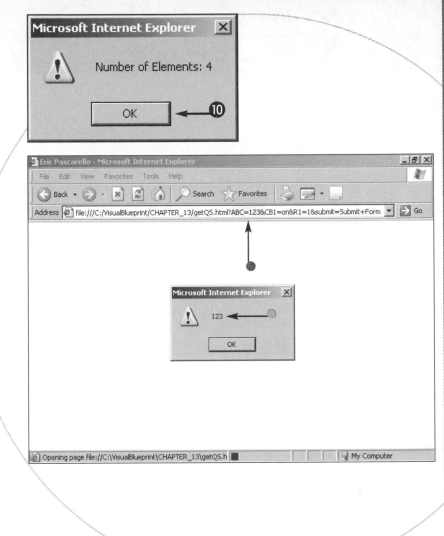

Apply It

Instead of referencing the array, you can reference the variable name that is in the query string. This eliminates the need to worry about the order of the array and allows you to use a variable throughout the page.

You need to still manipulate the string by removing the question mark and splitting the array into pairs. The difference lies in the `for` loop. Instead of separating the variable from the value, use the `evaluate()` method. To use this method, add quotation marks around the value with simple replace and string addition.

```
qStr = document.location.search;
qStr = qStr.substring(1,qStr.length)
theParts = qStr.split("&");
for(i=0;i<theParts.length;i++){
    theParts[i] = theParts[i].replace("=","='") + "'";
    eval(theParts[i]);
}
```

Link Style Sheets to a Web Page

You can use Cascading Style Sheets (CSS) to separate the Web page content from the rules that govern how a Web page looks. You can manage your Web site more easily by using style sheets to format your Web page.

You can add CSS to a Web page in three ways. The first method is to apply the style directly to the attribute. This allows you to format a single element with properties. You can apply the style directly to the element by using the `style` attribute.

The second method is to use the `<style>` tag, which allows you to apply the style class to the entire page. A class is a group of statements that affect the properties of the element to which they are applied. The MIME `type` should be added to the `<style sheet>` tag and set to `text/css`. This ensures that the browser processes it correctly. For example,

the statement `<style type="text/css">` adds a style sheet to the document.

The third method is an external style sheet. All the classes are assigned in a separate file to enable you to link to it from multiple pages. Therefore, you can share classes throughout the Web page and do not have to add them to every page individually. You can use the `<link>` tag to add an external style sheet file to your Web page. The link type should have a `rel` attribute set to `stylesheet`, a `type` attribute set to `text/css`, and the location of the style sheet defined by the `href` attribute. For example, `<link rel="stylesheet" type="text/css" href= "theSheet.css">` imports a style sheet into the Web page.

The external style sheet is just like an external JavaScript file. The external style sheet should only contain the style sheet rules.

Link Style Sheets to a Web Page

ATTACH CSS TO AN ELEMENT

1. Insert the `style` attribute into the element.

2. Add properties inside one of the quotes.

3. Save the file.

AFFIX A GLOBAL STYLE SHEET

1. Declare the `<style>` tag, adding the `type` attribute set to `text/css`.

2. Add `<! –` and `–>` to allow browsers to ignore the properties.

3. Add CSS rules with its properties.

4. Save the file.

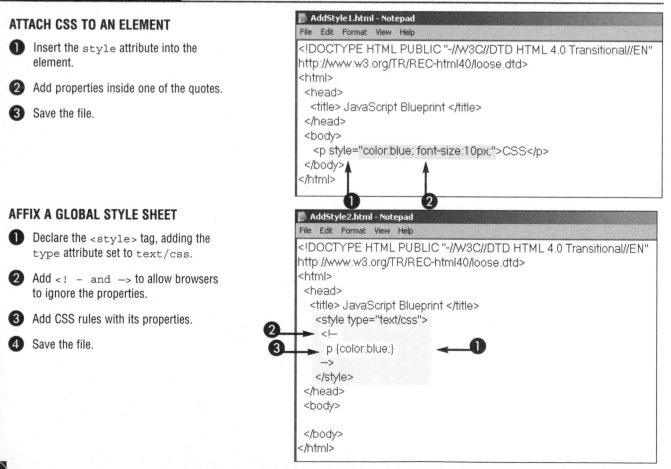

LINK TO AN EXTERNAL STYLE SHEET

① Add a `<link>` tag to the Web page.

② Add the `rel` attribute, and set the value to the `style sheet`.

③ Add the `type` attribute, and set the value to `text/css`.

④ Add the `href` attribute to the style sheet and link to an external style sheet.

⑤ Save the file.

CREATE THE LINK EXTERNAL STYLE SHEET

① Add rules to the file.

② Save the file with a .css extension.

Note: There are no tags entered into the style sheet other than the rules.

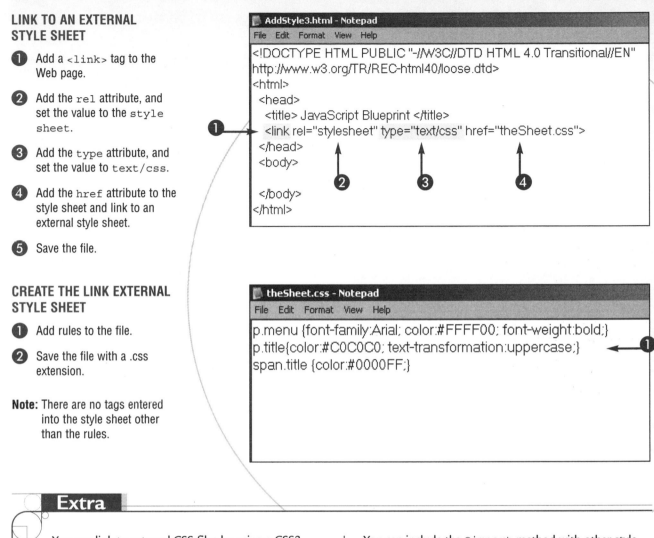

AddStyle3.html - Notepad

```
<!DOCTYPE HTML PUBLIC "-//W3C//DTD HTML 4.0 Transitional//EN"
http://www.w3.org/TR/REC-html40/loose.dtd>
<html>
 <head>
  <title> JavaScript Blueprint </title>
  <link rel="stylesheet" type="text/css" href="theSheet.css">
 </head>
 <body>

 </body>
</html>
```

theSheet.css - Notepad

```
p.menu {font-family:Arial; color:#FFFF00; font-weight:bold;}
p.title{color:#C0C0C0; text-transformation:uppercase;}
span.title {color:#0000FF;}
```

Extra

You can link to external CSS files by using a CSS2 specification, @import. This method excludes browsers that do not support CSS2. Netscape 4 browsers ignore the @import rule because they do not support CSS2. This is one way developers can have content specified to center browsers. The CSS2 uses @import to import the external CSS file into the document. Instead of using the `<link>` tag, the browser uses the `<style>` tag. Make sure that the MIME type is set for the `<style>` tag and that the browser is in standards-compliance mode. The file that the method is importing should also be a CSS file.

```
<style type="text/css">
 <!--
   @import url(theStyleSheet.css)
 -->
</style>
```

You can include the @import method with other style sheet rules without causing an error.

```
<style type="text/css">
 <!--
   @import url(theStyleSheet.css)
   #menu2_1 {color:black;font-
weight:bold;text-align:left;}
   #menu2_2 {color:blue;font-weight:bold;text-
align:center;}
 -->
</style>
```

Create Rules in a Style Sheet

Y ou can add rules to a style sheet to change the look and feel of elements on the Web page. The rules have a basic syntax that you must follow to correctly render the Web page.

A style sheet consists of rules. Each rule has properties that are used to customize an element. Each rule uses a selector to differentiate the rules. The selector can be a tag name, an element ID attribute, or a class name. Some examples of tag names are h1, h2, p, div, and input. Brackets that contain the properties and their values follow the selector.

The property values are case-insensitive, but the best practice is to use all lowercase values. Each property consists of a name and a value. A colon separates the name from the value. A semicolon and a space separate each property. For example, the statement selector {property1:value1; property:value2;} is the format of a CSS rule.

When the style is applied directly to an element, the properties are separated from each other with semicolons. For example, the statement <div style= "width:100px; height:30px;"> assigns width and height properties to a div element.

Certain properties accept more than one value, such as the font-family. This property checks to see if the font-family is available; if not, it selects the next name from the list. Separate the names with commas. For example, the property font-family; Arial, Georgia, Century; creates a list of values.

You can use spaces to separate other properties that accept multiple parameters. This group does not use the values as a fail-safe list; instead, it points to different properties. For example, the property border: solid 1px #FF0000; defines the border of an element by setting the style, size, and color.

Create Rules in a Style Sheet

CREATE RULES WITH THE TAG TYPE

1 Set the selector to a tag name.

2 Add properties inside the brackets.

3 Add the appropriate tag to the HTML body.

4 Save the file.

```
AddProperty1.html - Notepad
File  Edit  Format  View  Help
<!DOCTYPE HTML PUBLIC "-//W3C//DTD HTML 4.0 Transitional//EN"
http://www.w3.org/TR/REC-html40/loose.dtd>
<html>
 <head>
  <title> JavaScript Blueprint </title>
  <style type="text/css">
   <!--
    div {color:black; border: solid 3px #FF0000; width:300px; height:50px; }
   -->
  </style>
 </head>
 <body>
  <div>CSS Properties</div>

 </body>
</html>
```

5 Open the file in a Web browser.

● The tag appears with the properties in the CSS rule assigned to the tag name.

```
JavaScript Blueprint - Microsoft Internet Explorer
File  Edit  View  Favorites  Tools  Help
Back        Search    Favorites
Address  C:\VisualBlueprint\CHAPTER_14\AddProperty1.html        Go

CSS Properties
```

232

CREATE RULES WITH THE ELEMENT ID

1 Add the tag name in the HTML page and assign it an ID.

2 Set the selector with a hash mark with the ID of the element you want.

3 Add the properties inside the brackets.

4 Save the file.

5 Open the file in a Web browser.

- The tag appears with the properties in the CSS rule assigned to the tag name.

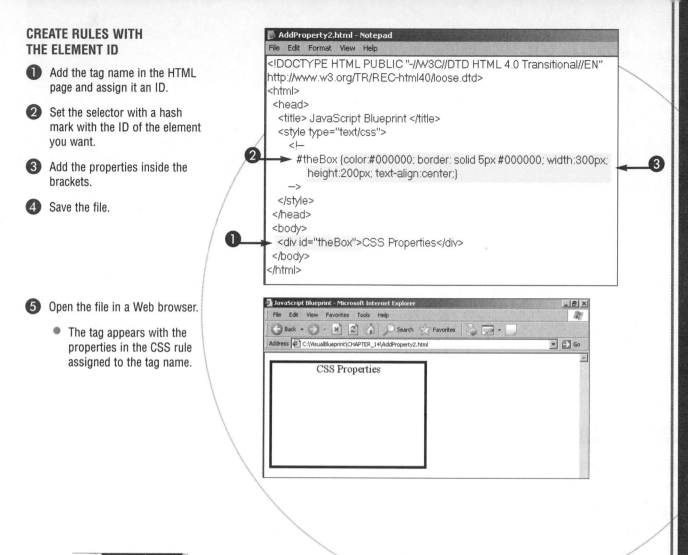

```
AddProperty2.html - Notepad
File  Edit  Format  View  Help

<!DOCTYPE HTML PUBLIC "-//W3C//DTD HTML 4.0 Transitional//EN"
http://www.w3.org/TR/REC-html40/loose.dtd>
<html>
 <head>
  <title> JavaScript Blueprint </title>
  <style type="text/css">
   <!--
    #theBox {color:#000000; border: solid 5px #000000; width:300px;
       height:200px; text-align:center;}
   -->
  </style>
 </head>
<body>
 <div id="theBox">CSS Properties</div>
</body>
</html>
```

```
JavaScript Blueprint - Microsoft Internet Explorer
File  Edit  View  Favorites  Tools  Help
Back  -        Search   Favorites
Address  C:\VisualBlueprint\CHAPTER_14\AddProperty2.html      Go

          CSS Properties
```

Apply It

You can do more than just apply a style to the entire group of paragraph elements, div elements, or any other element on the page. You can specify that certain types of elements get the CSS property by adding a class name to the selector.

```
p.menu {font-family:Arial;
color:#FFFF00; font-weight:bold;}
p.title{color:#C0C0C0;
text-transformation:uppercase;}
span.title {color:#0000FF;}
```

You can also apply multiple selectors to a single rule by separating them with a comma.

```
div, p {color:blue;font-weight:bold;}
span, p.title, em {color:#8800FF;}
```

The first rule applies to <div> and <paragraph> tags. The second rule applies to <span>, <paragraph> tags with the class title, and the <emphasis> tag.

Add Compliance Declaration

You can force newer versions of browsers to follow the current standards for style sheets instead of supporting all style behaviors. This allows you to have Web pages that appear correctly in all the modern browsers.

You need to add a `<DOCTYPE>` element to the uppermost line of the Web page document. If any information is above this declaration, it is ignored. The URL should be in standards-compatibility mode unless noted.

The element that you are most likely to use is the W3C HTML 4.0 recommendation. This element supports most depreciated tags that are not part of the standard. The statement `<!DOCTYPE HTML PUBLIC "-//W3C//DTD HTML 4.0 Transitional//EN" http://www.w3.org/TR/REC-html40/loose.dtd>` places the loose mode onto the document.

If your page is a frameset, then you should use the frameset mode. The statement `<!DOCTYPE HTML PUBLIC "-//W3C//DTD HTML 4.0 Frameset//EN" http://www.w3.org/TR/REC-html40/frameset.dtd>` places a frameset page into standards mode.

If your HTML document strictly follows the W3C HTML 4.0 recommendation, use the strict mode. The statement `<!DOCTYPE HTML PUBLIC "-//W3C//DTD HTML 4.0//EN" http://www.w3.org/TR/REC-html40/strict.dtd>` puts the standards mode into strict. You do not need the URL for strict.

If you follow XHTML 1.0 standards and it includes items from HTML 4.0, use `<!DOCTYPE html PUBLIC "-//W3C//DTD XHTML 1.0 Transitional//EN" http://www.w3.org/TR/xhtml1/DTD/xhtml1-transitional.dtd>`. The URL is not required.

If you use XHTML 1.0 standards and frames, use `<!DOCTYPE html PUBLIC "-//W3C//DTD XHTML 1.0 Frameset//EN" http://www.w3.org/TR/xhtml1/DTD/xhtml1-frameset.dtd>`. The URL is not required.

If you strictly follow XHTML1.0, use `<!DOCTYPE html PUBLIC "-//W3C//DTD XHTML 1.0 Strict//EN" http://www.w3.org/TR/xhtml1/DTD/xhtml1-strict.dtd>`. The URL is also not required.

If you use XHTML 1.1, use `<!DOCTYPE html PUBLIC "-//W3C//DTD XHTML 1.1//EN" http://www.w3.org/TR/xhtml11/DTD/xhtml11.dtd>`. The URL is not required.

Add Compliance Declaration

ADD THE LOOSE DOCUMENT TYPE DECLARATION

1 Add the `HTML 4.0 DOCTYPE` declaration.

2 Add the `loose.dtd` link.

3 Save the file.

● The document is in the loose declaration mode.

```
MakeComp1.html - Notepad
File  Edit  Format  View  Help
<!DOCTYPE HTML PUBLIC "-//W3C//DTD HTML 4.0 Transitional//EN"     —❶
http://www.w3.org/TR/REC-html40/loose.dtd>     ←❷
<html>
 <head>
  <title> JavaScript Blueprint </title>
 </head>
 <body>
 </body>
</html>
```

ADD THE STRICT DOCUMENT TYPE DECLARATION

1 Add the `HTML 4.0 DOCTYPE` declaration.

2 Add the `strict.dtd` link.

3 Save the file.

● The document is in the strict declaration mode.

```
MakeComp2.html - Notepad
File  Edit  Format  View  Help
<!DOCTYPE HTML PUBLIC "-//W3C//DTD HTML 4.0//EN"     ←❶
http://www.w3.org/TR/REC-html40/strict.dtd>     ←❷
<html>
 <head>
  <title> JavaScript Blueprint </title>
 </head>
 <body>
 </body>
</html>
```

Attach Multiple CSS Rules

You can make a CSS class and apply it to elements on a Web page. This enables formatting across the page that looks the same for different elements.

A CSS class is a selector that points that is assigned a rule. A selector can be a class name, a tag name, or an element ID. The rule consists of one or more properties that determine how the element that the rule is to apply to looks.

The class is added to an element by using the `class` attribute. For example, the statement `<span id="Menu" class="Menu1">` adds the rule set Menu1 to the `<span>` element.

You are not limited to the number of rules that are in a style sheet. You can have rules that apply to single or multiple elements. You can add multiple classes to a

`<span>` tag instead of creating a rule that makes one property different from the rest. To add multiple classes, separate them with a space. The statement `<span id="Menu" class="Menu1 BigText Boxed">` adds three classes to the `<span>` element. By using multiple classes, you can cut down on the size of the CSS file by eliminating repeating properties.

If a property repeats itself when multiple classes are applied to an element, the last property is used. For example, if text color of the Menu1 class is set to black and BigText is set to blue, the text color is blue because it overwrites the first value.

If you want to apply a style to an element ID rather then a class, use a hash mark (#) followed by the selector name. For example, the rule `#HOT {font: 12pt Arial italic}` is applied to any element with the ID HOT.

Attach Multiple CSS Rules

① Create one style that contains multiple properties.

② Create another style with additional properties.

③ Add a `class` attribute with the two rules names separated by a space.

④ Save the file.

```
AddClass.html - Notepad
File  Edit  Format  View  Help
<!DOCTYPE HTML PUBLIC "-//W3C//DTD HTML 4.0 Transitional//EN"
http://www.w3.org/TR/REC-html40/loose.dtd>
<html>
  <head>
   <title> JavaScript Blueprint </title>
   <style type="text/css">
     <!--
       div.black {color:white; border:dotted 5px #123123; width:300px;}   ①
       div.silver {color:#505050; text-align: center;}   ②
     -->
   </style>   ③
  </head>
  <body>
   <div class="black silver">CSS Two Classes</div>
  </body>
</html>
```

⑤ Open the file in a Web browser.

● The element appears with the second rule overwriting properties of the first rule.

```
JavaScript Blueprint - Microsoft Internet Explorer
File  Edit  View  Favorites  Tools  Help
Back  •  ⊗  ×  ⊠  ⬙  Search  ⭑ Favorites  ⬙  ⬙  •  ⬙
Address  C:\VisualBlueprint\CHAPTER_14\AddClass.html         Go

      CSS Two Classes
```

Override Rule Properties with Style Attribute

You can use two methods to overwrite the styles assigned to the element. This allows you to change the look and feel of a single element. You may want to change the color of the element and leave all the other properties assigned to it unchanged.

The first method is to use the style attribute of the element. The style properties are first applied from the global style sheet parameters, which are based on the element ID, class name, or element type. The properties in the style sheet overwrite the global values that are the same. For example, if the border width is set for two pixels in the global properties, the statement `<p id="Item" class="sale" style="border-width:4px;">` overwrites the two-pixel value with four pixels.

The second method to overwrite the global properties is to add a new rule in the style sheet. The new rule's selector

has to be different from the original selector. If the first selector is based on the class, then the second must also be based on the ID. For example, the statement `#Item {border-width:4px;}` needs to be added after the class `sale` in the style sheet. The new rule is located after the class so that it overwrites the properties that are the same.

Both methods produce the same results, but adding a new rule to the style sheet is easier to manage. If you want to make a change to the border in the future, you can make it on the style sheet instead of searching through the Web page code. If you have multiple pages that have this exception, you do not have to apply it to every page in the style sheet that is imported.

Override Rule Properties with Style Attribute

① Add CSS rules that you want to apply to the elements.

② Add the `class` attribute with the rule names to the HTML element.

③ Add the `style` attribute to the element assigning new properties.

④ Save the file.

```
ModClass.html - Notepad
File  Edit  Format  View  Help
<!DOCTYPE HTML PUBLIC "-//W3C//DTD HTML 4.0 Transitional//EN"
http://www.w3.org/TR/REC-html40/loose.dtd>
<html>
  <head>
    <title> JavaScript Blueprint </title>
    <style type="text/css">
      <!--
      div.black {color:white; border:dotted 5px #123123; width:300px;}          ①
      div.silver {color:#505050; text-align: center;}
      -->
    </style>
  </head>
  <body>
    <div class="black silver" >CSS Classes</div>
    <br/>
    <div class="black silver" style="border:solid 5px #123123;">CSS Classes</div>
  </body>
</html>
```

⑤ Open the file in a Web browser.

● The `style` attribute overrides the class rules that are assigned.

```
JavaScript Blueprint - Microsoft Internet Explorer
File  Edit  View  Favorites  Tools  Help
Back  ·  ·  x  2  ·  Search  Favorites  ·  ·
Address  C:\VisualBlueprint\CHAPTER_14\ModClass.html                Go

· · · · · · · · · · · · · · · · · · · · · · · · · · · ·
·             CSS Classes              ·
· · · · · · · · · · · · · · · · · · · · · · · · · · · ·

┌──────────────────────────────────────┐
│              CSS Classes             │
└──────────────────────────────────────┘
```

Modify Border Properties

You can modify the border on Web page elements by using CSS. CSS enables you to add or remove borders, adjust the style, change the width, and specify the colors.

The border property can be used to modify all four borders of the block, or you can specify the edges individually by using border-top, border-right, border-bottom, and border-left. You can specify the width, style, color, and size in one declaration. The statement border: 2px solid #FF0000; specifies a border that affects all four sides. The statement border-top: 5px inset #FFFF00; adjusts the top border and does not affect the others.

You can specify the border width, style, and color properties separately as well. The border-width, border-style, and border-color enable you to do this. You can also go one step further and specify each side individually. For example, border-right-color: #224466; changes the right border color.

The border-width property accepts the keyword values thin, medium, or thick. It also accepts a number value in pixels. For example, the statement border-width: thin; sets all the borders to a thin border. The border-style property affects the appearance of the border. The border-style property accepts one of these keywords: solid, dashed, dotted, double, groove, ridge, inset, and outside. The border-color property affects the color of the border. You can specify the rgb color, the hex value, or the color name keyword.

When using the border-width, border-style, and the border-color, you can specify multiple parameters inside the declaration. You can specify all four edges with border-property: top right bottom left;. You can specify three parameters with border-property: top sides bottom;. You can specify two parameters with border-property: top/bottom side;. For example, the statement document-width: 3px 5px 2px; sets the top border to 3 pixels, the right and left border to 5 pixels, and the bottom border to 2 pixels.

Modify Border Properties

① Create a CSS rule that applies to the element to which you want to add a border.

② Set width and height properties of the element if appropriate.

③ Add the border-top, border-right, border-bottom, and border-left properties, assigning the width, style, and color values.

④ Save the file.

⑤ Open the file in a Web browser.

● The border that appears has different properties on each side.

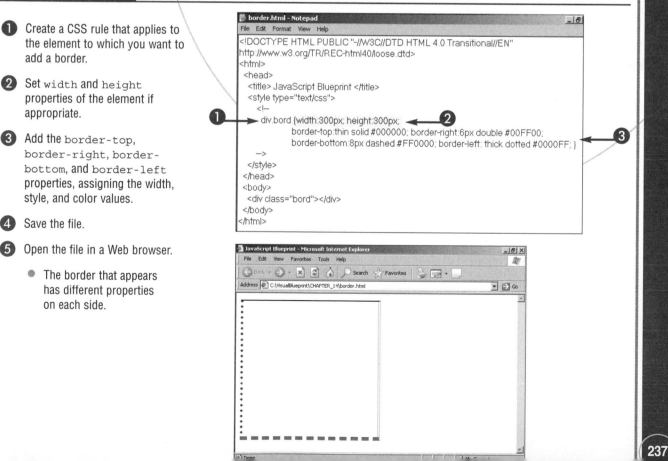

Customize a Link Style

You can modify text and links on a page to make them more appealing and easier to use. You can make links change properties as the mouse is hovering over a link or the link is active.

The `font-family` property is a comma-delineated list of `font-family` names. The `list` property uses the first available font from the list on the user's computer. A multiword font name should be quoted.

The `font-size` property is the height of the text that should appear. It can be a fixed size or a percentage. The value can even be a constant such as `xx-small`, `x-small`, `small`, `medium`, `large`, `x-large`, `xx-large`. The `color` property affects the color of the text.

The `font-stretch` is the amount of character spacing. Possible values are `normal`, `none`, `wider`, `narrower`, `ultra-condensed`, `extra-condensed`, `condensed`, `semi-condensed`, `semi-expanded`, `expanded`, `extra-expanded`, or `ultra-expanded`.

You can use the `font-style` property to affect the slant of characters. Possible values are `normal`, `italic`, or `oblique`. The `font-variant` is used for the small caps version of the font, which has two values: `normal` and `small-caps`. The `text-transformation` property also transforms the text's case. Possible values are `lowercase`, `uppercase`, or `none`.

The `font-weight` is the boldness level of the characters. Possible values are `lighter`, `normal`, `bold`, `bolder`, `100`, `200`, `300`, `400`, `500`, `600`, `700`, `800`, or `900`. You can also use the `text-decoration` property, which affects the display of the text. Possible affects are `line-through`, `none`, `overline`, and `underline`.

The font property combines one or more of the font properties into a list separated by spaces. You can create rollovers on links to display different properties. The classes are `a:link`, `a:visited`, `a:active`, and `a:hover`. By using these CSS classes, you can eliminate the need to use JavaScript to create rollovers.

Customize a Link Style

① Add links to the document of which you want to change the properties.

② Add `link` and `hover` classes to the global style sheet.

③ Add properties inside the brackets.

④ Save the file.

```
linkClass.html - Notepad
File  Edit  Format  View  Help
<!DOCTYPE HTML PUBLIC "-//W3C//DTD HTML 4.0 Transitional//EN"
http://www.w3.org/TR/REC-html40/loose.dtd>
<html>
 <head>
  <title> JavaScript Blueprint </title>
  <style type="text/css">
   <!--
    a:link {color:#000000; background-color:#FFFFFF;}
    a:hover {color:#FFFFFF; background-color:#000000;}
   -->
  </style>
 </head>
 <body>
  <a href="newPage.html">CSS Link Properties</a>
 </body>
</html>
```

⑤ Open the file in a Web browser.

● The link appears with the properties of the `a:link` rule.

```
JavaScript Blueprint - Microsoft Internet Explorer
File  Edit  View  Favorites  Tools  Help
Back  •  •  •  Search  Favorites
Address  C:\VisualBlueprint\CHAPTER_14\linkClass.html          Go

CSS Link Properties
```

6 Position the cursor over the link.

- The link changes to the properties in the a:hover rule.

7 Remove the cursor from the link.

- The link returns back to the a:link rule.

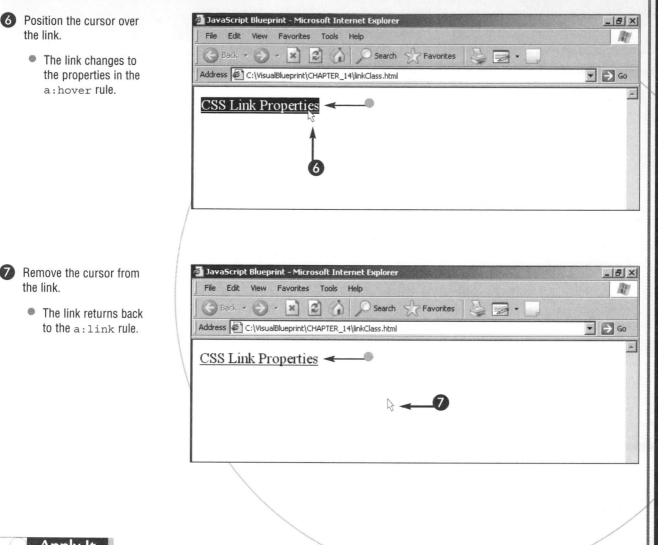

Apply It

You can remove the underline from links and the border around images used as links by applying CSS properties to them. Remember, however, that people recognize underlined information as a link, especially text that is blue and underlined. If you confuse users when they are visiting your site, they may not come back. To remove underlines from all the links on the page, use the a:link class. In this class, apply the text-decoration property with the value set to none.

```
a:link {text-decoration:none}
a:visited  {text-decoration:none}
a:active {text-decoration:none}
a:hover {text-decoration:none}
```

If you are using an image as a link, and you do not want the border around the image, then you need to set the border property of the image to remove the border. You can do this by setting it to none.

```
<a href="newPage"><img id="link1"
src="sunset.gif" style="border:none"></a>
```

Center Content on the Web Page

You can center form elements, text, images, and so on, in the center of the page by using two different methods. These methods require different amounts of CSS support; therefore, they cannot work for every browser, especially those that are not placed into standards-compliance mode.

The first method works in all browsers that support. Give the content that you want centered a set width. For example, the statement `<p style="width:80%">` sets the width of the content to 80 percent of the screen width. You can then place this element inside a block element like a `div`. The `div` would be set to have the `text-align` equal to `center`. The statement `<div style="text-align: center"><p style="width:80%; text-align:right; ">CSS</p></div>` centers the content on the screen.

If you do not use the `text-align` property on the `<paragraph>` tag, the format of the text centers. Using the `div` enables it to keep its normal formatting and margins on the left and right sides of the screen.

The second method relies on the browser following the CSS standards and being in standards-compliance mode. This time you do not need to use a block element to center the content. You still must give the element a set width. You need to use the `margin-left` and `margin-right` properties. Setting them to `auto` centers the content on the screen. For example, the statement `<p style="width: 80%;margin-left:auto;margin-right:auto;">` centers the content on the screen.

The method that you choose depends on what browsers you support. If you support earlier than version 5 of Microsoft Internet Explorer, then you should use the first method. If you only support the newest versions of the browser, however, use the second method.

Center Content on the Web Page

① Add a `div` to surround the element you want to center containing the style set to center the text.

② Add a `style` to the element to center, setting the `width` and `text` alignment.

③ Add a `style` attribute to another element inserting the centering code that requires compliance.

④ Save the file.

```
center.html - Notepad
File  Edit  Format  View  Help
<!DOCTYPE HTML PUBLIC "-//W3C//DTD HTML 4.0 Transitional//EN"
http://www.w3.org/TR/REC-html40/loose.dtd>
<html>
 <head>
  <title> JavaScript Blueprint </title>
 </head>
 <body>

  <div style="text-align:center">            ◀——①
   <p style="width:80%; background-color:#E0E0E0; text-align:left;">   ◀——②
     DIV centered  paragraph!
   </p>
  </div>

  <p style="width:80%;margin-left:auto;margin-right:auto;   ◀——③
background-color:#E0E0E0;">Centered Paragraph without a &lt;div&gt;</p>

 </body>
</html>
```

⑤ Open the file in a Web browser.

● The content centers on the Web page.

Note: Both methods are centered in the page the same. The compliance method required less coding.

```
JavaScript Blueprint - Microsoft Internet Explorer
File  Edit  View  Favorites  Tools  Help
Back ▼  ▼  ×  ▲  Search  Favorites
Address  C:\VisualBlueprint\CHAPTER_14\center.html          Go

DIV centered paragraph!

Centered Paragraph without a <div>
```

Add a Background Image to the Document

Y ou can allow users to select background colors and images so they can customize the look and feel of the Web page. The background properties are set before the page loads in the style sheet, but you can change them after the page has loaded.

Several CSS style properties control the background properties of the page and individual elements. You can apply the background properties to divs, spans, and so on. The first property is `background-color`. You can set this to an RGB color, Hex value, or the color name. For example, `document.body.style.background-color = "rgb(0, 0, 256)";` sets the background color to `blue`.

Another property is the `background-image` property, which displays an image in the background. The value of the property accepts the URL of an image. For example, the statement `document.body.style.background-image="url(BGpic.gif)";` displays a tiled image in the background.

You can keep an image fixed in position or scrollable by using the `background-attachment` property. You can set the property to `fixed` or `scroll`.

You can set the background image to repeat or not to repeat. The property values are `no-repeat`, `repeat`, `repeat-x`, `repeat-y`. The image can repeat in both directions or just on an axis.

The `background-position` property offsets the image to the edge of the element. A space separates the values. The values can either be a number or percentage value. They also can be a keyword such as `left`, `center`, `right`, `top`, or `bottom`. The first value is horizontal and the second value is vertical dimension.

The `background` property combines all the other properties into one specification. You can join the properties together with spaces between each value such as the statement `document.body.style.background-image="url(BGpic.gif) repeat-y fixed;"`.

Add a Background Image to the Document

① Add a `<body>` tag selector to the global style sheet.

② Add the `background` property and the URL.

③ Set the display parameters of the background image.

④ Save the file.

⑤ Open the file in a Web browser.

● The image appears in the background.

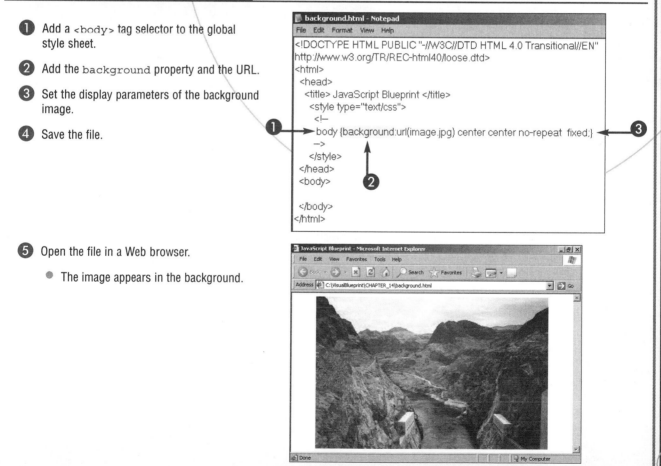

Add and Alter Elements to a Web Page

When you first look at the `<div>` and `<span>` tags there appears to be no major differences in the way they act with the browser. Developers tend to use them interchangeably, but there are reasons why you should use one over the other.

The `<div>` element is a block-style element. The content that follows a `<div>` element is placed on the next line. The div's container fills up the entire width of a line if no width is set. The div pushes content around so it fits.

The `<span>` element is an inline element. It flows with the document flow. Therefore, if you insert a `<span>` element in the middle of a sentence, the entire sentence appears on one line. If you enter a div in the middle of a sentence, the sentence appears on three lines.

A span is made to act like a `<div>` element by setting the display property to `block`. For example, the statement

`document.write('Hello,<span style= "display: block;">How are you</span>');` displays on two lines when the page executes.

You can make a div behave like a span by setting the width of a div to a set value. You also need to change the display value to `inline`. For example, the statement `document.write('Hello,<div style= "display:inline; width:50px;">How are you</div>');` displays the text on one line when the statement executes.

The `<div>` element is good for positioning data absolutely on the page. The `<span>` element is a great way to customize text without disrupting the program flow.

Div and span importance has increased significantly with DHTML and CSS. Spans are commonly used to change text properties in the middle of a sentence, and divs are commonly used to hold and position data.

Add Elements to a Web Page

① Add a `div` element in the document.

② Add a `span` element in the document.

③ Set the selector to the `<div>` tag name in the style sheet.

④ Set the selector to the `span` name in the style sheet.

⑤ Save the file.

```
divSpan.html - Notepad
File  Edit  Format  View  Help
<!DOCTYPE HTML PUBLIC "-//W3C//DTD HTML 4.0 Transitional//EN"
http://www.w3.org/TR/REC-html40/loose.dtd>
<html>
  <head>
    <title> JavaScript Blueprint </title>
    <style type="text/css">
    <!--
      div {color:black; font-weight:bold;}    ← ③
      span {color:black; font-weight:bold;}    ← ④
    -->
    </style>
  </head>                         ①
  <body>
    A div is a <div>block </div> element. <hr/>
    A span is an <span>inline</span> element.
  </body>
</html>
                          ②
```

⑥ Open the file in a Web browser.

● The `div` element inserts line breaks in the sentence that appears.

● The `span` element does not interfere with the sentence.

```
JavaScript Blueprint - Microsoft Internet Explorer
File  Edit  View  Favorites  Tools  Help
Back ·    ·        Search   Favorites
Address  C:\VisualBlueprint\CHAPTER_14\divSpan.html          Go

A div is a
block  ←
element.
_____
A span is an inline element.  ←
```

1. Add a `div` element in the document.

2. Add a `span` element in the document.

3. Set the selector to the `<div>` tag name in the style sheet with the `display` property set to `inline`.

4. Set the selector to the `span` name in the style sheet with the `display` property set to `block`.

5. Save the file.

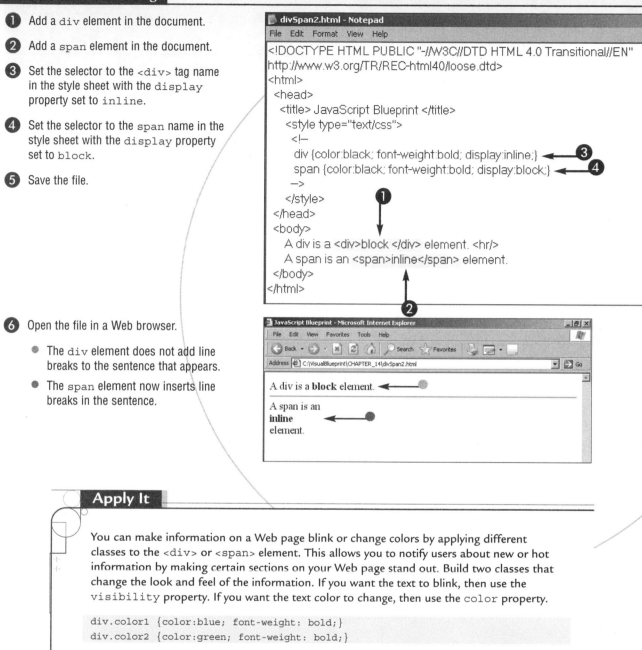

6. Open the file in a Web browser.

● The `div` element does not add line breaks to the sentence that appears.

● The `span` element now inserts line breaks in the sentence.

Apply It

You can make information on a Web page blink or change colors by applying different classes to the `<div>` or `<span>` element. This allows you to notify users about new or hot information by making certain sections on your Web page stand out. Build two classes that change the look and feel of the information. If you want the text to blink, then use the `visibility` property. If you want the text color to change, then use the `color` property.

```
div.color1 {color:blue; font-weight: bold;}
div.color2 {color:green; font-weight: bold;}
```

This function changes the element's class name.

```
function switchClass(elem,className1,className2){
  theClass = document.getElementById(elem).className;
  if(theClass == className1)document.getElementById(elem).className = className2;
  else document.getElementById(elem).className = className1;
}
```

A `setInterval()` method is needed to oscillate the classes. This function uses local variables so multiple items on the page can be changed.

```
switch1 = setInterval("switchClass('txt','color1','color2')",300);
```

Create a Scrollable DIV

Y ou can show and hide the scrollbars on the Web page. You can also add scrollbars to a `<div>` element to create a scrollable window at any location on the Web page.

You can set the `overflow` property to `scroll` to show scrollbars, or you can set it to `hidden` to hide the scrollbars. When the scrollbars are hidden, the scrollbar on the right-side of the screen is removed. Users cannot scroll down on the page using the scrollbar, but they use other methods to scroll down.

The `overflow` property has an `auto` property, which shows or hides the scrollbars depending on whether they are needed. If the content runs off the page, it shows the scrollbars. For example, the statement `document.body.style.overflow = "auto";` shows or hides the scrollbars depending on the situation.

Internet Explorer also has `overflow-x` and `overflow-y`, which you can use to show or hide scrollbars in either the horizontal or the vertical positions.

You can create a scrollable div on a Web page by setting three CSS properties: `width`, `height`, and `overflow`. You can set the overflow to `scroll` or to `auto`. Auto is the better choice because it does not show the horizontal scrollbar if the width is set properly. The statement `<div id="sDiv" style="width:200px;height:50px;overflow:auto">` creates a scrollable div.

By adding a border to the div, you can make it stand out from the rest of the content. You can customize it any way you want. You cannot add an external Web page to the scrollable div. If you want to include an external Web page, you should use an iframe.

Create a Scrollable DIV

① Add a `class` attribute to the div.

② Add the rule to the style sheet with the basic properties to format the div.

③ Set the `overflow` property to `auto` or `scroll`.

Note: In this example, the property has been set to `auto`.

④ Set the `width` and `height` of the div.

⑤ Save the file.

```
divScroll.html - Notepad
File  Edit  Format  View  Help
<!DOCTYPE HTML PUBLIC "-//W3C//DTD HTML 4.0 Transitional//EN"
http://www.w3.org/TR/REC-html40/loose.dtd>
<html>
 <head>
  <title> JavaScript Blueprint </title>
   <style type="text/css">
    <!--
     div.scroll {border:solid 2px black; overflow:auto;width:200px;height:50px;}
    -->
   </style>
 </head>
 <body>
   <div class="scroll">
   J<br/>A<br/>V<br/>A<br/>S<br/>C<br/>R<br/>I<br/>P<br/>T
   </div>
 </body>
</html>
```

⑥ Open the file in a Web browser.

● The div is scrollable.

```
JavaScript Blueprint - Microsoft Internet Explorer
File  Edit  View  Favorites  Tools  Help
Back •  •  •    Search  Favorites  •
Address  C:\VisualBlueprint\CHAPTER_14\divScroll.html     Go

J
A
```

Add an iFrame to the Web Page

Y ou can use iframes to create an HTML element that acts like a scrollable div and a frame in one package. Unlike a div, you can assign a Web page document to show in the window. Unlike a frame, you can add it anywhere on a Web page by setting its width and height. You can change the page in the iframe just like a regular frame.

You can assign the iframe to a certain Web page by using the `<src>` tag. The `<src>` tag is just like the `<src>` tag on a frame; whatever is assigned to the attribute is displayed in the frame. You can use JavaScript to change the location of the iframe by referencing the page. You can use the frame array or document object to reference the object. For example, `document.getElementById ("theIFrame").location.href = "newPage.html";` changes the location of the iframe named `theIFrame`.

You can specify the width and height of the iframe by setting the width and height attributes, or by applying CSS. For example, the statement `<iframe id="e"` `src="position.htm" style="width:100px; height:150px;"></iframe>` displays an iframe 100 pixels wide and 150 pixels high.

You can also make the iframe appear seamless on the page by adjusting its attributes. For example, the statement `<iframe id="menu" src="scrollTable.html" width=100% frameborder="0" vsapce="0" hspace="0" marginwidth="0" marginheight="0" scrolling="no" style="overflow:visible"> </iframe>` adjusts all the properties to make the iframe seamless.

One problem with using iframes is that some browsers do not support them. As a result, these browsers do not display the content. Another problem can occur when users use bookmarking content. The browser does not remember what information was loaded into the iframe. Therefore, do not use this to hold the site's main content.

Add an iFrame to the Web Page

1. Add the `<iframe>` tag to the document.

2. Set the `id` attribute to access the div.

3. Set the `src` attribute to the page you want to appear in this scrollable area.

4. Add a CSS rule to set the size of the iframe.

5. Save the file.

```
iframe.html - Notepad
File  Edit  Format  View  Help
<!DOCTYPE HTML PUBLIC "-//W3C//DTD HTML 4.0 Transitional//EN"
http://www.w3.org/TR/REC-html40/loose.dtd>
<html>
 <head>
  <title> JavaScript Blueprint </title>
   <style type="text/css">
    <!--
     iframe{width:450px;height:105px;}      ← 4
    -->
   </style>
 </head>
 <body>
  <iframe id="theStory" src="divSpan.html"></iframe>
 </body>
</html>
```

6. Open the file in a Web browser.

- The iframe displays another Web page inside the Web page.

```
JavaScript Blueprint - Microsoft Internet Explorer
File  Edit  View  Favorites  Tools  Help
Back          Search  Favorites
Address  C:\VisualBlueprint\CHAPTER_14\iframe.html          Go

A div is a
block
element.
```

Add Transparency to an Element

You can change the transparency of images and other elements on a Web page by using proprietary CSS properties. The main purpose in changing an image's transparency is to create a watermark or create effects with images on top of each other on the page. You can dynamically adjust the opacity of the elements, but it requires browser detection.

CSS is proprietary code. The CSS specifications do not support it, which means you have to deal with a different syntax for each type of browser. Netscape and Mozilla browsers use the `-moz-opacity` property. The value is set from 0 percent to 100 percent where 0 percent is transparent and 100 percent is completely opaque. The statement `#half {-moz-opacity:50%}` is 50 percent opaque.

Internet Explorer has two different proprietary codes to deal with transparency. The first is the `filter` property. The value for the opacity is set between 0 and 100. The statement `#half {filter:alpha(opacity=50);}` sets an element at 50 percent opacity.

The newer syntax that IE uses involves an ActiveX control that is part of IE5.5 or newer on Windows. The newer syntax also requires more information. For the same 50 percent opacity as before, it is written as `#half {filter:progid:DXImageTransform.Microsoft. Alpha(opacity=50));}`.

You can dynamically change the transparency of an element by referencing the object. With Netscape and Mozilla, it is `document.getElementById("elemID"). style.MoxOpacity = "75%";`. The first version of Microsoft Internet Explorer is `document.getElementById ("elemID").style.filter = "alpha(opacity=75) ";`.

The ActiveX version of Microsoft Internet Explorer is more complicated. Make sure the filter name is declared in the `style` attribute of the element or in the `CSS` attribute. The statement, `document.getElementById("elemID"). filters["DXImageTransform.Microsoft.Alpha"]. Opacity = 75;` changes the opacity level of the image with ActiveX.

Add Transparency to an Element

1. Add the elements to the page that you want to become transparent.

2. Assign a value to the `id` attribute.

3. Assign a CSS rule to the element to place it on the screen.

4. Create a CSS rule based on the element ID, and assign both browser specific opacity codes.

5. Save the file.

6. Open the file in a Web browser.

- The layer should appear transparent; verify that the transparency level is correct.

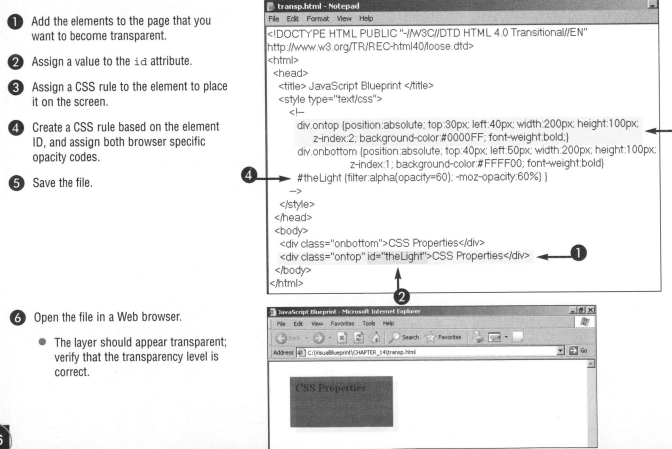

7 Reopen the file in a text editor.

8 Adjust the opacity level to desired settings.

9 Save the file.

Note: If you want the transparency to be more opaque, increase the value toward 100 or 100%.

```
transp.html - Notepad
File  Edit  Format  View  Help

<!DOCTYPE HTML PUBLIC "-//W3C//DTD HTML 4.0 Transitional//EN"
http://www.w3.org/TR/REC-html40/loose.dtd>
<html>
 <head>
  <title> JavaScript Blueprint </title>
  <style type="text/css">
   <!--
    div.ontop {position:absolute; top:30px; left:40px; width:200px; height:100px;
       z-index:2; background-color:#0000FF; font-weight:bold;}
    div.onbottom {position:absolute; top:40px; left:50px; width:200px; height:100px;
          z-index:1; background-color:#FFFF00; font-weight:bold}
    #theLight {filter:alpha(opacity=90); -moz-opacity:90%} }
    -->
  </style>
 </head>
 <body>
  <div class="onbottom">CSS Properties</div>
  <div class="ontop" id="theLight">CSS Properties</div>
 </body>
</html>
```

10 Open the file in a Web browser.

● The level of opaqueness increases.

```
JavaScript Blueprint - Microsoft Internet Explorer
File  Edit  View  Favorites  Tools  Help
Back           Search    Favorites
Address  C:\VisualBlueprint\CHAPTER_14\transp.html           Go
```

Extra

You can create a menu bar by using the transparency to show the mouse over an object. You need to develop three CSS rules for the menu: Set the basic color and size of the menu, set the opaqueness to the lower opacity level, and set a 100 percent opaqueness level.

```
<style type="text/css">
  <!--
  div.menu {width:200px; background-
color:#0000FF; font-weight:bold;}
  #theLight {filter:alpha(opacity=40);
-moz-opacity:40%;}
  #theSolid
{filter:alpha(opacity=100);
-moz-opacity:100%}
  -->
</style>
```

You need to create a menu that corresponds to the CSS rules for the menu. Set the classes to menu, and set the theLight. to id. Add onmouseover and onmouseout events to the div to switch the div's ID. This causes the style sheet properties to change for that element. By adding an onclick handler to the <div> tags, you can send the user to another page.

```
<div class="menu" id="theLight"
onmouseover="this.id='theSolid'"
onmouseout="this.id='theLight'">
CSS Properties</div>

<div class="menu" id="theLight"
onmouseover="this.id='theSolid'"
onmouseout="this.id='theLight'">
JavaScript</div>

<div class="menu" id="theLight"
onmouseover="this.id='theSolid'"
onmouseout="this.id='theLight'">
Games</div>
```

247

Change Style Sheet After the Page Loads

You can change the imported style sheet after the page loads to create different Web site skins. You can allow users to select style sheets that they prefer, and you can use a cookie to store their preferences for future visits.

To change the imported style sheet, you need to link to a new style sheet. To reference the style sheet link, give the `<link>` tag an `id` attribute. For example, the statement `<link id="theStyle" rel="stylesheet" type="text/css" href="basicStyle.css">` imports a style sheet and is referenced by using the ID `theStyle`.

You can change the style sheet by changing the link's `href` attribute. For example, the statement `document.get ElementById("theStyle").href = "fancyStyle. css";` changes the imported style sheet on the page.

Not all browsers import the new style sheet. Other browsers can import the new style sheet, but it can fail to change all the elements to the new style.

You can use a cookie to remember your users' selections so they can have the same style sheet when they visit your Web site or advance to other pages. If you do not use a cookie and the user moves from page to page, the user sees the default style sheet.

To save the user's choice, you need to set the cookie when the new value is selected. You can have a drop-down list full of choices, or even a group of radio buttons. When the page is loading, check to see if the cookie exists already. If the cookie is there, apply the style sheet of the user's choice. To set and retrieve cookie information, see Chapter 13.

Change Style Sheet After the Page Loads

① Add a style sheet `<link>` tag and assign a value to the `id` attribute.

② Set the style sheet to the default value for the style sheet.

③ Add a group of radio buttons, and assign the `value` attribute to a style sheet file.

④ Add `onclick` handlers to the radio buttons to pass the value to a function.

⑤ Create a function to receive the parameter passed from the `onclick` handler.

⑥ Create a reference to the location of the style-sheet link tag by using the `id` value.

⑦ Set the reference equal to the value passed to the function.

⑧ Save the file.

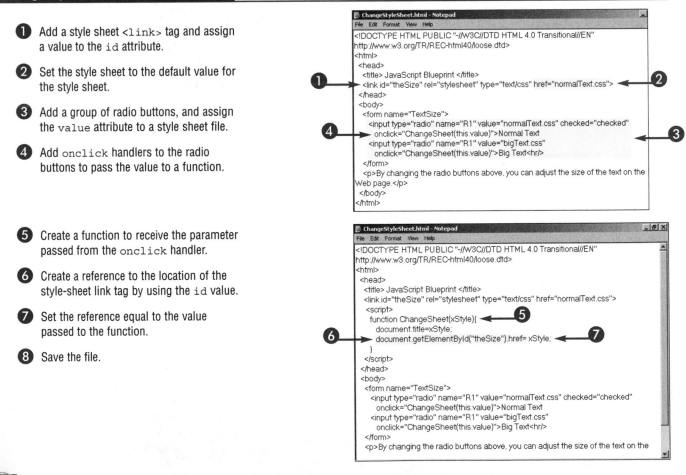

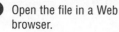

9 Open the file in a Web browser.

- The document is set to the default values.

10 Select another radio button option to change the style sheet.

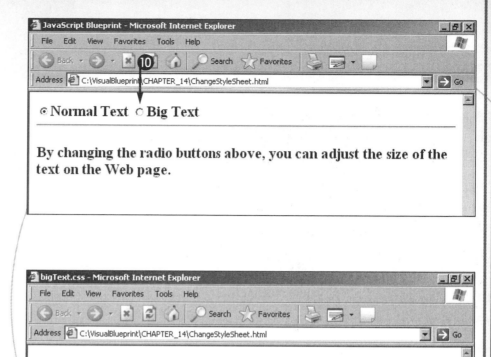

- The browser loads the new style sheet and changes the display properties on the page.

Extra

You can have a different style sheet based on the time of day. For example, you can make your Web site look darker at night or brighter during the day. This adds variety to your site and keeps it interesting for the user. To determine the time of day, you need to use the Date object to develop time ranges for each style sheet you want to have.

```
function GetSheet(){
  var sSheet = "dayTime.css";
  var theDate = new Date();
  var theHour = theDate.getHours();
  if(theHour<8 && theHour>17) sSheet = "nightTime.css";
  return sSheet;
}
```

You need to dynamically build the link to import the style sheet. This function calls the time function to figure out what style sheet it should import.

```
document.write('<link id="theSize" rel="stylesheet" type="text/css" href="' +
GetSheet()+ '">');
```

Turn Style Sheet Off or On

You can turn style sheets off and on to create different ways to display content on your page. You can have different Web page looks depending on the time of day, a user's interaction with the Web page, and so on. In order for this to work, you need to import multiple style sheets. Each style sheet should have the same class names or different class names depending on how you implement this.

If you are using the same class names, then you do not have to do any extra work. If you use different class names, you need to add multiple class names to the `class` attribute of the tag. For example, the statement `<div id= "man" class= "man1 man2 man3 ">` looks for three different classes to apply to that element.

You can use the style sheet array to disable the style sheets that are not in use. For example, `document.styleSheets`

`[2].disabled = true;` disables the third style sheet on the page. By assigning the disabled property to `false`, you enable the style sheet for use.

There are a couple of drawbacks to this method. The first one is that some browsers do not handle disabling and enabling style sheets. Some browsers ignore the fact that anything is happening. Another problem with this method is the Web page has to load every single style sheet into the memory when it is loading. Style sheets that have a large file size cause the loading time of the page to increase.

If the user is making the selection of what style sheet to view, the browser does not remember that when he visits another page or comes back to the site in the future. You can use cookies if you want the Web site to remember what option the user selected.

Turn Style Sheet Off or On

① Add an external or global style sheet to the document.

② Apply the style rules to the divs.

③ Add a group of checkboxes.

- The order of the check boxes applies to the order of the style sheets.

④ Add `onclick` event handlers to the `checkbox` elements calling a function to update the style sheets.

⑤ Create a function for the `onclick` handler to call.

⑥ Create a `for` loop that loops through the entire `styleSheets` array.

⑦ Find the check box checked state and store the opposite Boolean into a variable.

⑧ Reference the `styleSheets` array's `disabled` attribute and apply the Boolean value from the check box result.

⑨ Save the file.

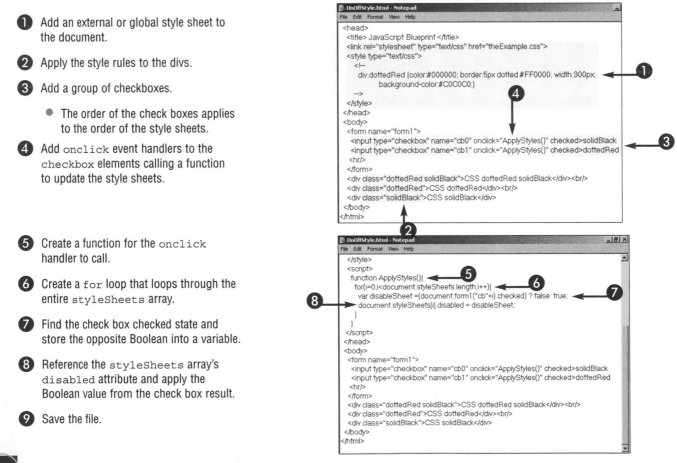

⑩ Open the file in a Web browser.

- The document is set to the default values.

⑪ Click a check box to deselect it.

- The browser disables the style sheet that corresponds to the check box.

Apply It

You can use radio buttons to determine what style sheet should be used. Build a form that contains radio buttons. The radio buttons need `onclick` event handlers to call a function to change the style sheets.

```
<form name="pick" >
  <input type="radio" name="sheet" checked onclick="PickSheet(0)">Night<br/>
  <input type="radio" name="sheet" onclick="PickSheet(1)">Day<br/>
</form>
```

The function loops through the `styleSheet` object array and disables them all. Then the correct style sheet is set to be enabled.

```
<script>
function PickSheet(numSheet){
  for(i=0;i<document.styleSheets.length;i++){
    document.styleSheets[i].disabled = true;
  }
  document.styleSheets[numSheet].disabled = false;
}
</script>
```

Reference an HTML Element

You can reference elements on a Web page using different methods depending on the information you have. When you create this reference, you can create dynamic content. By referencing Web page elements, you can change the text displayed, read values from tables, find property values, and more.

The first way to reference an object is to use a Document Object Method (DOM) `document.getElementById()`. This particular DOM can access every element in the document. The element ID is placed inside the parentheses. For example, the statement `var color = document.get ElementById("theBlock ").style.color;` accesses the element with the ID of `theBlock`.

Some elements that you may try accessing may not have an ID assigned to them. You can use the `document.get ElementsByTagName()` method to access the properties. The result is an array with all the elements containing that tag name. For example, `theDivs = document.get ElementsByTagName("div");` creates an array with all the div objects. You can access each element of the array by using the array syntax. For example, `theElem = theDivs[2];` stores the third element of the array into the variable `theElem`.

If you know the location of the object in the array, you can use it to reference the object. For example, the statement `var theMenu = document.getElementsByTagName ("div")[1];` references the second div on the page and stores the object into the variable `theMenu`.

Older generations of browsers do not use `document .getElementsById()` to reference objects. Netscape 4 uses `document.layers` and IE 4 browsers use `document.all`. Current IE browsers still support `document.all`, but not Netscape and Mozilla.

Reference an HTML Element

① Build a function.

② Add a `checkbox` element to control all other boxes.

③ Store all the `<input>` tags in a variable.

④ Loop through the `<input>` tag array looking for check boxes and setting the `checked` property.

⑤ Save the file.

⑥ Open the file in a Web browser.

⑦ Click the Check All check box.

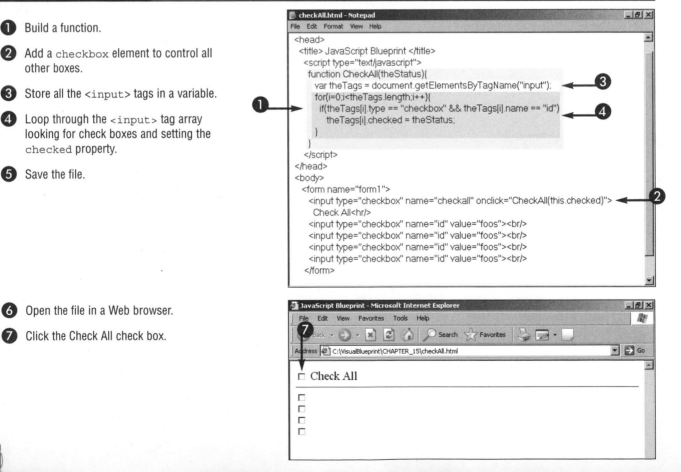

- The page appears with all the check boxes checked.

⑧ Click the Check All check box again.

- The page reappears with all the check boxes unchecked.

Apply It

You may need to reuse a `document.getElementById()` statement many times in one document. You can cut down on the amount of typing by storing the statement in a variable. You then can use this variable to reference the properties of the object. You can also add property references to the variable to reduce typing if required. Make sure that you assign the variable appropriate names so you can figure out what properties you are setting. Using variables lessens the chances of mistyping a statement. A missing quote or period can be hard to spot.

```
function UpdateDiv(theID){
  var theDiv = document.getElementById(theID){
  theDiv.style.visibility = "visible";
  theDiv.style.width = "150px";
  theDiv.style.background = "red";
  theDiv.style.color = "black";
  theDiv.innerHTML = "An error has occured.";
}
```

Create New HTML Elements

You can create new HTML elements on a Web page to insert new content into tables, forms, and more. This enables you to develop page content after the page loads and is initialized by an event handler.

To create a new element on the page, you can use the DOM `document.createElement()`. The `document.create Element()` method accepts the string value of the type of tag. You can use `p`, `h1`, `h2`, `input`, `div`, `span`, and so on.

After you create the element, you can set the attributes by using the `setAttribute()` method. The `setAttribute()` method has two parameters that are added in the parentheses. The first parameter is the name of the attribute. The name of attributes are `src`, `type`, `class`, `width`, `height`, and so on. The second parameter is the value of the first parameter. Attach the `setAttribute()` method to the element and the new attribute is added. For example, the statement `newElem.setAttribute("width", "100px");` adds the `width` attribute to the element.

To add the element to the Web page, you have three different choices: `appendChild()`, `insertBefore()`, and `replaceChild()`.

The `appendChild()` method receives one parameter in the parentheses, which is the new Element. This method adds the new element to the end of the *node tree* that is referenced. The node tree is a list of all the elements in the document. The statement `document.body.appendChild (newElem);` adds the element to the page.

The `insertBefore()` method accepts two parameters: the new element and the reference node before which you want to add the new element.

The `replaceChild()` accepts two parameters: the new element and the node reference that is replaced. This method replaces the node that is referenced with the new element.

Create New HTML Elements

① Create a new element.

② Set the appropriate attributes.

③ Add the new element to the Web page element.

④ Add an event handler and the element to the div.

⑤ Save the file.

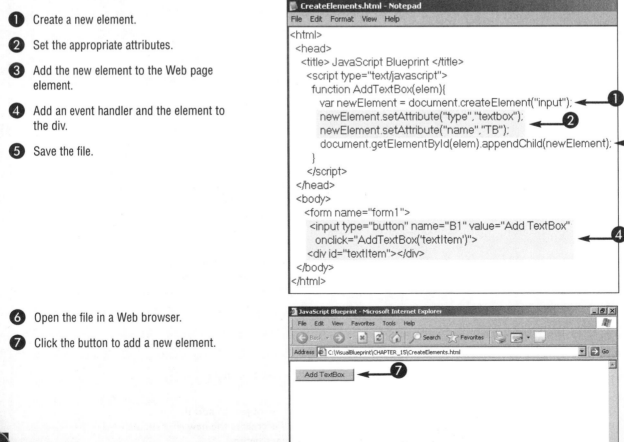

⑥ Open the file in a Web browser.

⑦ Click the button to add a new element.

- A new element appears.
⑧ Click the button again.

- Another element appears on the page.

Apply It

You can add text to a new HTML element to produce dynamic content on the page. This enables you to add content to the page, after it has loaded, that can interact with the user. You can add text to the new element by using the createTextNode() method. The createTextNode() method accepts a string parameter in the parentheses. Use the appendChild() method to add the text to a new element, which accepts the text parameter in the parentheses.

```
function AddTextBox(elem,newText){
    var theText = document.createTextNode(newText);
    var newElement = document.createElement("div");
    newElement.setAttribute("id","sp");
    newElement.appendChild(theText);
    document.getElementById(elem).appendChild(newElement);
}
```

The function accepts two parameters: the name of the object to add the new element, and the text to add to the new element. This creates the new element and adds it to the object specified in the function parameters.

Use innerHTML

You can add text, HTML tags, content, images, and so on, on a Web page as the content is loading or after the page has been completely loaded. By using the innerHTML of the document object, you can develop dynamic content that changes with user interaction.

The innerHTML tag is commonly used with `<div>` and `<span>` tags to change content in specified locations on the page. For example, the statement `document.getElementById("theDivId").innerHTML = "The new text";` replaces the content within the Web page element named theDivId with the text The new text. You can easily add HTML tags to the page instead of plain text.

The innerHTML property does not overwrite the entire HTML source code like the `write()` method does. The innerHTML property only replaces the information that is contained within the HTML tag that it is referring to.

When you use the innerHTML property while the page is loading, make sure that the innerHTML property is called after the element is loaded on the page. This is important because the innerHTML property relies on Web page objects, whereas the `document.write` statement does not. That means the `document.write` statement can be called at any time during the loading process.

To ensure that the element is loaded, use the `onload()` handler to initialize a function or place the script after the element that is being referenced. This eliminates a common error that may arise when developing DHTML scripts.

Developers tend to use innerText instead of innerHTML. The innerText method is not supported by all browsers. If you are developing an IE version of a Web site, then innerText will work. If you want to support other browsers, then you should use innerHTML.

Use innerHTML

① Create a div where you want the time to display.

② Retrieve the current time and convert it to a useable format.

③ Set the innerHTML property of the div to the time string.

④ Create an interval to update the time.

⑤ Save the file.

⑥ Open the file in a Web browser.

● A running clock appears on the Web page.

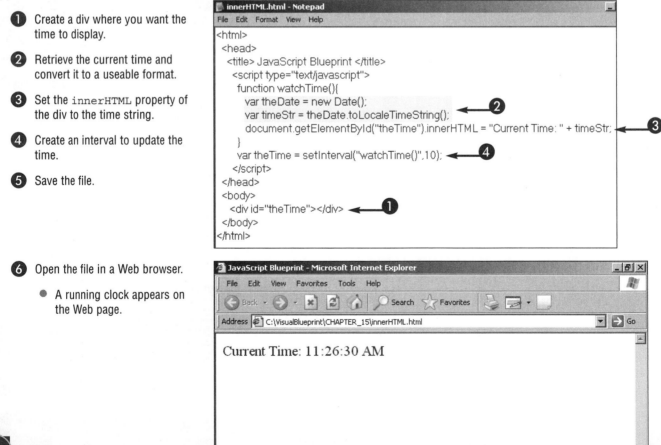

Set an Element Position

You can use DHTML to dynamically position Web page elements in the x, y, and z positions. The x position is measured from the left edge of the browser, y is measured from the top of the browser window, and the z position is measured out from the screen. The z-index places layers on top of each other. The z-index can be either a positive or a negative integer with the larger numbers placed on top of the smaller numbers. For example, an object with a z-index of 5 is displayed on top of an element with a z-index of 2.

To place the object, use the Cascading Style Sheet (CSS) properties `top`, `left`, and `z-index`. The element must have the position property set to `absolute` to place the object at any location on the page or set to `relative` to position the object relative to the parent object. For example, the statement `<div style="position:`

`absolute;top:10px;left:50px;z-index:0;">` positions the `div` at 10 pixels from the top of the page and 50 pixels from the left side of the page.

By using the `top`, `left`, and `z-index` properties, you can find the position of the elements on the page that are absolutely positioned. If the elements are not positioned on the page, then you have to use the nonposition script, which is shown later in this chapter.

The values of the `top`, `left`, and `z-index` properties are strings. Therefore, when you want to perform mathematical operations to the property values, convert the string to an integer. For example, the statement `var y = parseInt(document.getElementById("d1") .style.top);` converts the y coordinate of the element named `d1` to an integer.

Set an Element Position

① Create a div, setting the position to `absolute`.

② Create a function to access all the divs.

③ Reference the divs, and set the `top`, `left`, and `z-index` properties.

④ Create an event handler to adjust the element's position.

⑤ Save the file.

⑥ Open the file in a Web browser.

● The elements arrange dynamically on the Web page.

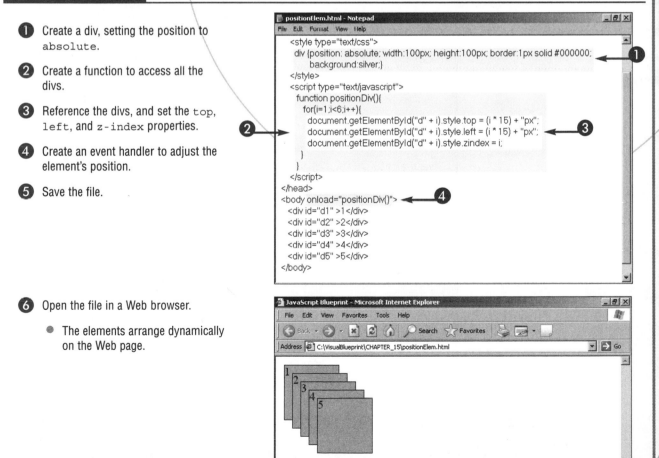

Find Nonpositioned Element Positions

Y ou may need to find the position of a nonpositioned element on a Web page. A nonpositioned element is an element that is not set by an absolute top and left position on the Web page. Finding the position takes extra coding because you cannot use the CSS properties to find the location.

The first step in finding the exact location of the image is to find the location of the element in relation to the location of the parent object. For example, if an image is contained inside a div, the parent object would be the div. If the image is not inside an object, then the parent object is the document. The offsetLeft and offsetTop properties allow you to find the location of the element in relationship to the parent.

After you find the location of the element in relation to its parent, you need to find the parent. To find the parent, use

the offsetParent property. For example, the statement parent = document.getElementById("theImg").offsetParent; stores the parent object of the element named theImg into the variable named parent.

You can then use the offsetParent object to get the offsetLeft and offsetTop properties to find the location of the parent. You can also use the object to retrieve other properties including id, width, height, and so on. After you find the location of the parent, you can get the location of the element by adding the parent's location properties to the element's location properties.

If the element's parent is a child element to another parent, then you have to repeat the process until there are no more parents. Because you may not know the number of levels of parent objects, you need to use a while loop to traverse the parent objects.

Find Nonpositioned Element Positions

① Determine the x and y location of the element in regard to its parent.

② Reassign the object reference to the parent.

③ Loop through all the element's positions.

④ Display the position on the screen.

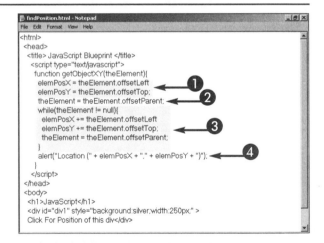

⑤ Add an event handler to an element to find its location.

⑥ Save the file.

7 Open the file in a Web browser.

8 Click the element to which you applied the event handler.

JavaScript Blueprint - Microsoft Internet Explorer

File   Edit   View   Favorites   Tools   Help

Back ▾ ▾ Search Favorites

Address C:\VisualBlueprint\CHAPTER_15\findPosition.html ▾ Go

JavaScript
Click For Position of this div ◄── **8**

● The position appears in the Web browser.

JavaScript Blueprint - Microsoft Internet Explorer

File   Edit   View   Favorites   Tools   Help

Back ▾ ▾ Search Favorites

Address C:\VisualBlueprint\CHAPTER_15\findPosition.html ▾ Go

JavaScript
Click For Position of this div

Microsoft Internet Explorer

⚠ Location (10,38) ◄──

OK

Apply It

You can position elements directly on top of other elements by finding the location of the element. This enables you to build multilayer images, add error messages to text boxes, and so on. To place an object dynamically on top of another element, give the upper element a z-index that is greater than the other object, and also set the positioning to absolute. Then develop the script to find the location of the object. After you find the location, position the second object. If you do not want the second object directly on top of the other element, you can add values to the position to offset it from the other object as in this example.

```
function getObjectXY(theElement){
  elemPosX = theElement.offsetLeft
  elemPosY = theElement.offsetTop;
  theElement = theElement.offsetParent;
  while(theElement != null){
    elemPosX += theElement.offsetLeft
    elemPosY += theElement.offsetTop;
    theElement = theElement.offsetParent;
  }
  document.getElementById("ErrorNote").style.left =  elemPosX - 15;
  document.getElementById("ErrorNote").style.top = elemPosY;
}
```

Show and Hide Elements

You can show and hide Web page elements to build dynamic menus, error messages, animations, and so on. Showing and hiding Web page elements is one of the most common things that is done in a DHTML script. You can use one of two methods to show and hide elements on the Web page, each of which produces different results.

The `visibility` property of the CSS is first method and is commonly used on most Web pages. You can set the `visibility` property to `visible` or `hidden` to either show or hide the element. For example, you can hide a Web page element ID named `t1` with the JavaScript statement `document.getElementById("t1").style.visibility="hidden";` or by adding it directly to the element `<div id="t1" style="visibility:hidden">`.

The `visibility` attribute hides the content and leaves the space the element normally fills, open on the page. You can use the `display` property method to hide the element if you do not want this space to remain blank.

The `display` property uses `block` or `inline` to show the element and `none` to hide the element. This method is great to use for tree menus where you want the other items to be moved down the page when the page is opened. For example, the JavaScript statement `document.getElement ById("t1").style.display="none";` hides the element `t1`. You can learn more about the difference between `block` and `inline` in Chapter 13.

If you want to hide an object on the Web page at the start, it is easier to set the `display` or `visibility` property of the CSS than it is to call a JavaScript function to hide it. Also, setting the CSS property allows the page to load much more quickly.

Show and Hide Elements

① Add a span beside each element, adding an error message and setting the visibility to hidden.

② Repeat step **1** for each form element you want to validate.

```
showHide.html - Notepad
File  Edit  Format  View  Help
<html>
 <head>
  <title> JavaScript Blueprint </title>
 </head>
 <body>
  <form name="form1" onsubmit="return validateForm()">
   <span style="width:150px;">User Name:</span>
   <input type="text" name="userName">
   <span id="error1" style="color:red;visibility:hidden;">User Name Required!</span>
   <br/>
   <span style="width:150px;">Password:</span>
   <input type="password" name="pass">
   <span id="error2" style="color:red;visibility:hidden;">Password Required!</span>
   <br/>
   <input type="submit" name="submit form">
  </form>
 </body>
</html>
```

③ Create a validation function.

④ Add an `onsubmit` event handler to the `<form>` tag.

⑤ Reference the span's visibility property to display the error message if the validation fails.

⑥ Repeat step **5** for each validation check.

⑦ Save the file.

```
showHide.html - Notepad
File  Edit  Format  View  Help
<html>
 <head>
  <title> JavaScript Blueprint </title>
  <script type="text/javascript">
   function validateForm(){
    allowSubmit = true;
    if(document.form1.userName.value.length == 0){
     document.getElementById("error1").style.visibility="visible";
     allowSubmit = false;
    }
    if(document.form1.pass.value.length == 0){
     document.getElementById("error2").style.visibility="visible";
     allowSubmit = false;
    }
    return allowSubmit;
   }
  </script>
 </head>
 <body>
  <form name="form1" onsubmit="return validateForm()">
   <span style="width:150px;">User Name:</span>
```

8 Open the file in a Web browser.

● The error messages do not appear.

9 Click the Submit Query button.

● The error messages appear.

Extra

You can easily toggle information from visible to hidden, and vice versa, with a button by using an `if` statement and an `onclick` event handler. You do not have to use a flag to keep track of whether the element is visible or hidden; instead, you can reference the element's `visibility` property. You can keep the script object oriented so you can use this on multiple items on the page. To do this, you need to pass the object that is to be toggled to the function and make sure the variables are all local.

```
<script type="text/javascript">
  function ShowHide(elem){
    var state = document.getElementById(elem).style.visibility;
    var newState = "hidden"
    if(state == "hidden")newState = "visible";
    document.getElementById(elem).style.visibility = newState;
  }
</script>
<div id="message">Welcome</div>
<input type="button" value="Change" onclick="ShowHide('message')">
```

You can use the `display` property instead of the `visibility` property just by changing the CSS property. Also, you can make things flash on the page by using a `setInterval` method and calling the function.

```
<body onload="setInterval('ShowHide(\'message\')',750)">
```

Find Browser Dimensions

Y ou can position an element directly in the middle of the browser window by detecting the window's width and height. This enables you to center content for scripts like the modal layer and custom alert.

The browsers do not have a set method or property to determine the browser size; therefore, some browser detection is required to see if a browser uses the property. Most browsers use the `innerWidth` and `innerHeight` properties. To determine the width of the browser window, apply it to the window object. For example, the statement `alert(window.innerWidth);` displays the browser's width. You can find the width of an individual element by referencing the object of the element. For example, the statement `var theWidth = document.getElementById("theItem").innerWidth` stores the height of the element named `theItem` into the variable `theWidth`.

Internet Explorer has two methods to determine the width of the browser. Both of the methods use the properties `clientWidth` and `clientHeight`.

When Internet Explorer 6 is in compliance mode, you can reference the browser width and height by using the `document.documentElement` object. The statement `pageH = document.documentElement.clientHeight;` stores the width into the variable `pageH`.

The other method to access the window width is the `window.body` object. The browser window's width is found by using the statement `window.body.clientWidth`.

When using IE, you can detect the width and height of an element by accessing the `clientWidth` and `clientHeight` properties of the element. For example, the statement `var theHeight = document.getElementById("theItem").clientHeight;` stores the height of the element into the variable `theHeight`.

Find Browser Dimensions

① Use `window.innerWidth` and `window.innerHeight` to obtain the dimensions of the browser in non-IE browsers.

② Use `document.documentElement.clientWidth` and `document.documentElement.clientHeight` to obtain the dimensions of the browser for IE in compliance mode.

③ Use `document.body.clientWidth` and `document.body.clientHeight` to obtain the dimensions of the browser for other versions of IE.

④ Display the dimensions with an `alert()` method.

● The dimensions of the browser appear in the alert dialog box.

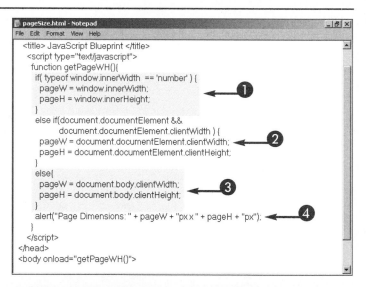

Find the Mouse Position

You can locate the position of the mouse on the screen by using JavaScript. You can use this method to build dynamic image maps, games, and much more. Detecting the mouse position on the screen in Microsoft Internet Explorer differs from other browsers. You need to verify that the browser is Microsoft Internet Explorer by using the statement `var IE = (navigator.appName == "Microsoft Internet Explorer")?true:false;`.

First, attach the mouse movement to the document. To detect the mouse movement, use the `onmousemove` event handler. The statement `document.onmousemove = getMouseXY;` attaches the event handler to the document. With the other browsers, you must attach another object to the document to catch the mouse movement event. The statement `if(!IE) document.captureEvents(Event.MOUSEMOVE)` allows the mouse position to be tracked.

When developing the function, it is important that you place a variable `e` inside the brackets of the function. For example, the statement `function getMouseXY(e)` allows Netscape and other browsers to use the event object.

Microsoft Internet Explorer uses the event object to detect where the mouse is located. The properties `clientX` and `clientY` detect where the cursor is on the screen. The `clientX` and `clientY` do not account for the amount the screen has been scrolled. As a result, you need to add `document.body.scrollLeft` and `document.body.scrollTop` to the `clientX` and `clientY` results. For example, the statement `tempX = event.clientX + document.body.scrollLeft;` displays the current mouse position.

With the other browsers, it is easier to find the mouse position. The statements `e.pageX` and `e.pageY` displays the current X and Y position of the mouse on the screen.

Find the Mouse Position

1. Detect if the user is using Microsoft Internet Explorer.

2. Attach the event handler to the document event.

3. Use a browser detection to detect the mouse position.

4. Use `document.title` to display the mouse `x` and `y` coordinates on screen.

5. Save the file.

6. Open the file in a Web browser.

7. Move the mouse around the browser window.

   • The mouse position appears in the title bar.

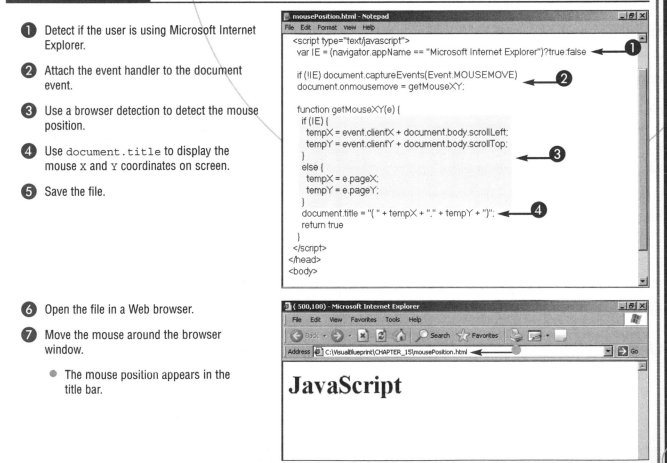

```
mousePosition.html - Notepad
File  Edit  Format  View  Help

<script type="text/javascript">
 var IE = (navigator.appName == "Microsoft Internet Explorer")?true:false   ——1

 if (!IE) document.captureEvents(Event.MOUSEMOVE)   ——2
 document.onmousemove = getMouseXY;

 function getMouseXY(e) {
  if (IE) {
   tempX = event.clientX + document.body.scrollLeft;
   tempY = event.clientY + document.body.scrollTop;
  }
  else {                                              ——3
   tempX = e.pageX;
   tempY = e.pageY;
  }
  document.title = "( " + tempX + "," + tempY + ")";  ——4
  return true
  }
 </script>
</head>
<body>
```

```
( 500,100 ) - Microsoft Internet Explorer
File  Edit  View  Favorites  Tools  Help
Back  ·  ·  ·  Search  Favorites
Address  C:\VisualBlueprint\CHAPTER_15\mousePosition.html   ——

JavaScript
```

Animate Elements

You can make objects move around the screen by using the top and left attributes of the object. You can animate menus to slide onto the screen, have dynamic slide shows that move images, create scrolling games, and so on. The key to making an object move around the screen is the `setTimeout()` method along with the help of CSS positional attributes.

First, make sure that the object's position property is set to absolute. If you do not do this, the object cannot be repositioned. To make the object move, set the left and top positional properties. Another thing you need to account for is the z-index of the animation and the other objects on the Web page. If you want the animation to be on top of everything, give the animation a higher z-index than any other element on the page.

The smoothness of the animation depends on the speed of the `setInterval()` and the amount of pixels the image is moved. If the amount of pixels and interval is large, then the image appears to shake as it moves, which is not a pleasant sight to the user. Smaller pixel movement with a fast refresh rate ensures smoother movement.

When you animate objects, consider the viewable area of the Web page. If an object goes off the viewable area of the page, the Web page does not follow it. The user must use the scrollbars to follow it.

Some browsers may cause the cursor to blink as the `setInterval()` is called. There is no way to stop the cursor from flashing.

Animate Elements

① Develop a function named `MoveObjX` that accepts multiple parameters.

② Determine the direction of the marquee movement.

③ Set the new location of the element by adding the step size to the current position.

④ Develop a `setTimeout()` method to call the function `MoveObjX`.

⑤ Create a function named `StartAnimation` to initialize the values for the marquee.

⑥ Add an `onload` event handler to initialize the function `StartAnimation`.

⑦ Save the page.

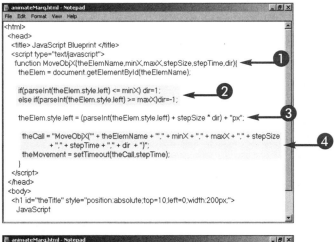

```
animateMarq.html - Notepad
File  Edit  Format  View  Help
<html>
 <head>
  <title> JavaScript Blueprint </title>
  <script type="text/javascript">
   function MoveObjX(theElemName,minX,maxX,stepSize,stepTime,dir){    ①
    theElem = document.getElementById(theElemName);

    if(parseInt(theElem.style.left) <= minX) dir=1;      ②
    else if(parseInt(theElem.style.left) >= maxX)dir=-1;

    theElem.style.left = (parseInt(theElem.style.left) + stepSize * dir) + "px";    ③

    theCall = "MoveObjX('" + theElemName + "'," + minX + "," + maxX + "," + stepSize
       + "," + stepTime + "," + dir  + ")";                                          ④
    theMovement = setTimeout(theCall,stepTime);
   }
  </script>
 </head>
 <body>
  <h1 id="theTitle" style="position:absolute;top=10;left=0;width:200px;">
   JavaScript
```

```
animateMarq.html - Notepad
File  Edit  Format  View  Help
    theElem.style.left = (parseInt(theElem.style.left) + stepSize * dir) + "px";

    theCall = "MoveObjX('" + theElemName + "'," + minX + "," + maxX + "," + stepSize
       + "," + stepTime + "," + dir  + ")";
    theMovement = setTimeout(theCall,stepTime);
   }

   function StartAnimation(){
    MoveObjX("theTitle",0,350,1,10,1);       ⑤
   }

   window.onload = StartAnimation;        ⑥

  </script>
 </head>
 <body>
  <h1 id="theTitle" style="position:absolute;top=10;left=0;width:200px;">
   JavaScript
  </h1>
 </body>
</html>
```

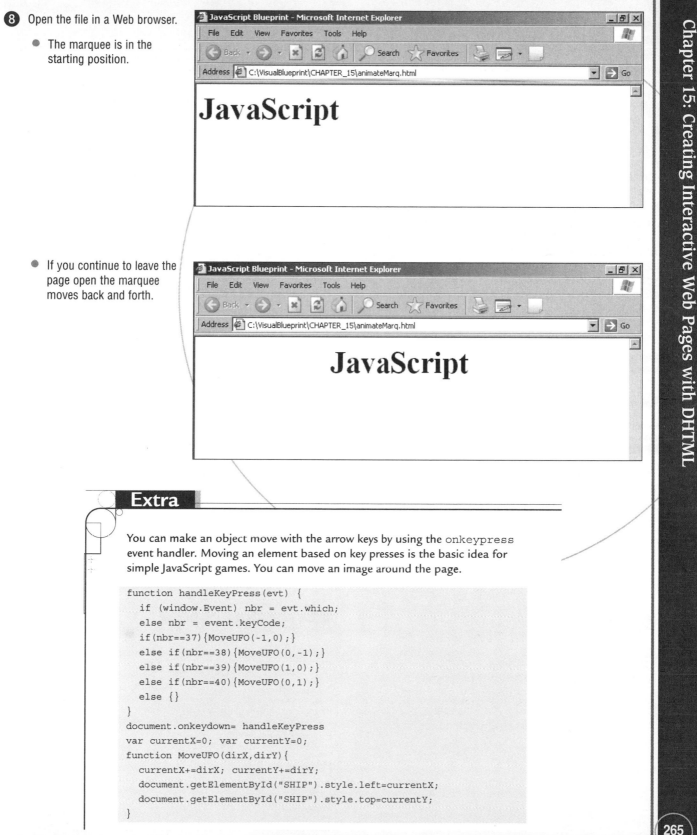

8 Open the file in a Web browser.

- The marquee is in the starting position.

- If you continue to leave the page open the marquee moves back and forth.

Extra

You can make an object move with the arrow keys by using the `onkeypress` event handler. Moving an element based on key presses is the basic idea for simple JavaScript games. You can move an image around the page.

```
function handleKeyPress(evt) {
  if (window.Event) nbr = evt.which;
  else nbr = event.keyCode;
  if(nbr==37){MoveUFO(-1,0);}
  else if(nbr==38){MoveUFO(0,-1);}
  else if(nbr==39){MoveUFO(1,0);}
  else if(nbr==40){MoveUFO(0,1);}
  else {}
}
document.onkeydown= handleKeyPress
var currentX=0; var currentY=0;
function MoveUFO(dirX,dirY){
  currentX+=dirX; currentY+=dirY;
  document.getElementById("SHIP").style.left=currentX;
  document.getElementById("SHIP").style.top=currentY;
}
```

Create a
Draggable Element

ou can make images or other Web page elements on a page draggable by combining a few DHTML concepts. By making elements draggable, you can give the users the ability to move objects around the page. This is handy for games or just a unique way to display information on the screen. Dragging elements combines multiple DHTML elements into one script: detecting the mouse position, detecting an element position, and repositioning an element. The most common elements that are made draggable are images and divs.

To create a draggable element, specify the position of the element as absolute so that you can change the location of the element according to the cursor. If you do not set the element to absolute positioning, then the script does not

work properly. The relative positioning does not allow the element to be placed in the right location due to its positioning restraints.

Along with setting the position to absolute, you also need to set the initial location of the element by adjusting the top and left properties of the object. You are also going to have to change the values in the top and left properties of the element when the element is being dragged.

You need to detect when the mouse button is held down or released on the elements which you want to be dragged. In order to do this, you can add onmousedown and onmouseup event handlers to the elements. The onmousedown event is used to initialize the dragging function and the onmouseup event is used to end the dragging function.

Create a Draggable Element

① Insert the code to detect the mouse position.

② Define the position variables outside the function to make them global.

Note: For a detailed description of the mouse position code, see the Find the Mouse Position section.

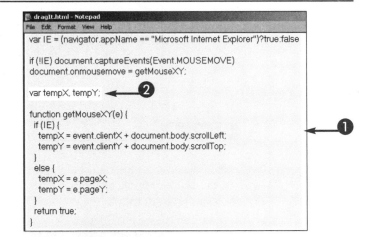

③ Insert the code to determine an element's position.

④ Define the position variables outside the function to make them global.

Note: For a detailed description of the element's position code, see the Set an Element Position section.

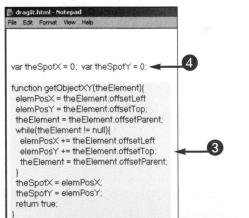

⑤ Develop a function that figures the difference between where the element is located and the position of the mouse.

⑥ Call the position function to find the element's position.

⑦ Calculate the new position of the element.

⑧ Add a statement to create an interval to call the positioning function.

⑨ Add a statement in front of the interval to cancel any previous intervals that might exist.

⑩ Develop a function that places the image according to the offset of the mouse.

⑪ Add statements to set the `top` and `left` properties of the image element.

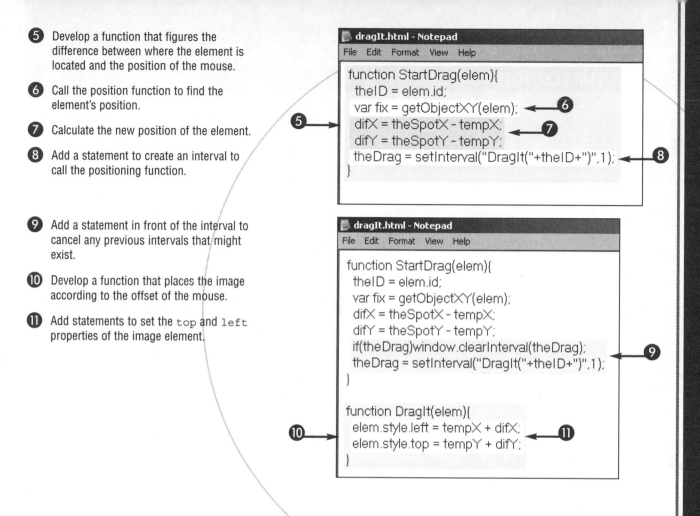

dragIt.html - Notepad
File   Edit   Format   View   Help

```
function StartDrag(elem){
  theID = elem.id;
  var fix = getObjectXY(elem);        ← ⑥
  difX = theSpotX - tempX;            ← ⑦
  difY = theSpotY - tempY;
  theDrag = setInterval("DragIt("+theID+")",1);   ← ⑧
}
```

dragIt.html - Notepad
File   Edit   Format   View   Help

```
function StartDrag(elem){
  theID = elem.id;
  var fix = getObjectXY(elem);
  difX = theSpotX - tempX;
  difY = theSpotY - tempY;
  if(theDrag)window.clearInterval(theDrag);       ← ⑨
  theDrag = setInterval("DragIt("+theID+")",1);
}

function DragIt(elem){
  elem.style.left = tempX + difX;                 ← ⑪
  elem.style.top = tempY + difY;
}
```

Extra

When you are testing the script, you may find that the element does not become unattached from the mouse when the button is released. The cause of this problem is the `onmouseup` event did not fire because the position of the mouse happened to be off the image. This problem normally occurs on a slower processor machine, or moving the image in a rapid motion while releasing the mouse button. To fix this problem, you can add an `onmouseout` event handler that cancels the dragging when the mouse leaves the element.

You can also add the `onmouseover` and `onmoueout` events to change the appearance of the element, so the user knows the element can be changed. By changing the CSS properties such as the border or background color, you can make the element easy to recognize. You can also set the cursor to `move` in order to show the movable crosshair mouse icon.

continued →

The current mouse position needs to be determined along with the position of the element to be dragged. The difference between the element and the mouse should be calculated so the distance remains the same during the dragging process.

The key to this script is to set an interval. The setInterval() method needs to be set when the initiation process begins in the dragging of the element. As the element is dragged around the screen, the setInterval() method calls a function to determine where the element should be in relation to the mouse. As long as the mouse button is held down, the setInterval() method needs to remain active.

When the mouse is released the dragging process is to be stopped. In order to stop the dragging process, the setInterval() method needs to be cleared by using the clearInterval() method. After clearing the timed interval, the element is no longer attached to the mouse movement and the element remains in the last calculated position.

The draggable element can be nested inside other elements. This allows for the parent element to move along with the child element. You need to use the parent id when you are initializing the function. This can allow you to create a layer pseudo-window that is able to be dragged by the toolbar just like a normal window.

After testing this on different browsers and different computers, you can see that certain computers handle the smoothness of dragging differently. Normally a computer with a slower processor can have a jumpy feel to the dragging of the images. Normally you do not see a major performance difference between different browsers like you do in other DHTML scripts.

Create a Draggable Element (continued)

⑫ Create a function to cancel the timeout when the button is released.

⑬ Add event handlers to the elements you want to make draggable.

⑭ Set the elements' initial position on the screen.

⑮ Save the file.

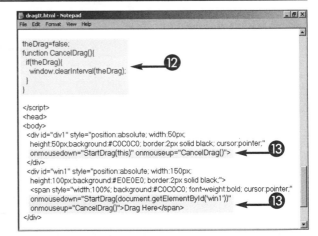

16 Open the file in a Web browser.

17 Click and drag an element that is draggable and move the mouse around the screen.

18 Release the mouse and the element remains in place.

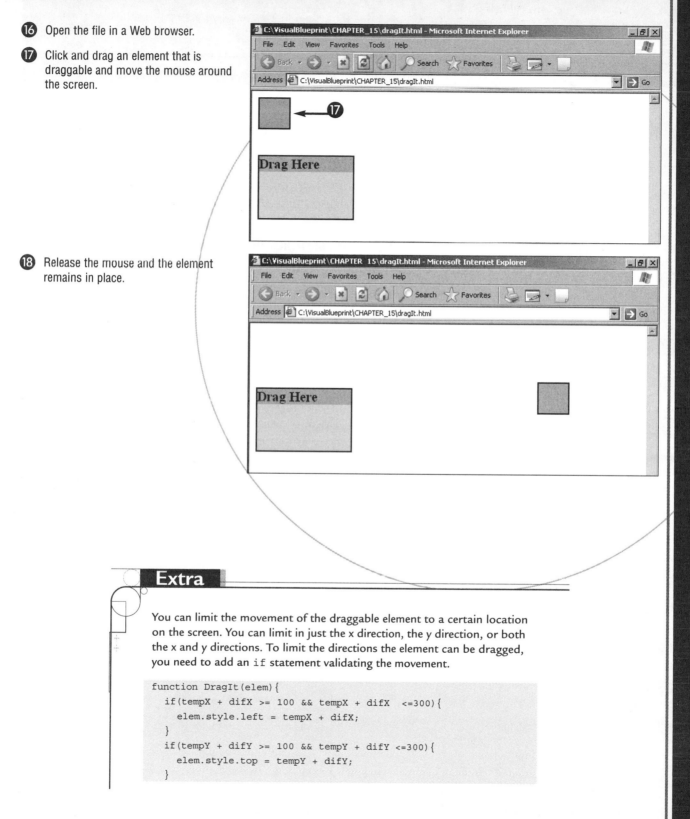

Extra

You can limit the movement of the draggable element to a certain location on the screen. You can limit in just the x direction, the y direction, or both the x and y directions. To limit the directions the element can be dragged, you need to add an `if` statement validating the movement.

```
function DragIt(elem){
  if(tempX + difX >= 100 && tempX + difX  <=300){
    elem.style.left = tempX + difX;
  }
  if(tempY + difY >= 100 && tempY + difY <=300){
    elem.style.top = tempY + difY;
  }
```

Create a Cross-Browser Layer Modal Window

You may want to use a modal window, which is only supported by Microsoft Internet Explorer. You can create a cross-browser version of a modal window by using layers to create the same effect.

The purpose of a modal window is to require the user to do whatever is in that new window. To get the same effect, you can create a layer that covers the entire document. The z-index of this new layer needs to be larger than any of the other layers. Therefore, you need to find the viewable height and width of the browser.

Add the content to this layer that you want to appear in the modal window. You can format the layer to look like a

browser window if you want. The important thing is to set a background color where the text is located. If you do not set a background color, the content under the modal layer will show through, making it hard for the user to read the content.

The function is called by any event handler or from the inside of a function. Develop a function that shows and hides the modal layer. Use the visibility property to show or hide the layer. Set the visibility property to hidden to hide this layer until it is called. If you do not set this property, the layer is visible when the page is loaded.

Create a Cross-Browser Layer Modal Window

① Create a function to determine the page dimensions.

② Adjust the layer's dimensions to fill the entire screen.

Note: Subtracting 20 pixels ensures that the layer does not run off the screen and activate the scrollbars.

③ Create a function that shows the modal layer and executes the sizing function.

④ Create a function that hides the modal layer by setting the visibility to hidden.

⑤ Add an event handler to display the modal dialog box.

⑥ Create the modal layer, setting the position to the top corner of the screen and adding an event handler to hide the layer.

⑦ Save the file.

8 Open the file in a Web browser.

● The modal layer covers the Web page.

9 Click the Close this layer link.

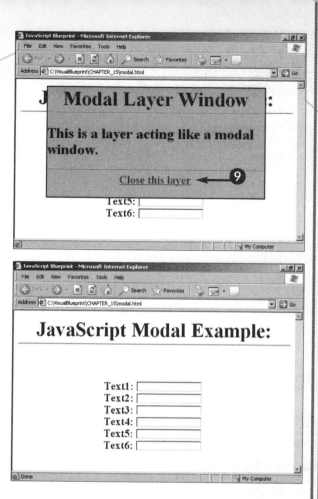

● The modal layer is hidden and the user can interact with the page.

Extra

You may find that certain browsers do not allow layers on top of form elements, especially select elements. The browser renders the select elements to have a top-level z-index. The solution is to hide all the select elements when the layer is placed on top of it. The select element does not show through the layer when the visibility of the element is hidden.

```
function ShowHideSelect(xHow){
  var theElems = document.getElementsByTagName("select");
  for(i=0;i<theElems.length;i++){
    theElems[i].style.visibility = xHow;
  }
}
```

The function loops through the tag name array stored in the variable theElems and sets the style attribute specified by the variable xHow. To show the elements, pass visible to the function. Passing hidden to the function hides all the elements from the user's view.

Create a Custom Alert or Confirm Dialog Box

You can create your own custom alert or confirm box so you can control its appearance. The normal browser alert and confirm dialog boxes are stuck with the default text on the buttons and in the header. You cannot add color or even add other buttons to the default alert and confirm dialog boxes, but you can create the same effect by using layers. Therefore you can have multiple buttons such as Yes, No, or Maybe. You can include dropdowns, text, radio buttons, checkboxes, and so on.

This code behind this script is similar to the modal window script; both scripts involve placing a layer over the entire window to keep people from interacting with the content underneath. The alert and confirm script goes one step further by adding another layer on top of the modal layer. This layer contains all of the content and also is centered in the window to produce the effect of the real thing.

The appearance of the customized alert and confirm dialog boxes is up to you. You can customize the layer to look like a traditional alert box, or you can create an alert box that fits the style of the document. You are not limited to a certain set of rules.

The main property that you need to utilize is the innerHTML property. The innerHTML method allows you to use the same layers multiple times by changing the content of the message. Therefore you do not need to have a bunch of extra layers lying around for different situations. You can add HTML formatting to the string that is used to display the information on the page. Therefore you can have the paragraph tag referencing a CSS class or an element being centered on the screen.

Create a Custom Alert or Confirm Dialog Box

 Develop the modal layer and the confirm box, making sure to set the position to absolute.

② Create an element to accept a string to display the value to the user.

③ Create a button or group of buttons to call a function and hide the modal layer.

④ Add an event handler to send a message to the layer, which appears and notifies that the layer should be displayed.

```
confirm.html - Notepad
File  Edit  Format  View  Help
<body>
  <div id="modalLayer" style="position:absolute; top=0;length=0; width:100%;
height:100%; z-index:100; visibility:hidden;"> </div>
  <div id="ConBox" style="position:absolute; width:400px; background:#E0E0E0;
border:2px outset">
    <h3 style="text-align:left;background:#C0C0C0">Custom Alert</h3>
    <h4 id="message" style="width:90%;margin:auto;"></h4>
    <div style="text-align:center">
      <form name="conf">
      </form>
    </div>
  </div>
  <h1>JavaScript Custom Alert Example:<hr/></h1>
</body>
```

```
confirm.html - Notepad
File  Edit  Format  View  Help
<body onload="ShowModal('The alert was called with the &lt;em&gt;onload&lt;/em&gt;
    handler! You can call the function anyway you want.');">
  <div id="modalLayer" style="position:absolute; top=0;length=0; width:100%;
height:100%; z-index:100; visibility:hidden;"> </div>
  <div id="ConBox" style="position:absolute; width:400px; background:#E0E0E0;
border:2px outset">
    <h3 style="text-align:left;background:#C0C0C0">Custom Alert</h3>
    <h4 id="message" style="width:90%;margin:auto;"></h4>
    <div style="text-align:center">
      <form name="conf">
        <button name="cB1" style="width:100px" onclick="push='Yes';HideModal()">
          Yes</button> 
        <button name="cB2"style="width:100px;" onclick="push='No';HideModal()">
          No</button> 
        <button name="cB3" style="width:100px;" onclick="push='Maybe';HideModal()">
          Maybe</button>
      </form>
    </div>
  </div>
  <h1>JavaScript Custom Alert Example:<hr/></h1>
</body>
```

5. Develop a function that accepts one parameter.

6. Set the `innerHTML` property of the div to display the message.

7. Change the `visibility` property to `visible` to display the confirm box.

8. Focus the default button by using the `focus()` method.

9. Call the function to center the content in the window and cover the page with a protective layer.

10. Create a function that hides the layers, setting the `visibility` property to `hidden`.

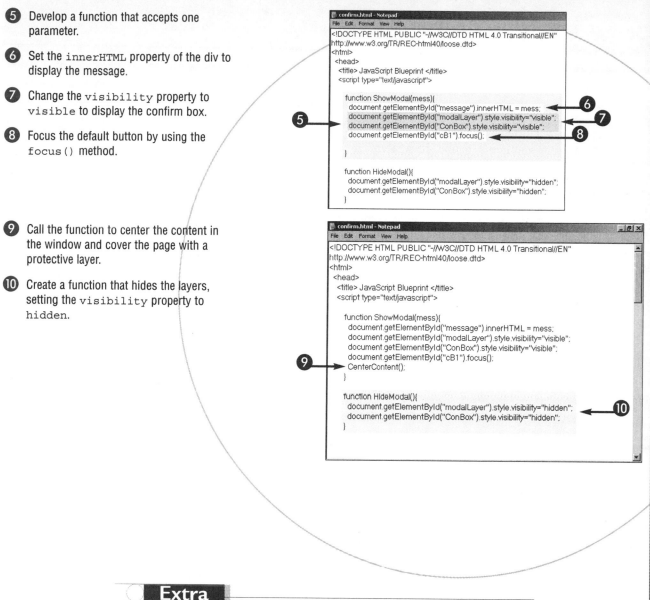

```
confirm.html - Notepad
File Edit Format View Help
<!DOCTYPE HTML PUBLIC "-//W3C//DTD HTML 4.0 Transitional//EN"
http://www.w3.org/TR/REC-html40/loose.dtd>
<html>
 <head>
  <title> JavaScript Blueprint </title>
  <script type="text/javascript">

  function ShowModal(mess){
   document.getElementById("message").innerHTML = mess;
   document.getElementById("modalLayer").style.visibility="visible";
   document.getElementById("ConBox").style.visibility="visible";
   document.getElementById("cB1").focus();

  }

  function HideModal(){
   document.getElementById("modalLayer").style.visibility="hidden";
   document.getElementById("ConBox").style.visibility="hidden";
   }
```

```
confirm.html - Notepad
File Edit Format View Help
<!DOCTYPE HTML PUBLIC "-//W3C//DTD HTML 4.0 Transitional//EN"
http://www.w3.org/TR/REC-html40/loose.dtd>
<html>
 <head>
  <title> JavaScript Blueprint </title>
  <script type="text/javascript">

  function ShowModal(mess){
   document.getElementById("message").innerHTML = mess;
   document.getElementById("modalLayer").style.visibility="visible";
   document.getElementById("ConBox").style.visibility="visible";
   document.getElementById("cB1").focus();
   CenterContent();
  }

  function HideModal(){
   document.getElementById("modalLayer").style.visibility="hidden";
   document.getElementById("ConBox").style.visibility="hidden";
   }
```

Extra

You can make the other items on the page appear to be grayed out by adding a transparency CSS property to the body of the document. Setting the opacity filter to about 40 percent changes the feel of the text, making it look like it is blurred out. Apply the CSS class to the body of the document when the alert or confirm dialog box is in view and remove it when the confirm dialog box is hidden.

```
transLayer {filter:alpha(opacity=40); -moz-opacity:40%}
```

continued ➡

A nother major part of the script is determining the center of the browser window. In order to do this, the screen width and height parameters need to be calculated along with the width and height of the custom alert box. By subtracting the screen width from the alert width and dividing by two, you are able to calculate the centered position of the window. You also need to perform the same operation for the height. These location parameters are then applied to the alert div and the window is positioned with the left and top properties.

When the layer is first loaded, you can set the focus of one of the buttons. The user can then press Enter instead of

having to click the button just like the real thing. In order to detect what button the user picked, you need to add an event handler to each of the buttons. After the button is clicked, you need to hide the layer so the user is able to interact with the rest of the page.

One downfall to using a custom alert or confirm is it cannot act the same as a real alert or confirm. A real alert can stop the operation of a function until the button is pressed. In order to perform the same operation with the custom method, the script needs to be split into two parts in order to stop the operation. The alert button needs to initialize the second function after the button is clicked.

Create a Custom Alert or Confirm Dialog Box *(continued)*

⑪ Find the dimensions of the screen and the custom dialog box for non-IE browsers.

⑫ Determine the dimensions of the screen and custom dialog box for IE in compliance mode.

⑬ Determine the dimensions of the screen and custom alert box for other versions of IE.

⑭ Set the modal layer to the new height to cover the page.

⑮ Determine the placement for the dialog box in the center of the browser window.

⑯ Set the position of the dialog box.

⑰ Save the file.

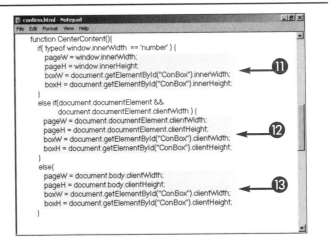

⑱ Open the file in a Web browser.

● The custom dialog box appears with the dynamic message.

⑲ Click a button.

● The custom alert box is hidden from the user's view.

Extra

Unlike a normal confirm dialog box, you can insert images into the text. This allows you to create your own error messages by using an error image that you can create. Images can be placed in the title bar or in the message body.

You can add text fields, select dropdowns, radio buttons, and check boxes in the confirm dialog box. You can use these form elements to collect extra data from the user, creating a modified prompt box. Instead of the usual prompt box, you can use this method.

You can force a user to agree to an agreement by using a custom prompt box. This guarantees that the user has seen an agreement before a form or function is executed. The agreement can be set in a scrollable div so the user can read the information. You can then add a submit button to submit the form or execute the JavaScript statement. You can have another button take the user to another page, or just have the page remain with no future action.

Insert and Remove Items in a Selection List

You can add and remove items from a selection list. This allows users to type information that may not be there when they are filling out a form. Instead of having another option in your selection list, you can allow users to add the missing information with the click of a button by accepting parameters from form elements.

A selection list is made up of options that have a text property and a value property. The text property is what is visible to the user. To add a new option you can add a new value to the option array of the selected item. The statement `document.form1.select1.options[3] = new Option (theText, theValue);` references a select element and adds a new value to the fourth element of the option array. If the element already exists at the index where you inserted the information, then the new information overwrites the old information.

Ideally, you want to add the option to the end of the list by finding the number of elements in the options array. To do this, you can use the length property. The statement `document.form1.select1.options.length` allows you to find the number of choices that are available to the user.

You can determine what option is selected by using the `selectedIndex` property. You can also pick the option that is selected by using this property. For example, the statement `document.form1.select1.options[0].selected = true;` selects the first element in the list.

You can remove items from the list by setting them to null. The statement `document.form1.select1.options[5] = null;` removes the sixth element of the selection list. The other options shift down on the index to fill the gap created.

Insert and Remove Items in a Selection List

① Create a function to add items to a selection list.

② Add a reference to the selection list.

③ Add two variables and obtain two text field values.

④ Create an option in the select element by using the `new Option()` method.

⑤ Select the new option by setting the select property to true.

⑥ Create a function to remove items from a selection list.

⑦ Add a reference to the selection list.

⑧ Determine if an option is selected; if it is, set the option to `null` and select a new option.

⑨ If no options are available, display an alert message.

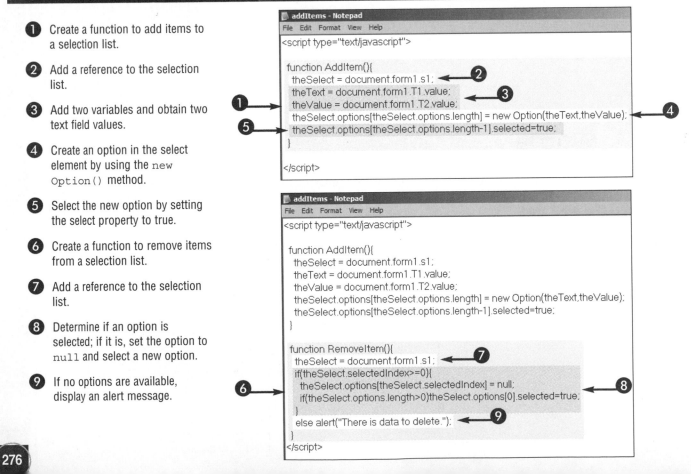

addItems - Notepad
File Edit Format View Help
```
<script type="text/javascript">

function AddItem(){
  theSelect = document.form1.s1;                                    ②
  theText = document.form1.T1.value;                                ③
  theValue = document.form1.T2.value;
  theSelect.options[theSelect.options.length] = new Option(theText,theValue);   ④
  theSelect.options[theSelect.options.length-1].selected=true;      ⑤

}

</script>
```

addItems - Notepad
File Edit Format View Help
```
<script type="text/javascript">

function AddItem(){
  theSelect = document.form1.s1;
  theText = document.form1.T1.value;
  theValue = document.form1.T2.value;
  theSelect.options[theSelect.options.length] = new Option(theText,theValue);
  theSelect.options[theSelect.options.length-1].selected=true;
}

function RemoveItem(){
  theSelect = document.form1.s1;                                    ⑦
  if(theSelect.selectedIndex>=0){
    theSelect.options[theSelect.selectedIndex] = null;             ⑧
    if(theSelect.options.length>0)theSelect.options[0].selected=true;
  }
  else alert("There is data to delete.");                          ⑨
}
</script>
```

10 Create the select element with one or more options.

11 Create two text boxes to accept user input.

12 Create three buttons to add a value, remove a value, and reset the text boxes.

13 Develop a function to reset the text fields to blank.

14 Save the file.

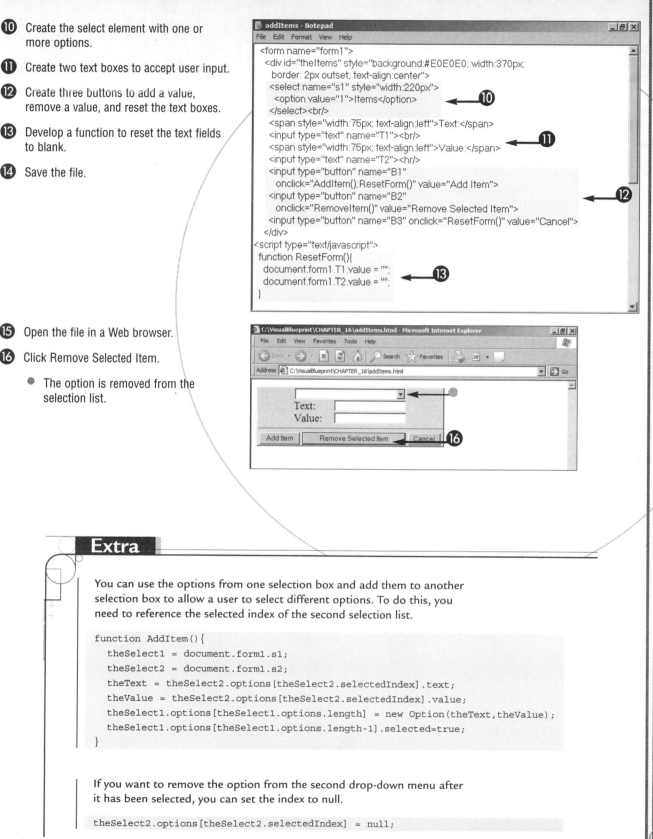

15 Open the file in a Web browser.

16 Click Remove Selected Item.

- The option is removed from the selection list.

Extra

You can use the options from one selection box and add them to another selection box to allow a user to select different options. To do this, you need to reference the selected index of the second selection list.

```
function AddItem(){
  theSelect1 = document.form1.s1;
  theSelect2 = document.form1.s2;
  theText = theSelect2.options[theSelect2.selectedIndex].text;
  theValue = theSelect2.options[theSelect2.selectedIndex].value;
  theSelect1.options[theSelect1.options.length] = new Option(theText,theValue);
  theSelect1.options[theSelect1.options.length-1].selected=true;
}
```

If you want to remove the option from the second drop-down menu after it has been selected, you can set the index to null.

```
theSelect2.options[theSelect2.selectedIndex] = null;
```

Create a Double Combo Selection List

O ne way you can generate dynamic forms is to use double combo boxes. You can make one selection list dependent on another list to develop customized data for the user. You can have users find Web page links that are suited for their needs.

A double combo box requires two select form elements. The first selection box contains the first level of information. This selection box data is static.

The second selection box is filled by a multidimensional array. The first index of the array corresponds to the index of the item in the first array. Setting the second array to `new Option` makes it easier to extract the data for the second array.

You need to capture the `onchange` event with the first select list. This event trigger starts the process of filling the

second list. First, remove all the items from the selection list. You need to do this from the last item to the first item in the list. To remove the item, set the value to null. For example, the statement `document.form1.select1 .options[0] = null;` removes the first item from the selection list.

After the selection list is cleared of all its options, it needs to be filled with the new options. To do this, loop through the multidimensional array setting the text and value parameters of the selection list.

If you are using the double combo box for a navigation system, you can add a button to send the user to a new location. By setting the second selection box's selected index value to the location object, you can change the page.

Create a Double Combo Selection List

① Create a select form element with options.

② Create a select element with no options.

③ Add a button with an `onclick` handler to call a function.

④ Calculate the number of options in the first drop-down list.

⑤ Create a new array and add the `new Option` based on the first drop-down list options.

⑥ Create a function and reference the select elements.

⑦ Set all the options in the second select box to `null`.

⑧ Place the new values into the second drop-down list.

⑨ Create a function to redirect users based on the second select element.

⑩ Add an `onload` handler to call the `SetOptions()` function.

⑪ Save the file.

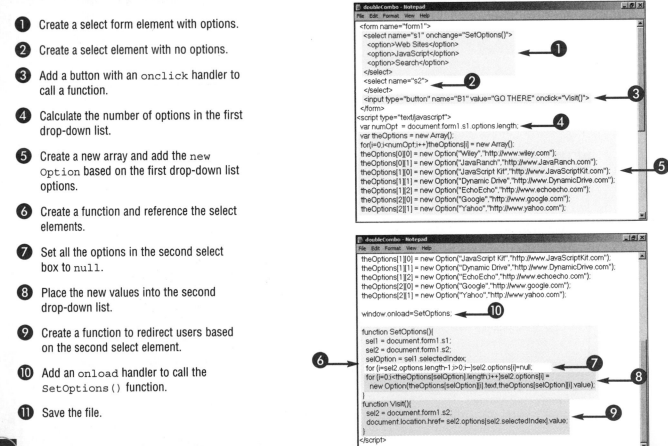

⑫ Open the file in a Web browser.

⑬ Click to select an option from the first drop-down list.

```
C:\VisualBlueprint\CHAPTER_16\doubleCombo.html - Microsoft Internet Explorer
File   Edit   View   Favorites   Tools   Help
Back       Search   Favorites   W
Address  C:\VisualBlueprint\CHAPTER_16\doubleCombo.html      Go

Web Sites    Wiley         GO THERE
Web Sites
JavaScript    ⑬
Search
```

● The second drop-down list contains values based on the first drop-down list.

```
C:\VisualBlueprint\CHAPTER_16\doubleCombo.html - Microsoft Internet Explorer
File   Edit   View   Favorites   Tools   Help
Back       Search   Favorites   W
Address  C:\VisualBlueprint\CHAPTER_16\doubleCombo.html      Go

Web Sites    Wiley         GO THERE
             Wiley
             JavaRanch
```

Extra

Instead of having the user leave your site, you can have the double combo box open into a new window. This allows your Web site to remain open while the user looks for more information on another site.

```
function Visit(){
   sel2 = document.form1.s2;
   newWin =
window.open(sel2.options[sel2.selected
Index].value,"newWin");
}
```

A double combo box does not have to be just for navigation; you can use it to allow users to select specific information for a form submission. The selected drop-down value is submitted with the form, but you can also place the value or text into another form element.

```
function PlaceText(){
   sel2 = document.form1.s2;
   text1 = document.form1.T1;
   text1.value =
sel2.options[sel2.selectedIndex].value;
}
```

Add New Table Rows

You can add rows to tables by using DOM methods. This allows you to build dynamic tables to display any information that you want. You can insert form fields, text, and other data into the cells of the row. The table rows and cells are formatted by adding CSS properties to the new elements. Additional attributes can also be added such as ID, width, and height.

The first thing you need to do is retrieve the table body reference. This allows you to add new rows to the table. The statement `var tRows = document.getElement ById("theBody");` stores the table body with the ID `theBody` into the variable `tRows`.

The first DOM method you need to apply to the table body is the `insertRow()` method, which accepts an integer parameter as a parameter. The parameter determines the position of the new row. The statement `tr = tRows .insertRow(tRows.rows.length);` adds a table row to the end of the table. The statement `tRows.rows.length` returns the number of rows that the table contains.

When the `insertRow()` method is executed, it returns the new table row element object. With this new object, you can use the `insertCell()` method. The `insertCell()` method also accepts an integer to determine the location of the new cell. The statement `td = tr.insertCell(tr.cells .length);` adds a new cell to the table row at the end of the current cells in the row.

You can also set attributes of a table row or cell by attaching the `setAttribute()` method to the object reference. The `setAttribute()` method accepts two parameters. The first is the name of the attribute and the second is the value of the attribute property. For example, the statement `td.setAttribute("align","center");` adds the attribute `align` to the table cell.

Add New Table Rows

① Create an HTML table.

② Add a header row to the table.

③ Add a `<tbody>` tag specifying an ID.

④ Add an event handler to a button that passes the ID of the `<tbody>` to the function `AddRow()`.

⑤ Create the function `AddRow()` with one parameter.

⑥ Create a reference to the passed table body element.

⑦ Create a new row with the `insertRow()` method.

⑧ Set any attributes for the table row with the `setAttribute()` method.

⑨ Create new cells with the `insertCell()` method and use the `setAttribute()` method and `innerHTML` property.

⑩ Save the file.

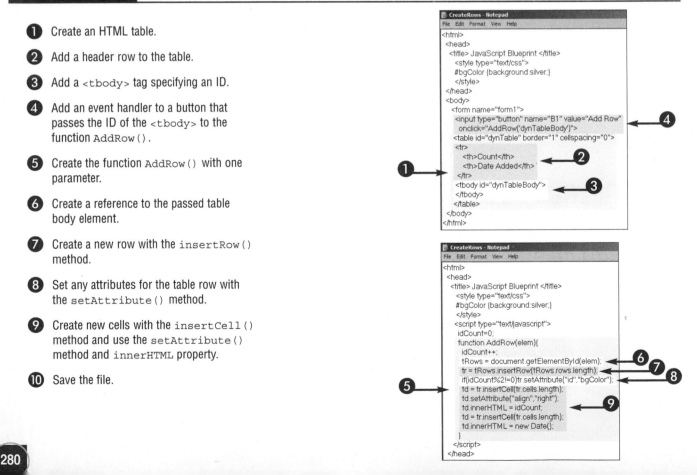

⑪ Open the file in a Web browser.

⑫ Click the Add Row button three times.

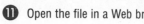

● Three new rows are added to the table.

Note: Each time you click the button, a new row is added to the table.

Apply It

You can use a two-dimensional array to hold the information from the table and dynamically build it. This allows you to build the table quickly and not have to hard code any of the values.

```
var tableArray = new
Array([1,"butter","$1.99"],[2,"cheese","$2.99"],[3,"pizza","$4.96"]);
function BuildTable(){
  tRows = document.getElementById("dynTableBody");
  for(i=0;i<tableArray.length;i++){
    tr = tRows.insertRow(tRows.rows.length);
    if(i%2!=0)tr.setAttribute("id","bgColor");
    for(j=0;j<tableArray[i].length;j++){
      td = tr.insertCell(tr.cells.length);
      td.innerHTML = tableArray[i][j];
    }
  }
}
```

Develop an Image Gallery

You can create an image gallery and eliminate the need to program hundreds of pages to display all your pictures. With an image gallery script, you can use one page to display an unlimited number of images. This script allows you to page through the images and set the amount of images that appear at one time. You can also display a description underneath the image.

First, develop a multidimensional array that contains the image name and the description. You can use bracket notation to save on the amount of space required to store the picture names.

Next, build the page to display the gallery. You can either hard code the image tags in the source code, or you can have JavaScript build the page. Using JavaScript can change the number of images that appear by changing a variable instead of adding or deleting hard coded HTML.

When you are building the code to display the images and text, you need to assign sequential IDs to the images and divs to make it easier to change the images.

You need two buttons to change the images. One button advances the page, the other enables you to move back to the previous page. By adding onclick event handlers to the button, you can pass a variable to inform a function to change the images.

The function contains a loop that steps through the image name and description array. By keeping track of the last image that appears on the page and looking at the button that was clicked, you can change the source of the image and the descriptive text.

Develop an Image Gallery

① Create a set of variables that set the default width and height of the images, plus the number of rows and columns you want to display.

② Create a 2D array with the picture source and the picture title.

③ Use the variables in step **1** to develop the gallery layout.

Note: Make sure to give the image and div sequential IDs.

④ Set the variable currentImg to negative one.

⑤ Create a function that accepts one parameter and sets the current image.

⑥ Create a for loop that changes the image's src, alt, and innerHTML.

⑦ Add an onload handler to initialize the script.

⑧ Add buttons to control the direction of the gallery.

⑨ Save the file.

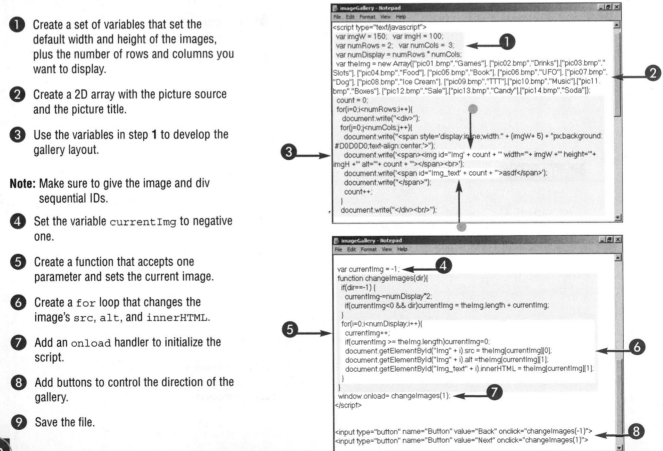

```
<script type="text/javascript">
 var imgW = 150;  var imgH = 100;
 var numRows = 2;  var numCols = 3;
 var numDisplay = numRows * numCols;
 var theImg = new Array(["pic01.bmp","Games"], ["pic02.bmp","Drinks"],["pic03.bmp","
Slots"], ["pic04.bmp","Food"], ["pic05.bmp","Book"], ["pic06.bmp","UFO"], ["pic07.bmp",
"Dog"], ["pic08.bmp","Ice Cream"], ["pic09.bmp","TTT"],["pic10.bmp","Music"],["pic11.
bmp","Boxes"], ["pic12.bmp","Sale"],["pic13.bmp","Candy"],["pic14.bmp","Soda"]);
 count = 0;
 for(i=0;i<numRows;i++){
   document.write("<div>");
 for(j=0;j<numCols;j++){
   document.write("<span style='display:inline;width:" + (imgW+ 5) + "px;background:
#D0D0D0;text-align:center;'>");
   document.write('<span><img id="Img' + count + '" width="'+ imgW +'" height="'+
imgH +'" alt="'+ count + '"></span><br>');
   document.write('<span id="Img_text' + count + '">asdf</span>');
   document.write("</span>");
   count++;
 }
   document.write("</div><br/>");
```

```
 var currentImg = -1;
 function changeImages(dir){
   if(dir==-1) {
     currentImg=numDisplay*2;
     if(currentImg<0 && dir)currentImg = theImg.length + currentImg;
   }
   for(i=0;i<numDisplay;i++){
     currentImg++;
     if(currentImg >= theImg.length)currentImg=0;
     document.getElementById("Img" + i).src = theImg[currentImg][0];
     document.getElementById("Img" + i).alt =theImg[currentImg][1];
     document.getElementById("Img_text" + i).innerHTML = theImg[currentImg][1];
   }
 }
 window.onload= changeImages(1);
</script>

<input type="button" name="Button" value="Back" onclick="changeImages(-1)">
<input type="button" name="Button" value="Next" onclick="changeImages(1)">
```

⑩ Open the file in a Web browser.

● The gallery is filled with the first set of images.

⑪ Press the Next button.

● The gallery changes to the next set of images.

Apply It

Instead of requiring the user to flip through the pages, you can have the script automatically do the flipping. Using a setInterval() method can automatically call the function to switch the images.

```
theTime=false;
theSpeed = 3000;
 function autoSwitch(theDir){
  if(theTime)window.clearInterval(theTime);
  if(theDir!=0)theTime = setInterval('changeImages('+theDir+')',theSpeed);
}
<input type="button" name="Button" value="Back" onclick="autoSwitch(-1)">
<input type="button" name="Button" value="Stop" onclick="autoSwitch(0)">
<input type="button" name="Button" value="Next" onclick="autoSwitch(1)">
```

Produce an Autoscrolling Window

You can use the `window.scrollBy()` method to make your Web page window scroll automatically. This enables information on the page to scroll, and the user does not have to scroll through it manually. Remember to adjust the speed so that the person can read it without any problem.

The `window.scrollBy()` method accepts two parameters: the x and y amount to have the page scrolled by. The x and y parameters are integers and represent the number of pixels to shift the page. A negative number moves up while a positive number moves down.

Use a `setInterval()` method to allow the window to continuously scroll to the bottom of the page. The statement `setInterval("window.scrollBy(0,1) ",100);` scrolls the window 1 pixel in the y-direction every 10 milliseconds.

You can also scroll the window to a specific spot by using the `window.scrollTo()` property. You can specify a location by identifying the x and y positions. For example, the statement `window.scrollTo(100,900);` moves the viewable part of the Web page.

A great use for the autoscrolling window is to display information in an `<iframe>` tag. You can show information in a dynamic manner without interfering with the rest of the page. You can also remove the scrollbars in the frame to make it look more interesting as it scrolls.

By adding the initializing controls to the main window, you have the ability to control how the data appears, instead of having to edit the iframe HTML page. The iframe page includes the function that scrolls the page.

Produce an Autoscrolling Window

① Add an `<iframe>` tag to the HTML page.

② Set the `name` attribute.

③ Set the `src` attribute to a Web page with lots of content.

④ Set the `style` attribute to give the iframe shape.

⑤ Create a `ScrollNews()` function that references the frame and calls a function called `ScrollPage(0,1)`.

⑥ Create a `PageStart()` function that creates an interval to call the `ScrollNews()` function.

⑦ Initialize the `PageStart()` function with an `onload` event handler.

⑧ Save the main page file.

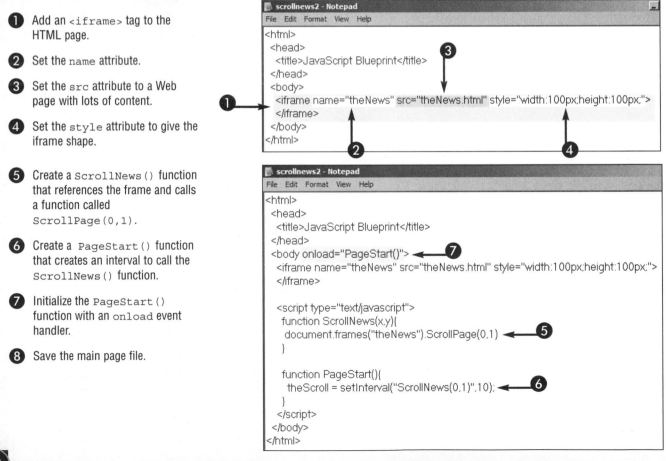

⑨ Open the Web page contained in the iframe in a text editor.

⑩ Create a function called ScrollPage() that accepts two parameters.

⑪ Add the window.scrollBy() method to the function using the passed parameters.

⑫ Save the iframe HTML page with the name referenced in step **2**.

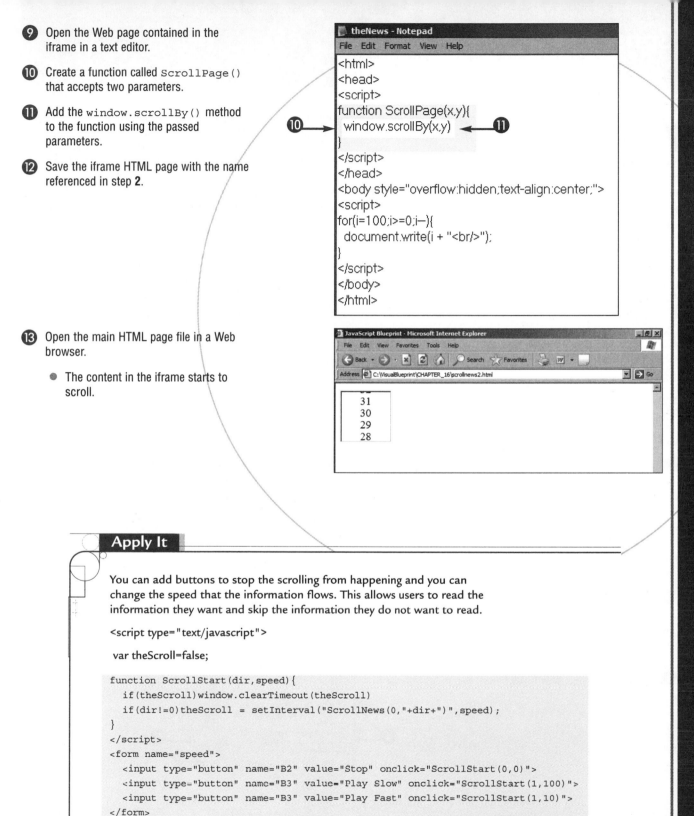

```
theNews - Notepad
File  Edit  Format  View  Help
<html>
<head>
<script>
function ScrollPage(x,y){
  window.scrollBy(x,y)
}
</script>
</head>
<body style="overflow:hidden;text-align:center;">
<script>
for(i=100;i>=0;i--){
  document.write(i + "<br/>");
}
</script>
</body>
</html>
```

⑩ →

⑪ ←

⑬ Open the main HTML page file in a Web browser.

● The content in the iframe starts to scroll.

```
JavaScript Blueprint - Microsoft Internet Explorer
File  Edit  View  Favorites  Tools  Help
Back ·       ·        Search    Favorites
Address  C:\VisualBlueprint\CHAPTER_16\scrollnews2.html        Go
    31
    30
    29
    28
```

Apply It

You can add buttons to stop the scrolling from happening and you can change the speed that the information flows. This allows users to read the information they want and skip the information they do not want to read.

```html
<script type="text/javascript">

 var theScroll=false;

function ScrollStart(dir,speed){
  if(theScroll)window.clearTimeout(theScroll)
  if(dir!=0)theScroll = setInterval("ScrollNews(0,"+dir+")",speed);
}
</script>
<form name="speed">
  <input type="button" name="B2" value="Stop" onclick="ScrollStart(0,0)">
  <input type="button" name="B3" value="Play Slow" onclick="ScrollStart(1,100)">
  <input type="button" name="B3" value="Play Fast" onclick="ScrollStart(1,10)">
</form>
```

Construct a Navigation Tree

You can create a navigational tree to allow users to navigate around your Web page. A navigation tree consists of a main link that can be drilled down to show a number of sublinks. The sublinks are hidden from view until the header link is clicked. The sublinks appear, pushing the content below the header downward.

The following script develops a two-level tree. The first level can either be a heading for the sublinks or just a link. The menu is created from a multidimensional array to make it easier to add the tree menu to other Web pages with a minimal amount of work. The first element of the multidimensional array is the header text. The next elements are the sublinks. The first item is the text for the link, and the second item is the link to a Web page or file.

For example, the statement `menuArray[2] = new Array(["Area 1"],["Link1_3","A.html"], ["Link2_3","B.html"]);` defines a multidimensional array that has a header text of `Area 1` and has two sublinks.

Next, set up a div element that sets the location of the menu on the screen. The `innerHTML` property of this div allows you to dynamically write the div to this spot with the information from the multidimensional arrays. This saves you time when developing each tier of the tree menu.

You can add an event handler that can detect the mouse click to open and close the sublinks. When the heading is clicked, it needs to check to see if it is just a link, or if it has subitems.

Construct a Navigation Tree

1. Create a series of CSS rules to apply to the tree.

2. Create default variables for how the menu initially will display.

3. Create a multidimensional array containing the header and sublinks.

4. Create a function `BuildMenu()` to build the menu and declare a blank string.

5. Create a `for` loop that loops through the menu array and develops the link.

6. Determine the link and image that will display.

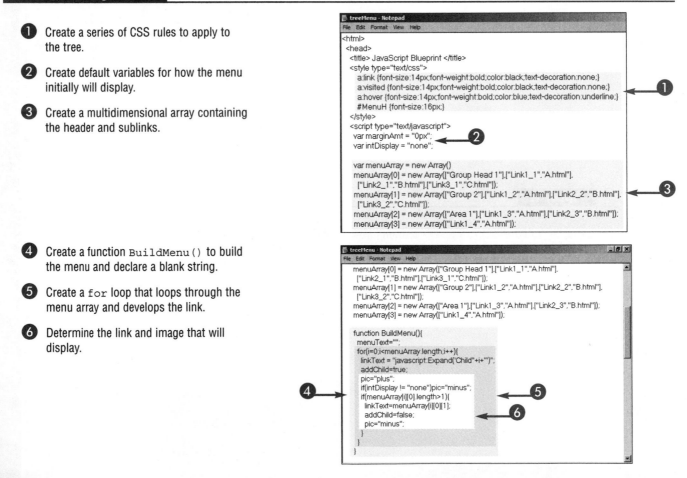

⑦ Develop the header link from the array along with the display image.

⑧ Create the Child Links if necessary from the array.

⑨ Set the `innerHTML` to display the menu.

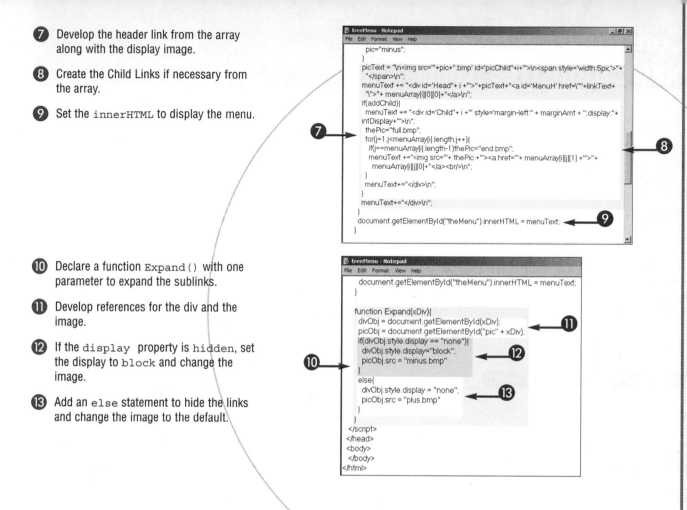

⑩ Declare a function `Expand()` with one parameter to expand the sublinks.

⑪ Develop references for the div and the image.

⑫ If the `display` property is `hidden`, set the display to `block` and change the image.

⑬ Add an `else` statement to hide the links and change the image to the default.

Extra

You can make certain that sublinks appear when the page loads by adding the Expand() function call after the BuildMenu() statement in the onload event handler. If you want to add more than one Expand() function call, you may want to build a separate initiation function to keep the code organized.

```
<body onload="BuildMenu();Expand
('Child0');">
```

The code executes after the menu is built, opening the first set of sublinks. Calling the Expand() function as the page is loading is equivalent to clicking the headers.

You can have all the links open by default by setting the variable declaration intDisplay equal to block instead of none. This eliminates the need to call the Expand() function for every header in the tree menu.

continued →

I f it is a link, then the link opens in the page. If it contains sublinks, then it determines if the sublinks need to be shown or hidden. You can do this by checking the display property state of the links.

If the display property is equal to none, the links are hidden. If the display property is block, the links are visible. When the menu is closed, setting the display property to none hides the sublinks. Using the display property is important because it does not leave a gap when information is hidden. If the visibility property is used, there are gaps where the data shows when it was hidden from the user's view.

To make it easier to know that a main heading has subheadings, you can add a picture beside the link. This

picture can also be changed when the submenus are visible. You can change the image that is displayed by adjusting the src attribute of the image. This image lets the user know if a menu is open, closed, or is a link. Common images are a plus (+) and minus (-) sign or an open and closed folder.

You can take advantage of the built-in CSS properties by using links as the Headers. CSS enables you to use the a:hover and a:link properties to change the look and feel of the links. By dynamically building the menu and using an external sheet, you can add this menu to any Web page without any problems. If you do not use links to do this, you have to add onmouseover and onmouseout event handlers to create the same effect.

Construct a Navigation Tree (continued)

⑭ Create an onload handler to call the function to build the menu.

⑮ Add the div where you want the menu to appear, assigning it the appropriate ID.

⑯ Save the file.

⑰ Open the file in a Web browser.

- All the sublinks appear in a collapsed format.

⑱ Click one of the headers.

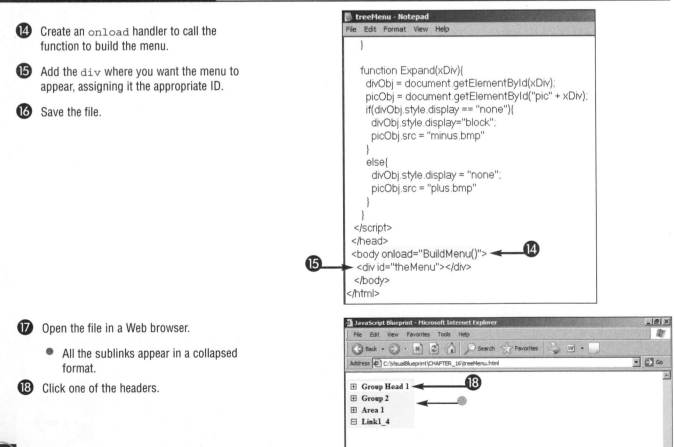

288

- The sublinks expand cascading the other headings downward.

⑲ Click the same header again.

- The sublinks are hidden and the menu collapses to its original state.

Extra

You can have all the tree headers show all their children links by developing a function that loops through the tree. The function needs to check to see if the menu contains any children and what the current status of the child is.

```
<script type="text/javascript">
function ExpandCollapseAll(xHow){
  for(i=0;i<menuArray.length;i++){
    if(menuArray[i][0].length==1){
      if(document.getElementById("Child"+i).style.display != xHow)
        Expand('Child'+i);
    }
  }
}
</script>
<input type="image" src="plus.bmp" name="expand" value="+" onclick=
"ExpandCollapseAll('block')">
<input type="image" src="minus.bmp" name="collapse" value="-" onclick=
"ExpandCollapseAll('none')">
```

Generate a Navigation Drop-Down Menu

You can create a navigation drop-down menu that uses layers. This script allows you to make any element turn into a drop-down menu. This enables you to create a menu anywhere on the page.

The first step is to create a function that grabs the X and Y positional coordinates of an object off the screen. Because the object is not required to be absolutely positioned, you need to find the coordinates for a nonpositioned element and not find the style properties.

The next step is to create a function that finds the position of the parent object by calling the positional script you just created. You then need to use this information to set the position of the submenu. The submenu is positioned away from the parent menu by adding an offset value, which allows for the header to show with the child window overlapping it.

You also need to set the display property to block so the menu is visible to the user. The function that shows the submenu needs a `setTimeout()` method to be initialized. The `setTimeout()` method is used to hide the menu if the user is inactive. If the user is inactive for the set period of time, the `setTimeout()` method initializes the function to hide the menu by setting the display to none.

If you did not include this timeout to catch the user inactivity, then the menu remains open and may be in the way of the user. You need to experiment to find out what time interval is needed in the `setTimeout()` method. You may prefer a longer or a shorter time limit depending on the preference of your Web site audience.

Generate a Navigation Drop-Down Menu

① Create two global variables to hold the element x and y coordinates.

② Create the get position of the non-positional elements script, `getObjectXY()`, using the `offsetLeft` and `offsetTop` properties.

```
menu2 - Notepad
File  Edit  Format  View  Help
<html>
 <head>
  <title> JavaScript Blueprint </title>
  <script type="text/javascript">
   var elemPosX = 0;          ①
   var elemPosY = 0;

   function getObjectXY(theElement){
    elemPosX = theElement.offsetLeft;
    elemPosY = theElement.offsetTop;
    theElement = theElement.offsetParent;
    while(theElement != null){
     elemPosX += theElement.offsetLeft;    ②
     elemPosY += theElement.offsetTop;
     theElement = theElement.offsetParent;
    }
   }

  </script>
 </head>
 <body>
```

③ Create a function `showSub()` determining the position of the header.

④ Set the position of the submenu according to the header.

⑤ Set the submenu's display to block.

⑥ Create a `setTimeout()` function to hide the submenu.

```
menu2 - Notepad
File  Edit  Format  View  Help
    elemPosY = theElement.offsetTop;
    theElement = theElement.offsetParent;
    while(theElement != null){
     elemPosX += theElement.offsetLeft;
     elemPosY += theElement.offsetTop;
     theElement = theElement.offsetParent;
    }
   }

   function showSub(xMenu,xSub){
    getObjectXY(xMenu);
    theDiv = document.getElementById(xSub).style;

    theDiv.left = elemPosX + 5;        ④
    theDiv.top = elemPosY + 20;

                                       ⑤
    theDiv.display="block";
    menuShow = setTimeout("hideSub('"+xSub+"')",2000);   ⑥
   }

  </script>
```

7. Create a function `hideSub()` that accepts one parameter and sets the `display` property to `none`.

8. Set a Boolean variable to `false`.

9. Develop a function `changeBG()` that changes the background properties.

10. Detect the status of the mouse, clearing the timeout if the mouse is over the menu.

11. If the mouse is leaving the menu, then create a `setTimeout()` method.

Apply It

You can alter the links to enable the menu to open them in the same browser window or in a pop-up window. This allows you to open pages that belong to other Web sites in other windows, enabling the users to navigate away from your page safely. In the `onclick` handler, you can add an additional parameter to specify how the link gets opened. Adding a Boolean is an easy way to handle this information.

```
<inout type="button" name="b1" value="search"
onclick="openLink('http://www.google.com',true)">
<script type="text/javascript">
  function openLink(xLink,xHow){
    if(xHow)newWin = window.open(xHow);
    else document.location.href=xLink;
  }
</script>
```

continued ➔

To make the menu more dynamic and appealing to the eye, add CSS to the sublinks. Adding onmouseover and onmouseout event handlers to the sublinks changes the background of the span tag so the item appears highlighted. This adds personality to your Web site and makes it easier to navigate.

Another thing you need to do when the mouse enters a sublink of the menu is cancel the setTimeout() method created by the function to hide the menu from an inactive user. You can cancel the setTimeout() method by using the clearTimeout() method.

When the user removes the mouse from the link, you need to reset the style properties back to their default state and reinitiate the setTimeout() method to hide the menu if the user becomes inactive. The setTimeout() calls the close

function when the mouse leaves the menu for a set period of time.

Because you are using functions to determine where the menu should appear on the Web page, the menu header can be placed anywhere on the screen. The header link does not have to be absolutely positioned. All you need to add is an onmouseover event handler that calls the function to show the menu.

The submenu on the other hand needs its position set to absolute. The z-index of the submenu needs to be set to the highest order on the Web page to ensure that the other elements on the page are located under it when visible. If any of the elements have a z-index higher than the submenu, then they appear on top of the submenu's links.

Generate a Navigation Drop-Down Menu (continued)

12 Create a function to open a link with two parameters.

13 If the Boolean parameter is true, open the link in a new window.

14 If the Boolean parameter is false, open the link in the same window.

15 Create the menu header with a mouseover to show the menu.

16 Create the submenu div setting the style attribute to absolute.

17 Create a link inside a <span> tag, adding the onmouseover, onmouseout, and onclick event handlers.

18 Repeat step 17 for the other links in the menu.

19 Save the file.

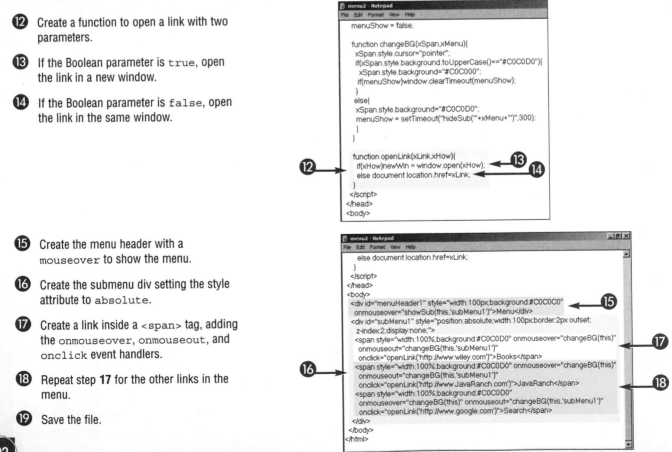

20 Open the file in a Web browser.

21 Position the cursor over the menu header.

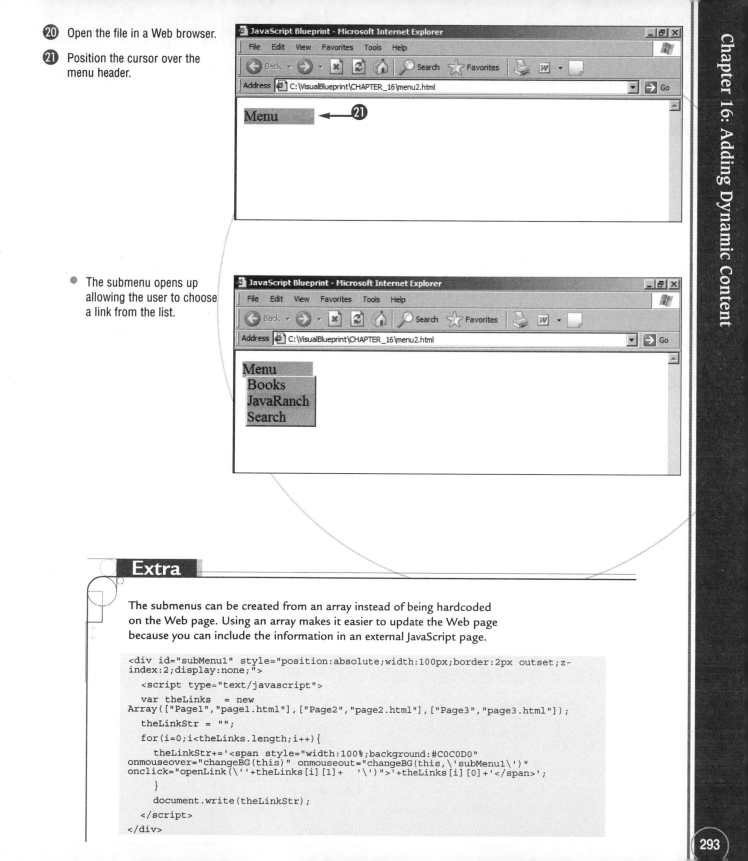

● The submenu opens up allowing the user to choose a link from the list.

Extra

The submenus can be created from an array instead of being hardcoded on the Web page. Using an array makes it easier to update the Web page because you can include the information in an external JavaScript page.

```
<div id="subMenu1" style="position:absolute;width:100px;border:2px outset;z-
index:2;display:none;">
  <script type="text/javascript">
  var theLinks  = new
Array(["Page1","page1.html"],["Page2","page2.html"],["Page3","page3.html"]);
  theLinkStr = "";
  for(i=0;i<theLinks.length;i++){
    theLinkStr+='<span style="width:100%;background:#C0C0D0"
onmouseover="changeBG(this)" onmouseout="changeBG(this,\'subMenu1\')"
onclick="openLink(\''+theLinks[i][1]+   '\')">'+theLinks[i][0]+'</span>';
    }
    document.write(theLinkStr);
  </script>
</div>
```

Insert Page Transition Effects

You can add page transition visual effects to a Web page for Microsoft Internet Explorer browsers. Microsoft Internet Explorer is the only browser that uses these effects so it does not work on Mozilla, Netscape, and the other browsers. The transition effects can be added to images, the page, or any other element. There are effects like barn doors, checkerboards, blinds, Iris, and so on. Transition effects add a unique feel to a Web site, especially for a slide show.

The IE4+ version of the transition effects is split into two families. The first set of effects is the blend family that uses the filter `blendTrans()` with one parameter, which is the duration in seconds. For example, the statement `img.blended {filter:blendTrans(duration=1.0)}` is a CSS rule applied to an image.

The second set of effects is the reveal family that uses the filter `revealTrans()`, which has two parameters. The first is the transition number and the second is the duration length. For example, the statement `img.blind {filter: revealTrans(transition=9;duration=1.0)}` applies a horizontal blind to the image. A list of filters is in the appendix.

If you want to control the filter type of an element on a page, assign the filter to the object. You can do this by adding it to the style tag. For example, the statement `style="Filter:revealTrans(duration=2);width:512 ;height:336;"` assigns a filter to an object when added to a tag. You need to use the filter object's `apply()` and `play()` methods when the filter is altered on the page. The statement `obj.filters[0].Play();` starts the transition.

You can dynamically change the transition of an element by specifying the transition number. For example, the statement `elem.filters.revealTrans.transition=1;` applies the `Box out` transition to the element stored in the `elem` object.

Insert Page Transition Effects

1. Develop a function that accepts two parameters.

2. Use the `Apply()` method on the element object.

3. Show or hide the image visibility depending on the current state applying filters.

4. Attach the `Play()` method to the element object to start the transition.

5. Give the element an ID to which the transition is applied.

6. Assign the element a `Filter`.

7. Add an event handler to initialize the function.

Note: Filter number 23 is a random filter.

8. Save the file.

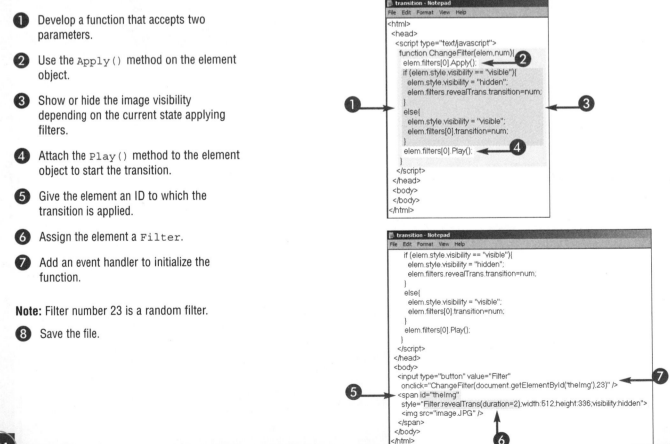

9 Open the file in a Web browser.

● The Web page appears blank.

10 Click the Filter button.

● The Image appears on the screen with a transitional filter.

Note: In this example, a random filter of a checkerboard displays.

Extra

You can add the effects when you enter or exit a page without using the `onload` and `onunload` event handlers. Instead, you can use `<meta>` tags to add the transition to the page. For entering the page, set the `<meta>` tag's `http-equiv` attribute to `Page-Enter`. The content needs to be set to the specified filter with its parameters.

```
<meta http-equiv="Page-
Enter" content="Reveal
Trans(Duration=2.0,
Transition=2)">
```

For exiting the page, set the `<meta>` tag's `http-equiv` attribute to `Page-Exit`. The content also needs to be set to the specified filter with its parameters.

```
<meta http-equiv="Page-
Exit" content="Reveal
Trans(Duration=1.0,
Transition=14)">
```

One thing you need to remember is to not set the transition duration time to a very large number because that makes the page load slower. Also, if you add a `Page-Enter` transition to every page, you do not need to add the `Page-Exit` transition.

Incorporate Sound with a Button

You can have sounds on a Web page, but it is difficult to have a cross browser solution. The code in this section is aimed at Microsoft Internet Explorer with Windows Media Player.

First, embed the sound file into the page by using an object tag. You can pick any version of Windows Media Player to play the sound. Most developers pick a very early version such as Media Player 6, which is the Microsoft ActiveMovie Control. The `classid` for this player is `CLSID:05589FA1-C356-11CE-BF01-00AA0055595A`.

You need to add an ID to the object tag so you can reference the sound. Set the width and height of the object to 1 pixel. Setting the `style` property `block` to `none` removes the object tag from the page. If you do not do this, the object tag takes up space on the Web page.

If you do not want the file to play when the page is loaded, set a parameter inside the object tag. The `name` attribute is set to `AutoStart` and the `value` attribute is set to `false` or `0`.

To play the movie from a JavaScript function, use the `run()` method. The statement

`document.getElementById("beep").run();` plays the sound clip that is stored in the object named `beep` when the statement executes.

You can also stop the sound clip from playing by using the `stop()` method. The statement

`document.getElementById("beep").stop();` causes the sound clip to stop playing when the statement executes.

You can have different sounds on the page by adding multiple object tags. Keep file sizes at a minimum so that pages load as quickly as possible.

Incorporate Sound with a Button

① Create a function to start playing a sound.

② Detect if the browser is Internet Explorer and add the `run()` method.

③ Create a function to stop a sound from playing.

④ Detect if the browser is Internet Explorer and add the `stop()` method.

⑤ Create the object that is for the Windows Media Player or another Application.

⑥ Set the parameters including `FileName`, `AutoStart`, `ShowDisplay`, and `ShowControls`.

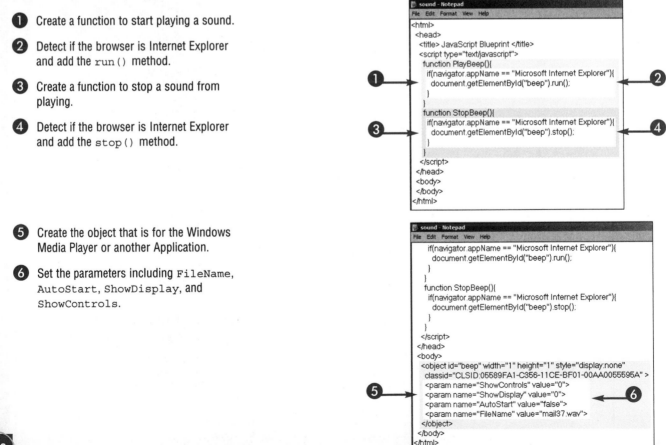

7 Add an `onmousedown` event to a button to play the sound file.

8 Add an `onmouseup` event to a button to stop the sound.

9 Save the file.

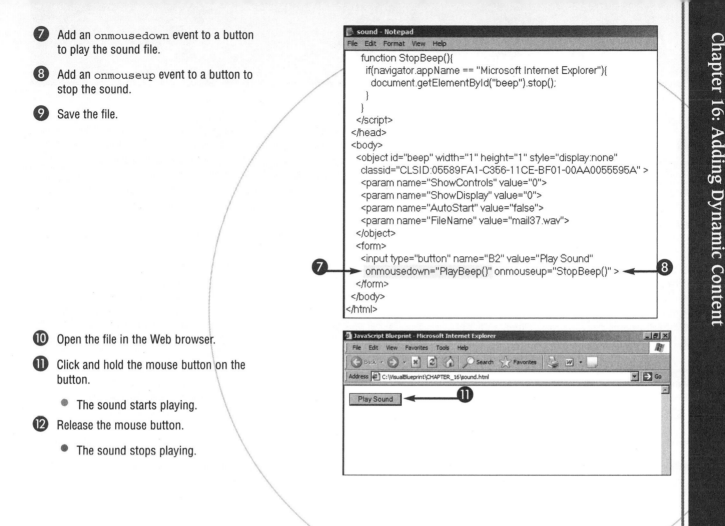

10 Open the file in the Web browser.

11 Click and hold the mouse button on the button.

● The sound starts playing.

12 Release the mouse button.

● The sound stops playing.

Apply It

You can add sounds to a link to resemble a flash-style link. This adds a new feature to the site. The important thing to do is keep the file size small so the site's performance is not impaired.

The first thing you need to do is to create a style sheet to make the links change appearance when the cursor is placed on top of the link. To do this, use the `a:link` and `a:hover` properties.

```
<style type="text/css">
   a:link {color:black; font-weight:bold; background:silver;}
   a:hover {color:blue; font-weight:bold; background:yellow;}
</style>
```

You then add `onmouseover` event handlers to the links. The event handler is used to call the function to play the sound. You can also add an `onmouseout` handler to play another sound when the mouse leaves the link or add an `onclick` handler to the link to play another sound.

```
<a href="movie.html" onmouseover="PlayBeep()" onmouseout="StopBeep()">The Movies</a>
<a href="music.html" onmouseover="PlayBeep()" onmouseout="StopBeep()">The Music</a>
<a href="books.html" onmouseover="PlayBeep()" onmouseout="StopBeep()">The Books</a>
```

Detect a JavaScript Error

You can encounter errors when you develop JavaScript applications, and finding what causes the errors may be difficult. The appearance of an error icon in the status bar when you load a page means there is a problem on the page, and the script will not run. Double-click the icon to view the error message. A dialog box appears where you can determine the error.

Errors are often caused by wrong syntax, misspelled keywords or variables, failure to define keywords, and so on. Syntax errors are the easiest to find because the error message normally shows you where the error is. Run time errors are more difficult to find because the error message shows the point at which the script stopped working properly, but it does not say what the exact error is.

Coding an application in small chunks and testing it in regular intervals can make it easier to find errors because

you have fewer lines to debug. Common errors to look for are a mismatch in brackets, quotation marks, and parentheses. It is very common to use a double quote instead of a single quote or to forget to add the matching quotation mark at the end.

A common error arises with `if` statements when the assignment operator (=) is used instead of the equality operator (==). An error message normally does not appear for this error, but you can spot it if you test your script correctly.

Other errors that occur are using properties or methods that do not exist in objects. For example, using `getDate()` on a string causes an error. Also, formatting a property or method name improperly may cause an error. For example, if you use `toString()` and do not capitalize the S, the script stops executing.

Detect a JavaScript Error

① In a Web page that has an error icon in the status bar, double-click the icon.

  ● The Error dialog box appears.

Note: You may have to click the show details button depending on your browser settings.

② Make a note of where the browser believes there is an error.

③ Make a note of whether the page on which the error occurred if you are using frames.

④ Check the check box to automatically open the error message.

⑤ Click OK.

  ● The error dialog box closes.

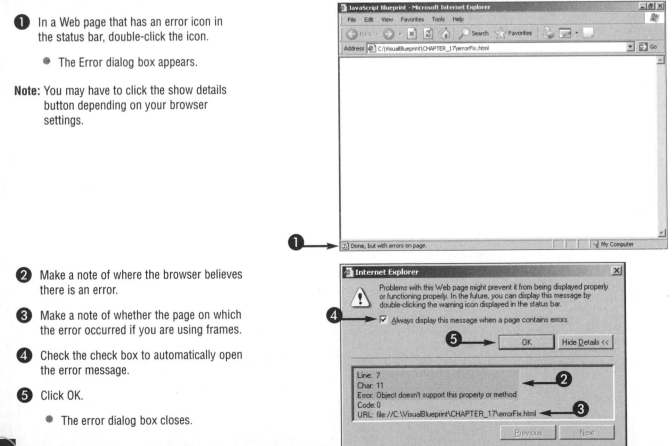

6 View the page source by clicking View➜Source

● The source code for the HTML page appears in the default text editor.

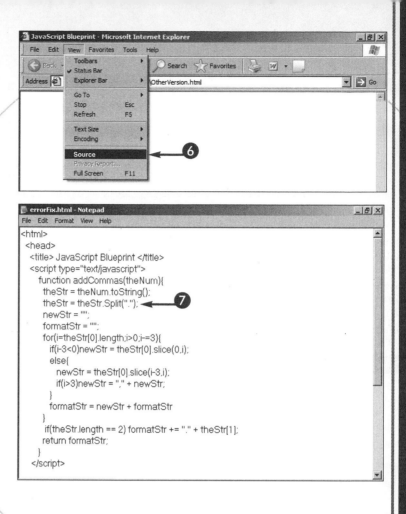

7 Locate the line on which the browser detected the error in step **2**.

Note: In this example, the error appears on line 7.

Note: The `split()` method has a capital S and changing it to lowercase solves the error.

Extra

You can use the error message, to guide you to the error by looking at the line number supplied in the dialog box. Certain errors do not show up on the line stated, causing you to have to search for it. The line number displayed in that case is the last line the browser was able to process correctly. This is typically the case when an event handler is called. If you investigate the function that it calls, you should find the error.

The error description in the dialog box gives you a good starting point to locate the area. The error message informs you when the string is not formatted properly or if a variable is not defined. A common message, `Object does not support method or property`, informs you that there is a problem with the method or property attached to a variable. A common fix for this error is to check the spelling of the property or method.

Debug through the Alert Dialog Box

You can spend hours trying to debug JavaScript code if you do not use a technique to find out what is causing the error. Two common methods developers use are commenting out code and using an alert dialog box. These methods enable you to find errors more quickly than simple trial and error. Over time, you may learn to spot errors without aids, but most developers have to use some sort of method from time to time.

By using comments, you can find the line of code that is causing the error. A common technique is to comment out every line of code in the script and uncomment them in small groups or one at a time until you find the error. You can comment the code by placing two slash marks (//) in front of the line. You can comment out multiple lines at once by using /* and */ marks. Both methods are used to debug the code.

You can also use alert statements throughout the page to debug the code. Alert statements show values of variables, property values, and notifications. You can use the alert dialog box to pinpoint where the script is executing and where it is not. By placing alerts inside loops, if statements, and functions, you can map out how the script is executing. When the alert dialog box appears, you can figure out what is executing properly.

If you are using multiple alert boxes in a script for debugging, it is important to give each alert method a good description. For example, the statement alert(" Inside if(A==B) statement "); gives you a better understanding of what is happening than alert(1);.

Debug through the Alert Dialog Box

Note: In this example, an error in the code has resulted in the Internet Explorer browser not being recognized. The browser says it is not Internet Explorer when the browser is.

 Open a page that has an error, but no error message is displayed.

② Click View→Source to view the source code.

● The source code opens in the default text editor.

③ Locate the areas that may be causing the problem.

Note: Problem areas normally include if statements, for loops, conditionals, and variable declarations.

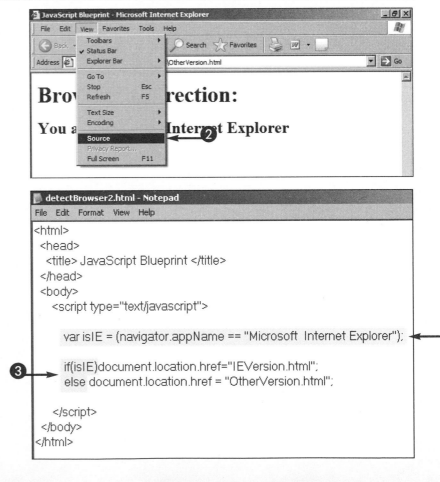

④ Add an alert dialog message to test the comparison expression.

⑤ Add scripting to test the first part of the expression.

⑥ Add scripting to test the second part of the expression.

⑦ Display the result of the expression.

⑧ Save the file.

Note: It is important that you copy and paste information and not retype it to spot spelling errors.

⑨ Reopen the file in a Web browser.

● The page loads with the alert message showing the problem.

Note: The problem with this script is there is an extra space in the comparison string; therefore, the values cannot be equal.

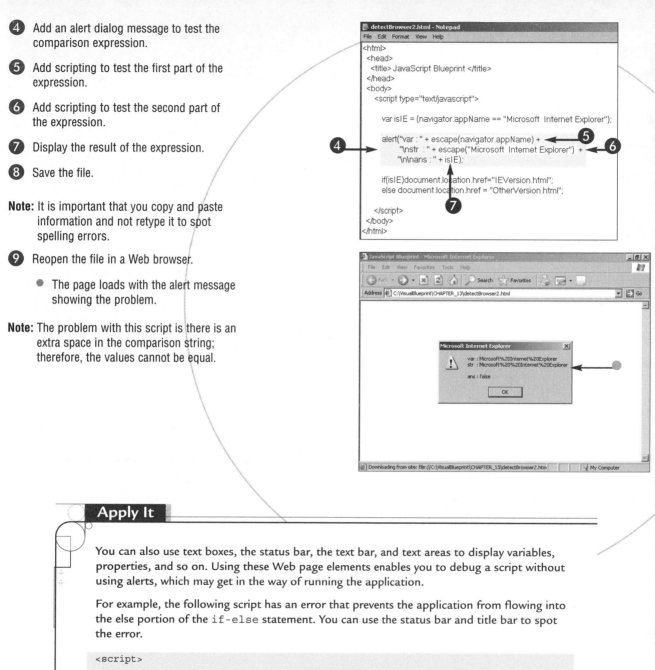

Apply It

You can also use text boxes, the status bar, the text bar, and text areas to display variables, properties, and so on. Using these Web page elements enables you to debug a script without using alerts, which may get in the way of running the application.

For example, the following script has an error that prevents the application from flowing into the else portion of the `if-else` statement. You can use the status bar and title bar to spot the error.

```
<script>
  var nCost = "1";
  document.title = "nCost: " + typeof nCost;
  window.status = (nCost + 10) + " > 20 = " + (nCost + 10 > 20);
  if(nCost + 10 > 20) theShipCost = nCost * 0.35;
  else theShipCost = nCost * 0.55;
  alert(theShipCost);
</script>
```

Checking the values in the title bar shows that the problem is that the value is a string and not an integer. The status bar shows that the addition process cannot run properly and that it is returning true.

Solve Problem with Page Onload Handlers

Y ou can face problems with the scripts running as the page loads and also with the `onload` page event handler. These problems occur as the page loads and do not allow any of the other scripts on the page to execute.

A common error occurs when the page starts loading and the script tries to access an element on the page, but the element has not yet been rendered. The script cannot access the element and normally has an error saying the object is not defined.

To correct this error, add the script after the Web page element that you are trying to access, or add the script to a function and call it with an `onload` handler from the Web page. This guarantees that the Web page has fully loaded and there are no errors accessing any part of the Web page.

Another common error is using multiple `window.open` declaration statements in one page. You can only use one

per Web page. That also includes the `onload` event handler in the `<body>` tag.

To correct this problem, you can use one statement that calls a loading function. Create a function that contains all the initiating statements. This allows all the functions to be called `onload` without this common error.

You can have only one event of the same type of event handler per element. You can have multiple event handlers. For example, it is safe to have an `onclick` and an `onmouseover` event handler in one element, but you cannot have two `onclick` handlers. Instead of including it twice, you can add both methods to the same `onclick` handler by separating them with a semicolon (`;`). For example, the statement `onclick="function1();function2()"` calls two separate functions.

Solve Problem with Page Onload Handlers

① Open a page that has an onload error.

● A common indication of an error appearing at Line 1, Character 1 is a page loading error.

② Open the source code of the page to find the error.

Note: To view the source code of the page, click View➜Source.

③ Locate the `onload` handlers that are conflicting with each other.

④ Create a new function.

⑤ Add the two loading expressions into the new function.

⑥ Create a single `onload` handler to call the new function created in step **5**.

⑦ Save the file.

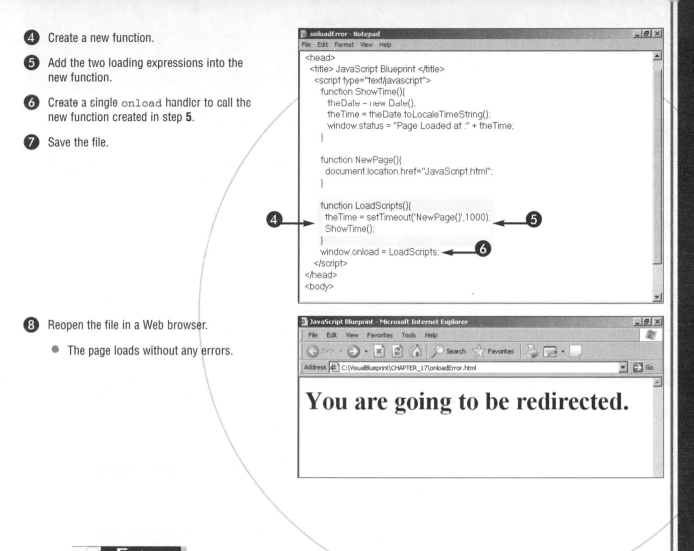

```
onloadError - Notepad
File Edit Format View Help

<head>
  <title> JavaScript Blueprint </title>
  <script type="text/javascript">
    function ShowTime(){
      theDate = new Date();
      theTime = theDate.toLocaleTimeString();
      window.status = "Page Loaded at :" + theTime;
    }

    function NewPage(){
      document.location.href="JavaScript.html";
    }

    function LoadScripts(){
      theTime = setTimeout('NewPage()',1000);
      ShowTime();
    }
    window.onload = LoadScripts;
  </script>
</head>
<body>
```

⑧ Reopen the file in a Web browser.

● The page loads without any errors.

```
JavaScript Blueprint - Microsoft Internet Explorer
File  Edit  View  Favorites  Tools  Help
Back  ·  ·  Search  Favorites
Address  C:\VisualBlueprint\CHAPTER_17\onloadError.html    Go
```

You are going to be redirected.

Extra

You may find that items to which you have linked on the page are not appearing. Check is to make sure that the image, JavaScript file, or Web page exists in the folder that you are trying to use to access the page. It is common to forget a file when uploading it to the server. Also make sure that the link to the file is correct and that the `src` attribute is spelled correctly. It is not uncommon to see `scr` mistyped as `src`.

Another problem that you may face on a Web site is a button or form element that fails to appear properly. If a form element does not appear properly on the page, it appears as a text box. The usual cause of the element appearing as the default text box is misspelling of element types or missing a quote.

Common Errors
```
<input name="big" type="button
value="Big">
<input name="R1" type="radoi"
value="r1">
```

Notice that the first statement is missing a quote after the type attribute and that the second statement has a misspelling in the type attribute.

Locate Common Errors

When you start coding or investigating another person's code, there are a few things that you should look for. Looking for and finding these common errors can save time in the debugging process.

If a problem appears to be located in a mathematical expression, make sure that all the brackets are there and in the correct locations. Second, make sure that all the variables are numbers and not strings. Also make sure that all the variables are defined and have values. If there is a math object property in the equation, make sure that the letter M is capitalized.

If a problem occurs in a string, the first things to check are the quotes. Make sure that there is a quote at the beginning and the end of the string. If there are extra quotes inside, make sure that they are escaped.

If you are performing a method or using a property that requires a string and is causing an error, verify that the variable that you are using is a string. The methods and properties developed for strings do not execute if it is an integer.

If a notification message appears saying that the object cannot be found, make sure that the object was referenced properly. Make sure that the document is using `document.getElementById` and not `document.all`. Make sure that the script is using the document object when referencing form elements. Also, check to see that the names of the objects are spelled correctly.

Problems with methods or properties are usually caused by misspellings. Make sure that if a character is supposed to be capitalized that it is. For example, the method `toString()` needs an uppercase S to execute.

Locate Common Errors

① Open a page that has a string-based error.

- A common indication of a string-based error is the error message `Unterminated string constant`.

② Open the source code of the page to find the error.

Note: To view the source code of the page, click View→Source.

③ Locate the string-based error.

- A double quote begins the string.

- A single quote ends the string resulting in an error.

Note: Changing the single quotation to a double quotation corrects the error.

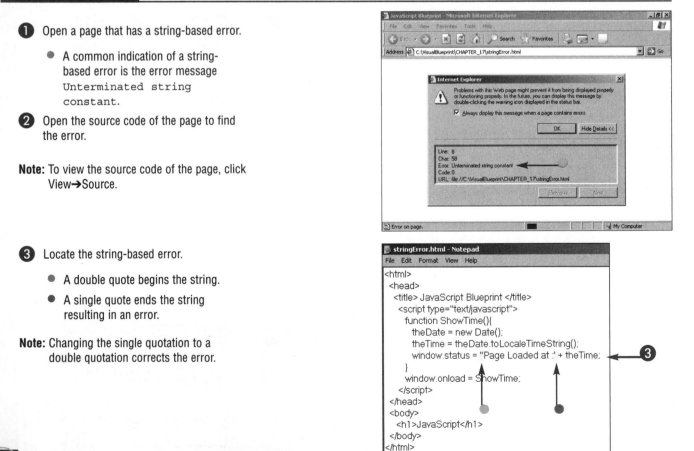

Avoid Errors with Try/Catch Statements

Y ou can detect if an error occurs when the JavaScript is executing by using the onerror() event handler or by using try/catch statements. The onerror() event handler fires when the page detects an error and is compatible with most older browsers unlike the try/catch statements that work only with browsers that support version 1.5.

Attach the event handler to the window object or place it in the <body> tag. The onerror() handler does not reveal to you or the user where the error occurs. You should only use this after the page has been fully debugged. The onerror() event does not stop compile-time errors from happening. If an error occurs while the page is loading, the error notification message appears.

In JavaScript version 1.5, try/catch statements were introduced. You can use the try/catch statements to

see if a certain statement or group of statements throws an error. The statements that are to be executed that may produce an error are placed in the try section. The catch section executes statements when an exception occurs in the try section. In the catch section, you can notify the user of an error, use an alternative method in the try section, end the script gracefully, and so on.

You are not required to have any statements in the catch statement in order for the try statement to work properly. If you do not include any statements in the catch section, you are just making sure that if any of the statements in the try section fail, they do not cause a fatal error. This is only true if the rest of the script does not depend on what is in the try section to perform other operations.

Avoid Errors with Try/Catch Statements

① Add a try statement to test a statement.

② Add one or more statements inside the try statement.

③ Add a catch statement, making sure to include the letter e inside the parentheses.

④ Add the statements inside the catch statement that you want to run if the try statement fails.

⑤ Save the file.

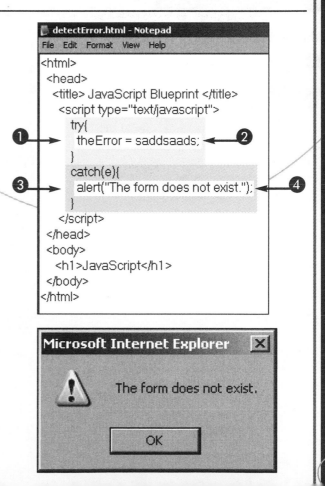

⑥ Open the file in a Web browser.

● The catch statement executes and runs the code to show an alert dialog box.

Test JavaScript
Code for Errors

One of the most important things that you can do is to test your JavaScript code. This is very important to make sure that there are no bugs that can cause errors when a visitor comes to the site. Depending on the size of the application you developed, testing can take minutes or hours.

The first step you should do is to note all the possible outcomes the script can produce. Check the script to see if any of the possible outcomes are missed. Sometimes you may overlook a big part of the code.

You should test nested `if` statements and `switch` statements with every possible combination. If the code has a lot of steps to get there, hard code a value in front of the statement to force each part of the conditionals to be checked. You may find out you missed an equal sign in one of the conditionals, or you used a greater than sign instead of a less than sign. These little mistakes can cause the program to execute wrong.

If you are using form validation, test every form element with multiple tests. If it is a text field, enter in random key combinations and special characters. Enter in negative numbers, click random buttons, click buttons multiple times, leave items blank, and so on to ensure that there are no bugs in the code.

The best tool is to ask a friend or family member to check your code. Because you coded the page you know what is supposed to happen. Other people tend to randomly do things without really knowing what is supposed to take place. These people can find errors that you missed. Using other people to check your work is great for catching spelling and grammar mistakes too.

Test JavaScript Code for Errors

TEST IF STATEMENTS

1 Open the source code of a Web page to test.

2 Add a value in front of the `if-else` statements to test the conditionals.

Note: You may have to add extra variables depending on the number of variables used in the conditionals.

```
    ifTest - Notepad
File  Edit  Format  View  Help
    <h1>Games Store</h1>
    <h2>The store is
    <script type="text/javascript">
      var theDate = new Date();
      var timeHour = theDate.getHours();

      timeHour = 4;        ←  2

      if(timeHour >= 11 && timeHour <=12){
          document.write("<span style='color:red'>AT LUNCH!</span>");
      }
      else if(timeHour >= 9 && timeHour <=16){
          document.write("<span style='color:green'>OPEN!</span>");
      }
      else{
          document.write("<span style='color:red'>CLOSED!</span>");
      }
    </script>
    </h2>
  </body>
</html>
```

3 Open the file in a Web browser.

● The `if` statement was tested producing the correct result.

Note: You need to test each conditional statement by changing the variable to test the code completely.

JavaScript Blueprint - Microsoft Internet Explorer
File Edit View Favorites Tools Help
Address C:\VisualBlueprint\CHAPTER_17\ifTest.html

Games Store

The store is CLOSED! ←

TEST FORM VALIDATIONS

1 Open the source code of a Web page to test.

2 Add a `document.write()` statement to verify the `for` loop is executing correctly.

Note: You may have to add extra `document.write()` statements if you are using nested loops.

3 Open the file in a Web browser.

● The `for` loop was tested verifying the correct result.

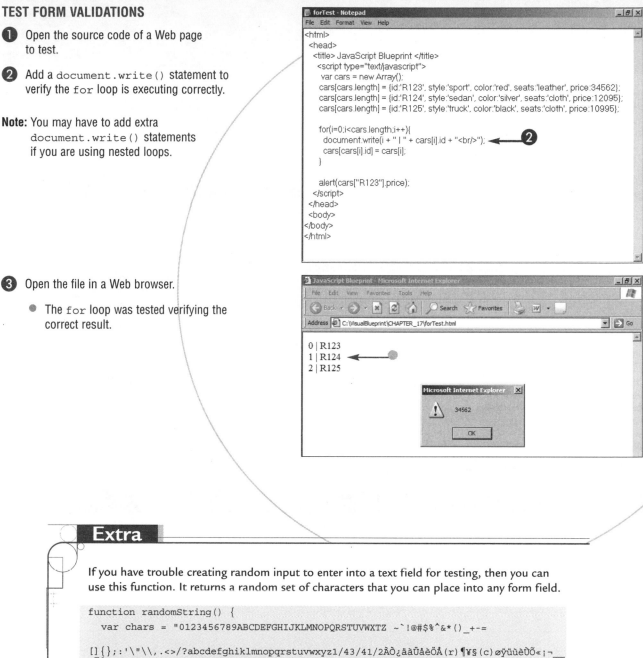

```
forTest - Notepad
File Edit Format View Help

<html>
 <head>
  <title> JavaScript Blueprint </title>
   <script type="text/javascript">
    var cars = new Array();
    cars[cars.length] = {id:'R123', style:'sport', color:'red', seats:'leather', price:34562};
    cars[cars.length] = {id:'R124', style:'sedan', color:'silver', seats:'cloth', price:12095};
    cars[cars.length] = {id:'R125', style:'truck', color:'black', seats:'cloth', price:10995};

    for(i=0;i<cars.length;i++){
     document.write(i + " | " + cars[i].id + "<br/>");          ◀──── 2
     cars[cars[i].id] = cars[i];
    }

    alert(cars["R123"].price);
   </script>
 </head>
 <body>
 </body>
</html>
```

```
JavaScript Blueprint - Microsoft Internet Explorer
File Edit View Favorites Tools Help
Address C:\VisualBlueprint\CHAPTER_17\forTest.html

0 | R123
1 | R124   ◀────
2 | R125

Microsoft Internet Explorer
⚠  34562
        OK
```

Extra

If you have trouble creating random input to enter into a text field for testing, then you can use this function. It returns a random set of characters that you can place into any form field.

```
function randomString() {
  var chars = "0123456789ABCDEFGHIJKLMNOPQRSTUVWXTZ ~`!@#$%^&*()_+-=

[]{};:'\"\\,.<>/?abcdefghiklmnopqrstuvwxyz1/43/41/2ÀÒ¿äàÜåèÖÅ(r)¶¥§(c)øÿüùèÙÕ«¡¬__
±¯°
  €_ö";
  var numChars = Math.floor(Math.random() * 15);
  var string_length = 8;
  var randomStr = "";
  for(i=0;i<numChars;i++){
    ranNum = Math.floor(Math.random() * chars.length);
    randomStr += chars.charAt(ranNum);
  }
  return randomStr;
}
```

Appendix

Transitional Effects

You can add transitional effects to a document and its elements to add dynamic effects. The following is a list of the Filters that Microsoft Internet Explorer supports.

NUMBER	FILTER	NUMBER	FILTER	NUMBER	FILTER
0	Box In	8	Vertical Blinds	16	Split Horizontal Out
1	Box Out	9	Horizontal Blinds	17	Strips Left Down
2	Circle In	10	Checkerboard Across	18	Strips Left Up
3	Circle Out	11	Checkerboard Down	19	Strips Right Down
4	Wipe Up	12	Random Dissolve	20	Strips Right Up
5	Wipe Down	13	Split Vertical In	21	Random Bars Horizontal
6	Wipe Right	14	Split Vertical Out	22	Random Bars Vertical
7	Wipe Left	15	Split Horizontal In	23	Random

Multifunctional Keyboard Keys

Each key on the keyboard has a unique keycode value, which is an integer. The integer value allows you to determine which key was pressed on the keyboard when monitoring key presses. The following is the list of the special keys and their key codes.

KEY	VALUE	KEY	VALUE	KEY	VALUE
Alt	18	Esc	27	;	186
Arrow Down	40	Home	36	=	187
Arrow Left	37	Insert	45	,	188
Arrow Right	39	Page Down	34	-	189
Arrow Up	38	Page Up	33	.	190
Backspace	8	Pause	19	/	191
Caps Lock	20	Print Scrn	44	'	192
Ctrl	17	Scroll Lock	145	[	219
Delete	46	Shift	16	/	220
End	35	Spacebar	32	]	221
Enter	13	Tab	9	`	222

Function Keys

The following is a list of the Function keys and their keycode values.

KEY	VALUE	KEY	VALUE	KEY	VALUE	KEY	VALUE
F1	112	F4	115	F7	118	F10	121
F2	113	F5	116	F8	119	F11	122
F3	114	F6	117	F9	120	F12	123

Numeric KeyPad Keys

The following is a list of the numeric keypad keys and their keycode values.

KEY	VALUE	KEY	VALUE	KEY	VALUE
0 (Number Pad)	96	6 (Number Pad)	102	- (Substract)	109
1 (Number Pad)	97	7 (Number Pad)	103	. (Decimal)	110
2 (Number Pad)	98	8 (Number Pad)	104	/ (Divide)	111
3 (Number Pad)	99	9 (Number Pad)	105	Num Lock	144
4 (Number Pad)	100	* (Multiply)	106		
5 (Number Pad)	101	+ (Add)	107		

Alphanumeric Keyboard Keys

The following is the list of alphanumeric keys and their keycodes.

LETTER OR NUMBER	VALUE	LETTER OR NUMBER	VALUE	LETTER OR NUMBER	VALUE	LETTER OR NUMBER	VALUE
A	65	J	74	S	83	1	49
B	66	K	75	T	84	2	50
C	67	L	76	U	85	3	51
D	68	M	77	V	86	4	52
E	69	N	78	W	87	5	53
F	70	O	79	X	88	6	54
G	71	P	80	Y	89	7	55
H	72	Q	81	Z	90	8	56
I	73	R	82	0	48	9	57

Appendix

Keywords are words that JavaScript reserves for specific use within the language. You cannot use keywords to name variables, functions, or labels. The following is a list of JavaScript keywords.

RESERVED KEYWORDS			
abstract	double	instanceof	switch
boolean	else	int	synchronized
break	enum	interface	this
byte	export	long	throw
case	extends	native	throws
catch	final	new	transient
char	finally	package	try
class	float	private	typeof
const	for	protected	var
continue	function	public	void
degugger	goto	return	volatile
default	if	short	while
delete	implements	static	with
do	import in	super	

Regular Expression Chart

Regular Expressions are made of many tokens that can build complex expressions. The following is a list of the common tokens explaining what they match when used in an expression statement.

TOKEN	MATCHES	TOKEN	MATCHES	TOKEN	MATCHES
\b	word boundary	\w	letter, numeral, or underscore	?	appear zero or one time
\B	non-word boundary	\W	not a letter, numeral, or underscore	+	appear one or more times
\d	numeral	\0	null	{x}	appear exactly x times
\D	non-numeral	.	any character except new line	{x,}	appear x or more times
\n	new line	[...]	any character in the brackets	{x,y}	appear at between x and y times
\r	carriage return	[a-e]	any character in the range	^	beginning of a line or string
\s	whitespace	[^...]	any character not in the brackets	$	end of a line or string
\S	non-whitespace	(abc)	match the string in the parentheses	\	denotes a special token or indicates an escaped character
\t	tab	*	appear zero or more times	|	or

| | (or) logical operator, 46
/ (slashes) in comments, 12
& (ampersand), string variables and, 23
&& (and) logical operator, 46
\ (backslash), string variables and, 23
: (colon) conditional operator, 80
$ (dollar sign), string variables and, 23
== (equals) comparison operator, 44
> (greater than) comparison operator, 44
>= (greater than or equal to) comparison operator, 44
< (less than) comparison operator, 44
<= (less than or equal to) comparison operator, 44
!= (not equal) comparison operator, 44
! (not) logical operator, 46
| (pipe), string variables and, 23
? (question mark), query strings and, 226
? (question mark) conditional operator, 80
_ (underscore), string variables and, 23

A

absolute values, positive value return, 153
acos function, 154–155
ActiveX, JavaScript disabled and, 11
addition (+) arithmetic operator, 40
address bar, 4–5, 195
alarm clock, countdown timer and, 149
alert dialog boxes
  create, 51
  custom, 272–275
  debug through, 300–301
alphanumeric keyboard keys, 309
altkey property, 64
ampersand (&), string variables and, 23
and (&&) logical operator, 46
animation, 264–265
arithmetic operators, 17, 40–41
arrays
  conversion to strings, 34–35
  declare, 28–29
  element addition, 39
  element removal, 38
  elements, number of, 32–33
  elements, reverse order, 33
  join( ) method, 34–35
  length property, 32
  multidimensional, declaration, 30–31

numeric variables, 29
pop( ) method, 38
push( ) method, 39
shift( ) method, 38
sort, 36–37
splice( ) method, 39
split( ) method, 38
split from string, 35
string variables, 28
two-dimensional, 30
unshift( ) method, 39
asin function, 154–155
atan function, 154–155
attributes
  <frame> tag, 182–183
  properties and, 196
  <script> tag, 6–7
  style, 236
autoscrolling windows, 284–285

B

Back button, disable, 211
background, images, 241
backslash (\), string variables, 23
blur( ) method, 66–67
<body> tag, <script> tag and, 6
bookmarklets
  Favorites folder, 5
  hidden elements and, 119
  source code security and, 14–15
Boolean variables
  display Boolean values, 22
  as flags, 17, 22
  introduction, 16–17
  typeof keyword, 24
borders, properties, 237
brand name, browser, 212–213
bread crumb navigation menu, 208–209
break in/out of frames, 188–189
break keyword, for loops and, 83
browsers
  Back button, disable, 211
  brand name detection, 212–213
  cross-browser layer modal window, 270–271
  cross browser scripting, 3
  dimensions, 262

events, cancel, 77
history object, 210
JavaScript support, 3
Mozilla, cross browser scripting, 3
native language, 216
non-JavaScript-enabled, 10–11
toolbars, remove, 15
window, maximize, 174–175
button elements, forms, 120
<button> tag, 120
buttons
Back, disable, 211
mouse, determine pressed, 76
radio, determining selected, 126–127
reset, 122–123
right-click, disable for security, 14–15
rollover, 60–61
sound and, 296–297
submit, 122–123

C

call functions, function keyword, 90
caller frame page, 184
cancelBubble event, 77
case sensitivity
strings, 100–101
variable names, 16
charAt( ) method, 102–103
check boxes, properties, 124–125
clearTimeout( ) method, 86–87
clicks, onclick event, 58–59
clock, 89, 150–151
close windows, 170–171
code tests for errors, 306–307
color
personalized Web pages, 7
Web pages, 20
commas, numbers and, 162–163
comments, 12–13
common errors, 304
comparison expressions, 44–45
comparison operator, 44–45
compliance detection, 234
conditional operators, 80
conditional statements, if-else, 22
confirm( ) method, 54–55

confirm dialog boxes, 54–55, 272–275
contant values, 16
continue keyword, for loops and, 83
controls. See user controls, forms
cookies, 220–225
cos function, 154–155
countdown timer, 148–149
counters, integer variables and, 17
createTextNode( ) method, 255
cross browser scripting, browsers and, 3
CSS (Cascading Style Sheets)
border properties, 237
change style sheets after page load, 248–249
elements, attach, 230
global style sheets, 230
introduction, 2
link style sheets to Web page, 230–231
link styles, 238–239
rollover buttons and, 60
rule properties override, 236
rules, 232–233, 235
style sheets off/on, 250–251
transparency and, 246–247
ctrlkey property, 64
cursor, focus( ) method, 66–67
custom methods, 200–201
custom object creation, 198–199

D

date, 138–143, 146
Date( ) object, 89, 138–139
dates, convert to strings, 144–145
debug
alert dialog boxes and, 300–301
comments and, 12
typeof keyword and, 25
decimal places
floating-point variables, 17
round numbers and, 161
decrement values, expressions and, 42–43
DHTML (Dynamic HTML), 2
dialog boxes
alert, 51, 272–275, 300–301
confirm, 54–55, 272–275
Error, 298–299
prompt, 52–53

INDEX

disabled JavaScript, browsers, 10–11
<div> element, 243–244
division (/) arithmetic operator, 40
do-while loops, 85
document object, write content to window, 164–165
dollar sign ($), string variables and, 23
DOM (Document Object Method), 2, 196–197
double combo selection lists, 278–279
drop-down navigation menu, 290–293

E

effects
  filters, 308
  page transitions, 294–295
elements, arrays, 32–33, 38
elements, event receipt, 74–75
elements, forms, 113, 118–119, 131
elements, HTML, 252–261, 264–269
elements, Web page, 242–243
embed, in HTML documents, 6–7
encodeURI( ) method, 105
encodeURIComponent( ) method, 105
Enter key, text field focus and, 136–137
enter key invoked form submission, blocking, 134–135
equal sign (=), variable value assignment, 19
error detection
  code tests, 306–307
  common errors, 304
  overview, 298–299
  try/catch statements, 305
Error dialog box, 298–299
escape, text strings, 104
escape( ) method, 104
eval( ) method, 50
event handlers
  events and, 56
  onclick, 6
  onkeypress, 62–63
  onload, 6
  onmouseoff, 6
  onmouseover, 6, 60
  onsubmit, 130–131
events
  attach to objects, 73
  browser events, cancel, 77
  cancelBubble, 77

element receiving, 74–75
event handlers and, 56
keyboard, 57
mouse events, 56
onchange, 68–69
onfocus, 66–67
onmousedown, 76
page, 57
selection, 57
Expand( ) function, 287
expressions
  arithmetic operator and, 40
  comparison expressions, 44–45
  decrement values, 42–43
  evaluate, 50
  increment values, 42–43
  logical operators, 46–47
  regular expressions, 106–107, 311
  shortcuts, 43
  tokens, 106
  variables and, 40
external code, hard-coded JavaScript on same page, 9
external files, link, 8–9

F

Favorites folder, bookmarklets, 5
fields, forms, password validation, 116–117
files, headers, 13
filters, transitional effects, 308
flags, Boolean variables as, 17, 22
floating-point variables
  arithmetic operators and, 17
  description, 17
  display numbers, 21
  fractional numbers and, 17
  shopping carts and, 17
  typeof keyword, 24
  values, assign, 19
floor( ) method, 158
focus
  set/remove, 66–67
  text fields, Enter key and, 136–137
focus( ) method, 66–67
fonts, operating system and, 215
for-in loop, properties and, 197

for loops
  arrays, reverse elements, 33
  create, 82
  integers and, 20
form fields
  address bar, 4
  query strings and, 226–227
<form> tag, 112, 130–131
forms, HTML
  button elements, 120
  development, 112
  disable elements, 131
  enter key invoked, blocking, 134–135
  hidden elements, 118–119
  password field validation, 116–117
  reference elements, 113
  submission, enter key, 134–135
  user controls, 112
  validation, 130–131
forward slashes (/) in comments, 12
fractional numbers, floating-point variables and, 17
frames
  break in/out, 188–189
  caller frame page, 184
  creation, 182–183
  dimensions, 186
  <frameset> tag, 182–183
  function frame page, 184
  hidden, 189
  menu frames, 182–183
  parent frames, 183
  print, 187
  reference, 184–185
  resize, 190–191
  security, 194–195
  write content to, 192–193
<frameset> tag, frame creation, 182–183
framesets, rows, hide/show, 191
function frame page, 184
function keys, 309
functions
  call, 90
  declaration, 90
  execution, 2–3
  numSort, 37
  parameters, pass to, 92
  source code and, 3

  special characters, 90
  value return, 93

G

generate random numbers, 158–159
getDate( ) method, 140
getMonth( ) method, 140
getYear( ) method, 140
global variables, 91, 184
go( ) method, history object, 210

H

hard-coded JavaScript
  external code on same page, 9
  HTML document, 4
  JavaScript files (.js), 4
hash tables, pseudo, 202–203
<head> tag, <script> tag and, 6
headers, files, 13
hidden elements, forms, 118–119
hidden frames, 189
history object, 210
HTML (Hypertext Markup Language)
  bookmarklets, 5
  create elements, 254–255
  draggable elements, 266–269
  element animation, 264–265
  element position, 257–258
  element references, 252–253
  embed JavaScript, 6–7
  execute statements from links, 72
  forms development, 112
  hard-coded JavaScript, 4
  innerHTML property, 256
  introduction, 2
  show/hide elements, 260–261
  text, 255
  user controls in forms, 112

I

if statements, 79, 218
if-else statements, 22, 78–79

INDEX

iframes, Web pages, add, 245
image object, 204–205
images
  background, 241
  clock with, 150–151
  gallery creation, 282–283
  preloading during page load, 205
  rotating, 155
increment values, expressions and, 42–43
infinite loops, 85
innerHTML property, 256
input, text areas, validation, 120
<input> tag, text box values, 114–115
integer variables
  arithmetic operators and, 17
  counters and, 17
  description, 17
  integer display, 20
  typeof keyword, 24
Internet Explorer, Modal windows, 178–179
isNan( ) method, 48–49

J

JavaScript
  browser support, 3
  disabled, 10–11
  version support, 217
javascript: keyword, address bar and, 4
join( ) method, 34–35
.js files, 4, 8–9

K

key press detection, 62–63
keyboard
  alphanumeric, keycodes, 309
  function keys, 309
  modifier key detection, 64–65
  multifunctional keys, 308
  numeric keypad keys, 309
keyboard events, 57
keywords
  break, for loops and, 83
  continue, for loops and, 83
  function, 90

javascript:, address bar and, 4
  reserved, 310
  this, 198, 200–201
  typeof, variable types and, 24–25
  var, 18

L

language attribute, <script> tag, 6
languages, browsers, 216
layers, cross-browser layer modal window, 270–271
length property
  arrays, 32
  string length, 96–97
links
  external .js files, 8–9
  HTML, execute statements from, 72
  locate all, 206
  style, 238–239
  style sheets to Web page, 230–231
local variables, handle, 91
location object, 207
logical operators, expressions, 46–47
look-up speed, statements, 94
lookup tables, arrays, multidimensional, 30
loops
  break, 83
  do-while, 85
  for-in, 197
  hash tables and, 202
  infinite, 85
  for loop creation, 82
  for loops, integers and, 20
  while loops, 84–85

M

Math object
  constants, 152–153
  maximum values, 157
  minimum values, 157
  powers, 156
  random number generation, 158–159
  round numbers, 160–161

square roots, 156
trigonometric functions, 154–155
mathematical constants, 152–153
maximize window, browser, 174–175
maximum values, 157
menus
  breadcrumb navigation, 208–209
  drop-down, construction, 290–293
  menu frames, 182–183
  select element, 132–133
<meta> tags, transitions and, 295
methods
  blur( ), 66–67
  charAt( ), 102–103
  clearTimeout( ), 86–87
  confirm( ), 54–55
  createTextNode( ), 255
  custom, objects, 200–201
  encodeURI( ), 105
  encodeURIComponent( ), 105
  escape( ), 104
  eval( ), 50
  floor( ), 158
  focus( ), 66–67
  getDate( ), 140
  getMonth( ), 140
  getYear( ), 140
  go( ), 210
  isNan( ), 48–49
  objects, 196
  onload( ), 166
  onunload( ), 166
  pop( ), 38
  push( ), 39
  replace( ), 110–111
  resizeTo( ), 173
  round( ), 158
  round numbers, 160–161
  scrollBy( ), 284–285
  setInterval( ), 88–89
  setTimeout( ), 86–87, 166
  shift( ), 38
  slice( ), 99
  splice( ), 38, 39
  submit( ), 123
  substring( ), 98–99

support verification, 218
toDateString( ), 144–145
toLowerCase( ), 100–101
toString( ), 27
toUpperCase( ), 100–101
unshift( ), 39
write( ), 164–165
writeln( ), 164–165
minimum values, 157
modal windows
  cross-browser layers, 270–271
  Internet Explorer, 178–179
modifier keys, detection, 64–65
modulus operator, 41
mouse
  button, determine pressed, 76
  onclick event, 58–59
  position location, 263
mouse events, 56
Mozilla browsers, cross browser scripting and, 3
multidimensional arrays, declaration, 30
multifunctional keyboard keys, 308
multiple line comments, 12
multiplication (*) arithmetic operator, 40

N

native browser language, 216
navigation
  drop-down menu construction, 290–293
  menu, bread crumb navigation, 208–209
  navigation tree construction, 286–289
  rollover buttons, 60–61
  select element navigation menu, 132–133
navigator.language property, 216
<noscript> tags, non-JavaScript-enabled browsers, 10–11
not (!) logical operator, 46
numbers
  commas and, 162–163
  conversion from strings, 26
  conversion to strings, 27
  random, generation, 158–159
  round, methods and, 160–161
  verify as variables, 48–49
numeric keypad keys, 309
numSort function, array sorts, 37

INDEX

O

obfuscated code, 15
objects
  custom, 198–199
  Date( ), 138–139
  events, attach, 73
  history object, 210
  image object, 204–205
  location object, 207
  methods, 196, 200–201
  properties, 196, 199
  reference with DOM, 196–197
  support verification, 218
onblur( ) event, pop-up windows and, 171
onchange event, 68–69
onclick event handler, 6, 58–59
onfocus event, 66–67
onkeypress event handler, 62–63
onload( ) handler, problem solving and, 302–303
onload( ) method, pop-up windows and, 166
onload event handler, 6, 70–71
onmousedown event, 76
onmouseoff event handler, <script> tag and, 6
onmouseover event handler, 6, 60
onresize event handler, 173
onsubmit event handler, 130–131
onunload( ) method, pop-up windows and, 166
Opera browser, verification, 212
operating system, determine, 214–215
operator precedence, 41
operators
  arithmetic, 40–41
  comparison, 44
  conditional, 80
or (| |) logical operator, 46, 201
order of precedence
  logical operators, 46
  sort( ) method, arrays, 36

P

page events, 57
page load
  image preload, 205
  onload event, 70–71

style sheet changes, 248–249
time, obfuscated code and, 15
page onload handlers, 302–303
page transitions, effects, 294–295
parameters, pass to function, 92
parent frames, browser properties and, 183
parent windows, close, 170–171
parseFloat( ) method, 25–26
parseInt( ) method, 25–26
password fields, validation, 116–117
password protection, user entered, 117
pathname property, location object and, 207
pattern matching, regular expressions and, 106–107
performance
  optimization, switch statement and, 81
  scripts, 94
personalized Web pages, <script> tag and, 7
PI constant, 152
pipe (|), string variables and, 23
pop( ) method, remove array elements, 38
pop-up windows
  close, 170–171
  content creation, 180–181
  creation, 166–167
  detect open, 168
  onblur( ) event, 171
  source code protection and, 15
powers (Math object), 156
precedence, operators, 41
print, frames, 187
prompt dialog boxes, create, 52–53
properties
  address bar, 4
  altkey, 64
  array length, 32
  assign to objects, 199
  attributes and, 196
  borders, 237
  check boxes, 124–125
  ctrlkey, 64
  for-in loop and, 197
  innerHTML, 256
  location object, 207
  navigator.language, 216
  objects, 196
  rule, override, 236
  selection lists, 128

shiftkey, 64
string length, 96–97
visibility, 260–261
protocol property, location object and, 207
pseudo hash tables, create, 202–203
push( ) method, add array elements, 39

Q

query strings, 226–229
question mark (?), query strings and, 226
quotation marks
convert numbers to strings, 27
string variables and, 17, 19, 23

R

radio buttons, 126–127
random number generation, 158–159
range, dates, 146
reference frames, 184–185
reference information from multiple windows, 169
RegExp( ) class, 106–107
regular expressions, 106–107, 311
reload( ) method, location object and, 207
replace( ) method, 110–111, 163, 207
reserved keywords, 310
reset buttons, apply, 122–123
resize, frames, 190–191
resizeTo( ) method, 173
reverse( ) method, 33, 36–37
right-click button, disable for security, 14–15
rollover buttons, create, 60–61
rotating images, 155
round( ) method, 158
round numbers, methods and, 160–161
rows (tables), add, 280–281
rules
properties, override, 236
style sheets, 232–233, 235

S

script, performance, 94
<script> tag, 3, 6–7, 18

scripts, header information, 13
scrollBy( ) method, 284–285
scrolling
autoscrolling windows, 284–285
<div> element and, 244
search property, location object and, 207
security
address bar, 4
frames, 194–195
JavaScript disabled and, 11
right-click button disable, 14–15
security, 14–15
source code, 14–15
select element navigation menu, 132–133
selection events, 57
selection lists
double combo, 278–279
item insertion/removal, 276–277
properties, 128
values, 129
semicolons
statements, multiple, 4
variable declaration and, 18
server-side languages, database and, 111
setInterval( ) method
draggable elements and, 268
image gallery, 283
introduction, 88–89
setTimeout( ) method, 86–87, 166
shift( ) method, remove array elements, 38
shiftkey property, 64
shopping cards, floating-point variables and, 17
sin function, 154–155
single line comments, 12
slice( ) method, 99
sort( ) method, 36–37
sorts, arrays, 36–37
sound, buttons, 296–297
source code
obfuscated, 15
protecting, 14–15
view, 3
<span> element, color and, 243
special characters
function names, 90
string variables, 17
splice( ) method, 38, 39

INDEX

split( ) method, split string to array, 35
spyware, JavaScript disabled and, 11
square roots, 156
statements
  address bar, 4–5
  execution from HTML link, 72
  if-else, limit executions, 78–79
  look-up speed, 94
  multiple, semicolons, 4
  switch, performance and, 81
  try/catch, 305
string variables
  as arrays, 28
  description, 17
  display strings, 23
  parseFloat( ) method, 25, 26
  parseInt( ) method, 25, 26
  quotation marks, 17, 19, 23
  special characters, 17
  typeof keyword, 24
strings
  case, 100–101
  character extraction, 102–103
  character matches, 108–109
  character replacement, 110–111
  combine, 97
  comparison operators, 45
  conversion from arrays, 34–35
  conversion from dates, 144–145
  conversion from numbers, 27
  conversion to numbers, 26
  display, 23
  initial caps, 101
  length determination, 96–97
  query strings, create, 226–227
  select portions, 98–99
  split into array, 35
  text, escape, 104
style attribute, rule properties override, 236
style sheets (CSS)
  link to Web page, 230–231
  off/on, 250–251
  page load, change after, 248–249
  rules, 232–233, 235
<style> tag, 230–231
styles, links, 238–239

submit( ) method, 123
submit buttons, apply, 122–123
substring( ) method, 98–99
subtraction (-) arithmetic operator, 40
switch statement, performance optimization and, 81

T

tables
  hash tables, pseudo, 202–203
  rows, add, 280–281
tan function, 154–155
text
  fonts, operating system and, 215
  HTML elements, 255
  string variables and, 17
text areas, input validation, 120
text boxes, values, 114–115
text fields, focus, Enter key and, 136–137
text strings, escape, 104
<textarea> tag, 120
text/javascript attribute, <script> tag, 6
this keyword, 198, 200–201
time, 140–147
timed intervals, 86–89
timers
  countdown timer, 148–149
  random number generation and, 158
  timed intervals, 86–89
toDateString( ) method, 144–145
tokens
  expressions, 106
  regular expressions, 311
toLowerCase( ) method, 100–101
toolbars
  chromeless windows, 167
  removal for source code security, 15
toString( ) method, convert numbers to strings, 27
toUpperCase( ) method, 100–101
transitions, 294–295, 308
transparency, add, 246–247
trigonometric functions, 154–155
try/catch statements, 305
two-dimensional arrays, 30, 202
typeof keyword, 24–25

U

unary operators, 42–43
underscore (_), string variables and, 23
unshift( ) method, add array elements, 39
URIs, encode, 105
user controls, forms, 112
user decisions, confirm dialog box, 54–55
user friendliness, page load, obfuscated code and, 15
user input, prompt dialog boxes, 52–53
users, direct based on browser brand, 213
UTC (Coordinated Universal Time), 141

V

validation
  forms, 130–131
  password fields, 116–117
  text area input, 120
values
  alphanumeric keyboard keys, 309
  assign, or (| |) operator and, 201
  cookies, 220–225
  function keys, 309
  multifunctional keyboard keys, 308
  numeric keypad keys, 309
  radio buttons, display, 127
  return from function, 93
  selection lists, 129
  text boxes, 114–115
  variable assignment, 19
var keyword, 18, 91
variables
  array declaration, 28–29
  as arrays, 29
  Boolean, 16, 17
  case sensitivity, 16
  constant values and, 16
  declare, 18
  expressions and, 40
  floating-point, 17, 21
  global, 91
  integer, 17, 20
  introduction, 16
  local, 91

for loops and, 82
  names, 16
  naming conventions, 16
  numbers, verify as, 48–49
  query strings, convert from, 228–229
  string, 17
  typeof keyword, 24–25
  types, 16, 24–25
  unassigned, 25
  value assignment, 19
version support, JavaScript, 217
visibility property, 260–261

W

Web pages
  add elements, 242
  alter elements, 243
  center content, 240–241
  clock on, 89
  color, integers and, 20
  CSS, link style sheets, 230–231
  iframes, 245
  <script> tag in personalized, 7
while loops, conditions and, 84–85
window object, write content to window, 164–165
windows
  autoscrolling, 284–285
  browser, maximize, 174–175
  center on screen, 176–177
  chromeless, 167
  modal, cross-browser layer modal window, 270–271
  Modal, Internet Explorer, 178–179
  onresize event handler, 173
  parent, close, 170–171
  placement, 172–173, 176–177
  pop-up, close, 170–171
  pop-up, content creation, 180–181
  pop-up, creation, 166–167
  pop-up, detect open, 168
  reference information from multiple, 169
  size, 172–173
write( ) method, 164–165, 192–193
writeln( ) method, 164–165

Read Less – Learn More®

![Visual]

Visual Blueprint™

For experienced computer users, developers, and network professionals who learn best visually.

Extra
Apply It

"Apply It" and "Extra" provide ready-to-run code and useful tips.

Title	ISBN	Price
Access 2003: Your visual blueprint for creating and maintaining real-world databases	0-7645-4081-5	$26.99
Active Server Pages 3.0: Your visual blueprint for developing interactive Web sites	0-7645-3472-6	$26.99
Adobe Scripting: Your visual blueprint for scripting Photoshop and Illustrator	0-7645-2455-0	$29.99
ASP.NET: Your visual blueprint for creating Web applications on the .NET Framework	0-7645-3617-6	$26.99
C#: Your visual blueprint for building .NET applications	0-7645-3601-X	$26.99
Excel Data Analysis: Your visual blueprint for analyzing data, charts, and PivotTables	0-7645-3754-7	$26.99
Excel Programming: Your visual blueprint for building interactive spreadsheets	0-7645-3646-X	$26.99
Flash ActionScript: Your visual blueprint for creating Flash-enhanced Web sites	0-7645-3657-5	$26.99
HTML: Your visual blueprint for designing effective Web pages	0-7645-3471-8	$26.99
Java: Your visual blueprint for building portable Java programs	0-7645-3543-9	$26.99
Java and XML: Your visual blueprint for creating Java-enhanced Web programs	0-7645-3683-4	$26.99
JavaScript: Your visual blueprint for building dynamic Web pages	0-7645-4730-5	$26.99
JavaServer Pages: Your visual blueprint for designing dynamic content with JSP	0-7645-3542-0	$26.99
Linux: Your visual blueprint to the Linux platform	0-7645-3481-5	$26.99
MySQL: Your visual blueprint to open source database management	0-7645-1692-2	$29.99
Perl: Your visual blueprint for building Perl scripts	0-7645-3478-5	$26.99
PHP: Your visual blueprint for creating open source, server-side content	0-7645-3561-7	$26.99
Red Hat Linux 8: Your visual blueprint to an open source operating system	0-7645-1793-7	$29.99
Unix: Your visual blueprint to the universe of Unix	0-7645-3480-7	$26.99
Unix for Mac: Your visual blueprint to maximizing the foundation of Mac OS X	0-7645-3730-X	$26.99
Visual Basic .NET: Your visual blueprint for building versatile programs on the .NET Framework	0-7645-3649-4	$26.99
Visual C++ .NET: Your visual blueprint for programming on the .NET platform	0-7645-3644-3	$26.99
XML: Your visual blueprint for building expert Web pages	0-7645-3477-7	$26.99

Over 10 million *Visual* books in print!

with these two-color Visual™ guides

Jan 04

M "Master It" tips provide additional topic coverage.

Title	ISBN	Price
Master Microsoft Access 2000 VISUALLY	0-7645-6048-4	$39.99
Master Microsoft Office 2000 VISUALLY	0-7645-6050-6	$39.99
Master Microsoft Word 2000 VISUALLY	0-7645-6046-8	$39.99
Master VISUALLY Adobe Photoshop, Illustrator, Premiere, and After Effects	0-7645-3668-0	$39.99
Master VISUALLY Dreamweaver 4 and Flash 5	0-7645-0855-5	$39.99
Master VISUALLY Dreamweaver MX and Flash MX	0-7645-3696-6	$39.99
Master VISUALLY FrontPage 2002	0-7645-3580-3	$39.99
Master VISUALLY HTML 4 and XHTML 1	0-7645-3454-8	$39.99
Master VISUALLY Office 2003	0-7645-3994-9	$34.99
Master VISUALLY Office XP	0-7645-3599-4	$39.99
Master VISUALLY Photoshop 6	0-7645-3541-2	$39.99
Master VISUALLY Web Design	0-7645-3610-9	$39.99
Master VISUALLY Windows 2000 Server	0-7645-3426-2	$39.99
Master VISUALLY Windows Me Millennium Edition	0-7645-3496-3	$39.99
Master VISUALLY Windows XP	0-7645-3621-4	$39.99
Master Windows 98 VISUALLY	0-7645-6034-4	$39.99
Master Windows 2000 Professional VISUALLY	0-7645-3421-1	$39.99

For visual learners who want an all-in-one reference/tutorial that delivers more in-depth information about a technology topic.

The Visual™ series is available wherever books are sold, or call 1-800-762-2974.

Outside the US, call 317-572-3993